The Women's Annual
1982 –1983

G. K. Hall

W★MEN'S STUDIES

Publications

Barbara Haber
Editor

The Women's Annual
1982 – 1983

Edited by Barbara Haber

G. K. HALL & CO. ● BOSTON, MASSACHUSETTS

This publication is printed on permanent/durable acid-free paper
MANUFACTURED IN THE UNITED STATES OF AMERICA

Contents

Introduction

Within the last year, the term "postfeminism" began to appear in the language, mainly in journalistic writing that announced the demise of the women's movement. Articles with this perspective on feminism are almost a genre, for they have been appearing from time to time since the mid-1970s. But what is new about the word "postfeminism" is that it contains implications that are contradictory and misleading. On the one hand, the term suggests that feminism is over because its goals have been accomplished; on the other, it implies that feminism is over without having achieved its goals. The most damaging aspect of this notion, however, is the suggestion that feminism is over at all. While the defeat of the Equal Rights Amendment lends itself quite handily to the belief that we have passed beyond the period of feminist activism, this setback and others that are occuring under the Reagan Administration are in fact leading to renewed commitment and organizational strategies on the part of activists for women's rights. This is one of the major messages expressed in this year's *Annual*.

Peggy Simpson's account of the political and legal situation illustrates how these setbacks are spurring women on to political activism. The picture, however, is still bleak. The Reagan Administration continued to reverse hard-won social and political gains by abandoning or cutting back such programs as nutritional, health, and income supports for poor women, special programs for women in business, job programs for displaced homemakers, and shelters for battered women. Simpson points out that women now make up 75 percent of the poor in this country. Instead of being helped, they have fallen victim to a government committed to disengaging from its role of providing social services and ensuring the civil rights of its citizens.

Such reverses are motivating women to renew their efforts, just as the antiabortionists have been a catalyst for the revitalization of the prochoice movement.

In her essay on women and health, Susan Reverby illustrates this theme when she points out that differing women's rights groups move into the front lines to do battle with a given political foe depending upon which specific issues are being challenged. In Reverby's analysis, the most controversial issues of 1982 centered around women's sexuality and reproduction. She describes, for example, the Reagan Administration's attempt to pass the "Squeal Rule," a law that would require family planning clinics to notify parents when teenagers request contraceptives. The concern of conservatives

I

over teenage sexuality is also expressed by what is being called the chastity program, another attempt to involve families in the sexual behavior of their daughters. Grants offered by the Office of Adolescent Pregnancy focus on encouraging abstinence and, failing that, on adoption, but not on birth control.

But the most controversial issue, of course, has been the continuing fight over abortion rights. While several proposed antiabortion measures came before the Senate, none so far has been passed. Still to be decided are three cases before the Supreme Court that will test the right of individual states to determine the legality of abortion. Throughout her discussion of these issues, Reverby points out that while feminist analysts separate sexuality and repro- duction, right-to-lifers insist on thinking of them as the same issue. Reverby agrees with writer Ellen Willis who pointed out some years ago that the abortion debate is really about sex and not about life.

It is clear that activists involved in the women's health movement have their work cut out for them. Less obvious, perhaps, is their ability to rise to the occasion. Ever watchful of the latest threat to public health and to the health of women in particular, feminists involved in this multiplying number of issues call attention to and rally support against unacceptable attitudes and practices.

The need to organize in order to improve conditions for women in the work force is one of the important themes of Karen Sacks's essay on women and work. Most employed women are earning money out of economic neces- sity, and many have the additional responsibility of caring for a family, a situation Sacks calls "the double work days of paid and unpaid work." Women have the additional disadvantage of earning less than men who do the same or comparable work. More women now head single parent households and do not have the option of staying home. This is a reality that has not yet been absorbed by conservative ideologues who preach nostalgically about the beauty of the nuclear family.

What will improve the lives of working women is better compensation for their labor, a safe and healthy work environment, freedom from sexual harassment, and a social structure that acknowledges the importance of child- rearing and offers more support to parents.

According to Sacks, the organized activity among women workers has been most successful in occupations and industries where women are concentrated—health care workers, including nurses, and clerical workers. For these groups, pay equity and improved working conditions are coming about through union sponsored collective bargaining and litigation. The in- creased militance of nurses is reflected in their movement toward unionization which sometimes results in strikes and the implementation of lawsuits. In professions where women are less concentrated—college teaching in particular—strategies involve affirmative action suits, especially class action suits, and the use of professional associations to seek equal pay and promotion.

Several issues are looming as major problem areas for women: the threat of job loss through automation, the growing prevalence of computer work in the home setting (which can be exploitive work reminiscent of the piece work system established by clothing manufacturers earlier in the century), and the potential dangers of video data terminal work. Research indicates that VDT operators are susceptible to back and eye problems and that office workers in general are suffering from alarming levels of stress.

Historians of women have been saying for years that in order to understand the relationship between women and work, one must also understand the role of women in the family. In their essay on parenting, Marjorie Bakken and Joan Bergstrom offer some perspectives on how these elements in women's lives fit together now and what they will be like in the future. They look at recent demographic changes and point out that women are having fewer children and are having them at a later age. Further, the rising divorce rate has resulted in more single parent households, a phenomenon that has increased by 100 percent since 1970. The working mother is now the norm rather than the exception; 54 percent of women aged sixteen and older now work, a statistic that is expected to increase to 74 percent by 1990.

The other major influence affecting the family is the women's movement, which has changed women's expectations about their roles. Women now feel that they should create and enjoy a life apart from their families and that they should be economically productive. Concomitant with these expectations is the belief that the responsibility for child rearing should be shared and that children benefit from the experience of knowing other adults in addition to their parents.

Although the development of support systems within industry on behalf of working parents has been slow in coming, some progress has been made. Among the benefits that exist in a few places are company day care centers, flex-time work schedules, job-sharing, maternity and paternity leave, and the option for child sick leave. One hopes that the availability of such benefits as these will become a trend.

Such external support systems are required to enable working couples to meet their day-to-day responsibilities; families with special problems need, in addition, an enlightened therapeutic setting. Offering a feminist perspective on the entire field of family therapy, Rachel Hare-Mustin points out that many therapists continue to reinforce the sex role stereotyping that feminists have been trying to resist. As most therapists are men who are living in traditional marriages, their failure to examine inequities in the family or in the society at large is not surprising.

This stereotyping inevitably leaves women feeling disadvantaged and that they are the emotional caretakers of the family. As Hare-Mustin points out, "defenders of the idealized family as a haven demand that the family and women make up for the indifference and hostility of the outer world. Rather than the family today being a refuge from activities that occur in common work and crowded urban areas, the anonymity and freedom of urban life may be a refuge from the intimacy, intensity, and responsibility of the private world of the family."

There are other implications inherent in the traditional role assignment of women as well. The gender-based roles that have been defined by the domestic activities of women have been carried into the occupational world. This has led to job segregation, with women getting the lower-paying jobs. Finally, Hare-Mustin makes the point that "without consciousness raising, women may be accepting their traditional lot and blaming themselves rather than outside sources such as the marriage for their unhappiness." Hare-Mustin emphasizes the importance to feminists of maintaining an activist role in approaching the issues that have been engaging them since the beginning of the women's movement.

Freada Klein certainly shares this conviction, as she illustrates throughout her chapter, "Violence Against Women." Of great concern to her is the split between scholarly researchers and the feminist activists who were the first to identify the issues that are now being studied. Klein points out that "research results are seldom made accessible to service providers. Activists are rarely allowed, let alone invited, to help determine what needs to be studied, how it should be studied, and by whom. The source of the problem, though, does not lie with researchers. The policy-making process ensures the division of research from services by equating expertise with professional credentials, by valuing research more highly than provision of service, and by funding the efforts separately." While this imposed division between researchers and practitioners surely exists in other areas of the social sciences, it is especially frustrating for feminists who, so to speak, invented the field.

Klein then surveys activism and the new scholarship on rape, incest, battering, pornography, and sexual harassment, and notes several positive trends: "First, the gap between research findings and feminist analysis is narrowing. For the first time, the link between the relative power and privileges of men in this society with acts of violence were at least noted in the majority of scholarly literature. . . . Second, the boundaries between types of violence have become more fluid. For example, battering and incest are being looked at under the rubric of family violence. . . . Finally, the movement exhibits growing sohpistication in its legislative and educative strategies, and in its quest to resolve internal dilemmas."

These measures of success do not belie the dismal fact that violence against women is prevalent in the society. While activists and professionals do their best to provide services to women who are victimized by one form of brutality or another, they also seek ways to help women to overcome their vulnerability. At the same time, they are influencing public opinion—especially through the media—to no longer tolerate crimes that have in the past been ignored.

Jeanne Speizer's examination of her topic, education, is comprehensive. In 1982, educational cutbacks occurred in almost every area that affects women. In treating her subject, Speizer steps back from the catalog of gloomy particulars in order to offer a perspective on what is fundamentally wrong with the educational system and what women can do about it. As part of her exploration of the current situation she says: "Thus far, little thought appears to have been given at any level of decision making to the goals of education as a whole and to the effects of severe cuts on its future. Expediency appears to rule behavior: officials make decisions based on budget considerations, and educators are interested primarily in conserving their own jobs. The needs of students, in general, now and in the future, do not seem to be of particular interest. Educational equity concerns have little, if any, bearing on decisions." To a great extent the fault lies with the present administration, which would prefer to withdraw the federal government entirely from matters of education and turn them over to the states. But, as Speizer indicates, the politics of education is more complex. With that perspective she looks at a whole range of issues—from how girls are educated to how women get jobs—and analyzes the ways in which women can not only succeed within the system but manage to change it.

To change the system is the central idea of Kathleen Barry's essay on feminist theory. At the core of her argument is the conviction that women can take command of their own lives through self-determination and by defining for themselves what it means to be a woman. In developing her argument, Barry distinguishes between socialist feminism, a major theoretical system espoused by one school of feminists, and radical feminism, the framework Barry herself advocates. She feels that radical feminism, unattached as it is to any preexisting philosophical system, is more appropriate for an analysis that seeks to place women at the center of concern. In her view, freedom for women is the ultimate goal.

In order to reach this goal, Barry describes the process called feminist *praxis*. It is the result of combining personal awareness with political awareness and confrontation. To sustain itself, the process requires consciousness-raising in order for women to continuously realize that the personal is indeed political, thus avoiding the age-old trap of women believing themselves personally at fault for adverse conditions that affect many other women. By understanding the sources of their grievances and by working collectively for change, women become empowered and rid of the feeling that they are the passive victims of a society that devalues women.

What is most compelling about Barry's point of view is its comprehensiveness. Her concern is for all women. Her theoretical framework takes into account the plight of poor women as well as rich, women of color as well as white women, lesbian women as well as heterosexuals, and uneducated women as well as the intellectually elite.

This comprehensiveness of outlook characterizes the essays considered here. In establishing perspectives on their subjects, the authors take an all-encompassing view so that when they speak about such issues as employment, health, or education, they include the special concerns of disadvantaged women and not just those of the privileged. This is perhaps a sign that feminist writing has matured in that writers are now more sensitive to the positions of minority groups.

This observation also applies to Heather McClave's review of the new scholarship in the humanities, in which she gives shape to an impressive array of material. In looking at women's studies, McClave sees as "the most pressing question in the field" the need for writers to determine what is authentic for women. In comparing feminist writing to other academic work she observes: "There could hardly be a greater contrast in approach and intent than the one we now find between feminist work on women—so conscious of individual traces surfacing out of buried generations—and fashionable academic theories that try to objectify human perceptions into autonomous texts and processes."

McClave then listens closely to the voices of feminist literary critics, historians, biographers, and other writers who offer their views of the truth about women's lives. By so doing, she isolates three trends that emerge from the material: the presentation of data that reveal women's experience through biographies, essays, journals, diaries, and letters; the active presence of some authors who offer insights about themselves as well as the subjects they write about; and the growing interest in exploring twentieth century material and popular culture.

The work that Heather McClave analyzes has been written by serious authors and is read, for the most part, by a serious feminist audience. Beverly Friend, in her essay on popular culture, concentrates on material aimed at the general public (that is, those who go to movies, watch television, and read popular fiction). Friend's analysis offers a sense of how women are being portrayed, however unflatteringly, for a popular audience and illustrates which issues are being popularized, which are distorted, and which are ignored by the media.

It is interesting and heartening to know, for instance, that ABC's After School Specials deal seriously with such topics as venereal disease, pregnancy, and difficult relationships. Less heartening is the knowledge that on prime time television, women's issues are often sensationalized, trivialized, and over-simplified.

Contemporary fiction is also a mixed bag. One finds masses of pulp romances written to formula with characters that could easily be interchanged from one book to another. Yet important fiction with memorable female characters also appeared in 1982, such books as *The Color Purple* by Alice Walker, *Dinner at the Homesick Restaurant* by Anne Tyler, and Ntozake Shange's *Sassafrass, Cypress, and Indigo*.

Friend asserts that the genre of science fiction is generally congenial to the handling of serious social questions. She makes the point that "science fiction sees and responds to what might be, and thus provides the most positive depiction of women in popular culture, not only for 1982, but for at least the twenty years preceding."

In sum, 1982 brought no tangible victories to women. The most serious and measurable set-backs were the results of devastating federal cuts in programs that would have provided more educational incentives and health and nutritional benefits for the poor. The year also brought with it failure of the passage of the Equal Rights Amendment. While antifeminists seized upon this defeat to proclaim the death of the women's movement, feminists are in fact reaffirming their commitment to its goals and are still actively engaged in the fight for women's rights. The writers of the essays included in *The Women's Annual: 1982* offer revealing accounts of the forms that fight is taking.

Barbara Haber
Cambridge, Massachusetts
April 1983

Publisher's Note

For a comprehensive list of special interest groups and women's organizations readers should consult previous *Annuals*. Those cited in this edition appear either for the first time or provide corrected or expanded information.

Domestic Life: Perspectives on Parenting

Marjorie Bakken and *Joan Bergstrom*

Although the family remains the primary focus of childbearing, parenting has changed during the last decade in the United States. Dramatic changes in the role include the fact that it now occurs throughout the life cycle, it takes place at the center of a public debate, and it has become more specialized.

There are two reasons for these changes: the significant shifts in demographic trends and the profound alteration in women's roles.

Demographic Trends

There are some notable and telling demographic changes. The fertility rate among all age groups, with the exception of adolescents and women aged thirty to thirty-four years, is down. Fewer children are being born and there are few children per family unit, only 1.8 at present. The divorce rate, which has risen steadily since 1950, continues to rise. Both women and men are marrying later and women are having their first child later. The number of households headed by a single person has increased. These households are headed by widows, young single adults who are not yet married, and divorced persons. More than three-fifths of them are headed by women. Women with children under the age of three to five years have entered the work force; in fact the working mother is becoming the norm rather than the exception.

Working Parents   The number of one-parent households has increased by 100 percent since 1970. Currently, one out of every eight children lives in a single-parent home, and that parent is most likely to be the child's mother. These women often must work to support their families because alimony has become a less frequent part of divorce settlements. Even when alimony or child support is available, inflation over the past decade and a half makes it absolutely necessary for a single parent to work (Bane 1980; Bronfenbrenner 1981; Lee 1981; Press et al. 1983; A portrait . . . 1983).

9

The number of working women has changed drastically from an earlier generation. In 1981, 54 percent of all women aged sixteen years and older worked outside the home, as did 52 percent of mothers with children under eighteen. These figures are expected to rise to 74 percent in 1990, and some have reported that these projections are conservative and will be exceeded. By 1990 only 27 percent of two-parent families will have one parent at home to care for the children; this compares to approximately 35 percent in 1982. Another way to think about this is that by 1990 three out of four mothers will be working outside the home, and two-thirds of all two-parent families will have both parents in the work force (Smith 1979). The fastest-growing segment of working mothers is among those with children under two years of age; for single mothers with preschoolers three to five years of age the rate of employment is over 61 percent. Also, almost 43 percent of mothers with children under age three and living with their husbands are employed.

Adoption   The Adoption Reform Act of 1978 was designed to help facilitate the adoption of waiting children (mentally retarded, physically handicapped, and emotionally disturbed) and those who are part of a group of siblings or of minority racial heritage (U.S. Department of Health and Human Services 1980). Through this legislation and because of the civil rights movement in the 1960s, more black children are finding homes with white families and international adoptions are increasing in number. In the private agencies in Massachusetts, a significant percentage of children adopted are children of color (Cronin 1980). Obviously, this means that multicultural families are becoming a definite part of society. These changes in family life have made parenting a more complex, more specialized, and more demanding task.

Women's Movement

Changes in parenting influenced by the women's movement have occurred in all social classes. There is a new belief that child rearing should be shared more equally by both parents, which influences the conviction that women's personal and social development depends on having a life beyond the household. It is also necessary for both women and men to be economically productive. This has led to a growing sense that it is good for children to experience a wide range of people outside of the home.

Motherhood itself has become a thorny issue. Women ask themselves whether to have a child or not, when to have a child, how many to have, if they should have a child when they do not have a husband, and whether to terminate a pregnancy.

Parenting Throughout the Life Cycle

The years of active parenting were once assumed to be from when the children were born to when they went away to college, found post-high school employment, or began their own families—from the parents' early twenties to their early forties. Until the 1980s most women finished childbearing by the age of twenty-six. Now children are frequently born to parents in their late twenties and early thirties. It is not uncommon for women to have their first child in their early forties, delaying parenting until closer to middle age. These changes in the timing of first parenthood can cause corresponding changes in the relationship between children and parents.

Couples who have children in their twenties condense the processes of becoming independent, getting married, and having a first child; the three events become nearly inseparable. Consequently, partners find it hard to establish an identity apart from their new nuclear family. When couples have their first child in their thirties, it is usually part of a deliberate design. They see the baby as a "reward" for hard work during their twenties. Couples who become parents for the first time in their forties have usually prolonged the process for a particular reason, such as feelings of personal unreadiness, problems of infertility, or difficulty in sustaining an intimate relationship (Weingarten 1983).

There are both sociological and technological reasons why parenting has become a lifelong task rather than one for a set period in the life cycle. The women becoming first-time parents in midlife were themselves born during the post-World War II baby boom and experienced the women's movement from their mid-teens to mid-twenties. They are now twenty-five to thirty-five years old and are more well educated than women older than themselves. They have often delayed marriage and first parenting until college or graduate study is completed and their careers are under way.

These women could delay pregnancy because of the development of successful birth control techniques, most notably, the pill. They have kept themselves fit, partly as a result of the recent popular concern about good nutrition and physical fitness. However, this group of women now in their thirties is currently experiencing difficulty in terms of the value changes of the 1970s. These women "grew up when values were traditional; they became young adults, however, when they were supposed to make choices and not passively accept tradition" (Bardwick 1980, 48). Their sense of what is expected of them in careers or as mothers is not as consistent as it was for both younger and older women.

The decision to delay pregnancy has become possible because of advances in medical technology, most notably thanks to the development of successful birth control techniques. Amniocentesis and sonar testing have increased the possibility for women of all ages to know if they are carrying a healthy infant. Amniocentesis, usually done in the third month of pregnancy, can detect Down's syndrome as well as other possible birth disorders. This is especially significant, as the chance of giving birth to a defective child increases proportionately as a woman ages.

Of equal significance to the extension of parenting from adolescence to middle age is the decision of women and men not to become parents. As a result of the women's movement, it became more evident that women could be involved in several roles, and motherhood became only one possibility. With advances in birth control and more liberal laws and attitudes about abortion, the option not to have children has been a possibility for all women, although it has principally been available to professional middle-class women. Very few couples consciously decide not to have a child; most simply drift into childless-ness (Whelan 1975).

Although there has been more research in adult development, beginning with Gail Sheehy's best-seller *Passages* (1974), writers and theorists pay very little attention to the parenting experience. Erik Erikson is an exception. The seventh stage of his life cycle theory is specifically related to his unique concept of generativity, the deep caring for other persons at different stages, but particularly the commitment to the growth and development of younger generations (Erikson 1968). Generally, however, the recent and major works in adult development focus on the continuing role of the adult who must separate from childhood consciousness and ties and who must deal with aging parents (Gould 1978; Levinson et al. 1978; Vaillant 1977). For example, two popular books for young and middle-aged women are Nancy Friday's *My Mother/My Self* (1977) and Signe Hammer's *Daughters and Mothers: Mothers and Daughters* (1975). Both books focus on how women come to terms with their own identity through understanding and resolution of their relationship with their mothers. The perspective is the daughter's and not the mother's. The child is the focus. Little attention is paid to the salience of one's life as a parent; rather the emphasis is on one's continuing role as a child. A more comprehensive theory outlining stages of parental growth has been devised by Galinsky (1981), who views parenting as a developmental, growing process. Parents have powerful effects on the growth and development of their children, but children engen-der profound psychological changes in their parents. Galinsky describes the effects that the child has on the parent as having six predictable stages: image-making, nurturing, authority, interpretive, interdependent, and depar-ture. A parent can be in any one, two, or three of these stages at the same time, depending on the ages and development of the children.

Image Making   This stage usually happens during pregnancy. It is a time when prospective parents begin to form and reform images of what is to come. They prepare themselves for new relationships with each other, their friends, and their newborn. When interviewed during this stage, prospective parents ask questions such as, "Am I ready?" "Can I afford it?" "Will I be able to take care of this child?" "Is this the right time?"

Nurturing   Between birth and toddler stage is when attachment takes place. Parents have a number of questions relating to their identity and to that of the child.

Authority   During the period from a child's second through the fourth or fifth year parents face the realities and illusions of power. They have the constant task of deciding what kind of authoritative persons they want to be. They ask questions like, "How am I going to handle this?" "What am I going to do about this issue in terms of controlling it?" "What kinds of controls are realistic?" "How am I going to decide what things really matter, what limits are really important to set?"

Interpretive   This stage begins when the child is of preschool age and extends approximately to adolescence. The psychological task for parents is one of interpreting: how to interpret all of the questions children ask, ways to respond to those questions, and what kinds of knowledge, skills, and values they want to promote. It is a time when parents constantly evaluate and reevaluate what might be important to their child. It is also a period in which they make decisions about whether to expose or not to expose their child to certain kinds of experiences they believe may have long-lasting influences on the quality of the child's lifestyle.

Interdependent   During the child's teenage years the issues are predominantly those of authority, particularly, "Who's the boss?" Parents and child must work constantly to reach new solutions. Parents develop new and more interdependent relationships with their child as he or she becomes an adult.

Departure   As the child leaves home, this stage typically involves parents evaluating themselves and their child. They are likely to try to assess their overall success or failure in the task of child rearing (Galinsky, 1981).

Extension of Parenting Roles

One of the most obvious and striking features of parenting today is the noticeable extension of the role from the mother to other family members— fathers and grandparents—and to persons outside the family—day-care teachers and family day-care mothers, persons who care for children in their homes. The role of grandparents has not been studied extensively (Neugarten and Weinstein 1973), but the role of the father has received considerable attention in the popular press and has been the subject of a number of research studies. It is his involvement with the children that, more than anything else, has changed the concept of "mothering" to the concept of "parenting."

Fathers make their most significant contributions to infants' well-being through play activities, while mothers spend more time in feeding and care taking. Research suggests that men really do interact with their babies differently than women: men are more tactile, more physical in their play, and much more robust, and it appears that infants and toddlers are aware of these differences. In one study of children at fifteen, twenty, and thirty months of age, babies actually appeared to prefer the father's play style over the mother's (Clarke-Stewart 1979). Numerous researchers have helped change the view of the importance of the father's role in child development from insignificant to significant. As one observer noted, "The impact of all this father-watching is beginning to be felt in courts of law, in hospitals and universities, which face the task of redirecting the training of a new generation of doctors, pediatricians, psychotherapists, health-care professionals and teachers" (Collins 1979, 31).

With young children—and most of the research reflects on the role of the father with infants, toddlers, and preschoolers—the primary psychological issue is their attachment to the parent. Most earlier studies addressed that issue solely as an issue between mother and child. John Bowlby's work (1969) solidified the view that the bonding between mother and infant "was an imperative of the very growth and development of the species" (Collins 1979, 49). This view of attachment has been directly challenged by new research (Brody 1983).

Becoming and Being a Parent: A Public Debate

In the 1980s the emphasis on parenting and its importance in the life cycles of adults have become subjects of a public debate. The involvement of the father as a concerned and informed parent is seen by many as a positive development. The movement of the mother out of the home and into the workplace, however, is not looked on so favorably in many circles. Can a woman have two careers—family and work? The answer after ten or more years of intense debate seems only maybe.

The experience of parenting became a public issue with the publication of Betty Freidan's *The Feminine Mystique*. What this book argued was that women did not and could not find satisfaction as wives and mothers, but they could and should assume other satisfying and demanding roles in society. In the 1950s, before Freidan's book was published, Spock's *Baby and Child Care* was a major source of support for many middle-class parents, the same audience that read and understood Freidan. Spock, writing about the mother's role, recommended that she be at home with her children (1946). In his 1968 revised edition, he suggested that "some mothers have to work to make a living," and that "a few mothers, particularly those with professional training, feel that they must work because they wouldn't be happy otherwise" (Spock 1968, 563). Fifteen years later the sense prevails that it is acceptable for mothers who must work to have both a home and work life, but that work is a taboo for those who do not need a job outside the home. This is reflected by Deborah Fallows, who thinks the joys of full-time mothers are a well-kept secret, lost to her generation because *The Feminine Mystique* closed off communications about parenting between her generation and her mother's (Fallows 1982, 1983). The letters to the editor and the editorial that followed Fallows's article were a face-off about the advantages of small children having their mother at home, versus the needs of women to work and mother (Letters 1982).

Betty Freidan wrote an antidote to her own position in 1981. *The Second Stage* is an argument that the concept of choice for women generated by the women's movement should be exercised by their return to the family, which will be regenerated by the strength they have found in the discovery of their own personhood. Ironically, the position of the opponents of the Equal Rights

Amendment (ERA), personified by Phyllis Schlafly, and that of Freidan appear to converge for some people. Both think that the family should be a haven; Freidan calls it the new feminine frontier. Freidan does not suggest, of course, that the Equal Rights Amendment is not significant for women, on the contrary. But the balancing of roles between men and women inside the home that she suggests may not be possible because of the reality of people's lives.

An interesting further effect of the public debate has been the private concern of individuals about living up to an increasingly articulated sense of parenting. Popular images of "super mother," "super parents," the "perfect American mother," and "perfect parent" place an added burden on mothers and fathers who feel that their role is not so much natural behavior as a mystifying profession. The concept of supermom is, in fact, a conservative backlash against women's new and multiple roles. Furthermore, the massive amount of information available about parenting has created a situation where parents may begin to be ambivalent about their behavior and constantly search for a "better way to do it." Turning to the literature, reading an article, talking to someone, listening to a lecture, or attending a workshop are only a few of the many ways that parents try to secure support. In doing so they are often even more overwhelmed and quickly develop a sense of helplessness. A tired phrase intended as consolation and reassurance to working parents, "It's not the quantity but the quality of time that counts," has become a kind of injunction always to perform well with their child.

At times the public expectations may well seem overwhelming to parents. A review of what is available in books, special magazines, newspaper columns, articles, and a host of other materials available at the newsstands today substantiates this fact. This extensive literature covers the broad topics of child development, child health, parenting, parent education, the single parent, and teaching basic skills to children beginning at infancy. Prenatal health and childbirth options are also topics about which there is a great deal of information. The deluge of materials, particularly those concerning young children, makes it impossible for parents to keep abreast of what experts and professional writers suggest. There are literally hundreds of books with complete and easy guides about every issue relating to parenting infants and preschool children, including separation, attachment, individual temperament, child nutrition, and effective means of communication. There are both individual books and entire series that illustrate and suggest ways for parents to interact, stimulate, motivate, play with, and advance the development of young children, a large percentage of which can be described as "how-to" books (Gilligan 1976). Topics closely parallel findings of studies about the problems that concern parents most. For example, Mesibov, Schroeder, and Wesson (1977) tabulated 672 parental inquiries to a pediatric office. The most common questions asked concerned discipline, toilet training, developmental delays, and school problems, topics well covered in popular literature.

For parents of school-age children there also are hundreds of books with complete and easy guides on every issue. As a result of the growing concern for basic skills in the mid-1970s and an increased interest in literacy, books are available that explain ways to teach children certain skills such as reading, writing, and mathematics using simple, varied, and practical experiences in the home. There is also a small group of parents who now educate their children at home, a movement headed by John Holt.

Popular magazines and newspapers frequently contain feature articles and special editions relating to child rearing, parenting, and educational themes for children and youth. Corporate business is also getting into the act. Diaper manufacturers and other baby product companies all see the possibilities of the growing market and either sell or provide free materials that have the purpose of promoting a happier, healthier, and brighter child. An example is the *New Parent Adviser*, created in the past two years with the sole purpose of guiding parents through the early weeks and years of their child's life.

Specialization of Parenting

Changes in demographic patterns and the increasingly public nature of parenting have led to the specialization of parenting. We now know that the care of children is not and cannot be an instinctual process, but must be differentiated by the age and stage of the child (Ilg and Ames 1962) and gender, race, or special learning needs (Comer and Poussaint 1975; Rivers, Barnett, and Baruch 1979; Featherstone 1980). People used to believe that all children should be raised in the same way and parents thought that they did so. Now a mother who feels confident that she has dealt comfortably with her newborn and infant may find that the child as a toddler will leave her exhausted and frustrated. Another example is the parent of a physically handicapped child who finds she cannot use developmental guidelines for normal children to assess the growth of her child or her own efforts.

Parenting did not become specialized in this way until the mid-1960s, when the tasks of mothering became noticeably distinct from the tasks of housework. Keeping a child's clothes clean was decidedly different from stimulating a newborn with bright colors and carefully crafted mobiles or playing games with a preschooler. Parenting was not taught through passive participation in the culture. Skills needed to be learned, not from parents and grandparents, but by reading books and magazine articles. Most authors, like Dr. Spock, stress the notion that parents can become more knowledgeable and more skilled at their role. A general thesis is that parents are the most salient and potent force in the child's life. It is ironic that most authors who write books for parents, including Spock, are white males (Brazelton 1974, Dodson 1970; Ginott, 1965; Gordon 1970). Only a few women have written such books (Fraiberg 1959; LeShan 1967; Lerman 1980), and even they made strong statements about why women should stay at home with the children (Fraiberg 1977). Furthermore, some of these authors are outspoken in their opposition to any child care out of the home, in effect, creating a greater sense of guilt for mothers.

Generally, parents are urged to take cues from their baby or child. "Your child knows best" is the motto, rather than "father or mother knows best." Books on the subject tend to fall into two categories. One type looks at the needs of the child as an example of a developmental stage or age. The other examines certain aspects of parenting such as discipline, providing appropriate toys, eating, and sleeping, usually written in an anecdotal, nontheoretical style. Advice to parents has increasingly become oriented toward encouraging cognitive and language development rather than affective growth. "Bringing up superbaby," (Langway et al. 1983) discusses what it calls "infant academics." Most of the experts are not in favor of pushing children to make them early academic achievers, and urge parents to let their children play. But the "super baby" idea is a natural outgrowth of the "super mom" idea.

There is no question that a generation of "on-line" children exists. While in some instances whole families are involved in computer-based activities, in others, parents stand aside, amazed by the technology and having little comprehension of it. Ironically, at the same time that more and more information that can help parents is becoming available, technology is creating a new kind of generation gap, which for some parents may lead to feelings of helplessness and confusion.

If parenting has become a highly specialized occupation, then it is not surprising that children, too, should be expected to be highly specialized people. Specialization breeds specialization.

Who Cares for the Children?

In the United States, as in other industrialized countries throughout the world, economic necessity and the women's movement are changing the daily lives of families. The United States is far behind European countries in being responsive and/or adaptive to the needs of working parents and their children. Drs. Sheila Kamerman and Alfred Kahn of Columbia University reported from their extensive studies that only the United States, Britain, and Canada at this time do not have "family policies." As described by Judy Foreman (1980), "A family policy would act somewhat like other American environmental impact statements in attempting to make sure that other governmental policies, laws and regulations on housing, working hours and salaries, for instance, do not have a negative impact on family life."

Given the burden of knowing that parenthood is a challenging task, we have to ask what kind of support is available for the great majority of parents who have no choice but to seek the help of other people in the bringing up of their children? It is apparent from all the demographic patterns and social forces that we have described, that parents need the help of others and that this is of benefit to the child also. Despite the obvious need, there is very little support for such a concept.

Over the past ten to fifteen years research has been conducted that begins to assist us in understanding the very complicated child-care system. Some major trends have been reported:

1. Parents of children under three tend to rely heavily on relatives and on family day care, as well as on sitters in their own homes.

2. The majority of parents prefer care facilities to be close to their homes rather than to their work. A small group of parents, however, tends to use child care near their place of work; these are primarily professional and working mothers.

3. Most parents combine several types of care in a single day and change the combination as the child grows. It is reported by researchers Sheila Kamerman and Alfred Kahn that there were seventeen million American children under the age of six years in 1978. Of these, 6.9 million had mothers in the paid work force (Foreman 1980). According to sociologist Sandra Hofferth of the Urban Institute, a Washington research organization, 60 percent of these 6.9 million children are cared for by relatives, including older siblings. About 10 percent are cared for in child-care centers, and about 30 percent by hired day-care mothers or in-home baby sitters (Foreman 1980).

4. Approximately 68 percent of all preschool children aged three, four, and five years go to some form of out-of-home care whether parents work or not. These include private centers and preschools, Head Start and other programs (Foreman 1980).

It is consistently reported that there is a tremendous shortage of programs available to serve children with working parents. The Child Care Resource Center in Cambridge, Massachusetts, reported that each month 400 to 500 Boston area families call for assistance regarding the locating and selecting of child care; 50 percent of these request care for infants and toddlers. There are also those who report that supply and demand are not fixed entities, but inseparable and dynamic. Cost, quality, openings for a given age, location of care, and time to search for and find the programs are only a few of the variables that influence a "match" between a family and a program. Also, a family may attempt to enroll the child in several centers and be unable to do so; it is possible that this child's name will remain on all of the centers' waiting lists. In the meantime, the family goes ahead and makes other arrangements, and this information does not become available to the other centers.

Unquestionably, research and statistics on the need for child care, taken piecemeal, are confusing. Some statistics apply only to children of working parents, others to children of all parents. Also, the terms used to define types of care, whether it be by relatives, in-home care, family day care, and centers have not been clearly delineated in some studies.

Over the past ten years a deeper understanding regarding day care for infants, toddlers, and young children has developed. Day care occurs in the child's home, in a family day-care setting, which is usually at the home of the caregiver, or in a center.

In response to criticism of mothers who work, research has demonstrated that quality day care does not undermine the parent-child attachment (Caldwell 1970; Kagan, Kearsley, and Zelazo 1978; Rubenstein and Howes 1979; Ricciuti 1974). In fact, when a mother believes that it is important for her child to be in day care while she is at work, her positive attitude is conveyed to the child. If the mother has ambivalent feelings, these too are conveyed to the child and can create problems (Rubenstein and Howes 1979). To enhance parent-child attachment, it is best to introduce a child to day care either before attachments are formed or after they are well formed. Hence, starting infant care at seven to twelve months of age is more difficult for the child than starting earlier or later (Kagan, Kearsley, and Zelazo 1978; Bergstrom and Gold 1974).

Young children's social relations are at the core of the controversy over day care. Children in day-care centers are more outgoing than those who are not, but they are also more likely to be loud, boisterous, competitive, and aggressive with their peers (Clarke-Stewart 1982). Infants and young children who are from what are classified or considered to be at-risk or disadvantaged families can benefit from day-care programs, as can their mothers. This is particularly the case if the child is in that environment for two years, especially between the ages of two and four years (Rescorla, Provence, and Naylor 1982). Perhaps this is because it is during these formative and critical years that a young child masters important cognitive and social skills, learns to manipulate objects, begins to express his thoughts, and develops a sense of curiosity (White 1975).

The caregiver is the most important aspect of day care. Good caregivers characteristically are actively involved with children in talking, teaching, demonstrating, playing, and responding to the child's and group's interest, and giving positive encouragement and suggestions. Research has shown that caregivers are most effective in their role if they have been involved in training and education that addresses the following subjects: child growth and development, child care programming and activities, design of physical space, health and safety practices, nutrition, and working with parents (U.S. Department of Health, Education, and Welfare 1980). Also of importance is the size of the total group. For children ages birth to two years, the maximum group size is six; for children from three to six years, it is sixteen. A smaller group creates a more homelike and personalized environment. The ideal staff:child ratio in center-based programs is one caregiver to three children from infancy to two, one caregiver to four children two to three years of age, and one caregiver to nine children three to six years of age (U.S. Department of Health, Education, and Welfare 1980).

The main problem with quality day care is that it is very expensive, in fact, beyond the means of the people who need it most. It is evident that many parents cannot afford quality day care and neither can they afford to stay home. The Bureau of Labor Statistics in 1980 showed that with a family income of $14,027 gross and with one preschool child in care ($2,000–$2,500), approximately 16 percent of family income goes to child care; if there are two children in care ($4,500–$5,000) approximately 32 percent of income goes to child care. In the Boston area, full-day care for infants and toddlers in a center ranges from $100 to $150 per week, and from $65 to $100 per week for preschoolers. At such prices many parents cannot afford to purchase the type of care that best meets the needs of their children.

There is no question that the topic is emotionally charged, especially as it relates to the care of infants and toddlers. Expert opinions, personal values, political and economic situations, the rights of women, and some fears regarding children's development all mesh together to create a debate around this difficult issue. Authorities who base their opinions on scientific evidence disagree, and perhaps this is bound to be the case, since the knowledge base is still somewhat limited.

The care of school-age children also remains a dilemma. Many families depend on a combination of resources for portions of the day. Sitters, neighbors, relatives, drop-in centers, Ys, local recreation facilities, public libraries, youth-serving organizations, and some school systems are among the resources that provide activities and/or care for children. The School-Age Child Care Project at the Wellesley College Center for Research on Women (1982) anticipates that the growing needs in this area will increase pressure for the use of empty classrooms. It is possible that more community and school groups will provide before- and after-school programs, extended day programs, and special enrichment activities. There is little evidence that the whole society is willing to accept responsibility for rearing children and supporting working parents.

Options for Support

There are, however, some supports for parents and families that are promising. For example, during the past three to five years, some companies have begun to design programs at the workplace that address the needs of working parents and are part of the benefits available to their employees. Some companies have work-site child care, family day-care systems, after-school child care, noontime seminars on family-related topics, information referral services for child care, and other employee assistance programs. Over eighty companies now sponsor their own day-care centers, and several hundred hospitals and many other companies are experimenting with addressing the needs of their employees who are working parents (Baden and Friedman 1981). Families profit from a flexible benefit plan from which they can select child care support instead of a medical, dental, or retirement plan. Among the possible options of flexible benefits that relate to families with children are:

> Flex-time, the employee has core hours to work each day
> Flex-place, some work can be done at home
> Job sharing, one position is shared by two people
> Full or partial sponsorship of on-site and off-site child-care centers
> Information and referral services for parents on child care and other family-related issues
> Specific times during the work day when employees may receive calls from their children, thus avoiding more costly, unplanned interruptions
> Summer camps
> Employee leave for adoption of a child
> Maternity leave
> Paternity leave

Child sick leave
Vouchers and vendor payments to off-site child-care services

The flexible benefits, referred to by many as the cafeteria plan, allow employees to choose those they want from a range of alternatives. In doing this, companies are beginning to address the special concerns of their employees with children and youth. While child-care programs and benefits, organized or subsidized by companies, are available to only a small percentage of the American work force—fewer than one million workers (Shenon 1983)—it appears there will continue to be a move toward more child-care subsidies. The Economic Recovery Tax Act of 1981 increased tax credits available to employees for child care expenses necessary for their continued employment. It also allowed an exclusion from gross income for the value of employer-provided day-care services, and provided depreciation incentive for employers who improve day-care facilities by creating on-site or nearby centers for employees' children (Child Care Resource Center 1982).

Conclusion

Parenting occurs across the life cycle, and this is especially so now because of the changes in demographic patterns. Parenting is a time of growth and has a developmental process of its own, and both mothers and fathers are involved. It is no longer viewed as something that everyone can do in a simple and natural style.

Parenting has become a public issue, although previously it was a private family matter. At the same time parents are encouraged to become more competent in their roles, there are a number of technological developments that make their jobs harder.

Locating adequate and appropriate child care is difficult and frustrating for parents, since the options vary a great deal and are often expensive. Furthermore, the care of infants and toddlers in child care settings remains an emotionally charged issue. The elements essential to providing quality care for children can be articulated; however, such care is costly.

There are many family forms and many patterns for family life, but support for families is hard to find. Programs and policies are being implemented in the work place and in the community, but this represents only a small effort.

References

A portrait of America. 1983. *Newsweek*, January 17, 20–33.

BADEN, C., and FRIEDMAN, D. E., eds. 1981. *New management initiatives for working parents*. Boston: Office of Continuing Education, Center for Parenting Studies, Wheelock College.

BANE, M. J., 1980. A profile of the family in the 1980's. In *Focus on the family*. Edited by C. Baden. Boston: Wheelock College Center for Parenting Studies.

BARDWICK, J. M. 1980. The seasons of a woman's life. In *Women's lives, new theory, research and policy*. Edited by D. B. McGuigan. Ann Arbor: University of Michigan Continuing Education for Women.

BERGSTROM, J. M., and GOLD, J. B. 1974. *Sweden's day nurseries: Focus on program for infants and toddlers*. Washington, D.C.: Day Care and Child Development Council of America.

BOWLBY, J. 1969. *Attachment*. New York: Basic Books.

BRAZELTON, T. B. 1974. *Toddlers and parents*. New York: Delacorte Press.

BRODY, J. E. 1983. Influential theory on "bonding" at birth is now questioned. New York Times, March 29.

BRONFENBRENNER, U. 1981. Children and families: 1984? *Society* (January–February):38–41.

Bureau of Labor Statistics. 1980. *Perspectives on working women: A databook*. Bulletin 2080. Washington, D.C.: Government Printing Office.

CALDWELL, B., et al. 1970. Infant day care and attachment. *American Journal of Orthopsychiatry* 40:397–412.

Child Care Resource Center. 1982. Tax incentives for employer-sponsored day care programs. Chicago: Commerce Clearing House.

CLARKE-STEWART, A. 1979. And daddy makes three: The father's impact on mother and young child. *Child Development* 49:466–78.

———. 1982. *Day care*. Cambridge, Mass.: Harvard University Press.

COLLINS, G. 1979. A new look at life with father. *New York Times Magazine*, June 17.

COMER, J. P., and POUSSAINT, A. 1975. *Black child care: How to bring up a healthy black child in America. A guide to emotional and psychological development*. New York: Simon & Schuster.

CRONIN, J. 1980. *A profile describing licensed adoption agency programs and their accomplishments*. Boston: Region I Adoption Resource Center.

DODSON, F. 1970. *How to parent*. New York: New American Library.

ERIKSON, E. 1968. Life cycle. *International Encyclopedia of the Social Sciences* 9: 286–92.

FALLOWS, D. 1982. Why mothers should stay home. *Washington Monthly* 13 (January): 50–55.

———. 1983. What day care can't do. *Newsweek*, January 10.

FEATHERSTONE, H. 1980. *A difference in the family: Life with a disabled child*. New York: Basic Books.

FOREMAN, J. 1980. Who will mind the children. *Boston Globe*, November 16–22.

FRAIBERG, S. 1959. *The magic years*. New York: Charles Scribner's Sons.

———. 1977. *Every child's birthright: In defense of mothering*. New York: Basic Books.

FREIDAN, B. 1981. *The second stage*. New York: Summit Books.

———. 1983. Twenty years after *The feminine mystique*. *New York Times Magazine*, February 27.

FRIDAY, N. 1977. *My mother/my self.* New York: Delacorte Press.

GALINSKY, E. 1981. *Between generations: The six stages of parenthood.* New York: Times Books.

GILLIGAN, C. 1976. The easy way to bring up children. *Harvard Magazine* 78 (April).

GINOTT, H. 1965. *Between parent and child.* New York: Avon Books.

GORDON, I. J. 1970. *Baby learning through baby play.* New York: St. Martin's Press.

GOULD, R. 1978. *Transformations.* New York: Simon & Schuster.

HAMMER, S. 1975. *Daughters and mothers: Mothers and daughters.* New York: New American Library.

ILG, F. L., and AMES, L. B. 1962. *Parents ask.* New York: Dell Publishing Co.

KAGAN, J.; KEARSLEY, R.; and ZELAZO, P. 1978. *Infancy: Its place in human development.* Cambridge, Mass.: Harvard University Press.

LANGWAY, L.; JACKSON, T.; and ZABARSKY, M. 1983. Bringing up superbaby. *Newsweek,* March 28.

LEE, G. R. 1981. Marriage and family. *Society* 18 (January–February):68–71.

LEVINSON, D. J.; DARROW, C. N.; KLEIN, E. B., et al. 1978. *The seasons of a man's life.* New York: Alfred A. Knopf.

LERMAN, S. 1980. *Parent awareness training: Positive parenting for the 1980s.* New York: A & W Publishers.

LESHAN, E. 1967. *The conspiracy against childhood.* New York: Atheneum.

Letters to the Editor. 1982. *Washington Monthly* 14 (March):1–3.

MESIBOV, G. B.; SCHROEDER, C. S.; and WESSON, L. 1977. Parental concerns about their children. *Journal of Pediatric Psychology* 2:13–17.

NEUGARTEN, B., and WEINSTEIN, K. 1973. The changing American grandparent. In *Middle age and aging.* Edited by Bernice L. Neugarten. Chicago: University of Chicago Press.

PRESS, A.; CLAUSEN, A.; BURGER, W., et al. 1983. Divorce American Style. *Newsweek,* January 10.

RESCORLA, L. A.; PROVENCE, S.; and NAYLOR, A. 1982. The Yale child welfare research program: Description and results. In *Day care: Scientific and social policy issues.* Edited by E. F. Zigler and E. W. Gordon. Boston: Auburn House, 982.

RICCIUTI, H. 1974. Fear and development of social attachments in the first year of life. In *The origins of human behavior.* Edited by M. Lewis and L. Rosenblum. New York: John Wiley & Sons.

RIVERS, C.; BARNETT, R.; and BARUCH, G. 1979. *Beyond sugar and spice: How women grow, learn, and thrive.* New York: G. P. Putnam's Sons.

RUBENSTEIN, J., and HOWES, C. 1979. Caregiving and infant behavior in day care and in homes. *Developmental psychology* 15:1–24.

School-age Child Care Project. 1982. School-age child care. In *Day care: Scientific and social policy issues.* Edited by E. F. Zigler and E. W. Gordon. Boston: Auburn House.

SHEEHY, G. 1974. *Passages.* New York: E. P. Dutton.

SHENON, P. 1983. Corporate kids. *New York Times*, March 6.

SMITH, R. E. 1979. *The subtle revolution: Women at work.* Washington, D.C.: The Urban Institute.

SPOCK, B. 1946. *The common sense book of baby and child care.* New York: Duell, Sloan, & Pearce.

—————. 1968. *Baby and child care.* Rev. ed. New York: Pocket Books.

U.S. Department of Health, Education and Welfare. 1980. Office of the Secretary HEW Day Care Regulations. *Federal Register* 42, no. 55 (March 19).

U.S. Department of Health and Human Services. 1980. *Children's bureau initiatives for the adoption of minority children.* Publication no. (OHDS) 81-30300. Washington, D.C.: Government Printing Office.

VAILLANT, G. E. 1977. *Adaption to life.* Boston: Little, Brown & Co.

WEINGARTEN, K. 1983. *Early and later parenthood: Interaction of developmental tasks with clinical issues.* Presented at Countway Medical Library, Boston, January 25.

WHELAN, E. M. 1975. *A baby . . . maybe: A guide to making the most fateful decision of your life.* New York: Bobbs-Merrill.

WHITE, B. L. 1975. *The first three years of life.* Englewood Cliffs, N.J.: Prentice-Hall.

Bibliography

Baden, C., ed. *Focus on the Family. New Images of Parents and Children in the 1980s.* Boston: Wheelock College Center for Parenting Studies, 1980.

Bane, M. J. *Here to Stay—American Families in the Twentieth Century.* New York: Basic Books, 1976.

Beck, R. "Beyond the Stalemate in Child Care Public Policy." In *Day Care: Scientific and Social Policy Issues.* Edited by Edward F. Zigler and Edward W. Gordon. Boston: Auburn House, 1982.

Bergstrom, J. M., and Joy, L. *Going to Work? Choosing Care for Infants and Toddlers.* Washington, D.C.: Day Care Council of America, 1981.

Bergstrom, J. M., and Lazar, I. "Electronic Learning Aids and the Family as Educator." *Journal of Educational Technology Systems* 2 (1982–83):23–33.

Borman, E., ed. *The Social Life of Children in a Changing Society.* Hillsdale, N.J.: Lawrence Erlbaum, 1982.

Brazelton, T. B. *On Becoming a Family.* New York: Delacorte Press, 1981.

Brazelton, T. B., and Vaughan, V. C., eds. *The Family—Can it be Saved?* Chicago: Year Book Medical Publishers, 1976.

Bruner, J.; Cole, M.; and Lloyd, B., eds. *The Developing Child Series.* 6 vols. Cambridge, Mass.: Harvard University Press, 1977–82.

Bureau of Labor Statistics. *Employment in Perspective: Working Women.* Report 675. Washington, D.C.: Government Printing Office, 1982.

Chess, S.; Thomas, A.; and Birch, H. *Your Child Is a Person*. New York: Viking Press, 1965.

Chodorow, N. *The Reproduction of Mothering, Psychoanalysis and the Sociology of Gender*. Berkeley: University of California Press, 1978.

Clarke-Stewart, A. *Child Care in the Family: A Review of Research and Some Propositions for Policy*. New York: Academic Press, 1977.

Cohen, Y. A. "Shrinking Households." *Society* 18 (January–February 1981):48–52.

Cummings, F. "Caretaker Stability and Day Care." *Developmental Psychology* 4 (1980):655–56.

Dearman, N., and Plisko, V. *The Condition of Education*. Washington, D.C.: National Center for Educational Statistics, 1980.

Dodson, M. "The Latch Key Child—Boy's Death Draws New Attention." *Los Angeles Times*, March 21, 1983.

Dullea, G. "Wide Changes in Family Life Are Altering the Family Law." *New York Times*, February 7, 1983.

Evans, J., and Ilfield, D. *Good Beginnings—Parenting in the Early Years*. Ypsilanti, Mich.: High-Scope Press, 1982.

"The Family." *Daedalus* 106 (Spring 1977).

Farrer, D., and Ramsey, C. "Infant Day Care and Attachment Behaviors toward Mothers and Teacher." *Child Development* 48 (1977):1112–16.

Fatherhood Project. New York: Bank Street College of Education.

Freud, A.; Goldstein, J.; and Solnit, A. J. *Before the Best Interest of the Child*. New York: Free Press, 1979.

Green, D. H., ed. *Parent's Choice*. Waban, Mass., 1978.

Hoffman, L. W. *Maternal Employment in the 1980s*. Presented at Wheelock College, Boston, November 15, 1982.

Kamerman, S. B. *Parenting in an Unresponsive Society*. New York: Free Press, 1980.

Kanter, R. M. *Work and Family in the United States: A Critical Review and Agenda for Research and Policy*. New York: Russell Sage Foundation, 1977.

Keniston, K. *All Our Children: The American Family under Pressure*. New York: Harcourt Brace Jovanovich, 1977.

Kent, G. B., and Kalkstein, K. *Smart Toys—For Babies from Birth to Two*. New York: Harper & Row, 1982.

Lasch, C. *Haven in a Heartless World, the Family Besieged*. New York: Basic Books, 1977.

Levine, J. A. *Who Will Raise the Children? New Options for Fathers (and Mothers)*. New York: J. B. Lippincott, 1976.

Lightfoot, S. L. *Worlds Apart: Relationships between Families and Schools*. New York: Basic Books, 1978.

McBride, A. B. *The Growth and Development of Mothers*. New York: Harper & Row, 1973.

McCall, R. *Infants*. New York: Vintage Books, 1980.

National Academy of Sciences. *Toward a National Policy for Children and Families*. Washington, D.C.: Advisory Committee on Child Development, 1976.

Nirenberg, S. "Life without Father." *Savvy*, March 1983, pp. 96–98.

Novak, M. "In Praise of Bourgeois Virtues." *Society* 18 (January–February 1981): 60–67.

Peters, C. "Tilting at Windmills." *Washington Monthly* 14 (March 1982):42–48.

Ragozin, A. "Attachment Behavior of Day-Care Children: Naturalistic and Laboration Observations." *Child Development* 51 (1980):409–15.

Reed, G., and Leiderman, P. "Age-Related Changes in Attachment Behavior in Polymetrically Reared Infants: The Kenya Gusii." In *Culture and Infant Interaction*. Edited by T. Field et al. Hillsdale, N.J.: Lawrence Erlbaum, 1981.

Rossi, A. S. "Transition to Parenthood." *Journal of Marriage and the Family* 30 (February 1968):26–39.

Rubin, N. *The New Suburban Woman: Beyond Myth and Motherhood.* New York: Coward, McCann & Geohegan, 1982.

Salk, L. *What Every Child Would Like His Parents to Know.* New York: Worker Paperback Library, 1973.

Sparling, J. J.; Lawman, B. C.; Lewis, I. S., et al. *What Parents Say about their Information Needs.* Chapel Hill: University of North Carolina, 1978.

Sparling, J. J., and Lewis, I. S. *Learning Games for the First Three Years.* New York: Walker & Co., 1977.

Steiner, G. *The Children's Cause.* Washington, D.C.: Brookings Institute, 1976.

United States Commission on Civil Rights. *Child Care and Equal Opportunity for Women.* Publication no. (OHOS) 80-30289. Washington, D.C.: Government Printing Office, 1981.

White, B. L. *A Parent's Guide to the First Three Years.* Englewood Cliffs, N.J.: Prentice-Hall, 1980.

Whitebread, J. "Who's Taking Care of the Children?" *Family Circle*, February 1979.

Zigler, E. F., and Gordon, E. W., eds. *Day Care: Scientific and Social Policy Issues.* Boston: Auburn House, 1982.

Resources

American Family, National Center for Family Studies, Cardinal Station, Washington, D.C. 20064. *American Family* is a monthly national newsletter on family policy programs published jointly by American Family, Inc., a nonprofit subsidiary of Wakefield Washington Associates and the National Center for Family Studies at the Catholic University of America. *American Family* is one of several cooperative efforts.

American Family Program, General Mills, Inc., Public Affairs Department, Box 5401, Dept. 830, Minneapolis, MN 55460. General Mills, Inc. instituted the American Family Program in 1974 in order to identify social concerns and communicate these to the private and public sectors. Published is a series of major research studies, the *General Mills American Family Reports* as well as *Digests of Proceedings* of American Family Forums.

Center for Parenting Studies, Wheelock College, 200 The Riverway, Boston, MA 02215. The Center was established by Director Frances Litman in response to the change in structure and substance of the American family. Programs provided are directed toward professionals and parents "who seek to understand and improve the quality of life for parents and children." Resources available to the public include courses, workshops, seminars, conferences, and publications.

Center for Research on Women, Wellesley College, 828 Washington Street, Wellesley, MA 02181. The Center's mission is to "develop wider opportunities for and new perspectives on women." They focus on five primary research areas: family employment, minority women, adult development and aging, and higher education. Outreach programs include working papers (available on request), research reports, conferences, a luncheon seminar series, and colloquia.

Child Care Resource Center, Chicago, Illinois: Commerce Clearing House, Inc. 1982. *Tax Incentives for Employer-Sponsored Day Care Programs* explores the various types of employer-provided child-care programs and looks at both their advantages and disadvantages. It describes various tax benefits available to employers and employees.

Child Care News, 24 Thorndike Street, Cambridge, MA 02141. A monthly newsletter distributed to parents, educators, and anyone else who has a genuine interest in the welfare of young children. It features information regarding current legislation, tax credit changes, job listings, conferences, books, and other relevant information dealing with young children. The newsletter is a collaborative effort of many organizations.

Coping with the Overall Pregnancy/Parenting Experience, 37 Clarendon Street, Boston, MA 02116. COPE is a nonprofit, nonpolitical organization that offers comprehensive services for both women and men. It is licensed by the Massachusetts Department of Public Health. "COPE addresses the issues of Pregnancy and Early Parenting at a time when dramatic social changes in the roles and relationships of women and men as people and parents are taking place."

Education Development Center, Inc., 55 Chapel Street, Newton, MA 02160. The Center (EDC) is a publicly funded nonprofit organization that supports educational research and development. Currently, EDC has thirty active projects grouped into four clusters: school and society, quantitative skills, continuing education, and international programs. Three projects of particular interest include exploring childhood, family and community health through caregiving, and young adulthood.

Fatherhood Project, Bank Street College of Education, 610 West 112th Street, New York, NY 10024. The Project's goal is to "encourage the development of new options for male involvement in childrearing." Main activities include a father-child play discussion group, an infant-care course for preadolescent boys, and a clearinghouse that distributes information about men in nurturing roles. Currently the project is in the process of preparing a catalog entitled *Fatherhood, U.S.A.* of innovative programs and resources around the country.

National Day Care Campaign, P. O. Box 28607, Washington, D.C. 20005. The Campaign began in 1979 with the initial construction of a platform statement. This platform is to serve as a "statement of principles behind which day care organizations with diverse views could unite." The central objective of the campaign is that quality day care for children must be available for all working parents who need it and want it at a price they can afford."

Perry, K. S., *Employers and Child Care: Establishing Services Through the Workplace.* (Washington, D.C.: U.S. Department of Labor, 1982). As the numbers of working mothers in the work force steadily increases, the need for reliable quality child-care services also does. This booklet provides valuable information for parents, educators, and planners of child-care programs in relation to business, industry, unions, employers associations, and community involvement.

Roth, L. E. *List of Employer-Supported Child Care Programs in the U.S. 1981–82.* NDNP, Child Care Information Service, P. O. Box 40652, Pasadena, CA 91104-7652. This guide was produced to facilitate sharing of information among employers, child-care professionals, public agencies, and others, as well as "to show the extent and variety of employer involvement in child care." Companies that support child-care centers, family day-care homes, information and referral services, voucher payment programs, care for sick children, care for school-age children, support for community child care programs, and parent education programs are presented.

Education

Jeanne J. Speizer

For women and education, 1982 will certainly be remembered as the year of the backlash, a time when the pendulum swung quickly to the conservative side. So much happened, so quickly, and most of it negative, that educators literally have been stunned and unable to react to even a portion of the losses. On all fronts there has been backsliding under the slogan that the way to solve problems is to return to the "good old days." The setbacks have been so extensive that the writer must struggle neither to focus on them nor to recount in petulant tone and lurid detail each and every resource and support that has been withdrawn from educational equity pursuits. Such an account could be construed as an admission of defeat and would most certainly devalue the advances of the past years to which we can justly point with pride. Rather, the task is to use this moment to step back from the fray, take stock, and make plans for future activities.

A view of education in 1982 was fittingly captured on the last day of the year under the newspaper banner, "Presidential panel recommends abolishing Education Department" (1982). The threatened loss of the Education Department came at the end of a long year of actual losses. A "last hired, first fired" policy meant the loss of jobs for many women and minorities who had successfully broken into the chain of command in educational institutions. Budgetary constraints led to the cancellation of curriculum reforms, action programs, and research studies that were designed to bring equity to education. Most difficult of all, perhaps, was the conservative trend that swept over every area of education and eliminated innovations that had been carefully planned and constructed to change the system to meet the needs of all students.

At first glance it would appear that twenty years of effort toward educational equity have been lost and the only way to proceed is to start over. That approach might indeed prove necessary, but only after we have gathered what can be learned as a guide for future steps. This chapter therefore focuses on a broad spectrum of educational change and on the internal and external forces that interact to impede or promote that change. Events of 1982 that illustrate the discussion are used where appropriate; however, a detailed account of programs, regulations, and activities is found in the resources section only.

Power in education is the focus of the analysis—who has it, how it is gained, and how it is exercised—in an effort to determine what forces enabled equity issues to be so easily set aside. In other words, what makes progressive change so difficult and slow and regressive change so easy and fast to achieve? The educational system is considered as a whole rather than as separate parts, as the power forces that interact are similar at every level.

External Institutional Power

Educational institutions are often greatly influenced or directly controlled by pressures from outside their boundaries. External power forces can emanate from the economic or political arenas, from actions of governing boards such as trustees or regents, from legal decisions, or from groups of people such as alumnae, parents, community representatives, and so on. Thus far, women and minorities have been underrepresented among those who can or have applied outside pressure, and in 1982 many of the changes have been to the detriment of those segments of society.

At the federal level, the year can best be characterized as a time when the foxes were let into the chicken yard. A conservative administration with an anti-intellectual, generally negative opinion of education and an even dimmer view of educational equity has been in control, with the result that educational issues have had relatively low priority. Appointments of officials to education positions have been given, more often than not, to individuals who have been publically in opposition to the goals of the programs for which they have been chosen. For example, Terrell Bell, Secretary of Education, has been committed to the destruction or demotion of his own department since he took office. To diminish or demolish governmental involvement in education, money has been cut back for research; programs have been eliminated, curtailed, or put into block grants to be administered by each state in its own fashion; student loans have been reduced; and regulations have been eliminated or changed. Most of the federal actions have been detrimental to the activities of those who are working to promote educational equity.

The "model" program for demonstrating the actions of the federal government in 1982 is the Women's Educational Equity Action Program (WEEAP). Initially WEEAP was targeted for block grants; when that step proved too difficult to accomplish, the administration requested that no money be budgeted to fund it. Community response to the possible loss of WEEAP was strong, so Congress reinstated its funds in the budget. The director of the program was moved to another area of government for ninety days, but again community response was immediate and vigorous and she was reinstated. Next, reviewers for grants were replaced by administration-chosen reviewers, many of whom had little knowledge of education and a less than positive attitude toward programs that support women, minorities, or the handicapped. Members of the National Advisory Council for WEEAP were changed; again, many of the appointees were people with little experience in education who represented political stances that were diametrically opposed to the aims and goals of WEEAP. The new council immediately ousted the executive director and selected a replacement who has been working to eliminate WEEAP since her appointment. Reactions to the government's steps to cancel, control, and subvert WEEAP have been extensive and thus the program has survived, although word of its potential demise was pervasive throughout the year. The fate of the program remains in the balance, but many remain optimistic that WEEAP will continue, as it is the only Federal program left that specifically addresses issues of importance to women and minorities.

Eligibility for federal loans has become more restricted and the amount of money available was reduced in 1982. Cutbacks in money to students has been devastating to all colleges and all students, except for the most wealthy. For women students, the effect of loan cutbacks is particularly difficult, as families with limited resources have traditionally supported the education of their sons in preference to their daughters. Those women who do attend college tend to receive less total aid than men, smaller grant awards, and smaller loan awards (Rosenfeld and Hearn 1982). Women are clustered in two-year and state schools, which may be an indication that they are now encouraged to attend colleges but mainly those that are closer to home and less expensive. Scholarships and grants are usually earmarked for younger students; thus adult women students are doubly handicapped in their ability to obtain funds to support their education.

States have responded to the shift in power away from the federal government by cutting back on money and programs. Cities and counties also have played their part by decreasing funds and eliminating programs. Trustees and school boards have been left with the task of overseeing the distribution of dwindling resources. Thus far, little thought appears to have been given at any level of decision making to the goals of education as a whole and to the effects of severe cuts on its future. Expediency appears to rule behavior: officials make decisions based on budget considerations, and educators are interested primarily in conserving their own jobs. The needs of students, in general, now and in the future, do not seem to be of particular interest. Educational equity concerns have had little, if any, bearing on decisions.

Parents, religious groups, and other special interest organizations have taken steps to enter the power vacuum thus created and have begun to battle over who "really" controls education. Each group has applied pressure to make changes to suit its views. Thus there have been court cases over adding "creation science" to the curriculum, and moves for a constitutional amendment (supported by the President) to have prayer in the classroom. Librarians have been inundated with requests to remove "controversial" books from the shelves, and teachers have been approved and reproved for teaching certain content areas. Hiring and firing of faculty, cancellation of programs, and a multitude of other areas of education have been considered fair game for lobbying groups who wish to control what happens in the classroom. In this atmosphere of competition for control, educators have had to spend so much time responding to each new challenge and encroachment that there has been little time or energy left over to work on educational equity issues.

Economic factors played havoc with education in 1982 and are predicted to continue to do so in the forseeable future. The number of students available to educate has declined in the past ten years. The brunt of the declining enrollments has been experienced at the elementary and secondary levels thus far, but each year brings a prediction that higher education also will be affected. The number of students at the postsecondary level has remained stable, because of the nontraditional aged students, primarily women, who have entered higher education in large numbers (Heyns and Bird 1982), and in 1982 because of increased unemployment. The increase in students has been in public higher education, with the greatest growth in community colleges (Magarrell 1982).

Many institutions have turned to continuing education as the panacea for money problems. There is widespread belief that an unending source of adult students, mainly women, with money and time to spare for education is available to fill the classrooms. In recent years, women students have been fulfilling these expectations and returning to school in large numbers; however, there can never be enough older students to come close to meeting the needs of all the colleges planning for them. Thus other solutions must be found.

Educators had to expend a great deal of energy in 1982 responding to a combination of pressures from outside their institutions that emanate from federal, state, economic, and public sources. These outside pressures tended to work to the detriment of women and minorities as the changes in regulations, declines in program and research resources, and lobbying efforts often revolved around issues that have been primary to educational equity. The response was muted, as those who might most appropriately respond often had their own positions in jeopardy. Programs for women and minorities tend to be add-ons outside the regular power lines; when educational institutions were cut back, the first to be eliminated were people and programs outside the traditional organizational structure. With such cuts have gone those groups most interested in equity. The next year will be a time of regrouping and collecting of power forces, political and otherwise, to redirect education toward a concern for all students and, in particular, toward the needs of women and minority students.

Intra-institutional Power

Who controls educational institutions is often a murky issue, but one fact is absolutely clear: women and minorities have not yet become part of that power structure, for if they had been there this past year in numbers large enough to be heard, the cutbacks, reorganizing, and difficult decisions would have more equitably affected all aspects of the organization. The paucity of women policy makers might be construed as a lack of effort to reach that level, or an indication that women's tactics have not been as extensive, or as effective, as needed to accomplish the goal. The latter explanation is most likely, as a large pool of women report themselves available, prepared, and interested in management positions. Few, however, have become part of the power structure of their institutions.

The organizational structure of education systems is different from that of business enterprises in that power does not flow upward in a pyramid fashion toward one person at the top. Rather, there are two centers of power—the faculty and the administration, each of which holds certain responsibilities for itself.* Faculty control the curriculum, teaching, and research, while administrators control money and the structure in which the primary functions of teaching and research occur. The power to hire and fire is usually held jointly. Each group reports frequently that power in the institution rests with the other, and, in fact, it is very difficult to pinpoint where policies are actually established. The use of committees lends an outward appearance of democracy, which masks by whom the final decisions are reached. Tension between the faculty and administrators over who has what power and how it is handled is a constant theme. In 1981 the Supreme Court ruled that at Yeshiva College, a private institution, the faculty were functioning as managers and could not therefore form a union separate from the administration. This ruling has not been applied to state institutions where faculty traditionally do not engage in management activities, or in other private institutions in which each group handles separate aspects of the organization. The question of who controls education must still be resolved, but whatever the outcome, faculty and administrators must devise new methods to work together to address this and other difficult issues, some of which are, in fact, related to survival.

Women and minorities rarely control the power centers of faculty or administration, with the exception of some women's colleges. In the faculty, representatives of these two segments are to be found on the lowest rung of the ladder, without tenure and with little power. The subject disciplines in which women and minorities concentrate, such as education, social work, and nursing, are likely to be those with the least prestige in the institution; thus even those women who have tenure and who are heads of their departments may have little actual power.

Administrators   The administrative positions held by women and minorities are also likely to be far from the decision-making centers. Power is inversely related to the closeness of the position to students: those farthest from students hold the greatest power, while those who work daily with students have the least. As might be expected, women and minorities hold

Postsecondary institutions serve as the model for this discussion, as many of the power forces are similar in elementary and secondary systems, and it would be too cumbersome to discuss them separately.

administrative positions that involve a large commitment to students and thus demand a great deal of interpersonal skills, time, and effort. Women most often work in student affairs rather than on business or academic issues. The career path in student affairs ends with the position of Dean of Students or Vice President for Student Affairs. Few job possibilities are available once an administrator has reached such an office, as there is little opportunity to change to another career track inside the institution. Power tends to rest in business or academic affairs tracks, two paths that are considered as leading to the presidency of an educational institution.

Women and minorities are likely to be found in staff positions where they must rely on their ability to act "behind the throne" to influence the person who holds the line position. If a staff person works for an influential administrator, her situation as "assistant to" can be very important. Power is in another person's name, however, and when that person leaves, the assistant can be stripped of her position with no obvious next job available.

As resources declined in 1982, many institutions began to cut back on student services, and those reductions led to the loss of positions for many women and minorities. The absolute number of administrators has increased, but the additions were not in the areas where women and minorities are traditionally found (*Chronicle of Higher Education* 1982). Thus the future for student affairs administrators is bleak unless a marked change evolves in response to the needs of students. There is an implicit belief that anyone can take care of students, so few skills are considered to be needed for related positions. Faculty are being "encouraged" to take over many of these responsibilities, allowing for further cutbacks.

Women administrators must move into nontraditional areas of management if they are to survive over the next several years of consolidation in education. Efforts to reach educational equity have concentrated on increasing the number of women and minorities who hold positions as faculty or administrators. Affirmative action guidelines have been enforced variously, depending on the individual institution and the dedication of those in power. Forward progress in this area stopped in 1982, and although this is a setback, there are those who argue that affirmative action is not the way to pursue educational equity. The requirement to announce jobs more widely has increased the chances for all to compete, however, women and minorities have benefited little from this; other avenues might more fruitfully be pursued.

If affirmative action had worked and the number of positions for women and minorities had been greatly increased, the power centers of education might still not have been altered. The mere presence of women and minorities does not ipso facto guarantee power, although counting people is an easy way to assess progress of sorts. A more important factor than absolute numbers is where the people are situated, but an analysis is not possible by title alone, as titles vary by institution, as does the power that accrues to each position (Moore and Sagaria 1982). A study of the centers of power in educational institutions is needed, such as the one done by Kanter (1977) for corporations, but the task will be a difficult one, as the power structure appears to be more variable among educational institutions.

Faculty The mandatory age of retirement for those who work in educational institutions has been extended to seventy years as of 1982. This places an extra burden on institutions that need to adapt to a decline in the number of students. Tenured faculty often are found in subject areas with decreasing student interest. Thus institutions must find a way to use these personnel.

There is also a question as to how much interchangeability of faculty members is possible. One example of the difficulties inherent in moving faculty from area to area was provided by the director of a women's studies program at a large eastern public university. She reported that courses in her department were oversubscribed and that the number of courses was growing at an ever-accelerating rate. With a decline in the number of students in other disciplines, she began to be inundated with requests, sometimes demands, from tenured faculty to teach women's studies courses. Some of the most importunate had initially shunned women's studies or had actively worked to keep them out of the curriculum. Yet these same faculty members insisted that they were now qualified because, for example, they had been teaching history and could easily change to women's history. Women's studies faculty members were equally adamant that women's history required special training and at least a feminist perspective. The power struggle was over numbers of students and the money and security that accrued to those who had sufficient students to justify their remaining in the institution. Women students represented money and thus power; however, their educational needs were being weighed in the light of the needs of tenured faculty to remain in their jobs. The solution is not simple or clear.

Tenure, and who receives it, is a crucial issue. There are fewer and fewer tenured slots available each year; thus the opportunity to add to the number of women and minorities who hold them decreases as the need, created by the addition of more women students, increases. The decision as to who receives the limited tenure positions rests with those who have been in the institution the longest and often have the greatest need to continue things as they have always been. Research on women is often downgraded or undervalued by the male establishment; thus women scholars must often decide whether they will continue their research on women or forego that interest to follow an alternate, safer, though not surer, path toward tenure, that is, an area of scholarship considered more important by the powers that be. Whatever they decide, few women or minorities have made it through the tenure maze. Lawsuits have been instigated as the decisions on tenure often appear to be discriminatory; however thus far the courts have left tenure decisions to the "professionals," and have been unwilling to intervene. Most cases that have become adversarial have been settled out of court, which means that few legal precedents have been set.

Women faculty members often experience pressures that do not exist for their male colleagues, as they are expected to be especially good teachers and are evaluated harshly when they do not take great care and time with students (Bennett 1982). As tenure often goes to those who do research rather than to those who teach, women must balance the demands of students against these other pressures. Women are also asked to serve on a plethora of committees as representatives of the so-called women's view. There is rarely time left over from teaching and committee work for the pursuit of research; and many women find at the end of their junior faculty status period that they have completed and published insufficient research to obtain tenure. Those who eschew committees and excessive demands from students so that they can give time to research are often denied tenure because they are considered to have let down the students and the community. Because of these, and sometimes even less subtle factors, achievement of tenure for women is difficult and few are successful.

Women's Studies   Women's studies programs have grown extensively in the past ten years, from 112 programs in 1972 to over 400 in 1982 (Howe and Lauter 1980). Many faculty members report that women's studies is the most exciting and interesting area of scholarship presently available. Women students continue to demand the programs, as they feel left out of a curriculum that focuses on men and male accomplishments.

Control of the curriculum is an important faculty prerogative. Despite, or perhaps because of, male domination of the curriculum, women's studies programs have grown extensively over the past few years to meet the needs of the increasing number of women students. Few women's studies teachers receive tenure, however, which means that the courses are often taught by a series of new professors who seem to enter and depart through a revolving door, and thus have little power or staying ability in the institution.

There is a recurrent question as to whether women's studies should be a separate discipline, program, or major, or be included in the mainstream of the curriculum. This discussion centers around whether the courses represent merely the addition of women to the established discipline, or whether the entire framework of the discipline needs to be refocused and redirected. Those who argue for the former believe that women's studies can be taught by any faculty member, while those who propose the latter believe that a total revision of the curriculum and extensive retraining of faculty is required.

Power struggles over women's studies heightened in 1982 as federal and foundation money declined. Institutions were required to make decisions whether or not to invest money to continue these courses and programs. Those who placed the women's studies courses into each discipline have been less affected than those who have designed separate, identifiable programs. It is much easier to discontinue a whole area than it is to eliminate course by course. This advantage must be balanced, however, by the fact that there is less clear power available to those who wish to promote women's studies if all decisions are made discipline by discipline, with only one or two women's studies faculty available in each department. If women students continue to choose women's studies courses to prepare themselves to enter the work world, and if this persists as an exciting area of endeavor, then whether the program is in the mainstream or separate will not matter, as the demand will be so high that either model will work. If cuts are made, however, then these courses are greatly at risk, as those who make the decisions are not often those who are interested in women's studies.

An evaluation is needed of the women who major in women's studies to determine if they pursue different careers from those who choose more traditionally female disciplines. If the former are found more often to enter fields that are nontraditional for women, that is, more lucrative and powerful, then women's studies may find a more permanent place in the curriculum or may be added to the curricula of all fields better to meet the needs of women students.

In summary, power inside an institution is determined by administrators who control space and resources, and by faculty who control curriculum and tenure. The presence of women and minorities must increase in both these bastions of power. As of 1982 there have been some inroads. The percent of women faculty members has grown very slowly, from 22 percent in 1972 to 26 percent in 1980 (Grant and Eiden 1981). Administrative advancement also has been very slow, and again, much of that growth has been into positions that have little power. Unions, especially in state institutions, have gained in status in the past few years, and with their rise have formalized the separation of power among faculty, administrators, and support staff. Union activity has tended to support seniority and status quo, both of which work to the detriment of women and minorities.

Women and minorities must concentrate on reaching positions that command resources and from which decisions are actually made. Quality of position, not quantity, must be demanded if equity is to be accomplished.

Power over Disadvantaged Groups

One important tool for keeping people out of power is to categorize them as "others" and then treat them as if they were all the same. If they internalize and accept the myths and stereotypes about themselves, they can be easily controlled. This section explores the ways in which beliefs and expectations are used by the powerless to control themselves and used by the powerful to keep "others" out of the important decision-making areas of the educational enterprise.

Limiting the Focus   Ralph Ellison (1952) provides an image of the oppressed and the oppressor that is very illuminating for a discussion of the powerful and the powerless in education. Imagine for a moment a boxing match with all the members of one team (women and minorities) inside the ring, intensely concentrating on each other's moves, poised to win and retain control of that space. Out in the arena is the opposing team (white males) who are quite content to rule the vast space outside the ring. If, or when, members of the inside team try to leave the ring, the white males will be attentive, but as long as they remain concentrated on each other, the men are not threatened. Representatives who leave the ring are expected to speak for the entire group left behind; however, most of them stay in the confined space, watching only each other.

In education there are specific areas (or boxing rings) traditionally occupied by women and minorities. The competition for these slots is fierce. In fact, there is often intense discussion and disagreement as to whether the person chosen should be a white woman, a minority woman, or a minority man. This competition succeeds in keeping members of these segments of society focused on a limited number of opportunities, those that are stereotypically associated with their group. Thus we find women and minorities in such jobs as Dean of Students, Chair of Home Economics, Social Work or Nursing Dean, Affirmative Action officers, and teachers of English. One or two women or minority people will have nontraditional positions and will be seen as representatives of all others like themselves. As such they may be replaced, but rarely will their numbers be increased, as that might tip the balance of power. These tokens experience intense pressure to work for those whom they represent, and an equal pressure from the power group not only to do a competent job but to respond to all matters of concern to the group from which they emerged.

One example of in-fighting among women and minorities is to be found in discussions about the "right" way to change the administrative structure of an educational institution. One recommendation is that they learn the rules of the game and behave in a fashion as similar to that of the power group as possible (Hennig and Jardim 1977). In other words, the outside group should learn to dress, talk, and in all other ways reflect the manner and attitudes of those currently in power. The assumption is, that by so doing, women and minorities can reach responsible, decision-making positions from which they will then be able to make changes that will be widespread and long lasting. Another approach is to recommend that those devoted to change stay outside the current power structure and try to build an entirely new system. The reasoning is that once they enter the existing structure, they will be co-opted and unable to change a system in which they have become an integral part (Rich 1979). We have little evidence that either approach is right; each appears to work sometimes and for different reasons. The struggle to prove that one is right and the other is wrong occupies a great deal of energy, however, and certainly prevents believers in either from supporting the other.

Another example of in-fighting occurred at a recent women's conference that was concerned with changing education to meet the needs of women and minorities. The attendees had limited resources, as they did not hold powerful slots in the educational world, so they needed the support of each other. At the conference, however, they focused on who should control the meeting, with each group splintering into finer and more elite fragments. Rivalries emerged between old and young, black and white, academic and activist, middle class and working class, ad infinitum. The energies of the participants were so dissipated that there was little mention of the people who were not in attendance. Those at the conference represented a small segment of the educational community, and they needed to act together if they were to have an impact on the system. They had to focus toward the larger arena—the source of real power; it was not necessary to change each other and become identical in their tactics and pursuits. They left the conference, however, still in competition, with each group intent on following its own path and ignoring or downplaying the work of others.

Now imagine how the power struggle might change if all the players inside the ring turned around, joined hands, and agreed to work together to equalize control of the available space. The group currently in power would have to respond more carefully, for no longer would those in the ring disempower themselves by intense competition for limited space. The power dimensions certainly might change and women and minorities might be able more effectively to control nontraditional areas of education.

Myths and Stereotypes   Myths and stereotypes have worked very well to keep educational institutions primarily in the hands of white males, with the assumption that all men are good managers and leaders. As women and minorities have pushed to enter the upper levels of faculty and administration, one of the most effective devices for denying them admission has been the nationwide search for "qualified" women to fill positions. Rarely does one seek "qualified" men, as maleness appears to be qualification in and of itself (Perun, et al. 1982). For some unspecified reason, qualified women are difficult to find despite repeated evidence that there is a large pool of experienced and knowledgeable women who are seeking such positions. Apparently "qualified" is a subjective criterion not easily filled by women or minority people, perhaps because they are not identical in all ways to the men who are searching for the candidate.

In theory, educational institutions are unable to discriminate in hiring practices, as the Supreme Court in 1982 ruled that the employment regulations of Title IX referred to employees as well as students (High court . . . 1982). This ruling may prove to be another example of the bittersweet happenings of 1982. As the present administration is moving with great haste away from regulating education, there is a chance they will take steps to cancel or alter Title IX regulations rather than try to enforce them. The power to discriminate in educational employment has been denied in theory but often permitted in practice, and there are presently few avenues for interfering with the privilege and prerogative of those in power.

Affirmative action requirements have placed pressures on educational institutions to explain why women and minorities have not been added to the ranks of upper-level faculty and administration. Widespread myths have developed that institutions are hiring minority women in great numbers because they can, for affirmative action purposes, be counted twice; as women and as minorities. As minority women in 1979 only held 2 percent of the top administrative positions, however, there is little evidence to support the belief that all the jobs are going to them (Frances and Mensel 1981, p. 3).

Another often-heard myth is that numbers of positions are being targeted for women and minorities. Unsuccessful male candidates are often told that they have all the qualifications for the job, and if times were different they would probably have been hired. Unfortunately, the position for which they have applied is being held for a woman or a minority person. Again, the facts belie the myth. A majority of positions go to white males, except for those that have been traditionally associated with women or minorities (Frances and Mensel 1981, p. 14). The male candidate is probably not hired because he is not the institution's choice. He leaves the competition feeling unfairly treated, however, and the institution does not have to provide him with any other reason.

Search committees more often than not select white males as their first choice and a woman or minority for the second or third place. The reason given for this order is that the three candidates are all excellent, but the white male had a slight edge. If the first choice turns the position down, however, committees often reopen the search rather than accept the woman or minority person. One can only conclude that placement on the list of candidates was for purposes other than selection.

Myths also work to change a position from traditionally female to male. For example, many elementary schools have replaced women principals with men, each school committee making an independent decision to choose a man to fill what had been a traditionally female position. The turnover has been from 55 percent women elementary principals in 1928 to 23 percent in 1981 (Jones 1982b). School committee members appear to be remembering times past when traditionally the elementary principal was a single woman who held the job forever. The encroachment of men into one of the only managerial positions associated with women has meant that the overall numbers of women in administration in school systems has declined despite extensive efforts to increase their representation (Haven 1980).

Stereotypical characteristics do not fit all or even a majority of people in a category, yet they continue to serve as external and internal controls on behavior as long as the members of the group accept them as individually determined. Power accrues to those who already have power; thus those who presently control educational institutions are not likely to move over meekly and share their positions with those outside their ranks who seek entrance. Status quo is a potent and difficult barrier to overcome. If and when people recognize that myths and stereotypes do not really fit anyone and are a device to control disadvantaged groups, then those in power may be forced to consider individual expertise.

Power over Individuals

In a hierarchical institution, power is exhibited on a day-by-day basis by one person having control or supervision over another. This is the modus operandi for most educational institutions and is rarely questioned by those involved. In general, this power is held by white males, making females and minority people dependent for their success and promotion on their approval and support. It is difficult to determine when a decision is based on individual characteristics or when a subjective evaluation related to sex or race has entered the interaction. Inability to decide what factors are involved in most supervision decisions has allowed the status quo to continue largely unimpeded, with those in power maintaining an overriding belief that they make objective, individual decisions, and those out of power continuing to be uncomfortable in their observations that individual decisions consistently lead to keeping them in their place.

As previously discussed, stereotypes and myths have some sway over who is considered for the full range of positions. Another factor is at play in decisions about whom to hire. Traditionally, these decisions are made by men or male-dominated selection committees. If these men are choosing a colleague who will function as their equal, they must consider how, or if, they will be able to work with the new person. As men have traditionally interacted with women as mothers, sisters, wives, or sex objects, there are few models for them to work with women as coequals. Thus a woman might be refused a position because of subjective factors that are not even noticed or consciously considered, yet that clearly sway the choice toward a man.

Historically, men have left fields or departments at a point when women or minorities become a majority, which thus shifts the entire field. This "tipping balance" of disciplines, departments, or areas of study can presently be observed in computer science. Over the past few years men have moved to the field of systems analysis, while women have become computer programmers. As an assistant professor of computer science said, "I used to know the console by heart, but no longer. Now I leave the typing to others while I concentrate on the more interesting area of systems analysis." Clearly, tenure will be for those who avoid the console. Computer programming, the action part of the field, is being left to females, while the more theoretical aspects are being "manned" by males.

Women are to be found in solo or token positions amid the upper levels of administration or faculty, and are often in the majority at the lower levels; vice versa for men. Thus, in 1978, 18 percent of the high level administrative positions were held by white women, 2 percent by minority women (Frances and Mensel 1981). There are two opposing theories for how or when women and men may begin to equalize in numbers at all levels. One theory (Kanter 1977) is that when there is a critical number of women in positions of power and authority (approximately 35 percent), pressures will abate and they will interact as individuals rather than as representatives of their sex. South and colleagues (1982) found, in contrast to Kanter's theory, that solo women faced less severe organizational pressures than women who were a larger percent of the work group. Harlan and Weiss (1981) studied two organizations, one with 6 percent females and the other with 19 percent females, and found as did South and his associates (1982) that merely increasing the number of women in an organization does not improve the work environment. In the organization with 19 percent women, there were many incidents of direct hostility, while in that with 6 percent the women reported few problems related to their sex. The women in the latter case were in numbers small enough that their presence was not considered a threat, so they could be treated as special cases; whereas in the organization where they represented 19 percent of the management staff, there was more open hostility toward women in general and toward these women in particular as they were viewed as direct competition for the limited number of high-level positions.

The environment in the organization with 19 percent women that Harlan and Weiss studied was certainly not productive for the females or for the males. What will happen when the number of women reaches the 35 percent point is yet to be determined, but Kanter predicts the impact will be so significant as to promote real change. The balance may tip and men may begin to leave the organization; the men may take over specific powerful areas and leave the rest to the women; or leadership positions may begin to be attained by employees who are most qualified regardless of sex. There are as yet few examples of women and men sharing power and leadership of organizations, so it is too soon to predict if the latter option is viable or even possible.

Power over Self

At the level of the individual, power is expressed through the choices available to and made by any one person. At that moment when a person makes one choice over another, she appears to have the power and control. Students make educational choices; faculty and administrators make professional and personal choices for advancement. An individual decision when viewed in the perspective of the person's sex and race, however, can lose all appearances of individuality.

In the 1980s for the first time in history the number of women students equaled the number of men, a much heralded accomplishment leading many people to announce that all is solved: an equal number of students a priori guarantees an equivalent education. As discussed earlier, numbers often mask the reality of the situation. Women students are not to be found in equal numbers in all types of institutions; in fact, they tend to be clustered in the less prestigious, two-year institutions (Heyns and Bird 1982). Even in the elite institutions, a mere equalizing of the numbers might not be an assurance of an equal education. The majors chosen by both sexes must be examined to determine if women students are clustered into those fields traditionally associated with women, which have lower status and fewer job possibilities. The same examination of major is required for women who choose nontraditional areas of study such as law, medicine, or business. Again, equal numbers do not represent the entire picture.

Career Choices   Students in the 1980s are career-oriented. As the availability of jobs after graduation has become severely curtailed their choice of major has a profound effect on their future. Women students have traditionally chosen between liberal arts or a technical field such as education, nursing, or social service. Rarely are they encouraged to be single-minded about a career pursuit or to explore an area outside these expected fields; rather, they are advised to be dabblers, to pursue a broad education so they can be "interesting" adults. Such an approach often leads to a general knowledge about a lot of things, but little specific information on which to base a career. One explanation for the underemployment of women is that their general education has not prepared them for the fields in which options are available. It is not that women should become single-focused as are many men, rather that their education should have multiple purposes: first, skills for a job; and second, a broad base of knowledge useful for all life's possibilities.

Female socialization affects women's performance in the classroom. In elementary school, teachers focus on children being good and tidy, a standard many female students find easy to accomplish. In secondary schools, the rules change, and students are expected to speak up and defend their ideas. Female students are confronted with a new expectation that runs contrary to the age-old assumption that women are not "supposed" to defend their point of view. They usually respond to the pressure by remaining silent and allowing the male students to dominate discussions which guarantees that their ideas and thoughts will not be verbally tested, but will be aired primarily in writing to an audience limited to the teacher. Women are therefore not experiencing ways to present their ideas out loud, and are ill prepared to defend them. Preparation by silence is not preparation for the work world, so even a woman with an identical course of study as a male peer may not be geared to active participation in a job situation.

A study at Brown University (1980) found that the self-appraisal and thus the self-esteem of female students appeared to drop with each successive year of college, while male students' self-esteem went in the opposite direction. As the survey did not question the same students over four years' time, the findings can only be considered suggestions for future explorations. Lowering of self-esteem for women may be related to the mounting pressure during college to find a career and a partner, as decisions about career and family are intertwined for women. Thus they may walk a tight-rope in vigorously pursuing a career while keeping all decisions subject to change dependent on marriage or family plans. Male students still do not weigh these decisions equally, but think of their careers independent of all other factors. Katz (1980) found that male students were planning to marry women who worked until they had children and then stayed at home for the first five years of the childrens' lives; meanwhile, the females were expecting to work without cessation as they planned to find a man who would share all responsibilities. Clearly, these two diametrically opposed expectations indicate a collision course for this generation of college students. Many women prefer not to discuss the family/career decision while they are in college because they assume they will have it all—a burgeoning career, a fulfilling marriage, and several happy children. They are preparing to take on the world alone, and they are magically assuming that all will work out well.

Students are perceived as having a plethora of choices; however, when a majority of women and minority students make the same choice, one must begin to examine what forces are influencing them. It is unlikely that sex or race alone makes one automatically good with children, or good at detail work, or good with machines, and so on. Clearly, socialization and stereotypes underlie such decisions, and they must be probed to see how deeply rooted they are. Despite an overabundance of teachers, or social workers, or counselors women continue to enter these fields in large numbers, even when they have been warned of the paucity of job opportunities. A certain percentage of them are "born" teachers, or helpers, or counselors and should be in that field if at all possible. For the majority, however, their decision is based on limitations of expectation caused by socialization, preventing them from examining a wide range of career options. Women often make stereotypical choices to drop science or mathematics in secondary school, and from that time on their options are limited.

Advisors can spend hours trying to help women look for broader choices, yet they will fail because at an early age women's vision was limited. Each woman considers herself to be making an individual decision, and she is certain that she will succeed where others have failed; for her the path will be different, and she will find an interesting and stimulating job. When she returns to her advisor in a despondent state, her shiny new degree in hand and no work options in sight, she cannot understand why she did not listen to the wealth of advice she received in advance. Her choice felt so individual to her when she made it, but, in fact, it was probably preordained by her socialization as a female rather than her abilities. Methods are clearly needed for intervening early and helping women seek wider horizons, individually determined, if they are to reach fields where there are real opportunities.

Role Models   Women who advance to high levels in education envision themselves, and are perceived by others, as representing all women. They have been labeled role models, mentors, or sponsors for all achieving women, and in that position many expectations are placed on their shoulders. There has been little research to show if role models, mentors, or sponsors promote success (Speizer 1981), but this lack of confirmation has not dampened the extensive, firmly held belief that women need each other's help if any are to advance. Women who move ahead and have responsible, all-consuming jobs expend a great deal of time for those who are striving to follow them. In return, little has been done to support and reinforce women in high-level positions. Those who are isolated in their positions are giving constantly to others who wish to emulate them and are themselves getting little support for their own survival. If role models, mentors, or sponsors are viable concepts that help younger women succeed, then they must become two-way supports to ensure that those at the top are not sacrificed for the striving.

Power over self is enacted in a framework of institutional and societal expectations and pressures. Counselors and teachers must recognize the potential traps that can prevent students from exploring their own abilities. The educational system must encourage students to develop their best qualities and strengths, so that when they enter society they are prepared to use those abilities to the betterment of all. For those who have left school, but not the educational system, the task is to recognize the past decisions that have led to stereotypical jobs, and to plan methods for changing the path that lies ahead.

If intervention is made early enough, women and minorities can be assisted to overcome the blinders of sex and race. The answer does not simply lie with helping them to make more comprehensive, individually determined choices, for there are many who have taken nontraditional positions and still have not made it into the power structure of an educational system. This lack of progress stems from power factors all along the path, and highlights the need to seek solutions that will have an effect throughout the chain of power.

Power Strategies for Future Progress

Educators tend to remain aloof from politics so as not to "soil their hands." The primary lesson to be learned from 1982 is that without federal government involvement, educational equity is too complicated and too cumbersome an issue to be resolved quickly or completely. The defeat of the Equal Rights Amendment (ERA) signals that, contrary to the myth, all women's problems are not solved, and efforts must be renewed in the political arena. In 1982 money poured into organizations working for the ERA and to other women's organizations as a result of the regressive steps taken by the federal government. One group reported that they had obtained enough money to send women to Washington to lobby for the ERA, but that they were unable to find women who had the time to spare for travel. Both time and money must be devoted to politics to ensure the involvement of federal, state, and local government officials in the task of eliminating discrimination.

Women and minorities also must become involved in the upper ranks of unions, professional associations, and governing bodies. The lack of such representation has resulted in decisions to the detriment of those not in the power group. Thus professional associations have not always lobbied for the causes that would assist women and minorities, and unions have negotiated perquisites that either work against women workers or, at best, do not meet their needs. There must also be a concerted effort to have women placed on boards of trustees or regents, and for them to run for school committee positions. With enough women at the upper levels of decision-making, their needs might be more carefully considered, and long-lasting, wide-ranging changes might be made.

One lesson which can be learned from 1982, using Ralph Ellison's image, is that the power group can dismantle the boxing ring if they so choose.

Discussions and arguments about the "right" tactics or people to support become irrelevant if the focus is not on the real target. We can no longer afford to be divided among ourselves; rather we must turn our united efforts against the outside where the real power resides. Support must be given to all people who are working to promote educational equity. That is not to say that all must be alike, or pursue the same avenues; rather, we must recognize that the "them" is "us," divide and conquer can no longer be tolerated. In particular, the split between minority and majority women must be ended for we share so many issues. We need all aspects of ourselves, the radical fringe as well as the conservative end, and there must be room for all to reach the end goal of equity.

The fact that women are half the population is a positive force for change, as it means "we are everywhere." Each can focus on her own particular areas of concern and be safe in the knowledge that there are women working in other arenas. Thus one person does not have to split her efforts into many small pieces. At the same time change will not be long-lasting or widespread unless there is cooperation and coordination among groups behind the banner of all women. The ease with which individual efforts and independent activities were blocked and eliminated in 1982 indicates that there must be protection and support for all efforts to promote equity. Numbers are in women's favor, and we should act on that fact.

Networks   One approach to isolation and tokenism has been the formation of networks of women. These networks provide support, information, and contacts for jobs, and may prove to be the most effective tool available for promoting change. Women are often found in marginal positions, outside regular communication channels, and far away from the decision-making process. Those who move to higher levels are often functioning as tokens, and as such do not have access to the information-sharing and support network that is available to their male peers. Women who work at the same level, in different areas of the same institution, or in other institutions can be invaluable resources for each other to overcome isolation. Information is power in educational institutions, and networks of women from all strata can be very powerful.

Networks can also be strategic tools for obtaining jobs, as administrative positions usually go to someone in the institution or someone who has inside contacts (Socolow 1978). Several studies have confirmed that administrators tend to get their jobs through contacts (Capek et al. 1982), and networks thus appear to be essential for administrators seeking jobs outside their present institution.

A caveat must be added, as there is little empirical support for the network concept. There is a widespread belief that there is an "old boys network" that helps men to advance. Such may, in fact, not exist, or if it does, it may be available to only a small percentage of men—those identified as bound for success in the first place. In any case, women have little knowledge about men's networks, and may be placing a great deal of reliance on an idea that may have little basis in fact.

A supportive network of peers and colleagues is certainly attractive and should be available for everyone, in particular for women who are in such small numbers in organizations. For them, a network may spell the difference between success and failure. There have been many "instant formula" schemes for networks devised in the past few years; such activities may raise expectations and promise successes that are not attainable. Network development, if it is to prove effective, requires time and trust, commodities not available on an instant basis. Issues related to status of position, institutional prestige, and level of position enter into most interactions, and an assumption that one meeting promotes the needed trust is not founded on the realities of how people develop contacts and provide supports. Women certainly experience relief when they find someone with whom they can share ideas and overcome isolation, but a single meeting is a far step from the long-term sustenance that is expected from a network contact.

Training Programs   Training programs that provide skills and opportunities to explore career paths have proved to be important intervention strategies to promote women and minorities. Examples in higher education are the administrative skills programs offered by Higher Education Resource Services—New England at Wellesley College, or Mid-Atlantic at Bryn Mawr. For elementary and secondary administrators, a summer institute has been shown to be effective in assisting career opportunities (Lyman and Speizer 1980), as has a series of career workshops (Jones and Montenegro 1982a). The long-range effects of such skills training has yet to be determined, but after two years one such program was found to promote advancement (Speizer 1983). A review of the research on women in school administration (Adkison 1981) suggests there is a wide range of change strategies that must be considered to assist women to advance.

Women are optimistic about education despite the general decline in status and resources that has befallen the profession. Thus we find the number of women students increasing at the postsecondary level, while those of their male peers decline; and the pool of women available for faculty and administrative positions increasing, while many men have sought other fields of endeavor. Women's optimism may be based on a reality not immediately available to the beholder; for as men leave the field, there is more room for women to advance. Women are perceived as good at managing decline, so when times get hard and men leave the arena, women are ready and available to take over. Such a phenomenon appears to be occurring in 1982 at the superintendent level. Male superintendents are staying on the job for fewer years, as this has become a very difficult job, and nationwide the number of women superintendents has increased (Jones and Montenegro 1982b). In Massachusetts, the increase is marked: presently there are twelve women superintendents while four years ago there were only three. An increase in the number of women administrators may continue over the next few years in all areas of education. Women will need to be creative maintainers instead of builders; a hard, though not impossible, task, especially for those who have been kept out of the leadership ranks for so long.

Feminism is like being "slightly pregnant"—just give it time. Once a woman has experienced sex-related barriers to advancement, she will begin the slow process of awareness that may finally result in her taking steps to eliminate such barriers for others. As women get older they often recognize or experience hindrances in their paths because of sex, age, and race, and many then begin to work to prevent such problems for the next generation. Men who might not consider a change in the power ratio for their generation, often feel quite differently for their daughters and granddaughters. Time is in favor of those who wish to promote educational equity.

References

ADKISON, J. A. 1981. Women in school administration: A review of the research. *Review of Educational Research* 51, no. 3:311–43.

BENNETT, S. K. 1982. Undergraduates and their teachers: An analysis of student evaluations of male and female instructors. In *The undergraduate women: Issues in educational equity*, edited by P. J. Perun. Lexington, Mass.: D. C. Heath.

The Brown Project. 1980. *Men and women together: A study of college students in the late 70s.* Brown University Office of the Provost, Providence, R.I.

CAPEK, M. E.; BENIGER, J. R.; BLACK, C., et al. 1982. *Higher education administrators in New Jersey: A preliminary report of research findings.* Princeton: Princeton University in Cooperation with American Council on Education.

Chronicle of Higher Education, 1982. February 3. Women and minority-group members in administrative posts, and Despite gains, women, minority-group members lag in college jobs.

ELLISON, R. 1952. *Invisible Man.* New York: Random House.

FRANCES, C., and MENSEL, R. F. 1981. *Women and minorities in administration of higher education institutions.* Washington, D.C.: College and University Personnel Association.

GRANT, W. V., and EIDEN, L. J. 1981. *Digest of Education Statistics, 1981.* National Center for Education Statistics. (Available from U.S. Government Printing Office, Washington, D.C. 20402.)

HARLAN, A., and WEISS, C. 1981. Moving up: Women in managerial careers. Working paper no. 86. Wellesley, Mass.: Wellesley College Center for Research on Women.

HAVEN, E. W. 1980. *Women in educational administration: The principleship.* Annandale, Va.: J.W.K. International Corporation.

HENNIG, M., and JARDIM, A. 1977. *The managerial woman*. New York: Anchor/ Doubleday.

HEYNS, B., and BIRD, J. A. 1982. Recent trends in the higher education of women. In *The undergraduate woman: Issues in educational equity*, edited by P. J. Perun. Lexington, Mass.: D. C. Heath.

High court rules title IX covers employees. *Peer Perspective* 8, no. 4 (July 1982):1.

HOWE, F., and LAUTER, P. *The impact of women's studies on the campus and the disciplines*. Women's Studies Monograph Series, National Institute of Education, February 1980.

JONES, E., and MONTENEGRO, X. P. 1982a. *Climbing the career ladder: A research study of women in school administration*. Office of Minority Affairs, American Association of School Administrators, Arlington, Va.

JONES, E., and MONTENEGRO, X. P. 1982b. *Recent trends in the representation of women and minorities in school administration and problems in documentation*. Office of Minority Affairs, American Association of School Administrators, Arlington, Va.

KANTER, R. M. 1977. *Men and women of the corporation*. New York: Basic Books.

KATZ, J. 1980. The new and old lives of men and women undergraduates. In *Men and women together: A study of college students in the late 70s*.

LYMAN, K. D., and SPEIZER, J. J. 1980. Advancing in school administration: A pilot project for women. *Harvard Educational Review* 50, no. 1:25–35.

MAGARRELL, J. 1982. 40,962 fewer students enrolled at private institutions this fall. *Chronicle of Higher Education*, November 24.

MOORE, K. M., and SAGARIA, M. A. D. 1982. Differential job change and stability among academic administrators. *Journal of Higher Education* 53, no. 5:501–13.

PERUN, P. J.; SPEIZER, J. J.; GAWALEK, M. A.; et al. 1982. Issues of educational equity in the 1980s: Multiple perspectives. In *The undergraduate woman: Issues in educational equity*, edited by P. J. Perun. Lexington, Mass.: D. C. Heath.

Presidential panel recommends abolishing education department. *Boston Globe*, December 31, 1982.

RICH, A. 1979. Toward a women-centered university. In *On lies, secrets and silence*. New York: W. W. Norton.

ROSENFELD, R. A., and HEARN, J. C. 1982. Sex differences in the significance of economic resources for choosing and attending a college. In *The undergraduate woman: Issues in educational equity*, edited by P. J. Perun. Lexington, Mass.: D. C. Heath.

SOCOLOW, D. J. 1978. How administrators get their jobs. *Change* 10, no. 5:42, 43, 54.

SOUTH, S. J.; BONJEAN, C. M.; MARKHAM, W. T., et al. 1982. Social structure and intergroup interaction: Men and women of the federal bureaucracy. *American Sociological Review* 47:587–99.

SPEIZER, J. J. 1981. Role models, mentors and sponsors: The elusive concepts. *SIGNS* 6, no. 4:692–712.

SPEIZER, J. J. 1983. A longitudinal evaluation of a skills training program to advance women in higher education administration.

Resources

Alliance of Independent Scholars, 6 Ash Street, Cambridge, MA 02138. An organization of scholars, particularly women, within and outside the academic profession who wish to continue intellectual exchange in a scholarly community. Memberships available.

Association of American Colleges, Project on the Status and Education of Women, 1818 R Street NW, Washington, DC 20009. Provides information concerning women in education; works with institutional government agencies and other associations and programs related to women in higher education; develops and distributes materials that identify and highlight issues and federal policies affecting women's status as students and employees; publishes *On Campus with Women*, a quarterly newsletter containing important and timely material about women and education (subscription $15 per year) and *The Classroom Climate: A Chilly One for Women?*, a comprehensive look at the classroom treatment of women. Complete list of publications available.

Bogart, Karen. *Resource Directory.* A listing of organizations and publications that promote sex equity in postsecondary education. Available from American Institute for Research, 1055 Thomas Jefferson Street NW, Washington, DC 20009. $10 per copy.

Brown, Linda Keller, *The Woman Manager in the United States.* Washington, D.C.: Business and Professional Women's Foundation, 1981, 2012 Massachusetts Avenue NW, Washington, DC 20036. A research analysis and bibliography.

But Some of Us Are Brave. Edited by Gloria T. Hull, Barbara Smith, and Patricia Bell Scott. Old Westbury, N.Y.: Feminist Press, 1982. Political theory, literary, social and historical essays, bibliographies, and syllabi on the lives of black women. $8.95 paper; $16.95 cloth.

Change Magazine: Special Section on Women's Studies. 14 no. 3 (April 1982):24–29. Article by Mariam Chamberlain, "A Period of Remarkable Growth on Women's Studies." Describes twenty-eight research centers devoted to the study of women. Article by Beth Reed, "Transforming the Academy: Twelve Schools Working Together." Using a consortial approach, the twelve small liberal arts colleges that participate in the Great Lakes Colleges Association have integrated women's studies into the curriculum of their schools.

Concerns, An informal organization of women administrators in colleges and universities established to promote the opportunities of women in academic institutions. Meets for discussion and workshop programs. Memberships available to interested individuals. For information contact: Concerns New England: Beverly Daniel, Executive Asst. to President, Wheaton College, Norton, MA 02766, Concerns California: Dean Margaret R. Bates, Treasurer, Sumner Hall, Pomona College, Claremont, CA 91711, Concerns New York, President Smith, Vassar College, Poughkeepsie, NY 12601.

Council on Interracial Books for Children. *Guidelines for Selecting Bias-Free Textbooks and Storybooks.* New York: Council on Interracial Books for Children. The Council also publishes a catalog entitled "Racism and Sexism Resource Center for Education." Both publications and others are available from the Council at 1841 Broadway, New York, NY 10023-7648.

Crocker, P. L. An analysis of university definitions of sexual harrassment. *Signs* 8, no. 4 (1983).

———, "Annotated Bibliography on Sexual Harrassment in Education." *Rutgers Law School Publication* 7, no. 2 (Winter 1982):91–106.

Displaced Homemakers Network, Inc., 1531 Pennsylvania Avenue SE, Washington, DC 20003. National advocacy organization publishing *Network News*, program directories, and offering referral services for nationwide training programs.

Eliason, Carol, and Edmondson, Gloria. *Women in Community and Junior Colleges.* 1980. ERIC: ED 196 456. Annotated review of works and programs relevant to educational opportunities for women at community colleges.

EQUALS, an organization that encompasses programs for teachers, counselors, administrators, parents, and scientific and technical workers. Contact: Nancy Kreinberg, Director, EQUALS, Lawrence Hall of Science, University of California, Berkeley, CA 94720. Publications include *Resource Directory Focusing on Careers in Science, Engineering and Technology* and *Math for Girls and Other Problem Solvers.* Catalog available.

Everywoman's Guide to Colleges and Universities. Edited by Florence Howe, Suzanne Howard, and Mary Jo Boehm Strauss. Old Westbury, N.Y.: Feminist Press, 1982. Profiles nearly 600 institutions—public and private, doctorate-granting, four-year and two-year—in state-by-state order. Provides the facts about the status of women and specific services for women on campus. $12.95 paper.

Federal Programs

Klein, Susan S., and Dauito, Kathleen. *What's Left of Federal Funding for Sex Equity in Education?* A detailed description of what happened to federal programs that support sex equity in 1982. National Advisory Council on Women's Educational Programs, Suite 821, 1832 M Street NW, Washington, DC 20036.

Title IX: "The Half Full, Half Empty Glass," a report on the results of the law that bans sex discrimination in educational institutions receiving federal money. Copies available from National Advisory Council on Women's Educational Programs, above address.

Feminist Press, Box 334, Old Westbury, NY 11568. Publishes materials for use in teaching women's studies at all levels. Also publishes *Women's Studies Quarterly*, a journal covering the field of education in traditional and alternative settings and at all levels from preschool to graduate school. Catalog available.

Gallagher, Kathleen, and Peery, Alice. *Bibliography of Materials on Sexism and Sex-Role Stereotyping in Children's Books.* Chapel Hill, N.C.: Lollipop Power, 1982. Available from the publisher at P. O. Box 1171, Chapel Hill, NC 27514.

Higher Education Resource Services (HERS). A network of three independently run organizations that provide a system of professional contacts for women in higher education.

Project HERS-New England, Wellesley College, Wellesley, MA 02181, Lilli S. Hornig, Executive Director. Activities include: Administrative Skills Program, a series of five weekend seminars for women administrators and faculty in higher education; *A Planner's Manual* by Jeanne J. Speizer for those who wish to run a skills program for women administrators; and *A Wo/Man's Guide to Academe* by Martha Tolpin, a self-help guide for career search.

HERS-Mid-Atlantic, University of Pennsylvania, 3601 Locust Walk/C8, Philadelphia, PA 19104, Cynthia Secor, Director. Activities include: Summer Institute for Women in Higher Education Administration; newsletter; workshops, mini-courses, and training programs.

HERS/West, Women's Resource Center, 293 Olpin Union Building, University of Utah, Salt Lake City, UT 84112, Shauna Adix, Director. Serves a six-state region: Arizona, Colorado, Idaho, Montana, New Mexico, and Utah. Services include: Annual institute; consulting to campuses on issue of equity; workshops and short training programs; *Connections*, quarterly newsletter with a calendar of events in region.

Hornig, Lilli S., Executive Director, Higher Education Resource Services, Wellesley College, Wellesley, MA 02181.

Climbing the Academic Ladder: Doctoral Women Scientists in Academe, 1979, reviews the supply of women doctorates, their postdoctoral training, academic employment, participation in the national science advisory apparatus, and future prospects, based on data available to 1977.

Climbing the Ladder II: Doctoral Women Scientists and Engineers in 1982, 1983, focuses on changes since 1977 in the status of women scientists in academe and includes a brief review of industrial employment as well. Reports may be ordered from the National Academy Press, 2101 Constitution Avenue NW, Washington, DC 20418.

Hornig, Lilli S., and Ruth Ekstrom. *Women in the Humanities* (forthcoming). A comprehensive study examining the participation and employment of women in humanities fields, the barriers to full professional status, and the strategies women have developed to overcome constraints, using statistical data, humanistic source material, and in-depth case studies. Publication information available from Lilli Hornig at Higher Education Resource Services.

Institute for Research on History, 432 Park Avenue South, New York, NY 10016. Organization of historians outside universities who share scholarly research and encourage publication of scholarship. Marjorie Lightman, Executive Director; Katherine Crum, Associate Director.

Jacobs, Ruth H. "Out of the Home to Where?" Wellesley, Mass.: Wellesley College Center for Research on Women, Working Paper No. 77, 1981. Available from the college. Checklist for counselors or displaced homemakers.

Learning Publications, Box 1326, Dept. 6, Holmes Beach, FL 33509.

Cain, Mary Alexander. *Boys and Girls Together: Nonsexist Activities for the Elementary Classroom*, 1981. Guide to inexpensive sex-fair games and activities available from publisher.

Stoddard, Cynthia. *Sex Discrimination in Educational Employment: Legal Alternatives and Strategies*, 1981. Concise guide to legal strategies on all levels of educational employment to counter sex discrimination.

Moore, Kathryn M., and Wollitzer, Peter A. *Women in Higher Education, A Contemporary Bibliography*. National Association of Women Deans, Administrators and Counselors, Washington, DC 20036.

National Council for Research on Women, Roosevelt Memorial House, 47-49 East 65th Street, New York, NY 10021. A network of 28 nationwide scholarly centers for research on women have joined to promote collaborative research projects and exchange people, programs and research ideas. Mariam Chamberlain, President.

National Identification Program, American Council on Education, Office of Women,

One Dupont Circle, Washington, DC 20036. Nationwide network to identify women candidates for administrative positions. Donna Shavlik, Director; Judy Touchton, Associate Director.

National Women's Studies Association, University of Maryland, College Park, MD 20742. Nationwide organization seeks to further the social, political, and professional development of women's studies throughout the country at every educational level. Memberships available.

Northeast Coalition of Educational Leaders, Inc. (NECEL). A coalition of women school administrators from nine states organized to exchange job-related information, establish mentor relationships, and collect and generate data on job openings. Complete list of programs and services available from NECEL, P.O. Box 637, Lincoln, MA 01773.

Project on Equal Education Rights (PEER), 1413 K Street NW, Washington, DC 20005. Project of NOW Legal Defense and Education Fund, publishes *Peer Perspective* and resource guides. An advocacy group especially concerned with implementation of Title IX.

Project AWARE, American Association of School Administrators, 1810 N. Moore Street, Arlington, VA 22209. Project AWARE coordinates six regional centers in Arizona, North Carolina, Oregon, Georgia, Massachusetts, and Texas. Effie H. Jones, Associate Executive Director.

Scott, Nancy A. *Returning Women Students: A Review of Research and Descriptive Studies.* (Washington, DC: National Association of Women Deans, Administrators, and Counselors, 1980) 1625 I Street NW, Suite 624A, Washington, DC 20006.

TABS Magazine: Aids for Ending Sexism in School, 744 Carroll Street, Brooklyn, NY 11215. Quarterly bulletin includes lesson plans, book reviews, biographies suitable for use in elementary and secondary schools; *Project SHARE* a national network for developing and exchanging practical nonsexist teaching ideas. Lucy Picco Simpson, Director; Liz Phillips, Associate Director.

Tittle, Carol Kahn, and Denker, Eleanor Rubin. *Returning Women Students in Higher Education: Defining Policy Issues.* New York: Praeger, 1980. Includes historical perspective and case studies on institutional and situational barriers to re-entry women.

Wider Opportunities for Women (WOW), 1511 K Street NW, Suite 345, Washington, DC 20005. Independent employment resource for women workers; provides technical assistance for training programs; publishes national directories.

Women and Minorities in Administration of Higher Education Institutions. Report of participation of women and minorities in higher education administration available from College and University Personnel Association, American Council on Education, One Dupont Circle, Washington, DC 20036.

Women at Work: The Myth of Equal Opportunity. Report presents a profile of women's economic status. Prepared by Women Employed Institute. From article appearing in *National NOW Times*, 15, no. 8 (October 1982).

Women's Action Alliance, Inc., 370 Lexington Avenue, Room 603, New York, NY 10017. A national center on women's issues and programs. Activities include: an information and referral service; workshops for nonprofit women's programs; and *Equal Play*, a quarterly resource magazine. *Project REED*, Resources on Educational Equity for the Disabled, develops nonsexist, multicultural materials for early childhood classroom.

Women's Educational Equity Act Program. Resources for Educational Equity, 1981–1982 catalog. Available from WEEAP Publishing Center, 55 Chapel Street, Newton, MA 02160.

Women's Equity Action League, 805 15th Street NW, Suite 822, Washington, DC 20005. National, nonprofit membership organization. Educational and legal defense fund whose goal is to eliminate sex discrimination in education and employment. Sponsors intern program for students in Washington, monitors Congress, holds conferences, publishes materials including *WEAL Washington Report* and *In the Running*, about women in sports. Complete list available.

Women's Studies Quarterly, a publication of the Feminist Press and the National Women's Studies Association, SUNY/Old Westbury, Box 334, Old Westbury, NY 11568. Journal features articles on the theory and practice of women's studies in the curriculum of colleges and universities. Fall 1982, Vol. 10, No. 3 contains complete list of Women's Studies Program—1982. Reprints available for $2.50 from above address.

Women's Research and Education Institute (WREI), 204 Fourth Street SE, Washington, DC 20003. Nonpartisan research arm of the bipartisan Congressional Caucus for Women's Issues.

Maria Collins, Administrative Assistant, Higher Education Resource Services, Wellesley College, assisted in the compilation of the resources list.

Feminist Theory: The Meaning of Women's Liberation

Kathleen Barry

Feminist theory has undergone major transformations since the late 1960s, the beginning of this new wave of feminism. By 1982 it is at a critical juncture; its relevance to a besieged women's movement must be established. Socialist feminist theory has taken its analysis of women's condition about as far as it can go and still remain within the marxist paradigm. Radical feminism, on the other hand, must reestablish its relevance to a movement that by 1982 has suffered the loss of the ERA, denial of many abortion rights, and loss of funding to many wife battery and rape crisis programs.

We look to feminist theory to reveal an analysis and a deeper understanding of women's situation. We also expect from it an understanding of the relationship of women's struggle to the political structure and to the behavior of society. Such a theory can only be derived from the active struggle of those engaged in the feminist movement.

In this chapter, that approach to theory is understood and explained as feminist *praxis*, the life force of both theory and action, rooted as it is in the origins of feminist consciousness. This provides a basis for analyzing and comparing the theoretical premises of radical feminism and socialist feminism, which (from the radical feminist perspective of this essay) reveals new questions and possibilities reconnecting feminist theory to the needs of women in the 1980s.

Theoretical Dimensions of Feminism

Despite all the efforts to trivialize women's liberation to "women's lib," or "those libbers," the intent of feminists was and continues to be to struggle for the liberation of women, to wrench women from domination to freedom; that is, feminism intends to make women free. Beginning with the assumption that

55

women qua women are unfree, living in conditions of oppression, and subjected to domination that effectively deprives them of their own self-determination, the women's liberation movement initiated the struggle. In the twentieth century, no other liberation movement has addressed the oppression of women as women. Feminist theory reflects this struggle, is derived from it, and is engaged with it. Consequently, the relationship between feminist struggle and theory is symbiotic. Thus the very idea of liberation and the quest for freedom is the core of feminist theory.

Liberation not only reflects on the past, it has meaning in terms of the future. The very demand for liberation means that the present is constituted by a struggle against domination in an effort to move the oppressed toward freedom. Women's liberation is a dynamic, forward movement; feminism finds "reality" is in the act of being created by those struggling for their freedom, which is always becoming and therefore is never finally determined.

As a movement for liberation, feminism is revolutionary. Freedom for women (and ultimately for everyone else) cannot begin to become a reality without radical restructuring of society, which necessitates that women recreate social relations and cultural life. For each and every feminist, the basis of this expansive revolutionary change requires the social reconstruction of self, moving individually and collectively from being oppressed objects to becoming active subjects. A woman's objective existence is given new strength as her subjectivity is asserted through self-determination and redefinition of the meaning of woman.

All-pervasive and all-powerful patriarchal ideology names women's oppression normal, natural, and feminine. In the face of their total objectification, the fact that women arose and began to comprehend the given "reality" as domination and began to assert a movement on their own behalf suggests the will to be free, by which any human group has refused to allow itself to remain in subjugation. It is this dynamic, daring, and demanding characteristic of the women's movement that is the essential quality of feminist theory. Reflecting on the connection between feminist theory and political action, French feminist theoretician and activist Christine Delphy (1980) noted that there is often much more feminist theory in one political slogan such as "A Woman Without a Man is like a Fish Without a Bicycle" or "Take Back the Night" than can be found in much of feminist theoretical writing. Certainly the theoretical impact of political action was clear when in 1982 French feminists demonstrated in Paris to display their solidarity with American women after the ERA was officially defeated in the United States. The French feminist demonstration demanded that the Statue of Liberty be returned to France!

Feminist theory begins with women's experience of oppression. What differentiates that from any other condition of domination such as capitalism is that it extends from the most private circumstances (the colonization of one's body in sex, reproduction, medical treatment, etc.) to the most public and political conditions. The latter range from sex discrimination in the labor force to state control of women's bodies and lives emanating from local to the highest levels of government. Patriarchy of the state is derived from and dependent on patriarchy of the family, that is, rule through male birthright. Early in this wave of feminism, Kate Millett (1970) characterized this condition and the issues it raises for a women's movement in the title of her book: *Sexual Politics*. She correctly identified the conditions of patriarchal domination as those that render sex (the genders of male and female*) to status categories. Thus *sexual politics* reveals the real nature of the relative status of the sexes (24). At the same time, the *Fourth World Manifesto* (Burris 1971) identified this "imperialism" of women's self as sex colonization: "Women, set apart by physical differences between them and men, were the first colonized group. The territory colonized was and remains our women's bodies" (8).

We have already stated that the conditions of women's oppression is found in their experience of private as well as public and political domination. In privatized domination women are subjected to experiences of oppression that are not accessible to public scrutiny (as is slave labor, national colonization, or imperialism, discrimination in labor force, or exclusion from governmental control). Privatized domination is most often located in the home or any other private setting; it is within the family, within private, intimate male-female relationships and among various male-female living arrangements. Privatized domination includes sexual exploitation (rape), physical abuse (wife and girlfriend battery), and unpaid labor (housework), but because it is inaccessible to public scrutiny, it can be manipulated, shaped, and reshaped, to meet private male needs and desires. It does not need to be made publicly accountable or subjected to rational scrutiny. Thus, in the face of each achievement women make toward their liberation, privatized domination adjusts itself to subvert the impact of that gain. For example, the "sexual revolution," with its claim to have freed sex from its repressive state, turned into yet another exploitative demand on women, as it was based on the expectation of their availability to male sexual needs.

Feminist theory begins with women in the actual, objective conditions of their situation. It provides a language and a framework as they confront this situation and in doing so, come to consciousness of their experience of domination, which annihilates their freedom and deprives them of their dignity. In other words, women come to consciousness and recognition of themselves as the objects of domination because they are women. This initial consciousness, like the experience of domination itself, is named and acted upon by women in isolation. Therefore it is likely to reflect only what impinges on their immediate life or limits their present existence.

Many women come to feminism from the consciousness of a particular experience of injustice (rape, sex discrimination, denial of abortion, contempt for lesbians, etc.), and from there they begin to realize that the experiences

---

**I do not follow the sociologic trend of linguistically replacing the word "sex" with the word "gender," as I assume it is meant to undermine the feminist definition of sex in all of its meanings as political.*

reflect a phenomenon that extends far beyond immediate personal experiences. Sonia Johnson (1981), for example, simply wanted the right to support the ERA. When the Mormon church denied her this political voice, her consciousness took a quantum leap from one issue and one aspect of experience to a critique of Mormonism, and from there to all patriarchal domination, an analysis that is the product of political consciousness.

Personal consciousness initially is limited by reflection of the individual only on herself in her situation. This consciousness is raised into a movement when it becomes political and collective. But how is this to happen for women whose basic experience of domination is in isolation, not visible to the world beyond private experience of it.

In the late 1960s women's political consciousness began with individuals, unmasking oppression in their personal situations as well as in its public manifestations. At that time, consciousness raising (CR) was the most manifest form of organizing in the women's movement. It gave a supportive, collective context to women coming from the isolation of their private experiences, whether those experiences were in the home, in the office, or in the streets.

Consciousness raising, or rap groups as they came to be known, involved group discussions through which individual self-consciousness of oppression was extended to collective, political analysis and understanding. Support among women gave the cohesive force which progressed consciousness from the personal to the political. Political consciousness was directed at naming, confronting, and challenging male domination both systematically and personally. CR or rap groups dealt with the consciousness of oppression in political terms, which expanded the analysis of women's oppression and at the same time retained its focus on personal support for women in their individual struggles to overcome specific circumstances.

Significantly, whether one was involved in trying to resolve personal turmoil, initiate political action, or write feminist theory and political analysis, each woman in the CR group confronted domination from her own as well as from other women's experiences of it. This was the central dynamic of consciousness raising.

With Millett's analysis of sexual politics (1970), feminist theory could define the conditions of women's oppression as political in nature and therefore their struggle would be political in action. CR or rap groups gave feminism its radical edge.* They established the context for the revolutionary critique of patriarchal power, and for activists they were the point of contact between the experience of oppression and direct political confrontation.

Consciousness-raising was the motivation for political actions. Some women used consciousness raising as personal therapy and returned to their

---

The only identifiable manifestation of feminism that existed at this point was the highly structured National Organization for Women (NOW), whose aim was specific and directed at much-needed change in public policy. At that time consciousness raising was not part of such structured organizations.

private situations to improve their marriages or enrich their own lives. But many more women realized the impact of consciousness raising by taking it to the next level of the struggle for liberation, political action. It was in political confrontation that feminists began to learn more about the deeper roots and wider manifestations of male power. Each new feminist demand, protest, or action produced a reaction from the many and diverse seats of patriarchal power that made it clear that the liberation of women was not going to come about simply because women demanded it. In turn, feminist actions escalated and continually expanded the dimensions of political action, leaving a clear message to patriarchy that women were not going to sit back and accept their inferior status. For example, original demands for abortion rights were met with rejection by one legislature after another. Women responded by expanding their demands, and a whole feminist health care movement came into being that aimed at taking the control of women's bodies out of the hands of men and traditional medicine.

When consciousness raising is taken into ongoing political action and confrontation and that action in turn feeds back and raises consciousness further, creating heightened political awareness and more challenging and confrontative political response, women find themselves no longer the passive objects of domination but acting subjects of their own liberation. This constitutes a new and genuine feminist praxis. It is in feminist praxis that women become acting subjects, no longer only acted upon, but instead acting from self-determination, and at the same time demanding revolutionary transformation of the oppressive social order which they are continually coming to know. Political tracts, manifestos, demands, and appeals constitute the most powerful evidence of women having become self-consciously reflective about structured power relations of patriarchy as well as the personal experience of male domination. Feminist praxis represents the dynamic force of feminist theory that negates the possibility that genuine feminist theory can be a product of an intellectual elitism that removes itself (usually to the academy) from the real conditions of women's oppression.

Feminist praxis that informs feminist theory engages women with social and political transformation which extends far beyond the limited marxist meaning of praxis, based, as it was, on the transformation of the workers' relations to production. Feminist praxis addresses economic domination but also includes systematized, albeit privatized, domination. In other words, for women, revolutionary transformation is extended to the most private and personal aspects of one's life, including seizing control not only of the means of production, but of one's body, one's reproductivity, one's sexuality, one's marital or other intimate relationships, one's family, one's domestic labor, in addition to all the external and public manifestations of domination.

Given the magnitude and dimensions of the meaning of women's liberation, it is not surprising that by 1982 feminist revolutionary transformation has not been accomplished; nor should it be surprising that the backlash against feminist action on issues of sexual politics is strong and severe. That in the last decade feminists have temporarily lost the ERA, experienced many retractions of hard-fought-for abortion rights, witnessed an escalation of rape and pornography, and seen the persecution of lesbians (particularly in child custody cases) does not detract from the revolutionary potential of these demands. Indeed, these backlashes are direct measures of the patriarchal resistance to the goals of women's liberation. That these political losses have surprised some feminists and sometimes confounded and discouraged their political action[1] is an indication of the problem in maintaining consistent links between consciousness raising, the experiences of oppression, and political action. Reflecting in 1982 on a decade of activism in which women have turned away from consciousness raising toward individual therapy, one can see that this loss of consciousness has diminished the dynamic forces of feminist theory to result often in self-righteous and deterministic politics (which is discussed in the last section of this chapter).

The political dilemma thus created reveals the extent to which reflection is prerequisite to revolutionary struggle and critical to the elaboration of theory. One of the effects of domination is to destroy opportunities to be reflective about one's immediate situation and instead leave one to live in it and respond to it. The severe backlash to feminism, at the moment of its new awareness of the meaning of that oppression is an attempt on the part of the oppressor to return the acting subject to a prereflective or subjugated state of existence.

With collective understanding that is not reduced to dogmatic beliefs and with courage to approach the future without predetermining it, reflection can dispel the sense of inevitability that characterizes the experience of oppression. Unless feminism breaks that sense of inevitability, the resurgence of domination in the form of backlash seems like it cannot be prevented or halted.[2] Thus reflection in consciousness raising frees women and allows them to begin to think of the struggle for liberation as an act in which they are engaged in conceptualizing a new and different future. By reflecting on the possible, the present becomes less tolerable and the dynamic forces actually to create the future become unleashed. Again, this is the basis for feminist praxis that opens the way for women to begin creating their own history and their own theory.

Thus theory is essentially connected to praxis but praxis can exist only in terms of a radical critique of society. Certainly in the initial stages of this movement not all feminists chose to participate in consciousness raising, nor did all women who considered themselves feminists adhere to a radical critique of society. When feminist theory is emptied of either feminist praxis or the radical critique, it is reduced to mere description of oppression. In that context feminist praxis devolves to reformism and political action turns into social services.

Many feminists engaged in projects have become aware of the political problems resulting from their emphasis on social services. At the 1982 annual conference of the National Coalition Against Sexual Assault, participants examined the question of whether or not feminist rape crisis and sexual assault programs should become political. This question is only possible because, like many other aspects of the women's movement, through the middle and late 1970s, consciousness raising as a part of political struggle was replaced with an emphasis on personal therapy and private solutions. Along with this, without the solid political base provided by CR groups, the threats raised by the economic recession and Reaganomics caused feminists to be concerned with loss of project funding. They began to think of ways to make themselves acceptable and therefore fundable without being aware of the political losses that could result and affect the whole movement. The major loss was that this kind of retraction displaced the feminist revolutionary critique of patriarchal power on which these programs were founded. In its place, many programs followed the direction of reform, that is, toward the therapeutic and to social services, and consequently away from radically confronting institutionalized sexism and male power.

It is a fact of sociopolitical movements that radicalism does not sustain them. For a movement to endure, its broad base and widespread influence must be assured. But radicalism is essential, as it will bring to the life of a movement the most uncompromising critique of the abusive, exploitative power that it seeks to undermine and overcome. It is the presence of radical critique that assures us that the movement will not be reduced to simple reform, that is, patchwork on an exploitative, corrupt, and ruthless power structure. Radicals insist on overthrowing the power structure. Reformists— activists in a movement that is without a radical critique—are content to make gains for themselves, their groups, and their issues within the power structure. In doing so they leave unquestioned many oppressive aspects of the dominant system.

Radical Feminism

The progression from personal experience of oppression to feminist praxis is the course of radical feminism and the basis of its theoretical orientation. Each theory that attempts to understand oppression in its particular manifestations produces a level of analysis that identifies the structure and character of that domination. Radical feminism identifies patriarchy and male domination as its level of analysis. Thus men as they individually dominate women and collectively operate through systems of domination constitute the group who by virtue of their birthright exercise power over women, individually and collectively. These power arrangements lead radical feminists to understand men as the political group who through their exercise of domination constitute women as the group they oppress.

Radical feminist theory is derived from, as it informs, issues of sexual politics that are based on objective and actual conditions of women's lives under domination. Patriarchal domination is enforced by deploying ideologies that justify the subordination of women to men, such as the media representation of woman's love of her unpaid labor in housework, its encouragement to women to make themselves into sexual objects, and pornography's redefinition of sexuality to its objectifying and violent manifestations (Barry 1979; Dworkin 1981; Griffin 1981). In other words, patriarchal domination does not result only from inequitable sex roles or from "feelings" of exploitation, or from some vague consciousness of oppression. It constitutes collective, systematized, and individual acts as well as structured social relations and ideological manifestations that shape and form the way life is lived. Domination consists of the interplay of each of these forces with the others, which causes them to be deeply embedded in social life:

> It causes domestic labor to be unpaid and exploited, and therefore it shapes the nature and conditions of housework (Warrior and Leghorn 1975). Delphy (1970) has named this the patriarchal mode of production. It consequently shapes a punitive welfare system to provide state control of women who are not individually dominated by men.
>
> It determines the conditions under which sex is used as the basis of male power, and therefore under domination it determines what sex is (Atkinson 1974; Barry 1979). Rich (1980) identifies the patriarchal rejection of lesbianism as compulsory heterosexuality.
>
> It controls women's reproductivity, and therefore it shapes and forms and in the process distorts and exploits her experience of childbirth (Arms 1975).
>
> It determines the places (jobs, positions) allocated to women in the labor force, and therefore it gives form to the organization of labor in the public economy, thereby making the external labor force dependent on private domination of women.

As patriarchal ideology interacts with the structures and individual acts of domination, it validates the social control of women by promoting sex-terrorism, which is actualized in rape (Griffin 1971, Brownmiller 1975), wife and girlfriend battery (Dobash and Dobash 1979), and incest assault (Butler 1978). It promotes and justifies such practices as sexual harassment (MacKinnon 1979; Farley 1978), which allow men the opportunity continually to remind women of their objectified status. It justifies the punitive welfare system, which keeps women below the poverty line and continually faced with the humiliating practices involved in receiving welfare assistance.

Each aspect of the patriarchal system is intensely dependent on all others. But in exploring each dimension of oppression we find its roots are embedded in private social life, thus the structures and interconnections among its various forms appear to be vague and unsystematic. Yet when taken together, as their interrelatedness is revealed through feminist theory, patriarchal domination appears as a totalization of social life.

Radical feminist theory then continually faces the difficulty of breaking through ideologies to name acts as oppression and thus reveal the structured, systematized nature of patriarchal domination. In feminist praxis, theory is always discovering, uncovering, disclosing aspects of domination. For example, sexual harassment for years has been a private, humiliating experience for many women, but it was not until radical feminists began to study and analyze it that the problem was even named in a way to convey its offensiveness. Until 1978, in Oregon, when Greta Rideout charged her husband with marital rape, the act did not exist either in social conceptualization or in patriarchal law. Now research documents this crime against women to be pervasive (Russell 1982).

Revealing the experiences, describing the conditions, and analyzing the acts of domination are all part of the central task of radical feminist theory: to pull oppression out from its embedded taken-for-grantedness and to name it as exploitation, and locate it in the structure of patriarchal domination. Thus radical feminist theory will be found in works that sometimes appear to be more descriptive than theoretical, more polemic than academic.

By taking patriarchy and male domination as its level of analysis, radical feminist theory is characterized by its emphasis on the common dimensions of women's oppression. It realizes that patriarchal oppression extends to women in all classes, races, ethnic, religious, and national groups. Therefore, radical feminist theory is oriented to the understanding of the dimensions of oppression which are common to all women. This is what is meant by understanding the oppression of woman qua woman. What makes it radical is that it continually seeks to go to the roots of male domination, particularly as those roots are located in private, intimate life and extended into public domination.

Radical feminism does not assume that all women's oppression is alike, that poor women on welfare fight against the same conditions of women who have access to economic security (of their own, or through their husbands). It does assert, however, that when each woman is subjected to patriarchal domination, it is because she is a woman, and therefore it is her femaleness that men seek to subdue, conquer, and reign over. This is the basis on which women from diverse class, racial, ethnic and national backgrounds understand the commonality of their oppression as women.

Thus radical feminist theory confronts the demands of patriarchal loyalty expected of all women in every racial, ethnic, religious and national group.

One of the central problems facing feminism in 1982 is the contradiction between the loyalty that each social group (dominated by men) expects of its women and the bonding that is essential if women are to act together in their own behalf. One of the major problems in women finding international unity is not in feminist politics per se, but in the way those politics conflict with that other loyalty that is demanded of women by each patriarchy. For them to give in to patriarchial loyalty is to remain separated from other women and to negate the demands for liberation of all women. But for women subjected to racist or imperialist oppression, distrust of other groups is essential to survival. The basis for distrust is established both by loyalty to one's racial, ethnic, or national group and from actual experiences of racism. Yet this loyalty as it separates and sets women against each other from different nationalities, races, or ethnic groups, ignores the fact that institutionalized racism and imperialism are functions of the power of men as they control all social institutions.

Radical feminist theory recognizes the colonization of women that separates them into opposing patriarchal categories. But the exigencies of life—in the face of war, in the face of active racial hatred—represent major problems and dilemmas to feminist praxis. As feminism is coming to be an international (global) force, the devisiveness among women fostered by each patriarchal unit is countered by the ability of women within those units to confront their oppression as women. From this action the unity of women is slowly being realized. The women of some African countries who are combating genital mutilation (Saadawi 1980) come to know that Western patriarchal medicine finds its own ways of physically mutilating women in unnecessary hysterectomies and disabling mastectomies. International feminism realizes the radical assertion that theory is found in these experiences of exploitation that women have in common.

The objective and actual conditions of patriarchal domination are in random acts, individual and institutional, systematized in the family or in the labor force. For radical feminism to produce coherent theory it must look beyond the immediate conditions of oppression to envision a future freed from present domination. Some social space removed from the most severe aspects of domination is necessary to allow one to see beyond the most direct and severe forms of oppression. Female bonding provides the social space and the basis of alternative visions of the world. It is both the personal and political support which allows women to face and rise up against their oppressive situations, and it establishes the theoretical point from which women begin to create and conceptualize their future in a world different from that which is characterized by the alienation of a woman from herself and as domination insists that she set herself up against others of her sex. As a major aspect of radical feminist theory, female bonding establishes women in a relationship to each other in a way that is based on self and same-sex affirmation and that stand against the misogynist contempt that characterizes patriarchy; it challenges the isolation that pervades private domination, and instead creates a collective base from which to confront oppression.

From this it follows that radical feminism will compassionately take the point of view of women, not in blind affirmation, but from political consciousness and in theoretical understanding. When all of society and the world appeared to believe that rape victims generally provoke rapists into something they wouldn't do otherwise, feminists insisted that it was an act of sexual politics and patriarchal domination to put the victim on trial for the crime committed against her. When all of society viewed housework as a "labor of love," feminists identified it as slavery and demanded "wages for housework."[3]

By compassionately taking woman's point of view and thus exercising faith and belief in she who has been deemed untrustable and unworthy, one breaks down the patriarchal categorizations of women and discards such male dichotomies as "madonna and whore." In the process, women are engaged in a new ordering of the social world in which female bonding insists on locating the agency of and responsibility for the oppression of women in the men and structures that perpetrate it instead of the women who experience it.

Among the many feminists writing with a concern for female bonding, Daly (1978) has found significant connections between conditions of women's oppression and the necessity of bonding (or in her term, "crones spinning," for example). She documents some patriarchal atrocities only to encourage women "to continue to unweave the prevailing dis-order, weaving our way deeper into the labyrinth" (109), or to tell crones to "spin closer to the Center of our Centering Selves" (409). In *Gynecology* Daly encouraged many feminists to find the potential for female bonding by separating themselves from the conditions of other women's oppression. In fact, Daly provides the excuse for woman-bonding to remove itself from the conditions of most women's lives and therefore she in effect severs female bonding from feminist praxis and from feminist theory.

This is not to say that all women have or continue to experience the most degrading aspects of patriarchal exploitation. While Faderman (1981) has clearly substantiated a history of women who have surpassed the love and privatized domination of men, while we recognize that many women continue to live free from that direct, oppressive experience, while many women have risen above the lower levels of economic exploitation to climb corporate or academic ladders, these achievements do not, in fact, objectively remove those women from the effects of living under patriarchal domination. Many of these women choose to see themselves as above, aloof to, or removed from that which dominates other women, and they choose to not use their "advantaged" position toward the benefit of those still in the tightest grips of patriarchal domination. It is these limited aspects of the women's movement that have made feminism appear to be self-serving, tending toward individual solutions, and worst of all, elitist; that is, a movement that achieves the liberation of a few at the expense of the many. One example of this has been the refusal among some lesbians to fight for what they consider "straight" women's issues such as abortion rights. (This does not characterize lesbian feminism, which finds many lesbians staffing feminist sexual assault and antipornography programs.) By refusing to work on or support action to protect and expand rights to abortion and to reproductive control, women who take this position deny that the liberation of all women, and hence revolution is the intention of feminism and the reason for feminist theory. From this apolitical stance, the fact that some women choose to withdraw from confronting abortion as a right at a time in the United States when it is increasingly denied to poor women is an example of what those opposed to radical feminism correctly identify as "privileged" because they effectively remove themselves from confrontation against the most severe aspects of the domination of women.

Daly-like feminists and other women who separate their goals and politics from the needs and concerns of the rest identify themselves as radical feminists. In turn, radical feminism is then attributed with the elitism and self-serving solutions of these minority tendencies. But feminist theory supercedes the ability of any group simply to assume any label it wishes, for theory requires one's engagement with feminist praxis and in a continually renewed analysis of domination that includes new realizations of a future that can be projected and fought for collectively.

Whether it is from this type of contempt for "straight" women, or on the other hand, the active fear among other women of a "lesbian menace" in the women's movement, or the benign neglect of racism that causes many feminist projects to exclude women of color, the liberation of women cannot and will not be achieved at the expense of any group. Each of these forms of objectification are antithetical to liberation and consequently, essentially antifeminist. Unlike every other social liberation movement in the history of the world, feminism, because it concerns itself with all aspects of the oppression of women, must leave no oppression untouched. For women, as an oppressed class, are also part of every other oppressed group which has militated action for its own liberation. Often ignored by other liberation movements, such women cannot be ignored by feminism or else feminist goals are achieved at the expense of the women most vulnerable to patriarchal domination.

The final characteristic that identifies radical feminism is that neither women nor their experiences can be reduced to artificially constructed social categories. The private nature of women's oppression and the commonality of that oppression necessitates that under patriarchy, every individual woman be recognized as a sociohistorical entity rather than artificially collectivized into theoretically constructed groups that primarily define men's economic, political, and structured relations with each other.

Socialist Feminism

Socialist feminists come to feminist theory with an already established, academically situated theoretical paradigm. However controversial marxism is as a political orientation, it is recognized as a substantive theory. Making marxism relevant to understanding women's oppression is the task to which socialist feminists address themselves in feminist theory.

Marx's conflict theory of society generated powerful categories of analysis that rest on clashes of interest, exploitation, and change. The sources of conflict are in the economic advantage of one group over another. The disadvantaged group or the working class possessing nothing but its labor power is viewed as a commodity to be bought according to a price. Under these circumstances, exploitation becomes a structural requirement of the whole social system as well as the basis for inequality and oppression; capitalists try to buy labor at the cheapest possible price in order to generate profits, and labor is exploited as a consequence. Class antagonisms and conflicts are generated.

The conflict between the major social groups, workers and capitalists, intensifies through polarizing skills, differentiating those held by capitalists from those assigned to labor, exploitative wages of labor, and monopoly of economic power by capitalists. Such intensification in Marx's opinion brings about the inevitable crisis whereby a counter-ideology develops. The counter-ideology constitutes a set of values and ideas that reflect the interests of the oppressed group and serves as the basis for a new consciousness and, ultimately, for the revolution.

The key category behind these processes is the idea of the social class. Class is a category in which the objective relationship of man to the means of production is determined and through which consciousness of this relationship is understood. The idea of class is further differentiated by reference to its objective formations in society (i.e., capitalists and labor) and by its subjective identity (i.e., the bourgeoisie and the proletariat as socially conscious entities). The division of society into these two distinct categories is viewed as encompassing all members of society, that is, the division is extended to include the wives and children of the primary actors—the capitalist and his workers.

Patriarchy and male domination constitute the level of analysis of radical feminist theory. In contrast, capitalism is the primary level of analysis in socialist feminist theory. Therefore it is not concerned with all women as objects of domination. Specifically, it excludes white women of the middle and upper classes, and practically speaking, it considers as among the bourgeoisie any white women who do not explicitly identify themselves as working-class. It rejects the idea that, for the most part, the "privileges" that acrue to nonworking-class white women are derived through women's economic dependence on men. Additionally, because it takes capitalism as its level of analysis and therefore identifies capitalist patriarchy as that which exploits women, it excludes women from socialist countries who are not seen to be the objects of domination.

It is working-class women who are understood to be primarily exploited by capitalism and secondarily oppressed by patriarchy (Eisenstein 1979). In the United States, socialist feminists extend their theoretical analysis to include women of color (marxism does not include a theoretical concern with racism) both in Western and Third World countries as they are victims of a racism that is the product of American capitalism and imperialism. It should be noted that in contrast to radical feminists who identify their concern with all women, socialist feminists are concerned only with one aspect of patriarchy and certain groups of women dominated by it. In their polemic they charge radical feminism as being without an economic analysis of capitalism and without concern for racism.

Juliet Mitchell (1971) found this to be the case of the women's liberation movement in the United States, which according to her, derived many of its numbers from discontented middle-class women who were unable to get professional jobs. She contrasts this with "a socialist stress on the working class as the revolutionary class" (52), which she found in many aspects of the women's movement when the movement was initiated in Europe. Finding that the oppression of women is intrinsic to capitalism but not to socialist systems (95), Mitchell framed the socialist feminist theoretical task: "We should ask the feminist questions, but try to come up with some Marxist answers" (69).

A major question that concerns socialist feminism is the sexual division of labor and how it corresponds to the capitalist division of labor as framed by Marx. Although Marx had little to say about the sexual division of labor, Engels, in *The Origins of the Family, Private Property and the State* (see Leacock edition 1972), did address this question. Finding his discussion to be problematic and limited, Gayle Rubin (1975) based her essay in part on Engel's intention to locate the subordination of women in the development of the mode of production (169). Rubin argued against the use of patriarchy as a theoretical construct because it obscures other distinctions. Instead she asserted a sex/ gender system that is "a set of arrangements by which society transforms biological sexuality into products of human activity, and in which these transformed sexual needs are satisfied" (159). Following Marx's analysis of commodity production, Rubin identified the "exchange in women" as the locus of women's oppression.

In this essay Rubin came close to identifying sex as the basis of oppression. But socialist feminists tend to disregard sex and sexuality, not finding it to be causal to the exploitation of women. Eisenstein (1979) found that while sex expresses an aspect of women's condition, "it doesn't connect women to the general power structure. It cannot explain the complexity of power relationships in our society" (19). Nevertheless, she does not dismiss the concept of patriarchy, although she does find it to be unstructured and vague in its manifestations of domination. As a logical conclusion of deemphasizing sex as a basis of domination, some British socialist feminists like Sheila Rowbotham now argue that the very idea of patriarchy should be abandoned in feminist theory (Alexander and Taylor 1980).

Rowbotham concluded that taking patriarchy as a level of analysis returns us to biology. This is the basis of current feminist debate over the validity of radical feminist theory as it was intensely discussed in the 1982 British Sociological Association meetings that were devoted to feminism. Among all the writings in radical feminist theory, socialist feminists most frequently cite Shulamith Firestone's *Dialectics of Sex* (1970) as the evidence of biological reductionism governing radical feminist theory (Friedman 1982).

It was Firestone's intention to use a marxist methodology but derive a radical feminist analysis of the sexual division of labor. By relying on marxism as a method to guide her analysis, she fell into the theoretical trap of having to identify the first cause of oppression. Marx established his monocausal method by finding that the rise of capitalism was caused by the origins of private property. Firestone found "the natural reproductive difference between the sexes led directly to the first division of labor" (11), and that "sex class sprang from biological reality" (8).

The problem Firestone produced by following Marx in identifying first (and only) cause is that we are left with women's subordination being traced back either to prehistory because of the long duration of patriarchy and therefore causality cannot be easily documented, or to biology and therefore not easily altered. This is but one example of the difficulty of modifying or following theories that in their original formulation exclude women as a historically oppressed group.

Biology is not the only problem socialist feminists had with Firestone's work. Eisenstein (1979) challenged Firestone's use of "sex class," asserting "she artificially separates the sexual and economic spheres, replaces capitalism with patriarchy as the oppressive system. . . . It is not that Firestone does not see economic oppression as problematic for women but that she does not view it as the key source of oppression" (11). Thus the division of labor that is sexual cannot be separated from that which is derived from capitalism, and capitalism must be understood as causal to both the sexual and economic divisions of labor. That Firestone rejected this causality presented particular problems to Zaretsky (1976) who argued that Firestone's formulations of the sexual division of labor located the cause of women's oppression in the family. He found that the family was oppressive only because of its connections to the origins of private property and capitalism. He concluded that capitalism was the cause of the exploitation of women's household labor and her relegation to the "private sphere."

In elaborating some important distinctions between radical feminist and socialist feminist theory from the perspective of the latter, Hartmann (1981) responded critically to Zaretsky and asked a significant and yet unanswered theoretical question: if capitalism created woman's private sphere "why did it happen that *women* work there, and *men* in the labor force?" (7).

This question focuses the problem of the sexual division of labor on women's domestic labor. Benston (1972) connected women's unpaid household labor with use-values (121) and found that "the support of a family is a hidden tax on the wage earner (male)—his wage buys the labor power of two people" (127). Thus the family and housework support capitalism and both husband and wife are exploited in the process. Gardiner (1976) supported this analysis but she found that "those engaged in domestic labour share a common class position" (119) as a result of their indirect contribution to surplus value by being a "source of surplus labor in capitalist society" (117). The exploitation of women's unpaid domestic labor is caused by capitalism and consequently the radical demand of "wages for housework" is seen by many socialist feminist analysts as merely subsidizing capitalism (Landes 1975). By assuming that men do not privately as well as publicly benefit from their domination of women in the home, this analysis levels the distinctions between the exploitation of men and of women in their relations to the public economy. From this one should be able to assume that with the overthrow of capitalism, domestic labor will no longer be exploitative. This logic highlights an important theoretical inconsistency in marxist analysis of domestic labor, as it has no way of accounting for the similarity in women's exploitation in the home (in unpaid labor, wife battery, marital rape, etc.) in both socialist and capitalist countries.

Considerable confusion has been introduced to feminist theory by attempts to distinguish revolutionary from reform feminism. In socialist feminist theory, the revolutionary potential of feminism (Eisenstein 1981) is seen only in terms of the marxist meaning of revolution. When measured by marxist criteria, many feminists engaged in reform work are considered "liberal" in the marxist sense because in their struggle for change they focus on individual rights, which is seen as not challenging the capitalist state. This kind of criticism reveals the socialist feminist rejection of a radical critique, as it insists that revolution be defined as an overthrow of capitalism and that women not engaged in that action are less than revolutionary. Patriarchal revolution is lost and so is the realization that feminists find that their work necessarily includes the demand for individual rights so as to enable them to demand deeper structural changes. Socialist feminism trivializes feminist praxis by subsuming much of it under the misleading label of "liberalism." While some feminists do not seek radical change, many find that there is a solid consistency between reform and radical politics in their work for women. Eisenstein (1981) recognized the need for feminists to demand individual rights, but when she evaluated this action she applied the marxist critique of liberalism and concluded that such women are ultimately supporting the capitalist state. Thus their work cannot be revolutionary, although according to her it holds that potential. In other words, reformists have the potential of becoming marxists—the ultimate undermining of a radical critique of patriarchy.

What differentiates feminism from marxism and all other movements is that it will not wage its revolution against the state without revolutionary confrontation against personally exercised privatized power. At its core, feminist political consciousness is derived from women's experience of oppression and not from Marx's teachings about domination. The expectation that women come from their conditions of oppression with a fully defined revolutionary consciousness that is "correct" in all of its politics and to all political orientations is a political expectation made of no other oppressed group. Insisting on this from women is a statement that their oppression is less significant, less exploitative, less destructive of the self than other forms of oppression. This kind of thinking is usually associated with "correct-line" analysis, which is often erroneously thought to be theory. The practice of imposing "correct" politics on a movement is not confined to marxism; it is identified in many aspects of the women's movement where correct politics, lifestyle, and behaviors are determined for women by women in the name of liberation.

Psychoanalysis Versus Consciousness

In addition to accounting for the material or objective conditions of oppression, feminist theory is left with the task of identifying how exploitation is accomplished on the psychological level.

Among the first criticisms radical feminists made of psychological theories was that beginning with Freud most psychoanalytical approaches locked women into the biological destiny of female subordination (Firestone 1970; Millett 1970). In rejecting these theories, radical feminism turned to its own understanding of women, to find her psychological or "inner" selves very understandable in the context of experiences of domination. Psychoanalysis had mystified women's psychology by not accounting for their response to domination. This was a radical theoretical critique but it was also the discovery made by one woman after another in consciousness-raising groups. Both theoretically and practically, feminists demonstrated the irrelevance of theory and therapy to women's liberation if it does not account for women's oppression. Thus freudian theory came to be understood as an ideological justification of male domination that placed the responsibility for women's oppression on women themselves.

Socialist feminist theory found that marxism too was notably without psychological explanation. Like many marxists, some socialist feminists turned back to Freud (Mitchell 1974) to find what they could salvage from his theory. Others went back to the French psychoanalyst Jacques Lacan.[4] Both Lacan and Freud equated rationality, order and discipline with the heritage of phallic symbolism. All psychoanalysts rely on Freud's formulation of the unconscious and thus develop an explanation of human behavior that is determined in and acted out from a state of existence unaccessible to the human being because it is *un*-conscious. This makes consciousness rely on the psychoanalyst's ability to assist the individual in discovering it. While some women challenged the more overt sexism and phallocentrism of these paradigms, followers of Freud and Lacan relied on the paradigm itself.

Some socialist feminists like Chodorow (1978) still had problems with the biological implications of psychoanalysis, and found that the object relations theory provided an account of instinctual determinism and thus the repressions and other unconscious motivations that result from it but without a biological base. Chodorow found object relations to be advanced over other psychodynamic theories because it is based on an analysis of social interactions with various erotogenic zones.

For many, these psychological theories find a compatibility with marxist economic determinism because they provide a deterministic framework (based on theories of unconscious motivation) that is imposed on psychological dimensions of existence and used to interpret it. As deterministic paradigms, when used by socialist feminist theory, they present major problems for feminist theory. First, when psychological conditions can be explained through predetermined constructs such as the oedipal complex, then consciousness as a phenomenon of liberation can be ignored and consciousness raising as it engages the self in its own determination is bypassed. Oppression, what it is, and how it operates, is no longer defined and articulated from the experience of it.

Removed from engagement with consciousness raising and feminist praxis, the proponents of these economic and psychological determinisms place themselves in the position of seeming to know what the oppressed who are not trained in these paradigms cannot know about their own oppression. From this position of received truths, theorists are then in a position to evaluate and judge the "correctness" of every other theoretical orientation from an assumed moral superiority over any that do not incorporate the determinism of these paradigms.

When theory takes as its responsibility the accounting of all the conditions of oppression, when it attempts to present the only systematic account of power relations, and when it predetermines how revolutionary change will come about as well as the consequences of it, then theory and its proponents are trapped in a closed and fully determined system. When one assumes that a specific theory is the only correct explanation of domination, the only correct formula for change, then theory has been established as a morally superior set of ideas. The proponents of these theories privilege themselves by establishing their distance from the actual conditions of women's lives, while identifying as incorrect analysis any explanation that does not agree with theirs. Finally, proponents of deterministic theories acting from moral superiority granted by the nature of the theoretical paradigm establish themselves as the intellectual leaders of the movement.

Obviously, these features of determinism characterize many theoretical approaches, including such orientations as lesbian separatism and socialist feminism. When lesbian separatism establishes itself as the sine qua non of female existence, a less theoretical but similar "correct-line politics" results, which imposes on women another oppressive determinism.

Against Determinism: The Acting Subject

These examples of marxism, freudianism, and lesbian separatism are used to demonstrate how determinism constitutes closed systems of thought and thus ushers in other forms of elitism, encouraging its followers to assume self-proclaimed moral superiority particularly in regard to those who hold different perspectives. To determine for a group the conditions of their future "liberated" state, and to shape the demand for liberation according to a derived analysis that understands that a predetermined future will result if the revolutionary struggle or the "spinning and weaving" are carried out according to certain established criteria is to deny those involved in fighting for liberation the opportunity continually to shape their own struggle and to envision their own future as a becoming—a going toward—that is created as it is being achieved, and therefore is always being created anew.

Determinism closes down thought and it reinstates the dogmatic character of oppression, which reflective consciousness raising seeks to surpass in the revolutionary struggle. Determinism then is the ability of any group through any theoretical orientation to impose a closed system of analysis on the social life it is attempting to understand. In contrast, liberation is a continuous struggle, and consequently our analysis of oppression and our projection of future possibilities must constantly be in the process of being formed in an open universe. Feminism requires an exploratory and constantly changing movement.

Causal theory that leads to determinism denies the ongoing dialectic in the quest for liberation, the tension between what is and what ought to be. It is in the loss of the dialectic between the possible and the actual that theory becomes rigidified and forecloses self-determination in approaching the future. Feminist theory should be constantly emerging from the dynamic interaction between the struggle for new consciousness and that of political action. It places women in the tension between what is, and what ought to be; that is, the future they are trying to create, not one they artificially devise and impose. In this sense "what ought to be" should be considered only as open possibilities.

Consciousness raising has been a critical aspect of feminist theory as it emerged within the women's liberation movement in the late 1960s, but there is no formula for how it must be done. It was appropriate for some women at one time, but it was fraught with problems such as "the tyranny of structurelessness" (Joreen 1972) and attacks on other women that led to "trashing" (Joreen 1976). Nevertheless, the ongoing creation of new consciousness in dialectical interaction with political action is essential for feminist theory and the continuation of women's struggle for their liberation. How this is actualized by any group of women, in any part of the world, at any time will undoubtedly be the consequence of their historical place in their struggle. But it can only be realized when their commitment to that struggle is revolutionary.

Theoretically, if we are to know feminist theory as it is continually emerging through feminist praxis, then we need to know how to view those who are engaged in that praxis. Rather than approach feminist theory from the analyses that determine it, we can learn much more about it and the meaning of liberation from those who are engaged in demanding it.

"Who is woman who demands her liberation?" *She is an acting subject*, by which is meant that she does not know herself as the passive object of forces of domination, but rather, she acts from herself, with others and against the annihilation of her self intended by those who dominate. Therefore her action in behalf of another (i.e., for abortion rights, lesbian rights, or any other feminist issue) is from her knowledge of herself not as an object but a subject who is active, not passive. (These are the philosophical origins of the meaning of "the personal is political.") She comes to others who are oppressed and victimized through domination not as "victim to victim" but as mutually engaged acting subjects.[5] From this stance, there can be no moral superiority. Acting subjects in command of their own liberation need no intellectual elite to lead the way.

Therefore, *she is engaged in self-determination* with her movement and its struggle for liberation. This means she is continually involved in creating and understanding the meaning of liberation.

Thus *she envisions the possible* by the very fact that as an acting subject she insists that the present in its patriarchal formulation and manifestations is neither the necessary present nor the inevitable future. In asserting that "women have a right to control their own bodies" or that "pornography is a lie about women" or that women must "take back the night" she implies a realization that another existence is possible in life that involves control of one's own body, a truth about women and sexuality, a movement away from confinement (during the night, for example). In other words, for her, human life and its subjective experience need not be the way they are, or their representation of it be a lie, rendered to ideological interpretation for the purpose of maintaining domination.

In approaching her future as a self-determining and acting subject she answers the age old question of "what do women want?" as she finds that the only possible answer is freedom.[6]

Notes

[1]At the 1982 Conference of the National Coalition against Sexual Assault it was noted that many sexual assault programs had become self-limiting in fear of losing public support and funding. In other words, there were many strategies program staff never tried because the present ideological climate promotes the belief that a conservative approach is necessary in order to protect the project. Thus they lived within self-imposed limitations that were not tested against reality.

[2]In discussions on reflection and its role in revolutionary transformation, I have found Jürgen Habermas's *Knowledge and Human Interests* (Boston: Beacon Press, 1971) to be of particular importance.

[3]The radical feminist demand for wages for housework is to be distinguished here from Selma James's organization, which adopted this originally feminist slogan as its name. James uses "wages for housework" only as a euphemism for a more generalized demand for a guaranteed annual income for everyone. In that sense, the organization does not follow the original radical feminist meaning of the term.

[4]Luce Irigaray and Helene Cixous are among the French theoreticians who critique Lacan and condemn some of his conclusions; nevertheless, with Julia Kristeva they apply his model to understanding the feminine subject. See "French feminist theory," *Signs* (Autumn 1981); also in this Bibliography, Marks and de Courtivron 1980, and Eisenstein and Jardine 1980.

[5]In *The Existential Sociology of Jean Paul Sartre* (Amherst: University of Massachusetts Press, 1980), Gila Hayim presents this idea of *"subjects* approaching *subjects"* (p. 41) in her sensitive discussion of the dialectics of the Self and Other.

[6]"Freedom" is used here in the full meaning of revolutionary radical feminism and therefore cannot be subjected to a marxist reductionism, which means only individual rights under the liberal state.

References

ALEXANDER, SALLY, and TAYLOR, BARBARA. 1980. In defense of "patriarchy." *New Statesman* February 1.

ARMS, SUZANNE. 1975. *Immaculate deception.* New York: Bantam.

ATKINSON, T. GRACE. *1974.* The institution of sexual intercourse. In *Amazon odyssey,* New York: Link Books, pp. 13–23.

BARRY, KATHLEEN. 1979. *Female sexual slavery.* New York: Avon.

BENSTON, MARGARET. 1972. The political economy of women's liberation. In *Women in a man-made world*. Edited by Nona Glazer and Helen Waehrer. Chicago: Rand McNally, pp. 119–28.

BROWNMILLER, SUSAN. 1975. *Against our will*. New York: Simon & Schuster.

BURRIS, BARBARA, with Kathy Barry, Terry Moon, Joann DeLor, Joann Parrent, Cate Studelman. 1971. *The fourth world manifesto: An angry response to an imperialist venture against the women's liberation movement*. New Haven: Advocate Press.

BUTLER, SANDRA. 1978. *Conspiracy of silence: The trauma of incest*. San Francisco: New Glide.

CHODOROW, NANCY. 1978. *The reproduction of mothering*. Berkeley: University of California Press.

DALY, MARY. 1978. *Gyn/ecology: The metaethics of radical feminism*. Boston: Beacon Press.

DELPHY, CHRISTINE. 1970. *The main enemy, a materialist analysis of women's oppression*. Translated by Diana Leonard. London: Women's Research and Resource Centre.

————. 1980. A materialist feminism is possible." Translated by Diana Leonard. *Feminist Review* 4:79–104.

DOBASH, R. EMERSON, and DOBASH, RUSSELL. 1979. *Violence against wives*. New York: Free Press.

DWORKIN, ANDREA. 1981. *Pornography: Men possessing women*. New York: Perigee.

EISENSTEIN, ZILLAH. 1979. Developing a theory of capitalist patriarchy and socialist feminism. In *Capitalist patriarchy and the case for socialist feminism*. Edited by Zillah Eisenstein. New York: Monthly Review Press, pp. 5–40.

————. 1981. *The radical future of liberal feminism*. New York: Longman.

FADERMAN, LILLIAN. 1981. *Surpassing the love of men*. New York: William Morrow.

FARLEY, LINN. 1978. *Sexual shakedown: The sexual harassment of women on the job*. New York: McGraw-Hill.

FIRESTONE, SHULAMITH. 1970. *Dialectics of sex*. New York: William Morrow.

FRIEDMAN, SCARLET. 1982. The marxist paradigm: Radical feminist theorists compared. British Sociological Association Conference paper, London.

GARDINER, JEAN. 1976. Political economy of domestic labour in Capitalist society. In *Dependence and exploitation in work and marriage*. Edited by Diana Leonard Barker and Sheila Allen. New York: Longman, 109–20.

GRIFFIN, SUSAN. 1971. Rape—The all-American crime. *Ramparts* (September) 26–35. Reprinted in *Rape: The power of consciousness*. New York: Harper & Row, pp. 3–22.

————. 1981. *Pornography and silence*. New York: Harper & Row.

HARTMANN, HEIDI. 1981. The unhappy marriage of marxism and feminism: Towards a more progressive union. In *Women and revolution*. Edited by Lydia Sargent. Boston: South End Press, pp. 1–41.

JOHNSON, SONIA. 1981. *From housewife to heretic*. Garden City, N.Y.: Doubleday.

JOREEN. 1972. The tyranny structurelessness. *Second Wave*, 2, no. 1:20–25, 42.

———. 1976. Trashing: The dark side of sisterhood. *Ms.* April, pp. 49–51, 92–98.

LANDES, JOAN. 1975. Wages for housework: Subsidizing capitalism? *Quest* 2, no. 2 (Fall):17–30.

LEACOCK, ELEANOR, ed. 1972. *The origin of private property and the state* by Frederick Engels. New York: International Publishers.

MACKINNON, CATHARINE A. 1979. *Sexual harrassment of working women.* New Haven: Yale University Press.

MILLETT, KATE. 1970. *Sexual politics.* Garden City, N.Y.: Doubleday.

MITCHELL, JULIET. 1971. *Woman's estate.* New York: Vintage.

———. 1974. *Psychoanalysis and feminism.* New York: Vintage.

RICH, ADRIENNE. 1980. Compulsory heterosexuality and lesbian existence. *Signs* 5, no. 4. (Summer):631–60.

RUBIN, GAYLE. 1975. The traffic in women: Notes on the "political economy" of sex. In *Toward an anthropology of women.* Edited by Rayna Reiter. New York: Monthly Review Press, pp. 157–210.

RUSSELL, DIANA E. H. 1982. *Rape in marriage.* New York: Macmillan.

SAADAWI NAWAL EL. 1980. *The hidden face of Eve.* Translated by Sherif Hetata. Boston: Beacon Press.

WARRIOR, BETSY, and LEGHORN, LISA. 1975. *Houseworker's handbook.* Evanston: Women's History Archives. Microfilm.

ZARETSKY, ELI. 1976. *Capitalism, the family, and personal life.* New York: Harper & Row.

Bibliography

Barrett, Michele, and McIntosh, Mary. "Christine Delphy: Towards a Materialist Feminism?" *Feminist Review* 1, no. 1 (1979):95–106. This paper is British socialist feminist response to Delphy's *Main enemy* (see References) in which the authors argue that Delphy has inappropriately applied marxist concepts to her articulation of the patriarchal mode of production. Delphy's essay "A Materialist Feminism is Possible" (see References) is a radical feminist response to this article.

de Beauvoir, Simone. *The Second Sex.* Translated by H. M. Parshley. New York: Bantam, 1953. Original publication 1949. The twentieth-century classic in feminist theory covering the oppression of women biologically, historically, in myth and through woman's life cycle. The work, written before a twentieth century resurgence of feminism, is remarkable for breadth of study, but necessarily disconnected from feminist praxis it is also limited in its depth of analysis.

Bunch, Charlotte, ed. *Building Feminist Theory: Essays from* Quest. New York: Longman, 1981. A collection of essays through the 1970s written by women who were and are committed to activism as well as theory. Discusses a wide range of issues from feminism in daily life to class analysis to feminist political strategies.

Daly, Mary. *Beyond God the Father: Toward a Philosophy of Women's Liberation.* Boston: Beacon Press, 1973. A radical feminist critique of patriarchal religion focuses the women's movement as a means of transforming human consciousness toward a human becoming.

Dworkin, Andrea. *Our Blood: Prophecies and Discourses on Sexual Politics.* New York: Perigee, 1981 (1976). A recently republished series of essays that were originally Dworkin's lectures. Strong, radical feminist discussions of diverse subjects from witches to the sexual politics of fear and courage to the intertwining of woman slavery and race slavery in "Amerika."

Eisenstein, Hester, and Jardine, Alice. *The Future of Difference.* Boston: G. K. Hall, 1980. This collection of theoretical papers from the Barnard College Scholar and Feminist series focuses on psychoanalysis and language. It is an exploration of female differences that examines the cultural presuppositions of women's experience. Particular emphasis is placed on French psychoanalytic thought.

Hall, Gloria T.; Scott, Patricia Bell; and Smith, Barbara. *All the Women Are White, All the Blacks Are Men, But Some of Us Are Brave.* Old Westbury, Conn.: Feminist Press, 1982. Oriented toward women's studies programs, the anthology contains writings on consciousness of black feminism, the interaction of racism and sexism, historical essays, and extensive bibliographies. Theoretical papers present critiques of social sciences, political statements, and literary criticism.

Janssen-Jurreit, Marielouise. *Sexism: The Male Monopoly on History and Thought.* Translated by Verne Moberg. New York: Farrar, Straus & Giroux, 1982. German edition 1976. Extensive theoretical and historical feminist analysis covers the origins of radical feminism in Germany, a radical analysis of both evolutionism and socialism, and issues such as division of labor, biology, and sexuality.

Koedt, Anne; Levine, Ellen; and Rapone, Anita, eds. *Radical Feminism.* New York: Quadrangle, 1973. Many of the political tracts, manifestos, and original theoretical papers of radical feminism from the late 1960s to early 1970s are collected in this volume. Covers major radical issues, actions and ideas as they emerged from feminist praxis of that period.

Kuhn, Annette, and Wolpe, Ann Marie, eds. *Feminism and Materialism: Women and Modes of Production.* London: Routledge & Kegan Paul, 1978. A collection of socialist feminist papers from England that examines women's relationships to production, division of labor, domestic labor, and the relationship of capitalism and patriarchy.

Latin American and Caribbean Women's Collective. *Slaves of Slaves: The Challenge of Latin American Women.* London: Zed Press, 1977. This work examines the situation of women from different social categories in several different Latin American countries. In each section it integrates theoretical issues such as women's relationship to the economy, the family, and revolutionary struggle.

MacKinnon, Catherine A. "Feminism, Marxism, Method, and the State: An Agenda for Theory," *Signs* 7, no. 3 (Spring 1982):515–44. Argues that sexuality is to feminism what work is to marxism, and explores the meaning of sexuality as power and finds that sexuality is a material reality of women's lives.

Marks, Elaine, and de Courtirvon, Isabelle, eds. *New French Feminisms: An Anthology.* Amherst: University of Massachusetts Press, 1980. A wide-ranging collection of recent French feminist writings that emphasizes writers who follow psychoanalytic theory and the politics of language. Minimal attention to radical feminist theory.

Morgan, D. H. J. *Social Theory and the Family.* London: Routledge & Kegan Paul, 1975. A theoretical analysis of the family critiques functionalism and kinship theory with feminist perspectives. Morgan approaches analyzing the family through "women as a social class" and by examining the intersection of sex and capitalism.

Morgan, Robin. *The Anatomy of Freedom: Feminism, Physics and Global Politics*. Garden City, N.Y.: Doubleday, 1982. Uses the "new physics" as an analogy for feminism and explores interconnections of gender, race, global politics, family structure, economics, and several other issues related to feminism. Explores issues of freedom in her own personal politics.

Rich, Adrienne. *Of Women Born: Motherhood as Experience and Institution*. New York: W. W. Norton, 1976. The first feminist critique of motherhood that draws from Rich's own diaries as she was rearing her children and extends to an analysis of the institution. Rich examines the history, childbirth, mothers and daughters, and mothers and sons.

Rosaldo, Michelle Zimbalist. "Woman, Culture, and Society: A Theoretical Overview." In *Women, Culture and Society*. Edited by Michele Zimbalist Rosaldo and Louise Lamphere. Stanford: Stanford University Press, 1974. Relates the universal aspects of male-female relations to a universal distinction in domestic and public spheres for each. Finds women's rise in status related to their ability to transcend domestic limits.

Rowbotham, Sheila. *Women, Resistence and Revolution: A History of Women and Revolution in the Modern World*. New York: Pantheon, 1972. A summary of the relevance of Marx's writings to feminism and the condition of women. Discusses the problems involved in integrating demands of feminism with marxist theory and in socialist revolutions.

————. *Woman's Consciousness, Man's World*. Baltimore: Penguin, 1973. Argues that revolutionary feminism is blocked by failure of equal rights strategies and the failure of marxism to come to terms with freudian insights and the progression of noncapitalistic societies. Discusses the nature of female production under advanced capitalism.

Rowbotham, Sheila; Segal, Lynne; and Wainwright, Hilary. *Beyond the Fragments: Feminism and the Making of Socialism*. Boston: Alyson, 1981. This work illustrates the fragmentation of the male-dominated Left and finds the relevance of feminism to be in it as a model from which the Left can learn to revive itself by following the loose, organizational structure and emphases on consciousness in the women's movement.

Sargent, Lydia. *Women and Revolution, a Discussion of the Unhappy Marriage of Marxism and Feminism*. Boston: South End Press, 1981. Heidi Hartmann's essay, "The Unhappy Marriage of Marxism and Feminism" prompted several socialist feminists to expand on different themes in the paper. This work includes the lead essay and papers covering the relationship of marxism and feminism to lesbianism, racism, the family, and the question of social structure.

Health

Susan Reverby

Women's bodies are the terrain upon which many of the crucial struggles over feminism have been fought in the last one hundred and fifty years. The alignments and strength of various forces, their "weaponry" and ideology, and the precipitating causes of the battles have, of course, changed considerably over time. In 1982 this seemingly "biological" or "god-given" battleground became the focus of political struggle over issues of women's sexuality and reproductive rights in particular. Differing women's health and women's rights groups continued to contest the onslaught from the New Right, conservative elements in the medical profession, the Reagan administration, and the media. At the same time, they sought to redefine women's health issues away from the battleground and onto a turf in which women's experiences and real needs can be ascertained and met (McBride and McBride 1981). This review suggests some of the parameters and key issues of this year's increasingly politicized struggle over who would define and control women's health and, ultimately, women's position in our society.

The "body battles" took place in the context of the country's worst recession/depression since the 1930s. As official unemployment figures jumped to over 10 percent and the "feminization of poverty" captured media attention, the crucial health issue became whether increasing numbers of women (and men) would have enough money to feed themselves and their families (Ehrenreich and Stallard 1982). Coupled to selective cutbacks in federal and state services that led to what a coalition of women's groups characterized as "the inequality of sacrifice," more and more women found it difficult to meet their most basic health and welfare needs. By early 1983, for example, the Washington-based Children's Defense Fund reported budget cuts were having "life-threatening" impacts on health services for poor mothers and engendering rising infant mortality rates (Group says . . . 1983).

In light of the increasing economic and health inequities facing women and their families, the focus on reproductive rights and sexuality among women's groups may appear on the surface as less critical. But it is through control over women's sexuality and reproductive capacities, and thus through our bodies, that the entry into our minds and consciousness is made. Our health and sexuality become the issues on which our subordination and return to more "traditional" roles is demanded.

More than in the realm of ideas and ideological argument, however, control over our sexuality and reproductive abilities is materially basic to women's demands for both "equality and autonomy" (Petchesky 1980, 662; 1981; Gordon 1977). It is thus no accident that in 1982, flush from her seeming victory over the ERA, Phyllis Schlafly and her Eagle Forum have moved on to the issue of herpes as the "reward" for sexual freedom. Nor is it surprising that the major issue of teenage sexuality this year focused on the administration's efforts to promulgate the so-called "squeal rule," requiring federally funded family planning clinics to notify parents when giving prescription contraceptives to teenagers.

Sexuality, reproductive rights, and health are also the issues that are manipulated to blame women and our demands for equality and paid labor, for the country's deep economic and cultural crisis (Gilder 1981, passim). Because easy solutions to the real difficulties of balancing work and commitments to family and friends cannot be found, women often find themselves divided and genuinely confused over questions of what it is "best" to do. In this arena of life so fraught with conflicting evidence and so open to deep feelings of guilt and neglect, medical expertise is being called on once again to make definitive statements about women's proper role.

The link between women's sexuality, reproductive rights, health, work, and family roles was forged in debates, in particular, over the fertility of women over the age of 30 and in the health of children in day care. According to the latest available figures, the greatest increase in births in 1979 occurred among women aged 30 to 34 (U.S. fertility . . . 1982). In February, a French study of the fertility of artificially inseminated women was published in the *New England Journal of Medicine;* it concluded that the risk of infertility in women was "slight but significant after 30 years of age and marked after 35 years" (Fédération CECOS, Schwartz, and Mayaux 1982, 406). Reports and editorials on the study in the newspapers suggested scientific evidence had been found for the necessity of women's childbearing in their twenties. The professional criticism of the study, however, was not widely reported as "news" (Bongaarts 1982).

Similarly, in early January 1983 the *Journal of the American Medical Association (JAMA)* reported and editorialized on the danger the nation faced from an epidemic of infectious diseases running rampant in day-care centers. In semihysterical tones, the editorial claimed the situation was "reminiscent of the presanitarian days of the seventeenth century." A number of Boston physicians interviewed on the report disputed the *JAMA* position calling it "absurd" (Matchan 1983, 7). Whether exaggerated or true, the critical point is that it is on the basis of health issues—both ours and our children's—that women's position and role in society is being debated.

The women's health movement has responded to these attacks in a number of different ways; however, it would be too simple to see 1982 as only a time during which women's health activists focused solely on defensive measures. Rather, it has been a year in which in more academic and theoretical writings and conferences, and in actual practice, many women have thoughtfully tried to formulate feminist-centered positions on sexuality, health, and science. This effort has been fraught with conflicts of the most deeply personal, and therefore, political nature. But it means women are seeking to understand how basic biological factors such as aging and reproductive capacities are linked in cultural and political terms to our position and role in this society (Nadelson and Notman 1982a, 1982b; Voda et al. 1982). It has also been a year in which women's concerns for health were broadly extended into the growing focus on disarmament and the necessity to stop the headlong rush toward armageddon (Cagan et al. 1982).

Both scholars and activists are attempting to rethink and redefine the meaning of women's health and women's relationship to science in a way that links self-knowledge to "rational inquiry" (Keller 1982, 594; Raymond 1982; Whitbeck 1982; Fee 1982). Feminists are continuing to seek new ways to define the human need for health and to carry on the political struggles necessary to obtain it. We have thus moved well beyond the simple, if necessary, "doctor bashing," which could be said to characterize the first thrust of this generation's health activism a decade ago.

While this search for a new understanding of need for all women continues, there has also been growing recognition of the "common differences" among women (Joseph and Lewis 1981). The issue of "compulsory heterosexuality" and lesbian existence was the focus of debate, for example, at the national meeting of reproductive rights groups. The National Women's Health Network, the Washington-based consumer advocacy wing of the women's health movement, is sponsoring a national conference on black women's health to be held in June 1983. The particular health and life-affirming needs of older, mid-life, and teenage women are beginning to have their own constituencies. The range of topics discussed at major health conferences in 1982 reflects the widening circle of concern and recognition of the complexity of the issues we face.

All these events testify to the growing sophistication and continued outreach on women's health issues. Despite the recession/depression and the continued effort to whittle (or hack) away at the hard-won, if minimal, rights women have obtained in the health arena, 1982 suggests that in this decade women's health rights and demands will be the continued focus of political and cultural struggle.

Sexuality

New York *Village Voice* writer Ellen Willis quipped a number of years ago that the debate on abortion wasn't about "life," rather it was about "sex." It has been around sex, and more generally sexuality, that controversy among feminists and antifeminists has swirled for over a decade now. As feminists have strived to separate sexuality and reproduction, and to search for and define female sexuality, antifeminists have attempted to limit and narrow that definition and to retie the bind to reproduction.

There is, however, no one clear feminist definition of female sexuality, nor, as it were, one feminist position on sex of whatever form. Critical of the link between sex and violence, many feminists have been organizing against pornography and the exploitation of women in films, magazines, books, and prostitution. But other women have begun to criticize the antipornography feminists for their narrow vision of sex, their failure to differentiate between the pornographic and the erotic, and their anticivil-libertarian positions on censorship.

Much of the debate on this topic and on conflict over forms of sexuality and sexual expression within the lesbian community surfaced at the ninth annual Barnard College conference on "The scholar and the feminist: Toward a politics of sexuality" in April. While difficult, tense, and explosive at times, the conference reflected the growing effort within the women's movement to explore more openly the complexities of the issues and to understand the differences between the more libertarian and social purity strains within feminism (Alderfer, Jaker, and Nelson 1982; Toward a politics . . . 1982; Gordon and DuBois 1983). Judging from the heated debates at this conference, and at similar discussions at the National Women's Studies Association meeting, the topic of female sexuality, so under attack from the New Right, will continue to be a, if not the, critical health-related issue for the 1980s.

Teenage Sexuality and Pregnancy   In the late 1970s and early 1980s, teenage sexuality, and in particular teenage pregnancy, became, in the words of the title of a national policy report, "the *problem* that hasn't gone away" (my emphasis) (Alan Guttmacher Institute 1981). While the birthrate among adolescents declined, the teenage pregnancy rate rose, signaling the continued increase in teenage sexual activity. By 1980 over 1.1 million young women became pregnant, with 38 percent of the pregnancies ending in abortion and 13 percent in miscarriages. Because about 5 percent of all American teenagers give birth, the United States has one of the highest teenage birth rates for developed nations. Our rate, in fact, exceeds that of such so-called less developed countries as the Philippines, Malaysia, Singapore, and Tunisia. The birth rate of unmarried white teenagers has continued to grow, and the majority of these women keep their children rather than give them up for adoption or abort (Alan Guttmacher Institute 1981). Because it is women who literally bear the consequences in social and economic, as well as biological, terms for sexual activity, it is around young women that much of the concern has been focused.

The policy debate on teenage sexuality has centered on the "problems" associated with early parenting: low birth-weight babies, school drop-out rates, welfare costs, and seemingly limited life opportunities for the mothers. In recent years, the question of familial control (primarily paternal control) over daughters and the necessity to limit and control sexuality in general has been more widely discussed. Liberal policy planners continue to amass evidence to prove that sex education does not increase sexual activity and that birth control information will help teenagers limit unwanted births (Zelnick and Kim 1982). They have argued for and developed specific family planning clinics for teenagers, sex education programs to encourage "responsible" sexuality, abortion services, support programs for teenage mothers, and so on (Yonas-Phipps 1980). As health planner Jeanette Valentine has queried, such programs must confront serious questions: "What is responsible sexuality, is abortion acceptable, and is a woman's career, job or schooling more important than her role as a mother?" (Valentine 1982, 3). Most important, who shall decide the answers to these questions, and under what conditions?

This question took on sharp focus this year when in February the Department of Health and Human Services (DHHS) proposed a regulation, quickly dubbed the "squeal rule" by opponents, that would require parental notification when unemancipated minors were given prescription birth control drugs and devices in federally funded family planning clinics. Such a regulation would affect 80 percent of the nearly one-half million young (primarily Third World and low-income) women using the 5,000 family planning clinics in the nation (Furstenberg et al. 1982). Despite the fact that the majority of clinics do make some effort to involve parents, and most teenagers do eventually tell their parents, the administration attempted to impose this regulation (Furstenberg et al. 1982). Republican Senator Jeremiah Denton, a leading Senate critic of adolescent sexuality, argued that the proposed regulation was "a long overdue step toward reestablishing what are legitimate, parental rights" (Administration proposes . . . 1982, 1).

The response to the proposed regulation was swift and overwhelming. A number of New Right groups decried the regulation as "useless" and demanded the federal government require parental *permission*, not just notification, for such services as sex education, counseling and abortion referrals (Administration proposes . . . 1982). By early May, however, the DHHS officials received over 50,000 letters running ten to one against the regulations, as the national debate raged on. A Lou Harris poll revealed that sentiment in the majority of people surveyed was similarly against the requirements (Majority opposes . . . 1982). Civil liberties and family planning groups announced they would challenge the regulations in court. By the year's end, the regulations had not been enacted, although family planning policy analysts expect their promulgation in early 1983.

With similar policy intent, in October, over a Reagan veto, Congress did allocate $10 million for sixty-two project grants under the so-called "chastity" program sponsored by Senator Denton. Funded through the Office of Adolescent Pregnancy Programs and its director, "right-to-lifer" Marjorie Mechlenburg, the grants are to encourage family involvement in teenage sexuality, adoption, and prevention of pregnancy (exclusive of family planning). The largest grant, nearly one-half million dollars, for example, went to a Catholic-run hospital, St. Margaret's, in Boston, Massachusetts.

Whether such policies can limit teenage sexuality or will encourage adoption rather than abortion, and young women keeping their children, remains to be seen. By late 1982 family planning clinics were beginning to report that the news coverage of the debate over parental permission was having a "chilling effect" leading to a drop in clinic visits by teenagers (Startling impact . . . 1982).

Other feminist analysts have suggested that teenage sexuality and pregnancies are related to broader factors that have to do with the development of sexual identity within specific cultural contexts and the "adaptive strategy" various teenage women take to their economic and cultural situations (Horowitz 1981; Valentine 1982; Schawb 1982). How much these more cultural and economic factors will be affected by the administration's "chastity" and familial policies will have to be evaluated in the future.

Herpes Simplex and the Moral Complex   Fear of venereal disease and unwanted pregnancies were historically two of the major restraints on sexuality (Brandt 1983). With antibiotics and the pill more widely available, these controls were loosened. By 1964 *Time* magazine heralded the change in sexual mores by making the sexual revolution its cover story. In 1982, however, a seeming scourge had returned. In bold, scary red letters, *Time* announced herpes was "today's scarlet letter" (Wallis 1982). Another magazine article more bluntly declared: "The sexual revolution may have officially ended this year, a victim of its own success" (Tierney 1982, 14).

Medically, the concern is over a type of virus, herpes simplex, that is transmitted primarily through sexual contact when one person has an active case. Genital herpes produces blisters, pain, and inflammation when it first appears; it then refuses to go away. It lodges itself in nearby nerve tissue and recurrences of acute episodes can be common or infrequent. Thus herpes unlike love, as the latest joke suggests, "is forever."

The Centers for Disease Control estimate herpes is now the most prevalent form of venereal disease affecting an estimated five to ten million Americans, with 600,000 new cases appearing this year. Although the lack of mandated reporting makes the statistics uncertain, it appears the virus is selective in its choice of hosts: white, middle- and upper-class, college-educated men and women. The class and race of its sufferers helps explain in part why herpes has made such a media splash in the last year. By early 1983 it even became the theme for a made-for-TV movie. While a new drug, acyclovir, has just been approved in ointment form to ease the pain and lessen the time of the initial outbreak, it cannot "cure" the virus (Crumpacker 1982).

Herpes is, however, being discussed more as a moral than a medical epidemic. Cynics have labeled it "Jerry Falwell's revenge," as Phyllis Schlafly intoned that "virginity and faithfulness" were the surest means of its prevention (Goodman 1982). Sex's most common partner, guilt, was once again in a menage à trois with disease-as-punishment.

Herpes has special meaning and presents specific difficulties for women. It has been linked to cervical cancer and can cause blindness and brain and neurologic damage in newborns whose mothers have active lesions at the time of vaginal delivery. But it is women who carry the moral, not just the medical, burden of herpes. It is changes in women's sexuality, not men's, that have been the basis for the sexual revolution. It is thus our increased sexual activity that is blamed for the herpes outbreak. Furthermore, emotionally, what could be worse than the thought that your child's neurologic damage was a consequence of your sexual activity? It is also women who find it more difficult to find new sexual partners once herpes becomes part of the information that has to be exchanged in new relationships (McWhorter 1982).

While medical researchers continue to search for yet another "magic bullet" cure, women will have to consider and confront the cultural assumptions, and the personal and political consequences of the virus. After all, what may be more recurring is not so much this virus as traditional views of women and our sexuality.

Reproductive Rights

Abortion   As the tenth anniversary of the Supreme Court decision in *Roe* v. *Wade* supporting legal abortion neared, abortion continued to be the focus of the political attack on women's rights. But there were at least a number of hopeful signs. As in the past, a number of different antiabortion bills or amendments came before the Senate proposed by Jesse Helms, Orrin Hatch, and Mark Hatfield. Power struggles for Senate leadership on antiabortion embroiled Hatch and Helms in debates that served to weaken their united front on the Senate floor. Helms's "fetal personhood" bill, which defines human life as beginning at conception, appeared to be too extreme to get clear Senate support. Hatch's "federalism" amendment, conferring on the Congress and the states the concurrent power to limit or ban abortion, passed through the Judiciary Committee in May. In July, Hatfield, a moderate Republican who took a relatively early stand in opposition to the Vietnam War, introduced another complicated bill permanently to restrict federal funds for abortion, limit abortion research, and suggest language for fetal personhood legislation in the various states (New abortion law . . . 1982).

In September, Helms's attempt to add an antiabortion amendment to the federal debt ceiling and Hatch's federalism amendment were both defeated by long filibusters led by prochoice Senators, backed by grassroots support from abortion rights groups. The legislation is expected to be reintroduced when the Ninety-eighth Congress convenes in January.

A similar victory was won against reproductive rights foes on the state level in Pennsylvania (Hunt 1982). An abortion control act, which would have mandated a twenty-four-hour waiting period, parental consent for minors, no payment for abortions of state employees, and limits on Medicaid coverage, was defeated through a governor's veto in late spring. A massive organizing campaign on the part of women's reproductive rights groups led to nearly 13,000 messages being sent to the governor at the end of the campaign. Tables to encourage writing of postcards were set up in neighborhoods in many of Pennsylvania's major cities, while rallies and press conferences concluded the blitz work.

The Supreme Court still has before it three cases that will make clear how far the retreat will be made from *Roe* v. *Wade*. Two of the cases involve the 1978 Akron, Ohio ordinance on abortion and one case is on a Missouri state abortion law. Both mandate waiting periods for abortion, require all abortions after the first trimester to be done in hospitals, and necessitate consent procedures for minors. The Akron law also requires the physician to tell a woman the fetus is an unborn child, describe its features, and warn her of the dangers of abortion "surgery." Although the administration has nothing to do with the judicial review of the cases, the Justice Department filed a friend-of-the-Court brief arguing each individual state's right to determine abortion legality. The Court's decision is expected early in 1983 (Hunter 1982).

Public opinion polls continued to say that a federal ban on abortion was generally opposed and that the majority of Americans supported the right to legal abortion (Henshaw and Martire 1982). Americans remained deeply divided on the moral question of abortion, however. The complicated relationship among moral stance, support for abortion rights, and political action and voting patterns remains tangled.

Perhaps sensing the tenor of the times, antireproductive rights groups continued to picket abortion clinics and harass women entering them. At Princeton University, feminists fought to keep antiabortion women from establishing a "pro-life" task force in the university women's center. During the summer, Dr. Hector Zevallos, the operator of a midwest abortion clinic, and his wife Rosalie were abducted for over a week by a group called the Army of God. Although the Zevalloses were unharmed, the kidnapping does suggest that terror tactics may be on the rise again (Senate Debate . . . 1982).

Reproductive rights activists who went underground at the National "Right to Life" Convention in July reported on a number of strategies being planned. They include: support for the congressional antiabortion legislation, as well as other bills on the cessation of treatment for handicapped infants and the terminally ill; stepped up nonviolent direct action; media campaigns; recruiting of "burned out" abortion counselors; and the establishment of problem pregnancy centers that would harass women seeking abortions (Fugh-Berman 1982; Sipe 1982).

Outside the "Right to Life" convention hall over 5,000 reproductive rights supporters came to hold a rally "in support of women's lives." Speakers stressed the connection between the reproductive rights struggle and the broad commitment to human life and political and economic self-determination. The rally was highlighted by the speeches of three women who had illegal abortions before 1973 (In support . . . 1982).

The same commitment to a comprehensive vision of women's reproductive rights linked to a broader feminist movement was in evidence at the November national meeting of the Reproductive Rights National Network.

Organized in 1979 in response to the abortion cutbacks, the Network represents a coalition of seventy-five reproductive rights groups. Debate continues within the group on how to develop a political stance and organizing strategy that joins various feminist issues to reproductive rights. But the national meeting reflected the Network's growing effort to understand the relationship among racism, the social determination of sexuality, and the denial of reproductive freedom. Local organizing on these issues, as well as nationally coordinated rallies to commemorate the tenth anniversary of the Supreme Court decision on January 22, 1983, were planned.

Sterilization   Since the mid-1970s reproductive rights groups have linked the attack on abortion to the continued availability and funding for sterilizations, particularly for Third World women (Teicher 1982). Statistics on sterilization suggest the scope of the issue: it is the most widely used, and generally irreversible, form of birth control for married women in the United States. The procedure is not, however, performed uniformly throughout the population. Between 1976 and 1980 the sterilization rate in the Medicaid population (which is one-third nonwhite) was 28 per 1,000 people age 15 to 44 years, in contrast to 12 per 1,000 in the general population. In the Medicaid groups in 1980, 98 percent of the sterilizations were on women; in the general population the figure was 53 percent (Johnson 1982).

The criticism of the finality of sterilization as a birth control technique coupled to medical interest in the science and technology of the procedure led to more work on the possibility of reversal surgery for women with tubal ligations and men with vasectomies. The success rate for women carrying pregnancies to full term after reversals appears to be about 62 to 64 percent (Saidi and Zainie 1980). Although exceedingly expensive, but technically "interesting," such procedures may become more available in the future for those who can afford them.

At the same time, the national and state provisions to guard against sterilization abuse are in danger. Such guidelines were passed after much political work was done by reproductive rights activists. State and federal health departments have continued to receive complaints from providers on the "burden" of the consent and data collection regulations. In 1983 and in the coming years, feminists will have to watch for the seemingly narrow rule changes that will prepare the way for more widescale, and often unnecessary, sterilization procedures (Stamm 1982).

Family Planning Services   Much of the nation's family planning services, as well as the research on birth control and population, are now funded out of the federal pocketbook. At the beginning of fiscal year 1982 (October 1981), a coalition of family planning organizations sued the Reagan administration for withholding family planning monies appropriated by the Congress. The lawsuit was withdrawn when funds, at a reduction of 22.7 percent from the previous fiscal year, were finally released. Family planning agencies argued for the continuation of categorical, rather than block grant, funding. If family planning monies are put into block grants, the levels of funding will be left to the states and the guarantee of more uniform provision of services will be undermined.

Family planning agencies were also subjected to a number of different forms of federal harassment and intimidation. Time-consuming and exhaustive audits of the programs continued to see if funds were used for any kind of abortion activity. Similarly, because of the agencies' outcry against the "squeal rule," federal administrators sent out "clarification" notices to remind agencies to "obey" the statute and regulations.

Although the family planning programs were cleared by the audits, draft guidelines were drawn up in late fall to separate even further any abortion activity from other family planning services, even when the agency or hospital can lawfully do both kinds of services because of separate funding sources. The pattern of continued effort to gain through administrative fiat and pressure what cannot be obtained through the legislative and judicial process seems to be the administration's strategy.

Birth Control Technologies   Research on the complications and advantages of particular birth control methods continued while several new pills and barrier methods were prepared for marketing. Federal support for biomedical research on fertility and contraception has continued to rise although there has been a 20 percent cut in constant dollar amounts between 1972 and 1979 (New contraceptives . . . 1982). New research has begun to suggest that the actual failure rates of the pill and intrauterine devices (IUDs), usually touted as quite low, were as high as 5 to 10 percent. Women discontinued their use over the course of a year because of the side effects, but did not use other forms of protection (Hatcher et al. 1982).

Debate on the link between the pill and other diseases continued. Since 1968 researchers have disagreed over whether or not the pill increases a woman's chances for skin and breast cancer and over which kind of pill puts a woman more at risk for uterine cancer. This year studies suggested the pill actually lessened a woman's chances of developing ovarian and uterine cancer (Rosenberg et al. 1982). Similar data from the Women's Health Study, a national multihospital case-control study, suggested pill users were half as likely to develop pelvic inflammatory disease (PID) as sexually active women who did not use contraceptives (Pill users . . . 1982). Whether such possible protections balance against the pill's other known medical, nutritional, and psychological side effects will have to be assayed by women considering its use.

New pills with lower estrogen content are beginning to be marketed. French researchers announced a pill that can be taken only two to four days a month and will act as an abortifacient in a very early pregnancy (Bell 1983; New birth . . . 1982). Population control groups and pill manufacturers are again pressuring the Food and Drug Administration (FDA) to rewrite the patient package inserts in less ominous tones. But the National Women's Health

Network has been urging the FDA to strengthen pill labeling. Women were urged by the Network to relay their experiences with the pill to FDA Commissioner Arthur Hill Hayes in Washington.

Reports this year on intrauterine devices continue to stress the greater risk of PID and ectopic pregnancy among women who used this form of contraceptive (Malhotra and Choudhury 1982). The Health Network's precedent-setting international class action suit against A. H. Robbins, manufacturer of the now discredited but still used Dalkon shield IUD, continued to be pressed through the courts. Robbins has never issued a comprehensive recall of the device, although it was linked by the FDA to a number of serious illnesses and deaths in 1974. It is estimated nearly 50,000 women in the United States and 500,000 women worldwide still carry this dangerous IUD in their bodies. New IUDs made of copper zinc, with synthetic hormones and without the "tail" string, appear to be on the horizon (Hatcher 1982).

Barrier methods—diaphragms, condoms, spermicides, foams, and cervical caps—are continuing to be in minor revivals across the country. The diaphragm, for example, was being "rediscovered," *Cosmopolitan* magazine reassured its readers in March, and was as chic to use as the latest entry in the designer jeans market (O'Malley 1982). Searle Laboratories is even currently test marketing a throw-away diaphragm to be called "Once," which will be available "thrice"—three to a package with packets of spermicidal jelly enclosed (Hatcher 1982).

Other barrier methods are being rediscovered, tested, and marketed. Cervical caps, thimble-like devices that fit snugly over the cervix and can stay in place for several days, are now being tested. They are available from selected health providers and clinics.* Issues under study include how long the cap can be kept in place; how much, if any, spermicidal jelly is necessary; "customized" versus standard-sized caps; and the dangers of infections. Similarly, a sponge of soft polyurethane containing a spermicide, which can be left in the vagina for forty-eight hours and then be thrown away, is expected to receive FDA approval for marketing early in 1983.

Research on the importance of the cervical mucus in making conception possible, coupled with feminist concern for woman-controlled noninvasive contraception, has spurred growing interest in fertility consciousness. Regular observation over a period of time of her cervical mucus allows a woman to determine her fertile days. It allows her either to avoid intercourse or use barrier methods during those times. When the method is carefully taught and regular observations made, it has a reported extremely high effectiveness rate with no side effects (Bell 1980).

Depo-Provera   A long-acting synthetic hormone given as an injectable contraceptive, Depo-provera has been controversial for nearly fifteen years. It is

---

*A cervical cap information packet and a list of health providers who offer the cap are available from New Hampshire Feminist Health Center, 38 South Main Street, Concord, NH 03301. Cost of the packet is $7.50.

currently available in over eighty, mainly Third World, countries. It is preferred by many population control experts because it can be injected and will remain effective for three months at a time. Depo's only manufacturer, the Upjohn Company, has been trying to gain FDA approval for its use in the United States.

Women's health groups, and the Health Network in particular, have fought approval of this drug on a number of grounds. Controversial animal studies have linked Depo to cancer. After the pill experience, in which a hormonal contraceptive was put into use by millions of women without adequate long-term testing, women's health advocates are wary of another hormonal drug. Evidence of coercive use of the drug and the inability of women to reverse its effects for months at a time have also been cited as dangers (Sun 1982; Gold and Wilson 1980).

This year the FDA convened a special board of inquiry to reconsider Depo's approval. The stakes at the hearing are quite high and have worldwide import; the Agency for International Development, one of the major suppliers of contraceptives to Third World countries, cannot export a drug without FDA approval. As the board of inquiry date set for January 1983 neared, the board tried to set the guidelines for consideration on seemingly nonpolitical scientific and technical issues. As the panel met, however, the controversy continued. The Health Network announced a class action suit against Upjohn on behalf of women harmed by the contraceptive. The outcome of the inquiry and the suit will not be known until later in 1983.

DES, Toxic Shock, Drugs, and the FDA   Research, political action, and legal suits continued around the drug diethylstilbestrol, commonly called DES. This artificial estrogen has been linked to numerous fertility problems, ectopic pregnancies and other reproductive complications, and certain kinds of cancers in the daughters of women who took the drug between 1941 and 1971 to prevent miscarriage. More recent research has begun to document the fertility and cancer problems of the DES sons as well.

Medical debate continued to focus primarily on the fertility and pregnancy difficulties of DES daughters. Researchers are attempting to find the mechanisms involved in determining these outcomes and to suggest proper monitoring and possible prophylactic procedures (Barnes et al. 1980; Herbst 1981). Although 81 percent of DES-exposed women have been able eventually to have children, about 50 percent had difficulty carrying pregnancies to term (Barnes et al. 1980; Herbst 1981). Studies into the psychological impact of DES exposure are also beginning to be promising avenues of research in helping us understand the human impact of the drug and the experience of living at risk (Bell 1983).

Concern was voiced for the half of the nearly three to six million men and women exposed in utero to DES who are not aware of the dangers. In some states, education announcements are being made through media spots, posters, leaflets, and notices in gas and electric bills. Eight states now have legislation that supports the funding of procedures to identify exposed men and women and the centers where they can be monitored on a sliding scale, to educate the public to the dangers of DES, to train professionals to deal with exposed people, and to outlaw insurance company discrimination against such men and women. The report of two DES daughters under special medical observation who developed cancers, but whose cervical Papanicolaou (Pap) smears had been negative, underlined the necessity for special careful palpation in screening and semiannual check-ups by DES knowledgeable medical personnel (Kaufman et al. 1982).

On the legal front a number of DES cases were settled. One woman won a $1.75 million case against E. R. Squibb and Sons. In Chicago, the University of Chicago settled out of court with three women who were unwitting participants in one of the DES drug trials. Joyce Bichler, a DES daughter and author of a book with that title, won her case against Eli Lilly and Co. The New York State Appeals Court upheld a lower court ruling that DES had not been properly tested, had caused Bichler's cancer, and that Lilly would be held accountable even when it could not be proved that it was specifically Lilly's product Bichler's mother had taken (Bichler 1982).

Bichler's case only underscored the danger facing consumers if a federal product liability bill now pending in Congress is passed. Among other provisions, the bill as now proposed would require an injured consumer to be able to identify the manufacturer of a defective product in all instances. In this case, where hundreds of different drug companies manufactured DES, such a limitation would close off legal action in most cases.

Lax drug testing and enforcement by the FDA were again questioned this year. The National Women's Health Network released its congressional report critical of the FDA's determination of drug safety (Haire 1982). The Network also petitioned the FDA to strengthen its proposed warning on the use of over-the-counter drugs by pregnant and nursing mothers. Similarly, in California, the work of health activist groups led to new labeling requirements on over-the-counter drugs (Network files . . . 1982).

Concern over FDA procedures and enforcement mounted in light of budgetary cutbacks and the nonregulatory stance of the Reagan administration. Certain estrogen-based drugs, for example, that are used to suppress lactation in post-partum women, were recommended for "withdrawal of approval" by the FDA's Committee on Obstetrics and Gynecology in 1978. Four years later the FDA still has not yet taken action (Clarkson 1982). Concern has also been raised over the necessity for a stronger warning label on Bendectin, the controversial drug used to treat nausea in pregnant women, which has been linked to serious birth defects in their children.

The FDA regulation to require tampon manufacturers to include package warnings on toxic shock syndrome (TSS) went into effect at the end of the year. Although the incidence of this still rare but serious disease is down from the 1980 high, the Centers for Disease Control have reported the rate has plateaued. All types of tampons, not just the Rely brand, have been associated with TSS, although the risk appears to be higher with the use of high-absorbency products. Because TSS has also been found in nonmenstruating cases, discontinued use of tampons is not a fool-proof way to avoid the illness (National Academy of Science 1982; Robertson 1982).

Diet, Drugs, Exercise, and Body Image

Eating Disorders   Why women, and particularly young women, more than men are obsessed by their body size and appearance has been the subject of increasing feminist and medical concern since the early 1970s (Orbach 1978; Bruch 1978; Wooley and Wooley 1979; Schwartz et al. 1980). Much attention in the medical journals and the media has focused on the eating disorders of anorexia nervosa, characterized by intense fear of obesity, vomiting, and extreme weight loss; and bulimia, episodic binge eating and food obsession.

Both physicians and researchers suggest that an epidemic of these disorders now faces the country and that the problem, once thought to be only an upper middle-class phenomenon, is becoming more universal among young women. While research and treatment on their clinical aspects continue, there has recently been growing concern with the social and cultural context of the disorders.

New work on this problem, and the related question of the culturally created norm for women's body image has led to the critique of what one author calls "the tyranny of slenderness" (Chernin 1982). Others have linked our cultural obsession with fatness and dieting to the "symbolic rejection of basic American values: self-discipline and self-control" (Bennett and Gurin 1982, 276). Psychologists are particularly interested in how eating obsessions relate to women's development into adulthood and their effort to gain control over their lives and relationships (Boskind-Lodahl 1976; Lesley College 1982). Research on why certain women at particular ages exhibit eating disorders and how they can be helped will be of critical importance in future studies (Brumberg 1982).

Exercise   Body image as well as concern for health and strength is linked to the increase in the number of women participating in various physical fitness and exercise programs. Women's gyms, exercise classes, and running stores are becoming financial growth centers in the economy, and *Jane Fonda's Workout Book* continues to be on the best seller list. While many of the pink-walled refurbished "figure salons" still focus on dieting, guilt-tripping, and the necessity to lose one-quarter inch off each thigh, some women are trying to find ways to develop exercise and running programs that support women in the effort to feel stronger and resilient at any size. More research on the relationship between body size, strength, and health will be done in the 1980s as "women in motion" continue to be of importance.

Dieting and Drugs   The danger from diet aids was highlighted this year when a 32-year-old Oklahoma mother in good health, trying to lose twenty pounds gained in pregnancy, died after being on the latest liquid protein diet, the Cambridge Diet, for only a month. Starch blockers, pills that are supposed to keep the body from absorbing complex carbohydrates, were pulled from the market by the FDA after hundreds of complaints were received on their side effects. The FDA was subsequently sued by thirteen of the over one hundred manufacturers and distributors of the pills (Liebman 1982). Criticism by physician and nutrition groups also continued of over-the-counter dietary aids such as Dietac because of their tendency to increase blood pressure and irritability, and to produce effects similar to amphetamines in some people. A general critique of dieting and its limitations was also published this year (Bennett and Gurin 1982).

Medical Care

Women's demands for more control over their medical care and less demeaning and dangerous encounters with physicians were given a special hearing this year by the American College of Obstetrics and Gynecology (ACOG). The annual clinical meeting in April capped the year-long effort of ACOG's president to open up dialogue between women and their obstetrician-gynecologists. Representatives from women's health groups spoke at the opening session while Ann Landers, a staple at AMA wives' luncheons in the 1960s, became the first woman and nonfellow of ACOG to deliver the annual memorial lecture (ACOG annual meeting . . . 1982). In another forum ACOG's executive director stressed the necessity of doctors meeting the demands of their "buyer-patients" (Pease 1982a). "If obstetrician-gynecologists do not meet . . . expectations," he warned, "these patients will turn to other health care systems and other practitioners."

If more women would read feminist physician Michelle Harrison's medical exposé of her training as an ob-gyn, ACOG fellows might indeed have much to worry about. She condemned the system of training and the brutalization of women patients (Harrison 1982). With physician over-supply looming by the end of the century, ob-gyns at particular risk for malpractice suits, and women becoming more vocal and certain of their needs, rights, and options in the medical encounter, some physicians are being forced to listen more openly to their patient's perspective. But the backlash against women's involvement in their own care was echoed by the physician editor of a newsletter:

> If we are to avoid being done in by the malpractice problem we must reassert our control over the patient and insist that we exclusively make the decisions relative to patient care, putting an end to the non-physician interference in this process. (Steward 1981)

Whether improvements on the level of individual care for women become translated into less institutional and professional control over medical care in general still remains problematical (Rothman 1982).

Birthing and Midwifery   Documentation of the increased danger of maternal mortality in both primary and subsequent cesarian sections (c-sections) and feminist organizing against the increase in the c-section rates continued this year (Petitti et al. 1982; Lavin et al. 1982). In 1970 only one out of every twenty births (5.5 percent) was by c-section; by 1980 the percentage had reached eighteen or nearly one out of every five births nationwide. Since physicians have been trained to assume each c-section requires another in subsequent deliveries, repeat procedures have been the norm for almost 99 percent of all women who went on to deliver other children after an initial section.

New ACOG guidelines issued this year after years of women health activists' pressure, however, may help to break this tradition. After reviewing over 28,000 cases of vaginal delivery subsequent to cesareans, ACOG has now suggested "under proper conditions" vaginal deliveries "may safely be considered" for women who have undergone previous sections (ACOG revises guidelines . . . 1982).

Interest in alternative birth centers and out-of-hospital birthing kept growing (Sumner and Phillips 1981; Romalis 1981). Recently released figures show that the rate of out of hospital births, as reported to the National Center for Health Statistics, stabilized at only 1 percent of all births between 1975 and 1979 (Pease 1982b). The economic recession, coupled with continued feminist criticism of hospital birth procedures, may change these figures in the coming years.

A historic alliance formed this year between lay and nurse-midwives may very well herald changes in birthing patterns for the 1980s. In recent years there has been often acrimonious division among physicians, nurse-trained midwives, and midwives who were not first nurses over the right and autonomy of the different kinds of midwives in practice. At an April meeting called "A conference to unite all midwives," the Midwives Alliance of North America was born.

The Alliance expects to be an umbrella organization for all midwives to promote guidelines, educational policies, and support for midwifery. Many nurse-midwives remain more closely aligned to physicians or seek autonomy and are critical of this alliance. Nevertheless, the new organization represents a real turning point in the turbulent history of midwifery in the United States (Downy 1982).

The legal status of nurse- and lay midwifery remains different in most states. In Washington, however, a model law went into effect in January that allows certified nurse-midwives and licensed, trained nonnurse-midwives to attend births in homes, hospitals, or birth centers. Changes in practice laws and legal suits between physicians and midwives can be expected in the future (Throne and Hanson 1981; Schoonmaker 1982).

Infant Feeding   Under attack worldwide for their pressure and unethical tactics in promoting infant formula use in Third World countries, the Nestlé company promised in March to comply with the World Health Organization's 1981 formula-marketing guidelines. In addition, Nestlé hired former Secretary of State Edmund S. Muskie to head their Infant Formula Audit Commission. Critics of the company's policy see the change and the commission as a new public relations strategy and have called for continuation of the boycott of its products.

The abuse in infant feeding is not limited to developing nations. In Canada, the Ministry of Health came out against the "gift packs" of formula that hospitals send home uniformly with new mothers. Public Advocates, a public interest law firm in San Francisco, filed a one hundred and eighty-page petition with the United States Government on infant formula use. The study reports on the disproportionate use of formula among low-income women and the continued evidence of greater illness among bottle-fed infants across class lines. Public Advocates is trying to get warnings on formula labels and to require federally funded hospitals to teach breastfeeding (Butler 1982).

Nurse Practitioners as Providers of Women's Health Care   Nurse practitioners are becoming increasingly common in the nation's family planning and health care clinics, private offices, and other ambulatory care settings. While debate over the quality, competence, education, and patient acceptance of such providers has lessened, nurse practitioners still face both legal and economic limitations on their practice.

In the spring, the Missouri State Board of Registration for the Healing Arts recommended that nurse practitioners in a family planning program be prosecuted for practicing medicine without a license. The circuit court in St. Louis ruled in November that the nurses were guilty because "providing oral contraceptives, IUDs, and vaginal medicines to patients . . . do [es] not constitute professional nursing" under the state law but is the "unauthorized practice of medicine" (Legal action . . . 1982, 1). The case is now on appeal. It will have far-reaching consequences for nurse practitioners in states in which the nurse practice laws do not yet encompass the real scope of these nurses' work. In many states, even rewritten practice laws that try and clearly differentiate between medicine and nursing leave nurse practitioners in a legal limbo or lock them into "binding liasons" with physicians (Thomas 1982).

Reimbursement policies almost as much as legal status will shape the future use and availability of nurse practitioners. In many localities, such third-party insurers as Blue Cross and Blue Shield have refused to cover nurse practitioners' services. In some states the insurers are writing serious limitations on the nurse practitioner's autonomy into the reimbursement laws or regulations. How well nurse practitioners and their allies can overcome the insurers and physicians' unwillingness to expand reimbursement coverage will determine whether or not women will be able to receive care from these providers in the future.

Cancer   The necessity and timetable for early detection procedures were the subject of controversy again this year (Morell et al. 1982). In 1980 the American Cancer Society proposed that cervical Pap smears be performed every three years for women aged 20 to 65 who were sexually active after 18, with single partners, and who had had two previous negative smears a year apart. ACOG, however, has continued to recommend yearly Pap tests for all women, while gynecologic cancer specialists stressed the necessity for frequent screening for women at high risk. The division in the medical community only illustrated the necessity for women to gain necessary information in order to make informed decisions on the appropriate risks in their individual situations. Women at high risk who do not have access to or cannot pay for the detection programs remain a serious problem.

The detection controversy spilled over into the feminist health community as well. In the spring the Women's Health Network published an article critical of early detection programs for breast cancer. "In view of the many unanswered questions on tumor biology, microscopic diagnosis, and even primary treatment of early disease," Maryann Napoli argued, "what really is the advantage of urging symptomless women to practice self-examination and to seek annual breast exams and mammography? (Napoli 1982, 4). Her views, which were basically a criticism of creating a disease focus in healthy women, generated more response, both critical and praiseworthy, than any other issue the Network has dealt with in seven years (Breast cancer . . 1982).

Endometriosis   Widening worry over the seeming spread of endometriosis also was discussed within the women's health community (Endometriosis 1982). This is a condition in which the presence of endometrial tissue, which normally lines the walls of the uterus, is detected in other areas of the body. The cause of this condition is unknown, but it can produce bleeding, pain, and infertility. Various theories link it to genetic factors, physiologic changes, and complications from PID. An Endometriosis Association has been formed to encourage research on the disease and to provide more information to women and their health care providers.

Premenstrual Syndrome   Interest in the connection between women's menstrual cycles and our physical and emotional behavior is probably as old as humanity. In 1931 there appeared the first medical description of what is now being labeled premenstrual syndrome, or PMS. Violent mood swings plus physical and other behavioral changes previously thought of as triggered by psychological "problems" are being seen by some as caused by hormonal shifts during the menstrual cycle. In England in recent years, two courts have accepted PMS as a defense in women's murder trials, leading to lessening of charges on the grounds of "diminished responsibility."

Much of the interest and care of women with PMS has been generated by the work of an English physician, Katharina Dalton, who has written extensively about PMS. She sees the condition as triggered by a progesterone deficiency during the menstrual cycle and treats women with natural progesterone. Her views remain controversial and new research on this problem can be expected to continue (Dalton 1979; Budoff 1980; Reid and Yen 1981; Gonzalez 1981).

In December 1981 a symposium on PMS was held in Cambridge, Massachusetts, and a clinic in Reading, Massachusetts, has been opened to study and treat PMS (*PMS connection* 1982). PMS Action, an educational and referral organization that supports Dalton's views, has been organized. It will be important to see that while women who need the help are given proper care,

PMS is not used politically as one more seemingly biological reason to deny women full equality.

Specific Groups of Women and Their Health Needs

Lesbians   In 1981 a medical journal published the first major article that dealt specifically with lesbian and bisexual women's gynecologic care (Johnson et al. 1981). No medical problem specific to lesbians was identified. The study concluded the women studied were healthier than their heterosexual counterparts, had lower rates of endometriosis, vaginal infections, depression, and sexual dysfunction. These women saw their biggest health difficulty in their physicians' negative attitudes toward their sexual preference. These attitudes affected the care they received and their willingness to seek it. Lesbians, for example, are estimated to have Pap smears only half as often as heterosexual women and to avoid contact with the health system longer (Peteros and Miller 1982). Issues of childbearing, alcohol use, and hospital visits to seriously ill and dying lovers and friends remain critical problems of the lesbian health care system relationship (O'Donnell et al. 1979).

Mid-Life and Older Women   The "medicalizing of aging" and the use of estrogen for postmenopausal women with osteoporosis were issues again this year. Osteoporosis, the decrease or thinning of bone mass, is considered a problem for one out of every four postmenopausal white women because of its implication in their greater tendency to sustain fractures in falls. Studies continued to support the use of long-term hormone treatments to prevent such bone loss (Jensen et al. 1982). But since bone loss is often more rapid once estrogen treatment has stopped, and because of the cancer dangers of estrogen replacement therapy, many of those concerned with older women's health have stressed other means of treatment (Findlay and Liebman 1982). Prevention through greater exercise, calcium supplements, and vitamin D, and lowered animal protein intake are all being discussed (Bruhn 1981). While younger generations of women more accustomed to physical exercise may be healthier when they age, concern remains focused on encouraging exercise and dietary changes among women whose sedentary lifestyles were shaped by an earlier period.

By the year 2000 it is estimated one out of every fourteen people in the United States will be a woman aged 65 years or older. As the population and women's health activists age, there will be increasing interest in the particular health and life needs of mid-life and older women. A national conference on these issues is being planned as groups organized specifically to support these women are continuing to form across the country. The effort to redefine menopause as a nonmedical event and to remove as much physician control over normal aspects of the aging process as possible seems to be gaining supporters.

A new book on menopause, although relatively academic and theoretical, addresses these issues (Voda et al. 1982). It contains the papers from an interdisciplinary conference among scholars in the newly formed Society for Menstrual Cycle Research. The book suggests the direction new feminist scholarship is going in the search for a more sophisticated understanding of the multiple dimensions of the female life cycle and the body–behavior relationship (Koeske 1982).

Women of Color   Medical researchers and epidemiologists have been tabulating mortality and morbidity statistics along racial, sex, and class lines for years. We still do not have a comprehensive understanding of how classism, racism and sexism affect women's health (Smith 1982). The first national black women's health conference is planned for June 1983 and self-help groups for black women are being formed in ten cities. A recent book compiles studies on different United States ethnic and racial cultures' medical understandings and how this affects the delivery of care (Harwood 1981). The problems of women are not specifically addressed.

Women with Disabilities   Women's groups continued to be particularly sensitive to their responsibility toward disabled women as signing for the deaf and access remained hallmarks of feminist concerts, conferences, and events. But the discriminatory treatment of disabled women and girls in education, medical care, and employment continued. Low expectations, parental overprotection, lack of role models, and sexism within the rehabilitation and health communities remained some of the worst handicaps disabled women faced (Fay 1982).

In June the Supreme Court ruled against a New York fourth-grader who needed interpreter services to increase her learning ability. The administration continued to chop away at the regulations in the Education of All Handicapped Children Act. The first national conference on Educational Equity for Disabled Women and Girls was held to discuss the special educational needs of this important minority among women (Fay 1982).

Women Workers   The health issues for two specific groups of predominately women workers were highlighted this year. The Women's Occupational Health Resource Center's research project on mortality among nonprofessional health care workers found there may be higher risk for certain kinds of cancer in this work force that divides along racial and sexual lines (Cancer risks . . . 1982). Growing criticism of the health dangers of office automation was central to the discussion at an international conference sponsored by Nine to Five, National Association of Working Women. Research in Europe and Canada on the problems associated with video display terminals, in particular, is well ahead of that being done in the United States. With five million word processors in use and ten million predicted by 1985, the dangers of this new technology will affect increasingly large numbers of women (Working Women 1981). Previous studies have already documented that the stress of clerical work, particularly for women with children, makes such workers more than twice as likely to develop coronary disease as other blue-collar and white-collar women workers.

In this area as well, the federal cutbacks are beginning to affect the National Industrial Occupational Safety and Health Administration. Withdrawal of support for standards and cutbacks on inspections and reporting requirements have already begun. With a number of major companies planning to begin genetic screening to reveal worker "predisposition" to workplace illnesses, the hard-won support for workers' rights on health and safety issues will be under continual assault from company initiatives and federal neglect.

Smokers, Alcoholics, and Drug Abusers   The studies of smoking and alcohol and drug abuse among women suggests we are gaining equality in the most unhealthy places. In 1982 more women adolescents than males of the same age were smoking, and by 1983 the female lung cancer death rate is expected to surpass that for breast cancer (U.S. Department of Health and Human Services 1980). Alcohol and drug use also had their female dimension. Nearly two-thirds of all women and 80 percent of all teenage women are estimated to use alcohol, while Valium continued to be the most prescribed drug, and one used predominately by women.

Most of the major women's magazines carry smoking ads and do not carry articles in their health sections on smoking's particular hazards for women (Zones 1982). Alcohol abuse by women continues to be seen as an invisible problem, although a new resource guide is now available to help those who deal specifically with women alcoholics (Sandmaier 1980, 1982).

In order to stem this dangerous development in substance abuse of various kinds, future prevention measures will have to focus less on blaming the individual for self-destructive habits and more on taking into account social factors that engender the habits. As one recent critic of prevention politics concluded, "As the attack on [Americans'] standard of living becomes more severe, they are likely to find less plausible the claim that health, like everything else, is simply a matter of willpower" (Taylor 1982, 41).

Environmental Hazards and Nuclear Holocaust

Women's health concerns have increasingly broadened to take on community environmental problems as well as the global threat of nuclear disaster. At Times Beach, Missouri, where another case of dioxin dumping has contaminated a whole community, and in Elizabeth, New Jersey, where toxic dumps and a major fire in a nearby chemical plant present serious hazards, it has been women who have led the demands for corporate responsibility for the cleanups and legal damages (Salazar 1982).

Women were active participants and planners in the march and rally for disarmament and human needs, which drew nearly one million people to New York on June 12. Feminists remained critical of the loosely defined politics of the march and the organizers' refusal to support the linking of the necessity for nuclear and overall arms reduction to a feminist perspective on life itself (Disarmament rally . . . 1982; Stephen 1983). The day before the march a Global Feminist Disarmament Meeting was held to bring together women working on disarmament issues worldwide to share their concerns and strategies.

Women's Health and the Future

Women in the health movement have continually expanded the breadth of their health concerns and their sophistication in fighting to transform medicine itself. Their ability to confront the institutions that control the health system has deepened as well. In the past year, for example, the Women's Health Network has, among many things: expanded its commitment to fund projects on women's health in Appalachia, opened a litigation information service for women considering law suits, and begun investigating nursing home abuse.

The recent past history of women's relationship to the health system has been a bleak litany of victimization and a monumental struggle, in individual and collective terms, to redefine the very nature of health care. At present, many women may reject current therapies and forms of care in search of new alternatives, while others will try to struggle to reorient the priorities and approaches of more traditional providers. In the future, reproductive rights, sexuality, control over drugs and the technology of medical care, and global environmental issues will continue to be the focal points of women's concerns as the struggle to control our bodies and minds takes on new appearances.

Acknowledgments

A number of women shared their knowledge and time with me in completion of this article: Belita Cowan, Tish Davis, Catherine DeLorey, Rachel Fruchter, Nancy Griesemer, Pamela Morgan, Judy Norsigian, Laura Punnett, Jeanette Valentine. The materials in the Boston Women's Health Book Collective Office were invaluable. Josslyn Gordon provided research assistance at a crucial moment. Susan Bell, in particular, contributed materials, analysis, her overwhelmingly sophisticated knowledge of women's health care issues, and her feminist support.

References

ACOG annual meeting opens with consumer-MD dialogue. 1982. *Ob.Gyn. News*, June 1–14, p. 1.

ACOG revises guidelines for vaginal delivery after cesarean. 1982. *Female Patient* 7 (July):39.

Administration proposes parental notification. 1982. *National Family Planning and Reproductive Health Association (NFPRHA) News*, February, pp. 1, 4.

Alan Guttmacher Institute. 1981. *Teenage pregnancy: The problem that hasn't gone away.* New York: The Institute.

ALDERFER, HANNAH; JAKER, BETH; and NELSON, MARYBETH. 1982. *Diary of a conference on sexuality.* New York: Faculty Press. (Available for $5.00 from "Diary of A Conference," 299 Riverside Drive, 9B, New York, NY 10025.)

BARNES, ANN B., et al. 1980. Fertility and outcome of pregnancy in women exposed in utero to diethylstilbestrol. *New England Journal of Medicine* 302 (March):609–13.

BELL, SUSAN. 1983. Birth control. In *Our bodies, ourselves.* 3rd rev. ed., Edited by Boston Women's Health Book Collective. New York: Simon & Schuster.

———. Living with risk: The social and emotional contours of the DES daughter experience. Department of Psychiatry, Massachusetts Mental Health Center, Harvard Medical School, in progress.

BELL, SUSAN, et al. 1980. Reclaiming reproductive control: A feminist approach to fertility consciousness. *Science for the People* 12 (January):6–9, 30–35.

BENNETT, WILLIAM, and GURIN, JOEL. 1982. *The dieter's dilemma.* New York: Basic Books.

BICHLER, JOYCE. 1982. DES daughter: The final chapter. *DES Action Voice* 4 (Summer):3.

BONGAARTS, JOHN. 1982. Infertility after age 30: A false alarm. *Family Planning Perspectives* 14 (March-April):75–78.

BOSKIND-LODAHL, MARLENE. 1976. Cinderella's stepsisters: A feminist perspective on anorexia nervosa and bulimia. *Signs: Journal of Women in Culture and Society* 2 (Winter):342–56.

BRANDT, ALLAN M. 1983. No magic bullet: The social history of venereal disease in the United States, 1880–1980. Unpublished PhD dissertation, Columbia University Department of History.

Breast cancer controversy. 1982. *Network News* 7 (November-December):10–11.

BRUCH, HILDE. 1978. *Golden cage: The enigma of anorexia nervosa.* Cambridge: Harvard University Press.

BRUHN, PEGGY. 1981. Osteoporosis. *Hot Flash* 1 (Fall):1.

BRUMBERG, JOAN JACOBS. 1982. Chlorotic girls, 1870–1920: A historical perspective on female adolescence. *Child Development* 53:1468–77.

BUDOFF, PENNY WISE. 1980. *No more menstrual cramps and other good news.* New York: G. P. Putnam's.

BUTLER, EDITH. 1982. Infant formula abuse in the U.S. *Women-Wise* 5 (Summer):1–2.

CAGAN, LESLIE, et al. 1982. Peace at any price?: Feminism, anti-imperialism and the disarmament movement. *Radical America* 16 (January-April):45–56.

Cancer risks found for hospital workers. 1982. *WOHRC News* 4 (September):1, 6.

CHERNIN, KIM. 1982. *The obsession: Reflections on the tyranny of slenderness.* New York: Harper & Row.

CLARKSON, FRED. 1982. TACE and DES daughters. *DES Action Voice* 3 (Spring):5.

CRUMPACKER, CLYDE. 1982. Genital herpes and acyclovir. *Harvard Medical School Letter* 8 (September):3–4.

DALTON, KATHARINA. 1979. *Once a month.* Pomona, Calif.: Hunter House.

Disarmament rally draws 1 million. 1982. *Off Our Backs* 11 (July):2.

DOWNEY, ALICE. 1982. Midwives unite in the U.S. and U.N. *Women-Wise* 5 (Summer):10.

EHRENREICH, BARBARA, and STALLARD, KARIN. 1982. The nouveau poor. *Ms.* 11, nos. 1 and 2 (July-August):217–24.

Endometriosis. 1982. *Santa Cruz Women's Health Center Newsletter.* (June). (Available from the Health Center, 250 Locust Ave., Santa Cruz, CA 95060.)

FAY, LISA. 1982. Disabled women confront educational discrimination. *Off Our Backs* 11 (December):2.

FÉDÉRATION CECOS; SCHWARTZ, D.; and MAYAUX, M. J. 1982. Female fecundity as a function of age. *New England Journal of Medicine* 306 (February 18):404–06.

FEE, ELIZABETH. 1982. A feminist critique of scientific objectivity. *Science for the People* 14 (July-August):5–8, 30–33.

FINDLAY, STEVE, and LIEBMAN, BONNIE. 1982. Brittle bones: Insufficient calcium one of many culprits. *Nutrition Action* 9 (June):12–13.

FUGH-BERMAN, ADRIAN. 1982. Undercover at the right-to-life convention. *Network News* 7 (September-October):12.

FURSTENBERG, FRANK F., et al. 1982. Parental involvement: Selling family planning clinics short. *Family Planning Perspectives* 14 (May-June):140–44.

GILDER, GEORGE. 1981. *Wealth and poverty* New York: Basic Books.

GOLD, RACHEL BENSON, and WILSON, PETERS D. 1980. Depo-provera: New developments in a decade-old controversy. *International Family Planning Perspectives* 6 (December):156–60.

GONZALEZ, ELIZABETH R. 1981. Premenstrual syndrome: An ancient woe deserving a modern scrutiny. *JAMA* 245 (April 10):1393–96.

GOODMAN, ELLEN. 1982. A new target for Schlafly. *Boston Globe,* October 14, p. 17.

GORDON, LINDA. 1977. *Woman's body, woman's right: A social history of birth control in America.* New York: Penguin.

GORDON, LINDA, and DUBOIS, ELLEN. Seeking ecstasy on the battlefield: Danger and pleasure in nineteenth-century feminist sexual thought. *Feminist Studies,* Spring 1983.

Group says budget cuts hurt health of the poor. 1983. *Boston Globe,* January 12, p. 6.

HAIRE, DORIS. 1982. *How the FDA determines the safety of drugs: Just how safe is safe?* Washington, D.C.: The National Women's Health Network.

HARRISON, MICHELLE. 1982. *A woman in residence.* New York: Random House.

HARWOOD, ALAN, ed. 1981. *Ethnicity and medical care.* Cambridge: Harvard University Press.

HATCHER, ROBERT, et al. 1982. *Contraceptive technology 1982–83.* New York: Irvington.

HENSHAW, STANLEY K., and MARTIRE, GREG. 1982. Morality and legality. *Family Planning Perspectives* 14 (March-April):53–62.

HERBST, ARTHUR, et al. 1981. Reproductive and gynecologic surgical experience in diethylstilbestrol-exposed daughters. *American Journal of Obstetrics and Gynecology* 141 (December 15):1019.

HOROWITZ, RUTH. 1981. Passion, submission and motherhood: The negotiation of identity by unmarried intercity chicanas. *Sociological Quarterly* 22 (Spring):241–52.

HUBBARD, RUTH, et al., eds. 1982. *Biological woman—The convenient myth: A collection of feminist essays and a comprehensive bibliography.* Cambridge: Schenkman.

HUNT, JEAN. 1982. Pro-choice forces win in Pennsylvania. *Network News* 7 (May-June):3.

HUNTER, NAN. 1982. Supreme Court focus: Retreats from *Roe* v. *Wade*. *CARASA News* 6 (September-October):4–5.

In support of women's lives: Abortion rights. 1982. *Off Our Backs* 12 (August-September):19.

JENSEN, GRETHE FINN, et al. 1982. Fracture frequency and bone preservation in postmenopausal women treated with estrogen. *Obstetrics and Gynecology* 60 (October):493–96.

JOHNSON, JEANETTE. 1982. Tubal sterilization and hysterectomy. *Family Planning Perspectives* 14 (January-February):28–30.

JOHNSON, SUSAN, et al. 1981. Factors influencing lesbian gynecologic care: A preliminary study. *American Journal of Obstetrics and Gynecology* 140 (May 1):20–28.

JOSEPH, GLORIA, and LEWIS, JILL. 1981. *Common differences: Conflicts in black and white feminist perspectives.* New York: Doubleday-Anchor.

KAUFMAN, RAYMOND, et al. 1982. Development of clear cell adenocarcinoma in DES-exposed offspring under observation. *Obstetrics and Gynecology* 59, no. 6 (Suppl.).

KELLER, EVELYN FOX. 1982. Feminism and science. *Signs* 7 (Spring):589–602.

KOESKE, RONDI DAIMON. 1982. Toward a biosocial paradigm for menopause research: Lessons and contributions from the behavioral sciences. In *Changing perspectives on menopause.* Edited by Ann Voda, et al. Austin: University of Texas Press.

LAVIN, JUSTIN P., et al. 1982. Vaginal delivery in patients with a prior cesarean section. *Obstetrical and Gynecological Survey* 37 (July):469–72.

Legal action on nurses is landmark. 1982. *NFPRHA News* 1 (December):1–2.

Lesley College. 1982. Adult development in women: Clinical perspectives. Interdisciplinary Conference, May 7–9, Cambridge, Mass.

LIEBMAN, BONNIE. 1982. Losing streak: Latest diet aids deemed dangerous to your health. *Nutrition Action* 9 (September):10–11.

MCBRIDE, ANGELA BARRON, and MCBRIDE, WILLIAM LEON. 1981. Theoretical underpinnings for women's health. *Women and Health* 6, nos. 1 and 2 (Spring/Summer):37–55.

MALHOTRA, MALCOLM, and CHOUDHURY, R. R. 1982. Current status of intrauterine devices. *Obstetrics and Gynecology Survey* 37 (January):1–8.

Majority opposes proposal as political views change. 1982. *NFPRHA News* 1 (June):1.

MATCHAN, LINDA. 1983. Is day care hazardous to children's health? *Boston Globe*, January 8, pp. 7–8.

MCWHORTER, DIANE. 1982. Truth and consequences. *Boston Phoenix*, September 21, pp. 6–9.

MORELL, NICHOLAS, et al. 1982. False-negative cytology rates in patients in whom invasive cancer subsequently developed. *Obstetrics and Gynecology* 60 (July):41–45.

NADELSON, CAROL C., and NOTMAN, MALKAH T., eds. 1982a. *The woman patient*. Vol. 2. *Concepts of femininity and the life cycle*. New York, London: Plenum Press.

———. 1982b. *The woman patient*. Vol. 3. *Aggression, adaptations and psychotherapy*. New York, London: Plenum Press.

NAPOLI, MARYANN. 1982. Breast cancer: A critical look at early detection. *Network News* 7 (May-June):4, 8.

NATIONAL ACADEMY OF SCIENCE. 1980. Toxic shock syndrome: An assessment of current information and future research needs. Washington, D.C.: National Academy Press.

Network files petition with FDA. 1982. *Network News* 7 (November-December):3.

New abortion law tries to nullify rights. 1982. *Off Our Backs* 12 (July):7.

New birth control pill developed. 1982. *Boston Globe*, April 21, p. 5.

New contraceptives seen if research continues. 1982. *NFPRHA News*, 1 (May):3.

O'DONNELL, MARY, et al. 1979. Lesbian health matters! Santa Cruz: Santa Cruz Women's Health Center.

O'MALLEY, SUZANNE. 1982. Diaphragms rediscovered. *Cosmopolitan*, March, pp. 171–72.

ORBACH, SUZY. 1978. *Fat is a feminist issue*. New York: Berkley Publishing.

PEASE, WARREN. 1982a. The obstetrician-gynecologist: A principal care physician? *Female Patient* 7 (April):10–11.

———. 1982b. Trends in out-of-hospital births. *Obstetrics and Gynecology* 60 (September):267–70.

PETCHESKY, ROSALIND POLLACK. 1980. Reproductive freedom: Beyond "A woman's right to choose." *Signs* 5 (Summer):661–85.

———. 1981. Antiabortion, antifeminism, and the rise of the new right. *Feminist Studies* 7 (Summer):206–46.

PETEROS, KAREN, and MILLER, FRAN. 1982. Lesbian health in straight world. *Second Opinion* April, pp. 1–2, 4–6.

PETITTI, DIANA B., et al. 1982. In-hospital maternal mortality in the U.S.: Time trends and relation to method of delivery. *Obstetrical and Gynecological Survey* 37 (August):528–30.

Pill users protected against PID. 1982. *Family Planning Perspectives* 14 (January-February):32–33.

The PMS connection. 1982. No. 1. Available from PMS Action, P. O. Box 9326, Madison, WI 53715 and PMS Program, 80 Main Street, Reading, MA 01867.

RAYMOND, JANICE G. 1982. Medicine as patriarchal religion. *Journal of Medicine and Philosophy* 7 (May):197–216.

REID, ROBERT, and YEN, S. S. C. 1981. Premenstrual syndrome. *American Journal of Obstetrics and Gynecology* 139 (January):85–104.

ROBERTSON, NAN. 1982. Toxic shock. *New York Times Magazine*, September 19.

ROMALIS, SHELLY, Ed. 1981. *Childbirth: Alternatives to medical control.* Austin: University of Texas Press.

ROSENBERG, L., et al. 1982. Epithelial ovarian cancer and combination oral contraceptives. *JAMA* 247, no. 23:3210–12.

ROTHMAN, BARBARA KATZ. 1981. Awake and aware, or false consciousness: The cooption of childbirth reform in America. In *Childbirth: Alternatives to medical control*, edited by Shelly Romalis.

SAIDI, M. H., and ZAINIE, CARLA M. 1980. *Female sterilization: A handbook for women.* New York: Garland.

SALAZAR, SANDRA. 1982. The night New Jersey exploded. *Network News* 7 (July-August):5.

SANDMAIER, MARIAN. 1980. *The invisible alcoholics: Women and alcohol abuse in America.* New York: McGraw-Hill.

———. 1982. *Helping women with alcohol problems: A guide for community caregivers.* Philadelphia: Women's Health Communications.

SCHOONMAKER, MARY ELLEN. 1982. Special deliveries. *In These Times* December 8–14.

SCHWAB, BRENDA. 1982. Teenage childbearing as adaptive strategy in rural New England. Paper presented at the American Anthropological Association Annual Meeting, Washington, D.C., December 7.

SCHWARTZ, DAVID, et al. 1980. Anorexia nervosa and bulimia: The socio-cultural context. *International Journal of Eating Disorders* 1(3):20–36.

Senate debate ends: Amendment tabled. 1982. *New Women's Times* 8 (October):1.

SIPE, LEE. 1982. Strategies mapped out. *Network News* 7 (September-October):12.

SMITH, BEVERLY. 1982. Black women's health: Notes for a course. In *Biological woman—The convenient myth.* Edited by Ruth Hubbard. Cambridge: Schenkman.

STAMM, KAREN. 1982. California strikes back. *CARASA News* 6 (November-December):3.

Startling impact in Oregon. 1982. *NFPRHA News* 1 (December):9.

STEPHEN, LYNN. 1983. Sex and the bomb. *Science for the People* 15 (January-February):37–39.

STEWARD, MARSH. 1981. Consumerism and the malpractice problem. *California Association of Obstetricians and Gynecologists* 3 (November):23.

SUMNER, PHILIP E., and PHILLIPS, CELESTE R. 1981. *Birthing rooms: Concept and reality.* St. Louis: C. V. Mosby.

SUN, MARJORIE. 1982. Depo-provera debate revs up at FDA. *Science* 217 (30 July):424–26.

TAYLOR, ROSEMARY C. R. 1982. The politics of prevention. *Social Policy* 13 (Summer):32–41.

TEICHER, ANNE. 1982. Linking abortion and sterilization abuse. *CARASA News* 6 (July):18–19, 28.

THOMAS, COURTNEY. 1982. State report on NP acts. *Nurse Practitioner* 7 (November-December):9–10.

THRONE, LINDA, and HANSON, LAURENCE. 1981. Midwifery laws in the United States. *Women and Health* 6 (Fall):7–26.

TIERNEY, JOHN. 1982. Herpes breaks out. *Science '82.* 3 (June):14–16.

Toward a politics of sexuality: Conference report. 1982. *Off Our Backs* 12 (June):2–25.

U.S. Department of Health and Human Services. 1980. *The health consequences of smoking for women.* Washington, D.C.: U.S. Government Printing Office.

U.S. fertility up slightly in 1979: Highest increase among women 30–34, lowest, among those 15–17. 1982. *Family Planning Perspectives* 14 (January-February):31–32.

VALENTINE, JEANETTE. 1982. Policy and programmatic issues in meeting the needs of pregnant and parenting adolescents of Hispanic background. Paper presented at the Critical Health Care Issues Affecting Mainland Puerto Ricans Conference, Boston, Mass., September 24–25.

VODA, ANN M., et al., eds. 1982. *Changing perspectives on menopause.* Austin: University of Texas Press.

WALLIS, CLAUDIA. 1982. The new scarlet letter, *Time,* August 2, pp. 62–69.

Warning: health hazards for office workers. 1981. Cleveland: Working Women Education Fund, 1224 Huron Road, Cleveland, OH 44115.

WHITBECK, CAROLINE, ed. 1982. Women and medicine. *Journal of Medicine and Philosophy.* Special issue. 7 (May).

WOOLEY, SUSAN, and WOOLEY, ORLAND. 1979. Obesity and women—A closer look at the facts. *Women's Studies International Quarterly* 2:69–79.

Working women. 1981. Race against time: Automation of the office. Cleveland: Working Women Education Funds, 1224 Huron Road, Cleveland, OH 44115.

YONAS-PHIPPS, SUSAN. 1980. Teenage pregnancy and motherhood: A review of the literature. *American Journal of Orthopsychiatry* 50 (July):403–31.

ZELNIK, MELVIN, and KIM, YUNG, J. 1982. Sex education and its association with teenage sexual activity, pregnancy and contraceptive use. *Family Planning Perspectives* 14 (May-June):117–26.

ZONES, JANE SPRAGUE. 1982. Getting the word out about smoking and women's health. *Second Opinion,* October, p. 1; 7.

Bibliography

ACLU. *Women's Legal Guide to Reproductive Rights.* 1982. Available from Janet Benshoof, Director, A.C.L.U. Reproductive Freedom Project, 132 West 43rd Street, New York, NY 10036, (212)944-9800.

Aiken, Linda H., ed. *Nursing in the 1980s: Crisis, Opportunities, Challenge.* Philadelphia: J. B. Lippincott, 1982. A good summary of current policy analysis of the nursing situation.

Alfin-Slater, R. B., and Kritchevsky, D., eds. *Human Nutrition: A Comprehensive Treatise.* Vols. 1–4. New York: Plenum, 1980. Technical, but just what its title promises.

Apfel, Roberta J. "How Are Women Sicker than Men? An Overview of Psychosomatic Problems in Women." *Psychotherapy Psychosomatics* 37 (1982):106–18.

Arney, William Ray. *Power and the Profession of Obstetrics.* Chicago: University of Chicago Press, 1982. A scholarly history of obstetrics.

Bluestein, Bill, and Bluestein, Enid. *Mom, How Come I'm Not Thin?* Minneapolis: Compcare, 1981. A short book dealing with many of the issues and feelings of overweight children.

Borg, Susan, and Lasker, Judith. *When Pregnancy Fails: Families Coping with Miscarriage, Stillbirth, and Infant Death.* Boston: Beacon Press, 1981. A sensitive sociologic study of these problems.

Buss, Fran Leeper. *La Partera: Story of a Midwife.* Ann Arbor: University of Michigan Press, 1980. The history of a New Mexico lay midwife.

California Urban Indian Health Council. *California Indian Maternal and Child Health Plan.* 1982. Available from the California Urban Indian Health Council, 1615 Broadway, Oakland, CA 94612. A model study of maternal and child health needs, problems and issues for Native Americans.

Campling, Jo, ed. *Images of Ourselves: Women with Disabilities Talking.* Boston: Routledge & Kegan Paul, 1982. An English study examines the lives of several disabled women.

CARASA. "Women under Attack: Abortion, Sterilization Abuse and Reproductive Freedom." New York: CARASA, 1979. An excellent pamphlet and introduction to the issues.

Carrillo, Ann, et al. *No More Stares.* 1982. Available from Disability Rights and Education Defense Fund, 2032 San Pablo Avenue, Berkeley, CA 94702. A tape in addition for the visually disabled is being prepared.

Chalmers, B. "Psychological Aspects of Pregnancy: Some Thoughts for the Eighties." *Social Science and Medicine* 16 (1982):323–31.

Chavkin, Wendy, and Welch, Louise. "Occupational Hazards to Reproduction: An Annotated Bibliography." 1980. Available from Health PAC, 17 Murray Street, New York, NY 10007. $5.00.

Childbearing Rights Information Project. "For Ourselves, Our Families and Our Future: The Struggle for Childbearing Rights." Boston: Red Sun Press, P. O. Box 18178, 02118. A political analysis of childbearing rights.

Coalition for the Medical Rights of Women. "Safe Natural Remedies for the Discomforts of Pregnancy." CMRW, 1638B Haight Street, San Francisco, CA 94117.

———. "The Rock Will Wear Away: Handbook for Women's Health Advocates." CMRW, 1683B Haight Street, San Francisco, CA 94117.

Cooper, Patricia, ed. *Better Homes and Gardens' Women's Health and Medical Guide.* Des Moines: Meredith Corporation, 1981. Factual and useful information from the folks who finally realized women have greater concerns than how to redecorate their gazebo.

Craig, Marianne. *Office Worker's Survival Handbook: A Guide to Fighting Health Hazards in the Office.* 1981. Available from Trade Union Book Service, 265 Seven Sisters Road, London, N4, England. $4.34. An English manual, but full of useful information for women in the United States.

Edlund, Barbara, and McKenzie, Carole Ann, eds. "Symposia on Women's Health Issues." *Nursing Clinics of North America* 17 (March 1982):111–88. A nursing perspective on women's health issues.

"Family Planning in the 1980s: Challenges and Opportunities." *Studies in Family Planning* 12 (June-July 1981):251–56. An overview of future issues.

Feldman, Silvia. *Choices in Childbirth.* New York: Grosset and Dunlap, 1978. A practical guide for the pregnant woman.

Felker, Marcia. "The Political Economy of Sexism in Industrial Health." *Social Science and Medicine* 16 (1982):3–18. A critical analysis of occupational health.

Gofman, John W. *Radiation and Human Health.* San Francisco: Sierra Club Books, 1981. A good discussion of this crucial issue.

Herbert, Wray. "Premenstrual Changes." *Science News* 122 (December 11, 1982): 380–81.

Holmes, Helen B., et al., eds. *Birth Control and Controlling Birth: Women-Centered Perspectives.* Clifton, N.J.: Humana Press, 1980. Feminist views from a conference on Ethical Issues in Human Reproduction Technology.

————. *The Custom-Made Child? Women-Centered Perspectives.* Clifton, N.J.: Humana Press, 1981. The companion volume from the Ethical Issues Conference.

Hunt, Vilma. *Work and the Health of Women.* Boca Raton: CRC Press, 1979. A careful, slightly technical, but excellent introduction to the problems, including a chapter on the influence of environmental agents on male reproductive failure.

Jacobson, Bobbie. *The Ladykillers: Why Smoking Is a Feminist Issue.* New York: Continuum, 1982. A feminist explanation.

Kalisch, Beatrice, and Kalisch, Philip. *The Politics of Nursing.* Philadelphia: J. B. Lippincott, 1982. A new overview on nurses and their political activities.

Kay, Margarita, ed. *An Anthropology of Human Birth.* Philadelphia: F. A. Davis, 1982. The "customs" of birthing in different cultures.

Kitzinger, Sheila. *The Experience of Breastfeeding.* New York: Penguin, 1980. A pro-breastfeeding book with helpful information, but not useful if you tire of it before the child is a year old.

Klerman, Lorraine V., ed. *Research Priorities in Maternal and Child Health.* Report of a conference, June 9 and 10, 1981, Brandeis University. Washington, D.C.: Office for Maternal and Child Health, Health Services Administration, Public Health Service, U.S. Department of Health and Human Services, 1981. Scholarly report on research issues.

Kushner, Rose. *Why Me? What Every Woman Should Know about Breast Cancer.* New York: Signet Books, 1977. The major feminist writing on the topic.

————. "Vital Support still Lacking for Breast Cancer Patients." *New Directions for Women* 10 (November-December 1981):5–10. A follow-up report to her book.

Liebman, Shelly. *Do it at Your Desk: An Office Workers' Guide to Fitness and Health.* Washington: Tilden Press, 1982. Office survival skills of a new kind.

MacLeod, Sheila. *The art of starvation.* New York: Schocken, 1982. An analysis of eating disorders.

MacKower, Joel. *Office Hazards: How Your Job Can Make You Sick.* Washington: Tilden Press, 1981. One of the best guides to office work health and safety problems and what can be done about them.

Marieskind, Helen. *Women in the Health System.* St. Louis: C. V. Mosby, 1980. A textbook introduction to the general issues in women's health with good tables and statistics.

Melosh, Barbara. *"The Physician's Hand": Work Culture and Conflict in American Nursing.* Philadelphia: Temple University Press, 1982. A historical account that begins to explain nursing's current dilemmas.

Meyer, Sharon I. "Bibliography." *Women and Health* 7 (Summer 1982):67–75. Bibliographical guide to women and health, especially useful for guide to other bibliographies.

Millman, Marcia. *Such a Pretty Face. Being Fat in America.* New York: W. W. Norton, 1980. A sociologist looks at the experience of being fat in America.

Menkin, Stephen. "Depo-Provera: A Critical Analysis." *Women and Health* 5 (Summer 1980):49–69. What the title promises.

Morgan, Susanne. *Coping with a Hysterectomy.* New York: Dial Press, 1982. A good feminist guide to the issues and problems with hysterectomies.

National Conference on Educational Equity for Disabled Women and Girls Report. 1982. Available from Project REED, Women's Action Alliance, 370 Lexington Avenue, New York, NY 10017.

Nathanson, Constance. "Social Roles and Health Status among Women: The Significance of Employment." *Social Science and Medicine* 14A (1980):463–71.

National Clearinghouse for Alcohol Information. "Spectrum: Alcohol Problem Prevention for Women by Women." (Rockville, Md.: The Clearinghouse) P.O. Box 2345, 20852.

Office of Technology Assessment. *World Population and Fertility Planning Technologies: The Next Twenty Years.* Washington, D.C.: Office of Technology Assessment, 1982. What the future holds in contraception.

Piercy, Marge. *Braided Lives.* New York: Summit Books, 1982. A feminist novel dealing with issues of abortion and reproductive rights.

Radical America, eds. "Facing Reaction." *Radical America* 15 (Spring 1981). A special double issue that serves as an excellent introduction to the New Right and how to cope with it.

Reverby, Susan, and Rosner, David, eds. *Health Care in America: Essays in Social History.* Philadelphia: Temple University Press, 1979. Historians examine the health care system.

Roberts, Helen, ed. *Women, Health and Reproduction.* Boston: Routledge & Kegan Paul, 1981. A primarily British feminist collection of essays on such issues as family planning, Depo-provera, pregnancy, well women's clinics, and women physicians. Contains Pauline Bart's history of "Jane," the feminist "illegal" abortion service in Chicago in 1969–1973.

Rosenbaum, Marsha. *Women on Heroin.* (New Brunswick: Rutgers University Press, 1982.) The special problems of women and addiction.

Rothman, Barbara Katz. *In Labor, Women and Power in the Birthplace*. New York: W. W. Norton, 1982. A sociologist's critique.

Sandelowski, Margarete. *Women, Health and Choice*. Englewood Cliffs, N.J.: Prentice-Hall, 1981. Primarily a text for health science students, it is a sensitive feminist introduction to women's health issues.

Santa Fe Health Education Project. *Menopause: A Self-Care Manual*. Available in both English and Spanish from The Project, P.O. Box 577, Santa Fe, NM 87502.

Scully, Diana. *Men who Control Women's Health: The Miseducation of Obstetrician-Gynecologists*. Boston: Houghton Mifflin, 1980. The demystification of how obstetrician-gynecologists are trained.

Silverman, Milton et al. *Prescriptions for Death: The Drugging of the Third World*. Berkeley: University of California Press, 1982. A devastating survey of the worldwide problem with specific sections on drugs used on women.

Solidarity. "1981 Discussion Bulletin on Socialist-Feminism." Available from Solidarity, 32 Lee Ave., #301, Takoma Pk., MD 20912. It includes a large section on reproductive rights.

Sours, John. *Starving to Death in a Sea of Objects*. New York: Jason Aronson, 1980. A psychiatrist's clinical view on the problem with a long psychoanalytic case history of one anorexic young woman.

Tabor, Martha. "Uses and Limitations of Male/Female Data." *Occupational Health and Safety*, November 1981, pp. 38–44, 51. A good journalistic overview of the problem.

Women: A Journal of Liberation (3):1981. On women and healing, essays and poems. Available from *Women*, 3028 Greenmont Avenue, Baltimore, MD 21218.

Young, Diony, and Mahan, Charles S. *Unnecessary Cesareans: Ways to Avoid Them*. Available from International Childbirth Education Association, P.O. Box 20048, Minneapolis, MN 55420. Just what the title says.

Resources

Periodicals and Key Organizations

American College of Nurse-Midwives. 1522 K Street NW, Suite 1120, Washington, DC 20005.

Boston Self-Help Center, 18 Williston Road, Brookline, MA 02146. Counseling and advocacy services for people with disabilities.

Boston Women's Health Book Collective, P.O. Box 192, West Somerville, MA 02144. Authors of *Our Bodies, Ourselves;* provide health and sexuality information to women.

CARASA (Coalition for Abortion Rights and Against Sterilization Abuse), 17 Murray Street, 5th floor, New York, NY 10007. Publishes *CARASA News*.

Center for Science in the Public Interest, 1757 S Street NW, Washington, DC 20009. Excellent resources, including posters on food and nutrition. Publishes *Nutrition Action*.

Coal Mining Women's Support Team News, Coal Employment Project, Box 3403, Oak Ridge, TN 37830.

Coalition for the Medical Rights of Women, 1638B Haight Street, San Francisco, CA 94117. Health advocacy and information resource. Publishes *Coalition News.*

Coalition for the Reproductive Rights of Workers (CRROW), 1917 Eye Street NW, Washington, DC 20006.

Disability Rights Education and Defense Fund, Inc. (DREDF), 2032 San Pablo Avenue, Berkeley, CA 94702.

DES Action National, 1638B Haight Street, San Francisco, CA 94117. Publishes *DES Action News.*

Do It Now Foundation, Box 5115, Phoenix, AZ 85010. Substance abuse information.

Emma Goldman Clinic for Women, 715 N. Dodge, Iowa City, IA 52240. One of the oldest women's health centers in the United States; offers literature; major center for fitting cervical caps.

Endometriosis Association, c/o Bread and Roses Women's Health Center, 238 W. Wisconsin Ave., Milwaukee, WI 53203. Provides information and support for women with endometriosis.

Feminist Women's Health Center, 6411 Hollywood Boulevard, Los Angeles, CA 90028. Resource for organizing information and teaching materials basic to movement and philosophy of self-help; literature list.

Health Facts, Center for Medical Consumers and Health Care Information, 237 Thompson Street, New York, NY 10012. General bimonthly newsletter.

Health/PAC (Health Policy Advisory Center), 17 Murray Street, New York, NY 10007. Analysis and study of health issues from radical perspective; produces variety of publications.

Healthsharing, Women Healthsharing, Box 230, Station M, Toronto, Ontario M6S 4T3 Canada. Quarterly newsletter covering wide range of women's health concerns.

Helper, American Social Health Association, Box 100, Palo Alto, CA 94302. About sexually transmitted diseases, particularly herpes.

Hot Flash: Newsletter for Midlife and Older Women, c/o Dr. Jane Porcino, School of Allied Health Professions, Health Sciences Center, SUNY Stony Brook, Stony Brook, NY 11794.

ICASC Information, International Contraception, Abortion and Sterilization Campaign (ICASC), c/o NAC, 374 Grays Inn Road, London, W.C. 1, England. Covers activities of governments, churches, the medical profession, drug companies, political parties, population control agencies, and antiabortion organizations, and what women are doing internationally to gain or preserve the right to control their fertility.

INFACT, 1701 University Avenue SE, Minneapolis, MN 54414. Organizers and information source on the Nestlé boycott.

International Childbirth Education Association (ICEA), Box 20048, Minneapolis, MN 55420. Offers extensive annotated lists of publications and audiovisual resources; monthly newsletter covers wide range of childbirth issues.

National Family Planning and Reproductive Health Association, 1110 Vermont Avenue NW, #950, Washington, DC 20005, (202)467-6767. Publishes *NFPRHA*

News and monitors federal changes in family planning support and other related issues.

National Women's Health Network, 224 Seventh Street SE, Washington, DC 20003. National membership consumer organization; monitors and works to influence government and industry policies. Publishes *Network News.*

New Hampshire Feminist Health Center, 38 S. Main Street, Concord, NH 03301. Publishes *Women-Wise,* which covers wide variety of topics on women and health.

Off Our Backs, 1841 Columbia, Room 212, Washington, DC 20009. Probably the best feminist monthly newspaper, with excellent regular coverage of women's health issues.

Older Women's League (OWL), 3800 Harrison Street, Oakland, CA 94611. Publishes *Gray Papers: Issues for Action.*

Ovulation Method Teachers Associated, 4760 Aldrich Road, Bellingham, WA 98225. They keep lists of women and groups able to teach fertility consciousness.

Practicing Midwife, quarterly publication of the Midwives Alliance of North America, c/o Concord Midwifery Service, 30 S. Main Street, Concord, NH 03301.

Reproductive Rights National Network (R₂N₂), 17 Murray Street, New York, NY 10007. Publishes *Reproductive Rights Newsletter.*

Resolve, Inc., Box 474, Belmont, MA 02178. Literature and resources on infertility, artificial insemination, and research into these and related issues. Publishes *Resolve Newsletter.*

Santa Cruz Women's Health Center, 250 Locust Avenue, Santa Cruz, CA 95060. Publishes excellent pamphlets on such topics as herpes and lesbian health care.

Science for the People, 897 Main Street, Cambridge, MA 02139. Bimonthly offering analyses of politics of science, frequently examines women's health issues.

Union WAGE (Union Women's Alliance to Gain Equality), P.O. Box 40904, Berkeley, CA 94701. Dedicated to fighting discrimination on the job, in unions, and in society. Publishes *Union WAGE,* which carries important articles on women and occupational health.

WIN News, Women's International Network, 187 Grant Street, Lexington, MA 02173. Carries wide range of topics of concern to women and reports from around the world.

Women and Health, Box 33790, Seattle, WA 98133 (editorial address); Haworth Press, 149 Fifth Avenue, New York, NY 10010 (subscription address). Academic journal with articles on all aspects of women's health.

Women for Environmental Health, 1747 Connecticut Avenue NW, Washington, DC 20009.

Women in Medicine Newsletter, Women in Medicine Task Force, American Medical Student Association, 14650 Lee Road, Box 131, Chantilly, Va 22121.

Women's Committee, Mass. Coalition for Occupational Safety and Health, 718 Huntington Avenue, Boston, MA 02115. Broad spectrum of activities focusing on occupational health of women and other workers. Many health and safety materials available.

Women's Occupational Health Resource Center, School of Public Health, Columbia University, 60 Haven Avenue, B-1, New York, NY 10032.

Recommended Films

Abortion. By Jane Pincus et al. 1970. Available from Boston Women's Health Book Collective, P.O. Box 192, W. Somerville, MA 02144. Thirty-minutes, 16mm, black/white. Produced in 1970–1971, this powerful film describes the plight of women denied access to legal abortion. Also covers sterilization abuse and experimentation on Third World women.

Blood of the Condor. 1970. Available from Tricontinental Films, 333 Sixth Avenue, New York, NY 10014. About the uprising of a Bolivian village after it is discovered that hundreds of their women were sterilized unknowingly at a U.S.-financed clinic.

Bottle Babies. 1976. Available from American Baptist Films, Valley Forge, PA 19481. 20 min., black/white. About infant feeding formula abuse in Third World countries.

The Chicago Maternity Center Story. By Jenny Rohrer and Suzanne Davenport. 1977. Available from Kartemquin Films Ltd., 1901 W. Wellington, Chicago, IL 60657. 16mm, 60 min., black/white. Details the struggle of a community group that unsuccessfully attempts to preserve community-based childbirth options.

Daughters of Time. By Ginny Durrin. 1981. Available from New Day Films, P.O. Box 315, Franklin Lakes, NJ 07417. 16mm, 24 min., color. About nurse-midwives.

Formula Factor. Available from California Newsreel, 630 Natoma Street, San Francisco, CA 94103. 16mm, 30 min., color. About infant formula abuse.

Healthcaring from Our End of the Speculum. 1976. Available from Women Make Movies, 257 W. 19th Street, New York, NY 10011. 35 min., color. Excellent introductory film covering many different women's health concerns.

The Last to Know. By Bonnie Friedman. 1980. Available from New Day Films, P.O. Box 315, Franklin Lakes, NJ 07417. 16mm and video cassette, 45 min., color. A compelling film focusing on four different women alcoholics.

Menopause: A Time of Transition. By Sheryl Brown. Available from San Francisco Planned Parenthood, 1660 Bush Street, San Francisco, CA 94109. Slide and tape show covering what to expect in menopause.

Nursing: The Politics of Caring. 1978. Available from Fanlight Productions, P.O. Box 226, Cambridge, MA 02138. 16mm, 22 min., color. Documentary about the struggles of nurses to increase their voice in the system, especially as advocates of patients. Explores attitudes of nurses toward their work.

La Operacion. By Ana Maria Garcia. Powerful documentary about sterilization abuse, particularly among Puerto Rican women. Further information available from the filmmaker, 733 Amsterdam Avenue, Apt. 12A, New York, NY 10025, or The Film Fund, 80 E. 11th Street, New York, NY 10003.

Our Lives on the Line. By Faye More and Linda Di Rocco. Available from the Media Group, Urban Planning Aid, Inc., 100 Arlington Street, 2nd floor, Boston, MA 02116. 45 min. Videotape explores abortion experiences of four black women living in Boston.

Period Piece. By Emily Culpepper. Available from the author. 3726 Lake Shore Avenue, Oakland, CA 94610. 16mm, 10 min., color. About menstruation.

Taking our Bodies Back: The Women's Health Movement. Available from Cambridge Documentary Films, Box 385, Cambridge, MA 02139. 33 min., color. Somewhat dated (produced in 1973), but still a good general film on women's health.

Trying Times: Crisis in Fertility. By Joan Finck Sawyer. 1980. Available from Fanlight Productions, P.O. Box 226, Cambridge, MA 02138. 16mm, 33 min., color. About infertility, produced in collaboration with Resolve.

VD and Women. 1978. Available from Perennial Education, 477 Roger Williams, Box 855, Ravinia, Highland Park, IL 60035. 16mm, 17 min., color. Includes good section on prevention.

Working for Your Life. By Andrea Hricko and Ken Light. Available from LOHP Films, Transit Media, 779 Susquehanna Avenue, Franklin Lakes, NJ 07417. 16mm, 60 min., color. Introductory film about women and occupational health.

Politics and Law

Peggy Simpson

The night of June 30, 1982, a glittering black-tie crowd of New Right luminaries celebrated the demise of the Equal Rights Amendment. They played "Ding Dong, the Witch is Dead." The editor of the *Conservative Digest* said, "We're here to celebrate a death, to dance on a grave," and anti-ERA strategist Phyllis Schlafly read a telegram of congratulations from President Reagan.

Hours earlier, white-garbed feminists gathered in Lafayette Park across from the White House, recalling the fifty-year fight that suffragists waged to win the vote and pledging to work as long as required to win full equality for women. They also vowed vengeance at the polls in November.

Four months later, pollsters and political analysts of both parties agreed that the 1982 elections proved that the historically unprecedented "gender gap" first detected in 1980 was not a fluke. Women favored Democratic candidates by far greater margins than did men; they shunned the Republican party by increasing margins as the political year unfolded; and in-depth exit interviews of voters and telephone interviews of probable voters showed that the growing antipathy of women toward Reagan was based not just on the fear of war but on issues of economics and sex discrimination as well.

The elections saw ERA supporters make major gains in the Florida and Illinois legislatures, two states that failed to ratify the amendment in the waning days of its life. A Schlafly protégée, Ann Bagnal, was upset in her race for a congressional seat along with four other GOP conservatives who had been backed by anti-ERA and antiabortion GOP Senator Jesse Helms of North Carolina.

Although the women's vote proved pivotal in the North Carolina defeats and in putting Democratic men over the top in close governors' races in Texas and New York, it was not enough to propel many new women into key national and statewide jobs. One exception was Ann Richards, who led the ticket in

Texas in her race for treasurer, the first woman in contemporary times to win a statewide contest. A notable casualty was Missouri state Senator Harriett Woods who attracted national attention in her near-upset of moderate GOP Senator John C. Danforth in a bid for a U.S. Senate seat.

Confrontations between civil rights and women's rights activists and the Reagan administration escalated in 1982. Shadow civil rights and budget-monitoring groups were formed to identify and publicize Reagan policy changes. In midyear, thirty-three of the fifty state advisory committees to the U.S. Commission on Civil Rights joined in a statement blaming Reagan's reversals on affirmative action and desegregation issues for a "dangerous deterioration" of civil rights enforcement.

As Reagan dramatically increased defense spending, he undertook equally dramatic efforts to scale back the rest of government—especially the giant retirement and social welfare programs that the United States had put in place in recent decades, the last of the industrial nations to do so. This had a disproportionate impact on women, who comprise 75 percent of the poor in America.

By late 1982 an analysis of what could be done to counter the gender gap was prepared for the White House Coordinating Council on Women. It concluded that the economic vulnerability of women, whose numbers heading single-parent families doubled to 6.6 million in the 1970s, may be a major factor. "Fear of losing government benefits appears to be causing women to oppose the administration," the twelve-page report said, based on findings from 20,000 interviews by Reagan's polling firm. It added that separated and divorced women feel "Reagan is a threat to the supports originating with government."

University of Maryland economist Barbara Bergmann testified in congressional hearings early in 1982 that the combination of budget cuts and abandonment of affirmative action advocacy "will reverse gains made previously and will make a basically bad situation worse. . . . It is not an exaggeration to say that the Reagan administration has declared economic war on women, particularly on those women who do not have a man to depend on" (Bergmann 1982).

By the spring of 1982, forty women's groups had formed a coalition to alert the grass roots, Congress, and the media about the damage done to women by the budget cuts and policy changes. A year later, when Reagan's budget for 1984 revealed even more severe cuts, the coalition was joined by an additional fifteen groups.

By his second year, it had become clear that the agenda of the Reagan revolution was based as much on ideological as fiscal conservatism. Programs that were minuscule in size were targeted for extinction. The hit list included virtually all programs that had been devised in the past fifteen years to help women become self-sufficient, overcome sex-based barriers in society, and break out of sex-segregated and stereotyped roles. Sometimes the goal was to drop an advocacy role and assume a hands-off "educating" or "observer" role instead; sometimes it was elimination entirely.

The budget and policy changes diluted nutritional, health, and income supports for poor women and infants; ended special business programs for women entrepreneurs; undercut new job programs for displaced homemakers; reduced support for emergency shelters for battered wives; limited aid to colleges and employers to change attitudes and workplace patterns that have kept women in sex-segregated cocoons; and greatly constricted the government's investigations into sex discrimination complaints and the class action and back pay remedies to resolve them.

Although Reagan continued to express his support for ending discrimination, he also escalated his rhetoric in seeking a ban on abortions, put his stamp of approval on the so-called squeal rule requiring parental notification when teenage girls are prescribed any form of birth control by federally funded clinics, reiterated his opposition to affirmative action, and made light of questions about federal investigations into sexual harassment.

The New Right coalition of religious and political fundamentalists, meanwhile, intensified its demands for ending sex equity programs they claimed were run by and for "radical feminists," which the White House then accommodated, by placing more conservative activists in high policy positions in two major departments. Despite Reagan's help, however, the New Right activists suffered major defeats in the Republican-controlled Senate in fruitless attempts to push through constitutional amendment proposals to ban abortion and require school prayer. Proposals to ban affirmative action and eviscerate sex-discrimination laws lay dormant.

As GOP moderates became increasingly alarmed about the course of the Reagan revolution and its impact on them and their party, they began to speak out and to form coalitions with feminists to blunt the budget cuts and preserve some agencies on the hit list, such as the Women's Education Equity Act Program in the Department of Education. A coalition of conservatives and liberals helped enact a major bill to overturn a 1981 Supreme Court ruling in *McCarty* v. *McCarty* and to require state divorce courts to consider military pensions a negotiable item in divorce settlements. A court had ruled that even though a military wife had followed her husband across the globe on his assignments, giving up her own career options (and future pension rights), she had no claim on his pension if they divorced.

Early in 1982 Oregon GOP Senator Bob Packwood warned that the Republican party could not survive if it continued to alienate women, minorities, and blue-collar workers. Although Packwood was ousted from his Senate campaign chairmanship in a White House-engineered retaliation move a year later, his basic message had been absorbed and heeded by his colleagues—and by the White House, with polls on the gender gap and the 1982 election results making the same point even more painfully.

Equal Rights Amendment

Despite millions of dollars of television and direct-mail advertising, supporters of the Equal Rights Amendment failed to push the amendment through any more state legislatures before the expiration date on June 30. Thirty-five states had ratified the amendment, thirty of them within the first year after it cleared Congress and before conservatives began to use it as an organizing tool for what evolved into a New Right coalition of religious and political fundamentalists. States that never ratified the ERA were Alabama, Arkansas, Arizona, Florida, Georgia, Illinois, Louisiana, Mississippi, Missouri, Nevada, North Carolina, Oklahoma, South Carolina, Utah, and Virginia.

The amendment was voted on in six of those states during 1982, with the last defeat coming June 21 in the Florida senate when it was rejected 23 to 17, after a debate that focused not just on the threat of women being drafted in the military but on the early 1970s themes that women needed to be "protected" from dangers that could result with full legal equality.

The National Organization for Women pioneered the use of cable television with its advertising message both for the ERA and for an increase in membership so it could continue to fight for women's equality. The New Right countered with ads of its own on television, featuring retired Army Brigadier General Elizabeth Hoisington saying women were not capable of taking on combat roles and would weaken the nation's overall defense if this occurred.

In Illinois, the only state with rules requiring a three-fifths rather than a majority vote on constitutional proposals, Sonia Johnson led a hunger strike in the capitol rotunda in Springfield for thirty-seven days in a fruitless attempt to persuade legislators to amend the rule and pass the ERA. Johnson, who was excommunicated from the Mormon Church in 1981 because of her ERA activism, and her colleagues called themselves the Grass Roots Group of Second Class Citizens. They were given scant national attention until the concluding days of their campaign when anti-ERA legislators made headlines by displaying candy bars and hamburgers in front of the hunger strikers. (Johnson subsequently lost a race for president of NOW on her platform to use more militant tactics in the equal rights fight, as the suffragists had done in Great Britain and in this country to get the vote early this century.)

In a letter to supporters shortly before the amendment expired, anti-ERA strategist Phyllis Schlafly said, "The libs thought they would dishearten us so badly when they passed their crooked time extension that we would give up. . . . How wrong they were! They didn't know that 'persistence' is our middle name." At a news conference on deadline day, she dated the ERA's demise to the 1975 International Women's Year activities funded by $5 million in federal money, which she said underwrote a "radical agenda" that included "tax-funded abortions, massive federal child care for all children, rights for lesbians to teach in schools and adopt children, affirmative action to get women into jobs instead of men, and a federal spending solution for every problem." She said supporters "never could show any right, any benefit, any advantage to women in ERA" and lost support when opponents persuaded the country that "the one certain effect admitted by everyone is that young women would be forced into the Army against their will—in the name of equality."

At a victory party that night, Schlafly's Eagle Forum paid tribute to major New Right leaders for their role in blocking the amendment, including Moral Majority founder Jerry Falwell; author George Gilder; cabinet Secretaries James Watt at Interior and James B. Edwards at Energy; direct-mail entrepreneur Richard Viguerie; Conservative Caucus leader Howard Phillips; retired generals John K. Singlaub, Andrew J. Gatsis, A. C. Wedemeyer, Elizabeth Hoisington, and Daniel O. Graham; television preachers James Robison and Tim LeHaye; and GOP Senators Orrin G. Hatch of Utah, Jesse Helms of North Carolina, Jeremiah Denton of Alabama, John P. East of North Carolina; and Jake Garn of Utah.

Viguerie called the ERA fight "a classic confrontation between the power elite and the people—and the people have won." Columnist M. Stanton Evans said, "When you hear the phrase 'gross national product'—that is not a reference to Bella Abzug." In a paraphrase to the music from Cole Porter's *Kiss Me, Kate*, the group heaped ridicule on two other feminist leaders, NOW president Ellie Smeal and *Ms.* magazine founder Gloria Steinem:

Where are you Ellie?
I'm sorry to tell you that your arguments were smelly.
Where are you Gloria?
Still pedaling your life style to housewives
    in Peoria?

Earlier on the deadline day of June 30, Reagan's daughter Maureen told the National Press Club a new era was just beginning for the women's movement, saying, "We are better organized and educated in the political process and we have long memories." Ellie Smeal, NOW president, told a rally, "We have just begun to fight. We are not even winded. . . . We are going to say to the men of this country: move over. Move over and make room for women." That same theme was reflected in signs carried by dozens of demonstrators that read "Women were not born Democrats, Republicans, or yesterday."

Two weeks later, on July 14, a coalition of fifty senators and 201 House members reintroduced the ERA in Congress.

Most leaders of the original fight had predicted it might be another decade before the amendment could be pushed anew with success. They were overtaken by events, however. The November elections proved that it had indeed become a major factor in the gender gap. Its defeat appeared to have had a far greater impact in alarming voters of both sexes about the goals of the Republican conservatives.

New political leaders came forth—Democratic Senator Paul E. Tsongas of Massachusetts and GOP Senator Packwood—to seize on the changed political climate to push the ERA forward before the 1984 presidential elections, gambling that Republicans could not risk lining up against it without considerable peril at the polls, when they have twice as many members up for reelection as do Democrats.

An analysis was launched to assess strength in state legislatures, including those where the ERA was approved swiftly and uncritically in the year after its congressional approval. The 1982 elections in Florida and Illinois included dozens of contests where the amendment was the front-burner issue—and the pro-ERA forces won control of the legislatures in both states. Early in 1983 the Illinois legislature scrapped the three-fifths rule that had blocked passage in Schlafly's home state.

The strength of the New Right as a major political force was called into question by the 1982 elections, which saw the popularity of its leaders such as Falwell plummet in polls and raised red flags about how much damage Reagan suffered from his association with the New Right.

Schlafly had not helped her own political credibility with the ERA victory party or with the Eagle Forum's delivery early in 1983 of quiches to senators sponsoring the ERA with a warning "Real Men Do Not Draft Women," an apparent play on the book title *Real Men Don't Eat Quiche*.

The draft-women question remained a key controversy; however, both sides conceded. Sponsors of the ERA insisted the laws now would permit women to be drafted and that the amendment would not change that option.

As 1983 opened, the ERA continued to be a major organizing tool both for conservatives and for women's rights advocates.

Elections

The gender gap proved to be a measurable phenomenon in 1982. It had been detected, but discounted by many in the 1980 presidential elections when women voted narrowly for President Carter while men voted in far larger numbers for Ronald Reagan. Exit polls in November 1982 showed that 53 percent of the women voted Democratic as opposed to 47 percent who voted Republican. The statistics were the opposite for men. The gender gap was detected in every region of the country and cut across age and income groups. It was wider for women workers.

The women's vote tipped the balance in many races tracked by pollsters. It was a key component in the unexpectedly tight governor's race in New York, where Democratic Lieutenant Governor Mario Cuomo upset New Right financier Lewis Lehrman due to a formidable get-out-the-vote effort and a gender gap that brought him women's votes that were between 6.5 and 8 percent higher than the men's votes for him. He won by 3.2 percent. In Texas, Democratic challenger Mark White upset the incumbent GOP Governor William Clements by a 7.6 percent margin. Again, the components were a strong get-out-the-vote drive and a women's vote that was between 7 and 8 percent higher for him than the vote of men. Abortion and the ERA were issues in both races, with the Democrats favoring and the Republicans opposing them. Clements, in addition, was haunted by a flip comment that he couldn't find a "housewife" capable of serving on the state's utility regulatory commission to help control soaring fuel bills.

After the 1982 election, it was clear that the gender gap had a potent negative power—to oppose a Clements or an anti-ERA activist such as Ann Bagnal, one of five GOP conservative congressional contenders beaten in North Carolina. But women candidates were the beneficiaries of this phenomenon only infrequently. In a race for a U.S. Senate seat, Missouri's Harriett Woods harnessed a statewide network of women and consumer advocates, but was hurt by a shortage of funds until the final weeks of the race against Senator Danforth. She fell victim to his last-minute barrage of mail and television ads questioning her stands on busing, abortion, and "liberalism." In New Jersey, seventy-one-year-old moderate GOP Representative Millicent Fenwick lost what had seemed a sure bet for a Senate seat, partly because she opted not to take funds from special-interest groups and was outspent five to one by an independently wealthy Democratic businessman, Frank Lautenberg. In Iowa, former United States attorney Roxanne Conlin blew a lead in her race for governor by bungling the issue of her own taxes (she and her husband had not paid any, taking advantage of tax loopholes through real estate holdings that she proposed to eliminate as governor). She remained short of money and was besieged by lukewarm support from Democratic party leaders. In Vermont, the polished Democratic Lieutenant Governor Madeline Kunin had little chance of winning the top office once GOP Governor Richard Snelling reversed his decision to retire and ran for reelection.

One congresswoman was defeated; GOP Margaret Heckler of Massachusetts lost a bitter contest with Democratic liberal freshman Representative Barney Frank when their districts were merged. Heckler lost her mainstay of conservative Democrats and much of her women's support when she voted down the line for Reagan's budget cuts. Heckler, an activist in the ERA and child-care fights of the last decade and a co-chair of the Congresswomen's Caucus, later was named to Reagan's cabinet.

Two women retired: GOP Representative Jean Ashbrook of Ohio, who had been named to fill the seat when her husband died the previous April; and fourteen-year veteran New York Democratic Representative Shirley Chisholm, the first woman to run for president in a 1972 race that was ignored by most other feminists, let alone by blacks. Chisholm, an influential defender of the social welfare programs under fire from Reagan, said she quit partly to be with her second husband who had been badly injured in a car accident, and partly because she was exhausted and embittered at fighting to save programs when her "moderate and liberal" colleagues were "running for cover from the New Right."

Five new women were elected, joining sixteen incumbents for a total of twenty-one in the House; the two women in the Senate, Republicans Paula Hawkins of Florida and Nancy Landon Kassebaum of Kansas, did not face reelection.

Women in Congress

Senate
The women holding U.S. Senate seats in the 98th Congress, neither of whom was up for reelection in 1982, are:
Paula Hawkins (R-Fla.)
Nancy Landon Kassebaum (R-Kans.)

House of Representatives
Women holding seats in the U.S. House of Representatives in the 98th Congress are:
*Barbara Boxer (D-Calif.)
Bobbi Fiedler (R-Calif.)
Patricia Schroeder (D-Colo.)
Barbara B. Kennelly (D-Conn.)
*Nancy L. Johnson (R-Conn.)
Cardiss Collins (D-Ill.)
Lynn Martin (R-Ill.)
*Katie Hall (D-Ind.)
Lindy Boggs (D-La.)
Olympia J. Snowe (R-Me.)
Barbara A. Mikulski (D-Md.)
Marjorie S. Holt (R-Md.)
Beverly B. Byron (D-Md.)
Virginia Smith (R-Neb.)
*Barbara Vucanovich (R-Nev.)
Marge Roukema (R-N.J.)
Geraldine A. Ferraro (D-N.Y.)
*Marcy Kaptur (D-Ohio)
Mary Rose Oakar (D-Ohio)
Claudine Schneider (R-R.I.)
Marilyn Lloyd Bouquard (D-Tenn.)

Source: Congressional Research Service, Library of Congress.
**Indicates newly elected Representatives.*

The House newcomers: Barbara Boxer (D-Calif.); Nancy L. Johnson (R-Conn.); Katie Hall (D-Ind.); Barbara Vucanovich (R-Nev.); and Marcy Kaptur (D-Ohio). Hall, who is black and a former Indiana state senator, won a special election to replace a white male Democrat who died. Kaptur was a domestic policy aide to President Carter. Vucanovich managed the Nevada congressional offices for Reagan confidante Senator Paul Laxalt. Johnson was a women's rights activist in the Connecticut state senate. Boxer had been a county commissioner in San Francisco. They shared in common a depth and breadth of political experience and clout in high places. Vucanovich opposed the ERA, the others supported it. She and Kaptur favored a ban on abortion, the others were vocal in supporting a pro-choice position.

No women were elected governor or were currently serving in the top office. Three of the seven women vying for lieutenant governor were elected, including the dogged hero of the ERA movement, former U.S. Representative Martha Griffiths, who was recruited to run for the second spot in Michigan by a gubernatorial candidate half her age, Robert Blanchard. Political experience in California Republican circles was not enough to pull through Carol Hallett as lieutenant governor in that state, however, although the GOP candidate for governor eked out a narrow victory. In Illinois the presence of ERA crusader Grace Mary Stern on the Democratic ticket as lieutenant governor could not put over a suprisingly unpopular Adlai Stevenson, Jr. The Stevenson-Stern ticket did, however, come within 8,000 votes of an upset against incumbent GOP Governor Jim Thompson, who had chosen as his running mate the architect of the anti-ERA move, assembly speaker George Ryan. The women's vote favored the Stevenson-Stern ticket, polls showed, and both sides conceded the ERA issue was key.

With ERA and abortion rights as organizing tools, women's rights groups made continuing strides in electoral politics. They were more generally accepted, if not integrated, into regular party organizations in many states. They were mastering fund-raising tools, but the sharply escalating costs of campaigns left them at significant disadvantages. In addition to Harriett Woods, who showed ability to attract major money, two candidates, Boxer in California and the victorious Texas state treasurer Ann Richards, pioneered in soliciting $1,000 donations from women supporters early in the process.

Women campaign strategists were in key positions in the 1982 elections. Nancy Sinnott was executive director of the Republican congressional campaign committee. Audrey Shepherd held the second spot at the comparable Senate Democratic campaign committee. At the Democratic National Committee, Ann Lewis was political director, Dottie Lynch was an on-staff pollster, and Angie Martin was a key field director. Wilma Goldstein was a top polling specialist at the Republican National Committee.

Ranny Cooper of the Women's Campaign Fund participated in the coalition of progressive political action committees that shared early knowledge and political judgments about potential candidates, and helped get them money and political support. The NOW political action committee and the National Abortion Rights Action League raised millions of dollars in 1982 on the strength of ERA, abortion, and fear-of-Reagan issues. The National Women's Education Fund held regional campaign technique seminars around the country. The Women's Campaign Fund and the National Women's Political Caucus raised more funds than in any previous years.

The amounts nevertheless paled compared to the money put into campaigns by conservative and New Right groups such as those controlled by Senator Helms. Women won more money and support from organized labor than in the past, but the enormous increase in business and industry PACs (political action committees) largely went to male candidates, with some notable exceptions such as Vucanovich, whose ties to Laxalt and top Republican party figures helped generate major donations from business and conservative groups.

Key questions for 1983–1984: how to strengthen women's PACs, stream-line and perhaps coordinate the resources of the diverse women's campaign lists, make further inroads into "regular" political funds, identify potentially winning contenders such as Harriett Woods and build her up with money and resources to scare off primary opponents—and how to marshal the most sophisticated polling and media resources, making the women candidates stronger against increasingly well-funded foes.

Reagan

Policies and Budget Cuts   With few exceptions, the Reagan administration in 1982 continued its efforts to reverse the government's historic role of advocating a broader role for women in society. It sought to dismantle or weaken almost totally the civil rights protections built up in recent decades to sustain and widen women's options. It not only all but abandoned its advocacy role on behalf of women and minorities, in many specific cases it took the lead in opposing such action.

The Justice Department's civil rights chief sought cases to take to the Supreme Court in hopes of outlawing affirmative action, and said class action suits no longer would be pursued; relief could be sought only for individuals able to prove the existence of discrimination damage and that it was inten-tional. The Secretary of Education worked to narrow the scope of Title IX, the law banning sex bias in education; a White House-orchestrated coup put conservatives in charge of the office they wanted abolished, the Women's Education Equity Act Program. The Labor Department limited probes of complaints about discrimination from government contractors and curtailed the use of proven remedial tools, back pay awards, and class action suits. The Equal Employment Opportunity Commission worked to water down regu-lations preventing sexual harassment. At the Defense Department, the Army reclassified more than half of its jobs as combat-related, thus putting them off limits to women; they initiated upper-body strength tests to screen out still more women.

A late 1982 report by Women Employed, a Chicago-based advocacy group, said the Reagan administration had combined budget cuts with policy changes in an assault on equal opportunity that threatened "to dismantle the entire federal enforcement apparatus" (Women Employed Institute 1982).

In an analysis of the Office of Federal Contract Compliance Programs (OFCCP), the Labor Department entity that oversees the 300,000 government contractors to monitor executive orders that ban sex or race bias, compliance review activity was at the lowest ebb since 1979, with only 56 percent of its own goals being met. Discrimination awards also were at low levels. Damage done to enforcement mechanisms put in place in the 1960s to eliminate job discrimination "will set back efforts toward that goal for years to come," Women Employed said (Women Employed Institute 1982).

Early in 1983 a federal judge reimposed timetables for action on the Labor and Education departments in dealing with complaints of sex, race, and handicapped discrimination. The order, by U.S. District Court Judge John H. Pratt, reaffirmed and stiffened a 1977 order in which timetables were set for dealing with discrimination complaints. The government had argued that these be lifted, after the Women's Equity Action League and other groups initiated contempt-of-court action against the government contending the agencies were not adhering to court-imposed schedules.

In addition to policy reversals, women were affected at all ranges in the income scale by Reagan budget cuts. Perhaps the most harm was done to poor and disadvantaged women who comprise 75 percent of the country's low-income population, a trend known as the feminization of poverty. By the end of 1982 major holes had been torn in the "safety net" of social welfare programs devised in recent years to help these women become self-sufficient and to care for their children. The Children's Defense Fund said early in 1983 that $12.5 billion had been cut from twenty key programs comprising the social safety net since 1981 or were proposed by Reagan for 1983 cuts (Rosenbaum and Weitz 1982). These ranged from child nutrition to maternal and child health, legal services, food stamps, foster care, education for the handicapped, and aid to families with dependent children. The 1981–1982 Reagan cuts in programs affecting low-income groups totaled 28 percent in real reductions. The Center for National Policy Review said the budget cuts and policy changes would return many social welfare programs to their 1950s status, although the needs and status of women are vastly different today (Pearce 1982).

The 1980 census showed dramatic changes in the status of poor and elderly women. In the decade of the 1970s, the number of women heading households doubled to 6.6 million, most of them poor. As the 1980s progressed, studies by the Labor Department and Congress proved that older women comprise the largest single bloc of low-income persons with an annual income of $4,757 in 1981 compared to $8,173 for men in the same over-65 age group. Two-thirds of the persons over the age of 75 are women. In this age group, 70 percent of the men are married but women are far more economically vulnerable with only 22 percent married.

Here are capsules of some budget cuts in social welfare areas:

1. Every state reduced Medicaid funding due to cutbacks of $1 billion a year from the federal government. Most states curtailed both coverage and services provided, and nearly 700,000 children lost Medicaid coverage when their families were terminated from the Aid to Families with Dependent Children (AFDC) program due to budget cuts.
2. $2 billion a year was cut from the food stamp program, with 1 million recipients cut off and benefits reduced for 20 million.
3. Most states cut back maternal and child health block grants after federal budget cuts, causing 725,000 persons (including 64 percent who were children or women of childbearing age) to be culled from community health centers.
4. 300,000 federally supported public service jobs were eliminated; half of the jobs had gone to women.

5. Child nutrition programs were cut 30 percent, or $1.5 billion, with 3 million fewer children receiving lunches at the school lunch programs and 350,000 fewer low-income children receiving school breakfasts.

6. 365,000 families were terminated from the AFDC program and benefits were reduced for another 260,000 families. In 36 states, AFDC mothers with three children earning as little as $5,000 a year lost benefits after their fourth month on the job.

7. Other cuts in programs affecting most women came in legal services, supplemental nutrition for pregnant women and their infants, community health services, preventive health programs, social services for low-income families, subsidized low-income housing, child care for low-income working mothers, job training for displaced homemakers and teenage single mothers, and energy assistance for low-income households.

Budget cuts took their toll in employment, too. In the federal government, women suffer twice the number of layoffs compared to their composition in the federal workforce.

Budget cuts also were targeted to eliminate programs or functions, sometimes with ideology rather than fiscal concerns the uppermost consideration. This was true of reductions in civil rights enforcement agencies in the half-dozen federal bodies. At the Education Department, for instance, a cutback in civil rights personnel reflected a shift "from a compliance effort to technical assistance," an internal memo showed.

Budget cuts also eliminated federal funds to enable government contractors to hire women as trainees in nontraditional fields such as construction; without the federal subsidies, nearly all trainee and entry-level programs ended. Another Labor Department program to require a minimum of 6.9 percent women in construction jobs also was under attack from within. After unsuccessfully trying to scuttle the program, the administration kept the current 6.9 percent target, but said contractors could hire women only for trainee and helper job slots and count them toward the total, with no need to integrate them into the more lucrative skilled trades. This proposal was withdrawn before the elections but was put forth again in mid-1983.

Another Reagan administration action also was aimed at lifting sex-discrimination compliance burdens from colleges and universities. Under pressure from conservative groups that had expected Reagan to abolish the Department of Education as he promised during the campaign, the administration moved to curtail application of Title IX. It attempted to exempt faculty personnel decisions from the scope of the law (but the Supreme Court disagreed in an early 1982 ruling). It then moved to argue that Title IX applied only to specific programs receiving federal funds; if a college received federal student loans, this did not mean the entire college activities were scrutinized under the law. When a federal district court in Richmond ruled in 1982 that Title IX did not cover intercollegiate athletics programs receiving no "earmarked" federal funds, the Justice Department refused to appeal the adverse ruling. This decision overruled advice from officials heading two sections in Justice's civil rights branch and from the U.S. Civil Rights Commission, as well as from private civil rights groups. The Supreme Court will decide the scope of Title IX in a ruling on a related case in 1983.

The Justice Department also intervened in two cases testing whether affirmative action under court-ordered hiring plans can abrogate traditional protection of seniority. The recession's layoffs forced increasing tests of the last-hired, first-fired principle, which has divided the labor and to a lesser extent the civil rights communities. The Justice Department sided with white policemen in New Orleans and white firefighters and police in Boston who challenged court-ordered minority plans that led to whites being laid off while less senior minorities were retained during job cutbacks.

In repeated instances, the Reagan administration pursued policies to curtail any funds that could encourage abortions or even use of birth control devices.

The Office of Personnel Management, directed by New Right activist Donald Devine, singlehandedly eliminated abortion coverage from insurance plans for federal workers (one union sued successfully to reinstate the coverage for their members, but the ban applied to 95 percent of all employees). He worked to purge most new groups from the federal charitable fund-raising drive, with Planned Parenthood being a specific target.

At the Department of Health and Human Services (DHHS), family planning funds were cut sharply and policies were adopted to prohibit centers such as those sponsored by Planned Parenthood from taking federal funds if they also performed abortions. A new rule proposed late in 1982 would preclude lobbying by groups that receive federal funds or by those that are in the federal fund-raising campaign.

Two policies came under political and legal fire that dealt with birth control and with government intervention in parental and medical decisions on deformed newborn infants.

Under the supervision of antiabortion leaders, DHHS proposed in early 1982 to require federally funded family planning centers to notify in writing parents of girls under eighteen (but not boys) for whom they prescribed birth control pills or devices. The so-called squeal rule was protested by more than 100,000 groups and individuals during the comment period, many of whom said it would scare teenagers away from the clinics but not away from sex—and ultimate pregnancy. Despite the controversy, and with Reagan's fervent support, the parental notification rule was put into effect early in 1983, days after the nomination of former Representative Heckler as DHHS secretary, who as a congresswoman had been among those objecting to the rule. Two federal judges blocked the rule from being enforced after Planned Parenthood and other groups filed suit; a full legal airing of the issue is due in 1983.

The second controversial intrusion came after an outcry in reaction to parents' decisions, backed up by doctors, in a Bloomington, Indiana hospital to not feed an infant born with severe mental and physical deformities. Antiabortion groups successfully prodded the administration into approving rules against "infanticides" similar to the Bloomington incident. This was protested by hospitals and medical professionals as an unwarranted intrusion by the government into areas where it has no expertise.

Perhaps no policy shift as graphically illustrates the administration's attitude toward women's role as the turnaround in the Defense Department, where the Department of the Army moved to bar women from three-fourths of all jobs, including work as carpenters, masons, electricians, and engineers. In revealing the actions, the Army cited a major study that justified such sweeping moves, which it said would reduce attrition among women because they now were unhappy in jobs beyond their competence. Months later, when challenged by the Defense Advisory Committee on Women in the Services (DACOWITS), the Army acknowledged it had no study to back up its claims that prompted the changes. Women veterans charged that the Army research was a "snow job," aimed at hiding other motives that could include a return to the abandoned separate-sex Women's Army Corps. Air Force Major General Jeanne Holm, the highest-ranked military woman when she retired and author of a major book on women in the armed services, said the Army action had caused severe morale problems among women soldiers who feared the military would make them scapegoats for lagging military performance.

Starting last summer, the Army also resegregated women and men in basic training, contending that "physiological differences" make integrated training impractical, thus reversing a four-year pattern. The Women's Equity Action League wrote Defense Secretary Casper Weinberger late in 1982 that the goal appeared to have been "to limit the role of women" and then to devise data to justify their decision. The New Right military leaders applauded the sharp curtailment of Army roles for women, however. It had been one of their key goals when Reagan took office.

In urging the new Reagan administration to curtail women in the Army, retired General Andrew J. Gatsis said that a strong defense is more than weaponry: "The most essential ingredients are esprit de corps, male-to-male bonding, high morale, strong discipline and the ability for people to redeploy and perform efficiently on the job. These are the basic elements that make a fighting unit. Without them, you lose. And these are the components the women's movement tends to destroy" (Gatsis 1982).

Appointments   As President Reagan's pollster showed evidence of continuing erosion in his support among women, a panel of senior White House officials was created to try and correct the "women's problem," with then-White House assistant for public liaison Elizabeth Dole in charge.

One significant change was the shift of Reagan's long-time personal secretary Helene Von Damm to become chief of personnel in mid-1982. For the first time, lists of desired appointees for specific jobs were rejected by the personnel office unless women were included in the pool. Von Damm, a native of Austria who has worked for Reagan since he was governor of California, thus put muscle behind Reagan's rhetoric about wanting to appoint women to top policy positions.

Although Reagan frequently claimed he had named more women to key jobs than any of his predecessors, his figures proved misleading. No women headed cabinet-rank agencies, nor were there any women as deputy secretaries or general counsels during his first two years in office, key management positions in which many women made their mark during the Carter administration. Reagan's appointees often were to part-time boards or to lower-ranked policy positions. Taken as a whole, his women appointees did not carry the weight of responsibilities and clout equal to those in the Carter administration.

While Von Damm set about to increase women appointees, her efforts did not bear fruit immediately, partly because there were no cabinet vacancies. When two occurred in early 1983, Reagan filled them with two veteran Republican moderates, Elizabeth Dole and former Representative Heckler. They were the first well-known GOP feminists to be included in his administration; virtually all other top contenders had been vetoed by conservatives advising Reagan or lobbying him from the outside.

The cross-fire between the conservative and moderate wings of the Republican party intensified in 1982, leading to some notable dismissals of entire women's advisory panels to be replaced by New Right ideologues. By the end of 1982, these conservatives had been put in charge of major segments of the Department of Education and the Department of Health and Human Services, supervising programs that ranged from sex equity in education to family planning and teenage pregnancy programs.

One notable skirmish of 1982 came in April, soon after the *Conservative Digest* put at the top of a must-go list of "radicals" a career federal executive in charge of the Women's Education Equity Act Program (WEEAP). The magazine said Leslie Wolfe was a "radical feminist," said she had turned the program "into a money machine for a network of openly radical feminists" and that she was "funding hard-Left women's groups," among them the University of Virginia, New Mexico State University, the Organization of Chinese-American Women, and Planned Parenthood (How Washington funds the left 1982).

Within days, Wolfe had been dethroned as the magazine wished, with her transfer coinciding with the deadline for grant applications for upcoming funds under the $6 million program that helps knock down sex barriers.

Soon afterward, the White House engineered a conservative takeover of the National Advisory Council on Women's Educational Equity and the dismissal of its executive director, Joy Simonson. She was replaced by Rosemary Thomson, a protégée of Phyllis Schlafly at the Eagle Forum headquarters in Illinois. Thomson had testified before Congress in favor of discontinuing the $6 million WEEAP, had recently joined in Schlafly's newest effort to ban certain objectionable books from schools and public libraries, and had been a substitute teacher and author of two books published by herself and a Christian publishing house. Holly Knox, executive director of the Project on Equal Education Rights that monitors compliance with sex equity laws, called the Thomson appointment "the most direct subversion of the law" next to killing the program, which Reagan had tried twice to do but which Congress had blocked.

The conservative coup at WEEAP caused such a political furor, with Simonson becoming a Democratic campaign draw in contested congressional races, that presidential assistant Wendy Borcherdt who carried it out was pushed out of the White House. Borcherdt, a former major fund raiser for Reagan in California, subsequently was appointed a deputy undersecretary in the Department of Education, drawing opposition from many normally non-political groups such as the American Association of University Women and the American Association of School Administrators, which broke a 115-year record to ask that she be defeated.

Similar replacements of advisory councils in vocational education programs also were made during 1982 with new members reflecting Reagan's views. (Reagan tried unsuccessfully for two years to eliminate the sex equity mandate of the voc. ed. program.)

In the Department of Health and Human Services, Marjory E. Mecklenburg, antiabortion leader and author of the squeal rule, was promoted in late 1982 to take charge of family planning and teenage pregnancy issues as deputy assistant secretary. At a family planning conference in early 1983 where she was featured speaker, she raised eyebrows with her call for increased use of "natural family planning methods," a modified form of the rhythm method of birth control.

Shortly before the 1982 elections, Reagan chose the wife of a conservative senator to become his liaison for women. Dolores "Dee" Jepsen, an antiabortion activist who had not worked previously, soon found herself on the firing line. In defending Reagan's jobs bill from criticism that the focus on construction and roadbuilding virtually eliminated prospects for the jobs bill to help women, she said wives would be helped when their unemployed husbands went back to work. She denied that the gender gap existed.

The bulk of Reagan's appointees to head regulatory agencies or functions came from business and industry, many times from the sectors they then would supervise. At the Equal Employment Opportunity Commission (EEOC), Michael Connally was named general counsel in 1981 but was eased out in late 1982, partly due to his usurpation of policy-making authority from the commission on such controversial issues as ending class action investigations. Connally had been on the legal staff at General Motors, which has been mired in major litigation with EEOC for years.

Reagan was forced to withdraw nominations of three persons to head the EEOC or be a member of the U.S. Commission on Civil Rights after their views proved to conflict with the mandate of the job. The future trend of appointments was unclear. The conservative backlash to the appointment of Heckler was second only to that after Reagan's rushed-up nomination in 1981 of Sandra Day O'Connor as first woman on the Supreme Court.

Schlafly remained clearly on the outside of the Reagan inner circle, despite placement of many of her allies in government posts. Antiabortion activists failed to persuade Reagan to fire a newly named director of the

National Institutes of Health, Dr. James Wyngaarden, after he disagreed with their (and Reagan's) views on outlawing amniocentesis and other prenatal tests to detect fetal abnormalities that could lead to decisions to abort.

The 1984 election pressures could prove an influential factor, with fear of the gender gap remaining high. Kathy Wilson, chair of the National Women's Political Caucus, heralded Heckler's appointment to head DHHS by saying, "I think they are finally beginning to realize over at the White House that it is not real wise to run the country like a men's club. We feel her appointment has given us another foot in the door of the administration which for two years was closed."

Congressional Action

The interests of women's rights activists and New Right conservatives collided again in Congress in 1982. The high point was the Senate showdown over several core conservative issues: banning abortion and requiring school prayer. The conservatives' loss on both proposed constitutional amendments may have marked a turning point in the power of the New Right, which suffered further blows in the 1982 elections.

As in 1981, the women's rights and civil rights activists wasted little time in trying to pass new legislation. Theirs was a defensive war against Reagan budget cuts and against regulatory changes that would dilute the structures of civil rights enforcement mechanisms within the federal government.

At the urging of the Congressional Caucus on Women's Issues, and with the backing of New Right GOP Senator Roger W. Jepsen of Iowa (a leader in the "profamily" movement), Congress overruled the court on the *McCarty* v. *McCarty* ruling. It ordered that states consider military retirement pay as joint marital property if the marriage had endured at least ten years. Medical care was extended to former spouses whose marriage had lasted twenty years while the military member was on active duty.

The Former Military Spouse Protection Act was the second major segment enacted from the Economic Equity Act introduced in 1981 by a bipartisan group of women's rights advocates. In 1981 similar pension rights were guaranteed for former spouses of foreign service officers.

Hearings continued in 1982 on a third key part of the Economic Equity Act: to ban discrimination in insurance rates. Life insurance companies routinely charge women more in monthly payments but pay them less in retirement benefits because they live longer than men, contending that the total amounts equal out in the end. Women's rights advocates argue that this violates the law: that blacks live shorter life spans on the average than do whites, but that the law would not sanction separate pay-out systems based on that generalization.

The Senate Commerce Committee approved the insurance equity bill in 1982, setting the stage for 1983 when the Supreme Court accepted a key case brought by Nathalie Norris of Arizona. Norris, a mother of three, took out a deferred annuity plan at work and put $100 a month into it—but sued the state, her employer, when she discovered that she would be paid $33.95 a month less than male colleagues putting an equal amount into the pension fund. Shortly before the court heard arguments on the Norris gender-based insurance case, the Economic Equity Act was reintroduced for the third time.

The bulk of the year, however, was spent trying to dramatize the impact of Reagan budget cuts to rally the grass roots and congressional advocates to blunt those cuts when possible in social welfare areas where they were concentrated. The same pressure was applied to ward off Reagan administration attempts to eliminate special programs for women, such as the Women's Education Equity Act Program (WEEAP) in the Department of Health and Human Services, the sex equity mandates in the Vocational Education Act in the Department of Education, and the governmentwide system of flex-time, which had been of most help to working mothers. The WEEAP was salvaged for a second year, but with major budget cuts. The sex-equity mandates of vocational education (which required states to teach girls more than sewing and cooking, to prepare them for the real world along with the high school boys) were kept intact for another year after a congressional showdown, and flex-time was extended for three years despite Reagan's opposition. Other programs fell victim, including a special program in the Small Business Administration that had helped women entrepreneurs get on their feet. Pilot programs in the Women's Bureau and in other entities of the Department of Labor also were ended, although in the weeks before the 1982 elections many minuscule programs were launched to help women prison inmates and single women heading households.

With the phase-out of the government's most elaborate public service jobs bill, the Comprehensive Education and Training Act, that at its height had provided a federal underpinning for several million low-income workers (half of them women), the Reagan administration put in place a jobs bill late in 1982 that essentially would speed up existing heavy construction work already authorized for years in the future. Virtually no women were likely to be hired for these jobs, especially since the Reagan administration had abdicated the federal role of trying to push open the employment door for women in nontraditional jobs such as bridge building and road repair. The Congressional Caucus on Women's Issues belatedly made that point as the jobs bill was rushing through Congress. It made a priority for the next jobs bill in 1983 to ensure that women also shared in the federal job-creating program.

Other major congressional hearings included the Joint Economic Committee examination of budget and regulatory cuts on women's economic standing; on the impact of cuts in nutrition supplements for pregnant women and for low-income mothers with newborns; the impact of alcohol on pregnancy; the value of a federal jobs program for the elderly; and the pattern of layoffs in the federal government that showed women and minorities were put off the payroll at nearly twice the rate of their work participation.

Congress wrote into tax laws for the first time a provision for pension benefits for homemakers with no independent income, giving a household head the right to set aside up to $2,000 a year not just for his or her own Independent Retirement Account (IRA), but the tax exemption of up to $2,000 if an IRA was set up for a nonworking spouse.

There was no movement on the proposed Family Protection Act with its suggested censorship of textbooks and its mandate that schools return to teaching "traditional" family values. Senator Orrin G. Hatch (R-Utah) dropped plans to weaken Title IX significantly after women in his home state protested during his tight reelection campaign. He also did not push his proposed constitutional amendment to ban affirmative action.

Abortion   The fight over abortion rights was a major issue in 1982, both in the courts and in Congress, as well as in many election skirmishes. Antiabortion activists who took major credit for electing Reagan two years earlier had been put off by the White House until Reagan could put his economic program in place. When the economy remained a major preoccupation in 1982, they insisted that their social issues still should be front and center, as Reagan and the GOP Senate leaders had promised.

The antiabortion movement was divided internally, however, about the form their attempt should take to overturn the 1973 Supreme Court ruling that said women had a legal right to abortion. The historic *Roe* v. *Wade* decision limited states' rights to regulate abortion to the later months of pregnancy and only in ways that are "reasonably related to maternal health." In the years after the Court ruling, the Census Bureau and the Alan Guttmacher Institute said the number of abortions performed annually had more than doubled, from the 1973 total of 744,600 abortions to 1.55 million in 1980, making it one of the nation's most commonly performed surgical procedures.

Political action increased on both sides of the issue. The right-to-life lobby has held annual marches on Washington since the 1973 ruling, with the peak being a 100,000-strong march in 1980. They drew 50,000 demonstrators in 1982 on the eve of what they thought would be major legislative victories in the Senate. Months after the Senate defeats, the tenth-anniversary march on January 22, 1983, drew only 26,000 participants.

In August of 1982 an antiabortion group called the Army of God kidnapped the owner of an Alton, Illinois abortion clinic and held him and his wife captive for eight days. The kidnappers, who were disavowed by national antiabortion leaders, later were convicted.

Militant antiabortion groups took an increasingly active role in the 1982 elections but found that the overwhelming preoccupation with economic issues diluted their single-issue influence. Noting that thirteen million abortions had been performed in the decade since the Supreme Court ruling, they began to compare abortions to killings during the Nazi Germany Holocaust against Jews.

Antiabortion forces gained considerable political ground within the Reagan administration in 1982, especially at the Department of Health and Human Resources and at the Office of Personnel Management.

Prochoice forces rallied the grass roots with new appeals for funds and political support using personally worded direct-mail letters from such luminaries as Katharine Hepburn, urging support for Planned Parenthood in their battle with the Reagan administration. The National Abortion Rights Action League formed dozens of state-issue chapters to build support for potential constitutional amendments.

The conservatives' pressure for constitutional bans on abortion did not end with the 1982 battles, which they lost. But their tactics—especially the overriding goal of stripping lower courts as well as the Supreme Court of any abortion scrutiny jurisdiction—alienated many erstwhile supporters, including those within the hierarchy of the Catholic Church. As a result, the 1982 showdowns may have been the pivotal test.

The U.S. Catholic Conference of Bishops and the National Right-to-Life Committee defined human life as beginning at the moment of conception, and they coalesced behind Hatch's proposed amendment as the most workable option, as it would let states legislate antiabortion restrictions. The Senate vote ultimately came, however, on the competing measure by Senator Helms, whose "human life statute" would strip the courts of all jurisdiction on abortion by overturning the 1973 ruling. Helms put his amendment as a rider onto the measure raising the federal government's debt limit: a must-pass measure or the government would have to halt work. After a surprise and prolonged filibuster by Senator Packwood, the Senate voted 47 to 46 to table the Helms amendment. Subsequent debate of the Hatch amendment ended when the Utah Republican withdrew it for lack of votes.

Early in 1983, Senator Thomas F. Eagleton (D-Mo.) proposed a ten-word constitutional amendment that would state: "A right to abortion is not secured by the Constitution," and return the legal situation to the pre-1973 Supreme Court situation where most states outlawed abortions.

The abortion issue became so divisive that early in 1983 the legislative director of the national right-to-life lobby, Douglas Johnson, contended in a private memo to his associates that Helms had become so unpopular as a result of his antiabortion leadership that he no longer could function effectively as chief strategist, and might be in danger of losing his 1984 reelection fight as well. When the memo became public, Johnson's superiors apologized and said his statements did not represent their views.

The court fights on the abortion issue also intensified during 1982. For the first time since its 1973 landmark decision, the Supreme Court reviewed five state cases that would substantially narrow the scope of the previous ruling. Cases tested the validity of laws in Missouri and Virginia and in Akron, Ohio and went to the core of how much power state and local governments retain to regulate abortion: can they require that all abortions after the first three months be performed in a hospital (where costs averaged $850 to $900 compared to the clinic cost of $350 to $400); may authorities spell out detailed warnings that doctors must give women seeking abortions as part of obtaining the legally necessary "informed consent"? The Reagan administration filed a friend-of-the-court brief urging the Supreme Court to uphold these restrictions.

In response to conservative pressure, Reagan had spoken out with increasing regularity on the issue. After 16,500 fetuses and embryos were discovered in a huge storage container outside of what had been an abortion center in Los Angeles, he suggested holding a memorial service for the fetuses, saying, "On such an occasion we must strengthen our resolve to end this national tragedy."

Pressures were also telling at the Supreme Court. After the abortion hearings late in 1982, Justice Harry A. Blackmun gave an unusual interview to Daniel Schorr of the Cable News Network, saying he had been pilloried as a "butcher" and "murderer" for his original 1973 ruling. He said: "You can think of any name to call someone and I have been called it. Butcher of Dachau, murderer, Pontius Pilate, King Herod, you name it. . . . Well of course, it hurt at first. It doesn't hurt so much anymore because I think one's hide gets a little, a little thick to use that old phrase. On the other hand, I like to know what people are thinking. And the fact that 75 percent of the correspondence was critical doesn't mean that represents 75 percent of the people."

Legal Aspects

Despite a dramatic reversal by the federal government away from the historic advocacy role on behalf of women and minorities, women continued to break new legal ground in 1982.

Generally, courts supported women in their efforts to knock down barriers to sex-segregated occupations despite a backlash during the hard economic times from white males. Back pay and punitive damages to remedy past workplace discrimination were at historic levels, with the largest settlement to date coming in a $52 million ruling against Northwest Airlines for paying stewardesses less than stewards, and holding them to more rigid weight and dress restrictions. Courts upheld the arrival of eleven women as firefighters in New York City, although the union fought them down to the swearing-in ceremony itself, where Mayor Ed Koch took note of the occasion by saying, "Someday one of the women or men who are graduating today may be called on to carry a 206-pound mayor out of a burning window—and what's important is that you've all demonstrated that you're equal to the task."

Society's changing attitudes about women continued to be reflected in rulings that included action on protests about skimpy attire required on the job, sexual harassment complaints against top athletes on campus, and outcries against judges who took rape or sexual abuse lightly. When a New Jersey Superior court judge freed a 565-pound rapist for health reasons, the national furor that resulted included calls for the judge's imprisonment. The rapist was returned to jail. A recall effort was launched, with national publicity, against Wisconsin Circuit Judge William Reinecke after he said a five-year-old victim of sexual assault was "sexually promiscuous." The judge apologized, in effect, and was reelected. A NAACP protest came after Mayor D. C. Master of Charles Town, West Virginia, suggested that low-income mothers who undergo repeated abortions be "spayed."

Another major Supreme Court case in 1982 ruled that men could not be barred from women-only nursing schools in a suit challenging the Mississippi University for Women nursing school policies. The Court, in the first major sex discrimination opinion written by Justice Sandra Day O'Connor, applied a heightened standard of scrutiny to the sex-bias case. It said the university did not prove that its gender-based classification for the nursing school showed "exceedingly persuasive justification" and, in an argument that closely tracked that filed by a coalition of women's groups in a friend-of-the-court brief, warned against "the mechanical application of traditional, often inaccurate assumptions about the proper roles of men and women." Limiting admissions to women could hurt rather than help them because it "perpetuated the stereotyped view of nursing as an exclusively women's job" where wages have been depressed.

In other action, the Supreme Court threw out a case brought by ERA supporters that Missouri's attorney general tried to damage "the entire women's movement" by a suit challenging the economic boycott of unratified states. It dismissed as moot an Idaho ruling that ERA ratification procedures were unconstitutional because they did not permit state legislatures to rescind their approvals. The Court also ruled that employers who have discriminated against job applicants can minimize their liability from sex-bias suits by making belated job offers, and it broadened the time period for unwed mothers to sue purported fathers for child support.

A significant appeals court ruling was delivered on the sensitive issue of whether companies can bar women—but not men—from jobs where products being manufactured could be harmful to their reproductive capacity. The Olin Corporation had restricted women's access to jobs requiring contact with toxic substances it said could endanger fetuses. Women argued that growing medical evidence showed that men's reproductive organs also were affected by the work, but that only women were screened out of the high-paying chemical plant jobs. The Fourth U.S. Circuit Court of Appeals said the employer must prove that the risks to unborn children of women workers make the restrictions necessary, returning the case for another hearing.

A growing family-law issue concerns divorce cases where the woman (in virtually all cases) put her husband through school and then was divorced by him. The question was whether or not she could claim a portion of his future earnings. Courts were divided on the issue in 1982. In California, the Fourth District Court of Appeals initially said that Janet Sullivan was entitled to a share of the lucrative earnings her doctor-husband could expect in the decades to come because she put him through medical school. Eight months later it reversed itself and said professional training "is not property" and therefore is not divisable if the marriage dissolves. In New Jersey, the state supreme court skirted the issue of whether the degree itself represented dividable tangible "property," but said three former wives could claim "reimbursement alimony" if educational support had been given in expectation of sharing future benefits.

Also in New Jersey, the attorney general late in 1982 ordered the state's Sports and Exposition Authority to require the New York Giants to admit women sports reporters to comply with "a constitutional mandate to offer male and female reporters equal access to information." The *New York Daily News* had sued to secure equal access to locker rooms for its female reporter, who had been forced to wait outside for up to an hour while male reporters were allowed inside dressing rooms to interview players immediately after the games. The Giants complied—by closing locker rooms to all reporters. Basketball, football, and hockey leagues all have equalized access to coaches and players for women and men reporters in recent years, under legal pressure.

Comparable Worth and Pay Equity   Pay equity became a prominent legal and political issue in 1982. The term, an umbrella phrase that goes beyond the concept of "equal pay for work of comparable value," became more generally understood. Hearings were held on the issue in Congress to spotlight the still-prevalent pattern: that pay is far less for jobs in fields dominated by women than for male-dominated fields, even when skills or management tools are higher than those required for the men's jobs.

The Department of Labor's Bureau of Labor Statistics compiled the most recent statistics on the average wages paid in sex-segregated occupations that women's groups said proved their contention: in fields where women dominate such as nursing or clericals or waitress, the wages are low; in fields where there are few women, wages are higher even when adjusted for skills and education (Table 1).

The Minnesota legislature approved the most sweeping wage-adjustment action to date, using data gathered by the Council on the Economic Status of Women to order state budgets earmarked to fund a realignment of wages. A list of "underpaid (job) classes" was ordered drawn up for the legislature's action in 1983.

In Boston, an employers group signed a consent decree denying it had violated antitrust laws against wage-fixing for clerical workers, but agreeing that members of the Boston Survey Group no longer would share detailed data on individual wages. The women's advocacy group Nine to Five had instigated the wage-fixing probe, which the state attorney general subsequently pursued.

The Hawaii and Kentucky legislatures ordered studies of how the comparable worth premise would affect state workers. In New York, a study funded by the state and by the American Federation of State, County, and Municipal Employees (AFSCME) was to contrast wages and promotion options for women-dominated and minority-dominated fields with those dominated by white males. The results were due in early 1983.

AFSCME, which is using the pay equity issue to recruit women members, is the only union actually filing suit. It filed charges against the state of

Table 1

Average Wages in Sex-Segregated Occupations

Occupation	Average Annual Salary	Percentage in Occupation Who Are Women
Secretary	$12,000	99
Sewer/stitcher	8,200	97
Practical nurse	11,800	97
Pre-kindergarten and kindergarten teacher	13,600	97
Registered nurse	17,300	96
Private household worker	5,600	95
Lodging cleaner	7,400	95
Bank teller	9,800	94
Bookkeeper	11,800	91
Child-care worker	7,900	87
Waiter/waitress	7,800	85
Cashier	8,700	85
Hairdresser	9,300	85
Librarian	16,600	85
Nursing aide/orderly	9,100	84
Elementary school teacher	16,700	82
Health technician/technologist	15,000	69
Social worker	16,100	61
Retail sales clerk	9,300	60
Secondary school teacher	18,300	49
Stock clerk	13,700	34
College and university teacher	23,100	29
Computer specialist	23,600	26
Pharmacist	24,100	26
Shipping and receiving clerk	12,800	22
Stock and bond sales agent	27,800	17
Janitor	11,400	15
Sales representative	15,000	12
Mail carrier	21,100	12
Taxicab driver	12,500	7
Butcher/meat cutter	16,400	7
Police	18,900	5
Welder	17,400	5
Engineer	28,100	5
Truck driver	16,300	2
Plumber	21,000	0
Airplane pilot	27,600	0

Source: U.S. Dept. of Labor, Bureau of Labor Statistics, March 1982.

Washington in mid-1982, after the state failed to remedy the pay inequities discovered with the first study in 1974 and confirmed with each subsequent study. It also has complaints against the cities of Philadelphia, Los Angeles, and Chicago and the states of Connecticut, Wisconsin, and Hawaii.

As the tenth anniversary of the Equal Pay Act approached in mid-1983, the Women's Legal Defense Fund launched a pay equity educational campaign with radio spots dramatizing why it "pays to be a man"—literally, with women earning fifty-nine cents for every dollar earned by men. An early 1983 Census Bureau report on lifetime earnings projected for today's high school and college graduates provided further proof: men can expect to earn nearly double that of women during their lifetime.

Single-Sex Clubs   President Reagan, Vice President Bush, and top cabinet secretaries continued to patronize male-only clubs. Secretary of State Schultz took visiting heads of state, for instance, to the Bohemian Club in San Francisco where he, Reagan, Bush, Defense Secretary Casper Weinberger, and Attorney General William French Smith are members. Reagan and cabinet secretaries attended the male-only banquet at the Alfalfa Club in Washington. At the Washington branch of the English-Speaking Union, women members were excluded in 1982 from a men's lunch to hear a speech from diplomat Charles Yost. At a political barbeque near Fort Worth, Texas last year, the male-only sponsoring club invited statewide candidates to a forum, but barred women candidates, including Ann Richards, who ultimately led the overall Democratic slate in votes in her successful bid for state treasurer.

There were no major changes in memberships at male-only clubs, but legal efforts against their policies intensified. The Minnesota Supreme Court ruled that the Jaycees violated the state ban on sex discrimination by denying full membership to women, because they operate as a public business without the constitutional protection of the "right to associate" of genuinely private groups. They appealed the ruling to the circuit court. The Jaycees also remained locked in legal battle in Massachusetts, where the state's Commission Against Discrimination ruled against their male-only policy in 1981 and the state supreme court heard the appeal in 1982. The Jaycees had fostered pilot projects allowing local chapters to admit women as full members in the late 1970s, but then rescinded that authority and have threatened local chapters with expulsion from the international group if they keep their women members, who number 500 of the 1,800 members in Massachusetts.

The American Bar Association, which had gone on record condemning exclusionary policies at private clubs that function as major business conduits for members, reversed its stand in 1982 after vigorous lobbying by private-club owners. The outgoing Carter Administration had put into effect a so-called country club regulation that would have disallowed business deductions for discriminatory private clubs patronized by the 300,000 government contractors. The regulation was revoked by the incoming Reagan administration before it could take effect.

By year's end, efforts were being mounted in Maryland to attack the male-only country club bastions through another route: by revoking its tax-exempt status. The elite Burning Tree Country Club in a Maryland suburb of Washington and patronized by most politicians and presidents, pays only

$13,000 of the $165,000 in taxes that it would be assessed if it had no tax exemption (granted for providing "open space" in the Washington area).

Another simmering dispute on single-sex clubs broke into the pages of the *New York Times* late in 1982 during a drive to drop the male-only membership at the 1,900-member Century Club in New York City. Former Undersecretary of State George W. Ball insisted the club was "a male haven for pleasant, if not always cosmic, communion among authors, artists and amateurs." An editorial, written in the form of a letter to the Centurians, contended that the club was not so much a forum for camaraderie as for business, and asked, "Do we pose that much of a threat to male bonding or are we really a threat to—please be honest, gentlemen—a status quo that has served you very well?"

Legal Appointments   By the end of two years, President Reagan had made eighty-nine appointments to lifetime federal judgeships. All but seven were white males. Women, black, and Hispanic groups protested the termination of structures used by President Carter to help him find nominees for appeals judges and district judges. Reagan officials said that process reduced the quality of appointees. The women and minorities retorted that the return to "business as usual" has shut them out.

Women Presently Serving on the Federal Bench

Key (presidential appointment): * Reagan, † Carter, ‡ Ford, / Nixon, // Johnson

* Sandra O'Connor (Supreme Court)	† Patricia Wald (D.C.Cir)
† Betty Fletcher (9th Cir)	† Ann Aldrich (N.D. OH)
† Ruth B. Ginsburg (D.C.Cir)	† Susan Black (M.D. FL)
† Amalya Kearse (2d Cir)	† Patricia Boyle (E.D. MI)
†/ Cornelia Kennedy (6th Cir)	† Ellen Burns (D. CT)
† Phyllis Kravitch (5th Cir)	† Carmen Cerezo (D. PR)
† Dorothy Nelson (9th Cir)	† Barbara Crabb (W.D. WI)
† Carolyn Randall (5th Cir)	† Orinda Evans (N.D. GA)
† Mary Schroeder (9th Cir)	† Helen Frye (D. OR)
† Stephanie Seymour (10th Cir)	† Susan Getzendanner (N.D. IL)
† Dolores Sloviter (3rd Cir)	† Joyce Green (D. D.C.)
// June Green (D. D.C.)	† Mariana Pfaelzer (C.D. CA)
* Cynthia Hall (C.D. CA)	† Sylvia Rambo (M.D. PA)
† Norma Johnson (D. D.C.)	‡ Mary Anne Richey (D. AZ)
† Shirley Jones (D. MD)	† MaryLou Robinson (N.D. TX)
† Judy Keep (S.D. CA)	† Barbara Rothstein (W.D. WA)
* Elizabeth Kovachevich (M.D. FL)	† Elsijane Roy (E&W D. AR)
* Shirley Kram (S.D. NY)	* Pamela Rymer (C.D. CA)
* Carol Los Mansmann (W.D. PA)	† Norma Shapiro (E.D. PA)
† Mary Lowe (S.D. NY)	† Anna Taylor (E.D. MI)
† Consuelo Marshall (D.C. CA)	† Anne Thompson (D. NJ)
† Gabrielle McDonald (S.D. TX)	† Zita Weinshienk (D. CO)
// Constance Motley (S.D. NY)	† Veronica Wicker (E.D. LA)
† Diana Murphy (D. MN)	† Rya Zobel (D. MA)
† Marilyn Patel (N.D. CA)	† Helen Nies (Ct. of Appeals for the Fed. Cir.)

Source: National Women's Political Caucus, March 15, 1983.

State Courts

Women on the Highest Court in the State

Shirley Abrahamson	Wisconsin Supreme Court
Ruth I. Abrams	Massachusetts Supreme Judicial Court
Rose Elizabeth Bird	California Supreme Court
Mary S. Coleman	Michigan Supreme Court (Chief Judge)
M. Jeanne Coyne	Minnesota Supreme Court
Rita C. Davidson	Maryland Court of Appeals
Carolyn Dimmick	Washington Supreme Court
Jean Dubofsky	Colorado Supreme Court
Christine Durham	Utah Supreme Court
Marie Garibaldi	New Jersey Supreme Court
Catherine B. Kelly	District of Columbia Court of Appeals
Blanche Krupansky	Ohio Supreme Court
Julia Cooper Mack	District of Columbia Court of Appeals
Kay E. McFarland	Kansas Supreme Court
Florence Murray	Rhode Island Supreme Court
Ellen A. Peters	Connecticut Supreme Court
Lenore Prather	Mississippi Supreme Court
Betty Roberts	Oregon Supreme Court
Susie Sharp	North Carolina Supreme Court
Janie L. Shores	Alabama Supreme Court
Rosalie Wahl	Minnesota Supreme Court
Alma Wilson	Oklahoma Supreme Court

Two-thirds of the states still do not have a woman on their highest court.

There are approximately 700 women judges (in positions requiring a law degree) in the United States.

Source: National Women's Political Caucus March 15, 1983.

Of Reagan's nineteen appointments to federal appeals courts, none was a woman. Of the sixty-nine appointees to federal district courts, three went to women. In 1982 his appointments included two women among the forty-eight selected.

Carter had made twelve appointments to the appeals courts and fifty-two to district courts, including six women, during his first two years in office. The passage of the 1978 Omnibus Judgeship Act gave him 152 new federal judgeships to fill. By the end of his four years, he had named forty women (and thirty-eight blacks and sixteen Hispanics) to the federal bench—more than any other president.

Reagan's most noted appointee, Sandra Day O'Connor to be the first woman on the Supreme Court, continued to take a strong role in the Court's public and behind-the-scenes deliberations. She asked pertinent questions on sex discrimination cases. She was uncharacteristically reticent when the court heard five abortion cases in late November, giving few clues to her views on an issue that had prompted antiabortion groups to oppose her nomination in 1981.

O'Connor strengthened the conservative bloc where states' rights were the central question. In sixty-six decisions that pitted the Court's most conservative jurist, William Rehnquist, against the liberal William Brennan, O'Connor sided with Brennan 15 times; in the 139 decisions in which she took part, she voted more often with Rehnquist (123 times) than even conservative Chief Justice Warren Burger.

Outside the court, O'Connor enjoyed a popularity that crossed political lines, with the symbolism of her appointment giving her a power and a presence that suprised her colleagues on the court. By the year's end, with the gender gap a proven political phenomenon, Republican moderates began to talk with some wistfulness about the bonus it could be to have O'Connor on the 1984 presidential slate in second spot.

Conclusion

As 1982 ended, the Reagan administration clearly had become aware of the hazards of continuing to alienate working women, especially. The appointment of two feminists to head cabinet agencies reflected the administration's intention to remedy the gender gap if it could. Continuing budget cuts and additional U-turns in lawsuits on behalf of white males against minorities (and presumably against women) continued to make the headlines, however, and reinforced the initial impression of an ideological administration committed to reversing many of the gains from the past two decades.

Women's rights groups rose to the challenge, with Reagan as an organizing catalyst. The loose coalition of old-line and more contemporary women's groups from the early 1970s came together again in 1982 to fight Reagan's budget cuts, to organize opposition factions in Congress, and to educate the public about what was at stake. Shadow women's rights and civil rights groups were formed to track conservative actions in the Reagan administration and to rally the grass roots. They managed to hold the line—but barely. The basic civil rights laws remained intact but were not enforced, and regulations were weakened. Budgets for poor women, the elderly, and for children were cut by billions of dollars, but the bulk of the basic program structures was preserved.

The women's movement took new strides forward in activism in all forms of society. The League of Women Voters broke a historic position of neutrality to come out for a pro-choice position on abortion as the constitutional fight to ban all abortions heated up again in 1983. The National Organization for Women continued to pioneer in direct-mail and television fund-raising and membership drives, aiming to expand from its 1982 base of 260,000 to 1 million members by the 1984 presidential election. The Women's Campaign Fund, the National Women's Political Caucus, and the National Women's Education Fund, along with most older groups, also aimed their fund-raising and educational efforts toward 1984, warning Democratic candidates as well as Republicans that the gender gap could work against them if they were not responsive to women's issues.

Across all levels of society, women were challenging previous definitions of their "place," from nuns in Catholic schools protesting their arbitrary ouster, to the 1982 Miss Connecticut who was dethroned after refusing to sing at a truck stop—and who was reinstated after the publicity rallied the people on her side.

The 1983 and 1984 years promise to be full of political ferment and controversy.

References

BERGMANN, BARBARA R. 1982. Women's economic condition in the 1980s: Bad and getting worse. Joint Economic Committee of Congress, February 3.

Children's Defense Fund. 1982. A children's defense budget: An analysis of the president's budget and children. February.

FRIEDAN, BETTY. 1981. *The second stage.* New York: Summit.

GATSIS, ANDREW J. 1982. ERA would mean women in combat role, devastation of our fighting forces. *Conservative Digest*, October.

HOLM, JEANNE. 1982. *Women in the military: An unfinished revolution.* Novato, Calif.: Presidio Press.

How Washington funds the left. 1982. *Conservative Digest*, April.

PEARCE, DIANA M. 1982. The poverty of our future: The impact of Reagan budget cuts on women, minorities and children. *Center for National Policy Review*, May.

ROSENBAUM, SARA, and WEITZ, JUDITH. 1982. Children and federal health care cuts: Impact of federal health budget reductions on state maternal and child health services during 1982. Children's Defense Fund, January.

Women Employed Institute. 1982. Damage report: The decline of equal employment opportunity enforcement under the Reagan administration. November.

Bibliography

Books

Gilligan, Carol. *In a different voice: Psychological theory and women's development.* Cambridge: Harvard University Press, 1982. An influential analysis of women's psychological composition and motivations, which Gilligan shows to be strengths rather than weaknesses.

Holwill, Richard N., ed. *Agenda 83: A mandate for leadership report.* Washington, D.C.: Heritage Foundation, 1983. A report on what still needs to be done for the New Right "Reagan Revolution."

Journals, Magazines, and Pamphlets

Benenson, Robert. "Women and politics." *Congressional Quarterly Editorial Research Reports* September 1982. An analysis of Reagan's "woman problem" including evidence of the gender gap and the president's record on women's rights issues. Analyzes women as potential force in winning more offices.

Berkson, Larry; Carbon, Susan; and Houlden, Pauline. *Judicature* December-January. Special issue on the history of women on the bench, profiles of women judges at state and federal levels, and analysis of Justice Sandra Day O'Connor.

Bolotin, Susan. "Voices from the post-feminist generation." *New York Times Magazine*, October 17, 1982. Controversial article about how the thirty-five-and-younger generation of women sees no need for "feminism" and, although they have absorbed many of its lessons, have taken it for granted and see no need for linkages with women's rights groups or with other women.

Bureau of the Census. "Lifetime earnings estimates for men and women in the United States: 1979." February 1983. Lifetime earnings for women would be less than half that of comparable earnings for men with equivalent education.

Cohadas, Nadine. "Reagan's judicial selections draw differing assessments." *Congressional Quarterly*, January 15, 1983. Sums up Reagan's judicial appointments: sixty-nine federal district court appointments, three to women, two to Hispanics, and none to blacks.

Federal Education Project, Lawyers' Committee for Civil Rights Under the Law. "A good start: Improving opportunities for women under the Vocational Education Act." Thirty-six-page booklet summing up December 1981 testimony before House subcommittee on economic and social issues facing women in breaking into vocational education training using the sex equity provisions in the law.

Health and Human Services Department, Public Health Service. "Parental notification requirements applicable to projects for family planning services." *Federal Register*, January 26, 1983. The Reagan administration's requirement to notify in writing parents of women under eighteen prescribed contraceptives by family planning agencies.

Gladstone, Leslie. "Women: Selected issues in the 97th Congress." *Congressional Research Service, Library of Congress*, January 7, 1983. Summary of budget, taxes, reproductive rights, employment, pension, and insurance issues as they affect women.

Glenney, Daryl. "Women in politics: On the rise." *Campaigns and Elections*, Winter, 1982. The president of a bipartisan campaign consulting firm outlines strides made by political women inside major campaign groups of both parties. Summary of women's political success stories, advice for novices.

"Inequality of sacrifice: The impact of the Reagan budget on women." May 6, 1982. Analysis of Reagan budget cuts by coalition of forty women's groups based in Washington.

Kasun, Jacqueline. "The international politics of contraception." *Heritage Foundation Policy Review*, Winter 1981. An attack on U.S. foreign aid programs on family planning. Questions the core premise that there is a population explosion that should be curbed.

Labor Department. "Government contractors: Affirmative action requirements." August 25, 1981. The initial Reagan administration outline of dramatic restrictions in affirmative action mandates for government contractors. This was a proposed rule.

Labor Department. "Government contractors: Affirmative action requirements." April 23, 1982. Another Reagan administration proposal (not implemented) to curb back pay and class action remedies for sex and race discrimination, and to exempt three-fourths of the contractors from scrutiny.

Ladd, Everett Carll. "Reagan and women." *Public Opinion*, January 1982. Discusses the historic evolution of a gender gap against Reagan.

Leadership Conference on Civil Rights. "Without justice: A report on the conduct of the justice department in civil rights." February 1982. An overview of civil rights reversals in the first year of the Reagan administration.

McLellan, Vin. "We're going to be right again." *Savvy*, July 1982. Describes the purge of women members from the Jaycees.

National Coalition for Women and Girls in Education. "Title IX: Ten years of progress." Update and analysis of Title IX and the erosion occurring under Reagan administration policies.

National Commission on Working Women. "Women, work and age discrimination: Challenging the workplace myths." 1982. Analyzes trends that pressure older women to retire early, difficulty women over forty find getting work, problem of lacking pensions.

Norwood, Janet L. "The male-female earnings gap: A review of the employment and earnings issue." Bureau of Labor Statistics, Department of Labor, September 1982. She shows that a "pay equity" gap of at least 26 percent exists after all other factors are equalized.

Rix, Sara E. "Saving social security: An equitable compromise. An analysis of how women would fare under the recommendations of the national commission on social security reform." The Women's Research and Education Institute, prepared for the Congressional Caucus for Women's Issues. January 25, 1983.

Rytina, Nancy F. "Earnings of men and women: A look at specific occupations." *Monthly Labor Review*, April 1982. Women are breaking into some nontraditional fields but remain segregated into lower-paying jobs.

Schroeder, Patricia. "National call for equality: Mother's day sermon." Given at the Washington Cathedral, May 9, 1982. "It is not the Bible that denies women equality—it is the Constitution of the United States."

Simpson, Peggy. "The fight for pay equity." *Working Woman*, April 1983. Summary of 1982 congressional hearings on pay equity and roundup of legal, political, and organizing efforts to remedy workplace inequities where women still earn only 59.8 percent to every man's dollar.

Stasz, Clarice. "Room at the bottom: Why 17 years of civil rights laws have had little impact on the ghettoization of most women's work." *Working Papers*, January-February 1982. A sociologist's analysis of the pay equity and sex-segregation problems faced by working women.

Stone, Anne J., and Rix, Sara E. "Employment and unemployment issues for women." January 1983. Women's Research and Education Institute. Analyzes working women's economic and job problems, how the recession hit them extra hard, impact of two-worker families, and the fast increase in female-headed families.

Tourfexis, Anastasia. "Waking up to the gender gap: GOP dilemma: Why can't a woman vote more like a man?" *Time*, October 18, 1982. Overview of fund raising, polls, projections in key 1982 general elections, where record number of women were nominated: 56 for Senate and House seats, 1,620 for state legislative seats (an increase of 206 for state legislative candidates).

U.S. Commission on Civil Rights. "Affirmative action in the 1980s: Dismantling the process of discrimination." November 1981. Makes a case for affirmative action, including goals and timetables, to correct past and continuing patterns of bias against women and minorities. Found disparities actually rose in the 1960s, that black women were group with highest rate of workers in poverty.

U.S. Commission on Civil Rights. "The federal response to domestic violence." January 1982. A companion report to the one below, with an in-depth study of nineteen federal programs that did or could respond to needs of abused women.

U.S. Commission on Civil Rights. "Under the rule of thumb: battered women and the administration of justice." January 1982. Examination of police and judicial treatment of spouse abuse, concluding this is too often treated as a family matter rather than as a crime.

Wider Opportunities for Women, the Women's Work Force. "A territorial issue." 1982. Research report on women in the construction industry, from confidential monitoring of four construction sites to study attitudes toward and sexual harassment of women workers.

Women Employed Institute. "Women at work: The myth of equal opportunity." 1982. Challenges myths surrounding women's economic status, including argument that affirmative action is no longer needed because women have "made it."

Women Employed Institute. *Women Employed* v. *Harris Bank:* A case study. 1982. Blow-by-blow description of the eight-year campaign to achieve equal employment at Chicago's Harris Bank. The administrative law judge at the Department of Labor ruled that the bank owed the women $12.2 million, but the judgment has been held up by the Reagan administration.

Resources

Films

How We Got the Vote, depicting the Suffragists' fight for the Nineteenth Amendment. Narrated by Jean Stapleton. Produced by the National Women's Party, 144 Constitution Avenue NE, Washington, DC 20001.

With Babies and Banners: Story of the Women's Emergency Brigade. Profile of women pioneers of the labor movement. Directed by Lorraine Gray and shown on Public Broadcasting System on May 7, 1982.

Organizations

American Association of University Women, 2401 Virginia Avenue NW, Washington, DC 20037.

American Civil Liberties Union, Women's Rights Project, New York, NY.

National Federation of Business and Professional Women, 2012 Massachusetts Avenue NW, Washington, DC 20036.

Catalyst, 14 East 60th Street, New York, NY 10022.

Center for the American Women and Politics, Eagleton Institute of Politics, Rutgers—The State University, New Brunswick, NJ 08901.

Children's Defense Fund, 122 C Street NW, Washington, DC 20001.

The Federal Education Project, Lawyers Committee for Civil Rights Under Law, 733 15th Street NW, Suite 520, Washington, DC 20005.

Leadership Conference on Civil Rights, 2027 Massachusetts Avenue NW, Washington, DC 20036.

League of Women Voters, 1730 M Street NW, Washington, DC 20036.

National Abortion Rights Action League, 1424 K Street NW, Second Floor, Washington, DC 20005.

National Council on Pay Equity, 1201 16th Street NW, Room 615, Washington, DC 20036.

National Federation of Business and Professional Women, 2012 Massachusetts Avenue NW, Washington, DC 20036.

National Organization for Women, Inc., 425 13th Street NW, Suite 1048, Washington, DC 20004.

National Women's Education Fund, 1410 Q Street NW, Washington, DC 20009.

National Women's Law Center, 1751 N Street NW, Washington, DC 20036.

National Women's Political Caucus, 1411 K Street NW, Washington, DC 20005.

Older Women's League, 3800 Harrison Street, Oakland, CA; Washington Office, 600 Maryland Avenue SW, West Wing 100, Washington, DC 20024.

Planned Parenthood of America, 810 7th Avenue, New York, NY 10019; and 1220 19th Street NW, Suite 303, Washington, DC 20036.

Religious Coalition for Abortion Rights, 100 Maryland Avenue NE, Washington, DC 20002.

Wider Opportunities for Women, Inc., 1325 G Street NW, Lower Level, Washington, DC 20005.

Women Employed Advocates, 5 South Wabash, Suite 415, Chicago, IL 60603.

Women's Campaign Fund, 1725 I Street NW, Suite 515, Washington, DC 20005.

Women's Equity Action League, 805 15th Street NW, Washington, DC 20005.

Women's Research and Education Institute (data research arm of the Congressional Caucus on Women's Issues), 204 4th Street SE, Washington, DC 20003.

Wonder Woman Foundation, 75 Rockefeller Plaza, New York, NY 20019.

Major Congressional Hearings

Printed transcripts of hearing records are available from the U.S. Government Printing Office.

Abortion. Senate Judiciary Subcommittee on the Constitution, on Sen. Orrin Hatch's S.J. Res. 110 to prohibit abortions.

Family Planning and Teenage Sex Education. Senate Labor and Human Resources Subcommittee on Aging, Family, and Human Services. On Title X: Sex education and health aspects of teenage contraception. March 30 and April 19. By Sen. Jeremiah Denton (R-Ala.).

Senate Labor and Human Resources Subcommittee on Aging, Family, and Human Services. March 2. Sen. Denton's concern about women working "who don't really need to"; Heritage Foundation's Onalee McGraw saying the feminist movement "issued an appeal that rapidly spread through our culture urging women to liberate themselves from the chains of family life and affirm their own self-fulfillment as the primary good."

Women in the Military. Senate Armed Services Subcommittee on Manpower and Personnel. March 10. Hearings on the Uniformed Services Former Spouse Protection Act, which ultimately was approved to overturn the Supreme Court ruling that had left former military spouses with no share in pension.

Women's Economic Status. On February 3, 1982, the House-Senate Joint Economic Committee held the first oversight hearing in eight years on women's economic status, entitled "The Economic Status of Women and its Effect on Family Income." Includes testimony from economist Barbara Bergmann on impact of Reagan programs on poor women.

The House Post Office and Civil Service Subcommittees on Civil Service, Human Resources, and Compensation and Employee Benefits held a series of oversight hearings on pay equity and comparable worth issues in September and October 1982. These highlighted the sex segregation of women in lower-paying jobs, the persistence of discrimination as a factor even when all education and skills factors are equalized, and the slowdown of federal enforcement and advocacy efforts on behalf of women.

Senate Subcommittee on Employment and Productivity, and House Subcommittee on Employment Opportunities held joint hearings March 16–18 on job training bills that would help never-employed, underemployed, and older women. The Older Women's League (OWL) testified about the compounding impact of ageism, sexism, and racism on older women looking for work.

Health and Nutrition. Senate Labor and Human Resources Subcommittee on Alcoholism and Drug Abuse. September 21, 1982. One aspect concerned the impact of alcohol on pregnancy.

House Education and Labor Subcommittee on Elementary, Secondary, and Vocational Education. March 16–18. Hearings on the Reagan budget cuts in the Women, Infant and Children proposal and the child nutrition block grant proposal.

Senate Select Committee on Aging. February 25, 1982, on proposed budget cuts on food stamps and nutritional programs for pregnant women and infants.

Senate Agriculture Subcommittee on Nutrition. February 25, 1982. Impact of budget cuts on federal nutritional and low-income energy aid programs.

Women's Economic Equity Act. Senate Commerce, Science and Transportation Committee held hearings and subsequently passed out one key segment of the omnibus bill, the Fair Insurance Practices Act, S.2204. July 15, 1982.

Popular Culture

Beverly Oberfeld Friend

Men succeed. Women get married.
Men fail. Women get married.
Men enter monasteries. Women get married.
Men start wars. Women get married.
Dull, dull.

Joanna Russ, The Female Man (1978)

Movies

Looking like a cross between a knight in shining armor and an exceptionally well-turned-out Good Humor man, Zack (Richard Gere) walks into the dingy factory, lighting up a path before him gleaming from his white officer's uniform with its shiny buttons and sharply creased pants. He strides between the lines of dull, gray machines, and every female worker turns haunted eyes toward him, envying the one who is his goal. He sees her! Sweeping Paula (Debra Winger) into his strong, masculine arms, he carries her forth from the factory, away from the drudge and toil, her unfulfilling work and life, and into a brighter tomorrow, which she deserves, you see, because she is very beautiful, quite sexy, and—most important—has never lied to him.

Thus ends *An Officer and a Gentleman*, which, had it been titled after the heroine of the story might have been more aptly called *A Lady and a Nincompoop*.

But it's the Cinderella story, critics protest. What's wrong with that?

Nothing, when Cinderella is presented as a fairy tale, but much when it attests to be a desirable reality.

Cinderella, now as always, is a recurrent theme in popular culture: films, television programs, and fiction setting women into passive roles where they worry and wait, hope and dream. Moreover, it is the one depiction that

149

feminists must fight if the role of women is ever to achieve anything like realistic portrayal.

All the women in *An Officer and a Gentleman* are Cinderellas, living in hopes of being rescued by men who will take them out of their poverty, out of the drab ugliness of their lives. Zack's mother was a failed Cinderella, who, long before the film opens, had committed suicide because her Prince Charming deserted her, leaving her to cope as best she could. She couldn't. Paula's mother, on the other hand, settled for the frog, unable to get the Prince, a pilot-trainee who impregnated her and then refused to wed her. Paula's friend Lynette (Lisa Blount) is an unworthy Cinderella, really more like one of the stepsisters, who lies about being pregnant in order to capture a mate. Only Paula is true to the fairy-tale princess, and thus deserving of rescue.

Zack might equally have turned out to be a Cinderfella. His life has not been easy; his mother died when he was very young, his dad has become a womanizing alcoholic. But Zack has taken life into his own hands, rising from emotional and economic poverty to make something of himself by entering the military to become a jet pilot.

Men become pilots. Women get married (to paraphrase Joanna Russ). If the women are lucky (and it helps if they are good, true, beautiful, and good in bed), they marry pilots.

To be absolutely fair, one woman in the film appears to be able to initiate rather than respond to circumstances. She is the token woman pilot-trainee (equivalent to the token black and the token Latino on the base). Even she can't really make it on her own, needing Prince Zack to help her over the hurdles of the obstacle course much as he will ultimately (as only a man can) help any woman who needs to surmount life's literal and figurative obstacles.

Critic Michael H. Seitz (1982), writing for the *Progressive*, stated that the movie is "as sophisticated in its grasp of the realities of military life as a recruiting film" (55). He has missed the point. This is not a recruiting film for men, it is a recruiting film for women—not to get them to join the military, but to reinforce their willingness to play the passive role of Cinderella. The success of this recruitment can be seen in an essay in *People Magazine* (1983), which, purporting to examine "How to Tell a Real Woman," lists *An Officer and a Gentleman* among the movies Real Women watch, along with *Norma Rae, Annie Hall, Julia*, and *A French Lieutenant's Woman*.

Critic Gene Siskel (1983) has said that the film is "a working-class love affair between a young man . . . who wants to fly jets so he can forget his past, and a young woman . . . in a Seattle papermill who wants to get married so she can forget the present."

What about the future? What about using the present to prepare for the future? What happens after the Ball?

One answer is provided by *Best Friends*, which examines the problems faced by two professionals who decide to change their status from roommates to husband and wife. This is no Cinderella story. Paula McCullen (Goldie Hawn) and Richard Babson (Burt Reynolds) are both successful writers, working as a team turning out Hollywood screenplays. More important, this Paula, the antithesis of the other Paula, is extremely reluctant to take the big step, not only because she is leery of the change in the relationship but, more important, because she fears she will lose her identity. She does not want to become merely Mrs. Richard Babson.

The film opens ambiguously as Richard and Paula are reading their latest script to each other. They are playing the roles of two sisters, yet the audience does not, at first, understand that they are not enacting their own life roles, creating an interesting set of expectancies. In how much of their relationship do they resemble siblings as well as lovers?

They formalize this relationship in one of the most significant moments in the film, the wedding scene. During the ceremony itself, in a quickie-wedding chapel, the minister who is more accustomed to delivering the sacred words in Spanish than in English mispronounces "and thee endow" so that they become garbled into the meaningless "dee and do." Paula and Richard are mystified when they are asked to repeat the words, but dutifully do so—never actually endowing each other. It is an interesting symbolic moment that seriously examines keeping back something of one's own autonomy.

Supposedly based on the relationship of the film's married authors, Valerie Curtin and Barry Levinson (who are responsible for *And Justice for All*, and *Inside Moves*, with Levinson also the writer-director of *Diner*), the film moves from the realistic to the comic as the couple tries to adjust from being best friends to being married, examining their current status as it is juxtaposed against the relationships of their parents, whom they visit right after the wedding.

Paula's mom and dad are eccentric recluses. The father is impotent yet interested in reading pornography and pinching maids, and the mother frankly admits her longing for sex in a rare but realistic confession not often seen in films about women her age. Richard's parents (who live in the biggest condo in Virginia) are, of course, the antithesis of Paula's, outgoing eccentrics. The mother, for example, is continually snapping flashbulbs in people's faces in a rather sad attempt to freeze present moments for future reflection (and nostalgia).

What do all these marriages mean? The older couples claim happiness. Richard's sister is in the midst of a divorce. Richard and Paula fight, make-up, fight, and threaten to dissolve the relationship. What saves their marriage, and what saves their integrity as individuals, ultimately, is their professional commitment. Richard and Paula must write the last act of a screenplay no matter what their current personal problems or pains. They are locked into a room to do so and, of course, resolve all their own problems in the process. The story is more than just another cliché of marital battles. What we are dealing with here is friendship and professionalism, both of which ultimately prove more important than romance.

Friendship is also the keynote of one of 1982's most visually beautiful films: *Personal Best*. This film celebrates personal worth and endeavor as it examines the lives of two athletes amid the complicated themes of growing up, self-discovery, the joys of one's own body, and the joys of another's body—which may or may not be the same sex as one's own—all captured within the framework of sports competition.

The two heroines, Tory and Chris (Patrice Donnelly and Mariel Hemingway) play mentor and student as well as friends and lovers. Both are winners. Pauline Kael (1982a) has called them warrior women, and the term fits. "Warrior women," she says, "who care for each other."

At last, 1982 has provided one response to all those male bonding films starring Redford and Newman, Gould and Sutherland, Hoffman and Mc-Queen, Hoffman and Redford, or Hoffman and Voight. It seems that two women *can* be as great friends, lovers, and competitors as men. The film is also unique in that, like *Julia*, it is commercially willing to test whether or not women can carry a picture without a presumably indispensable male star.

But something is still lacking. As Kael also noted in her review: "Watching this movie, you feel that you really can learn something essential about girls from looking at their thighs" (118).

How does one learn about women if not by watching them? Another answer provided in 1982 is, either by watching one pretend to be a man (as in *Victor/Victoria*) or, more provocative, by watching a man take on a female role (as in *Tootsie*.)

In *Victor/Victoria*, Julie Andrews plays a penniless, starving soprano, desperate for employment, successful only when she pretends to be a man pretending to be a woman. That is, she agrees to a double-switch, pretending to be a young Polish count enacting the role of a female impersonator. Complications arise when James Garner, as a big-time Chicago gangster, falls for what he initially believes to be a man.

While the film does give lip service to the women's movement, with Julie spouting forth an impassioned speech about how much more liberated she is as a man, the role portrayal is still stereotypical. As Kael (1982b) pertinently asked, why doesn't Julie express any rage when her skills as a singer are rejected by managers who prefer to employ a female impersonator rather than a real female?

In addition, Julie, even in the guise of a man, is stereotypically female: sickened at a prize fight, bravely inhaling and choking on a cigar, and, naturally, giving up her male guise and her career for a man!

Furthermore, is she really more liberated as a man? No. Not even if she thinks and says so. Actually she is more of an effete homosexual than a plausible man. In fact, it is difficult if not impossible to suspend disbelief and consider her as a man at all—or as anyone other than Julie Andrews, for that matter.

The same is not true of *Tootsie*, the success of which emanates from the audience's forgetting that Dustin Hoffman really is a man, even though they've seen him make-up and don female garb right before their eyes.

As Gene Siskel (1983) perceptively notes, while Julie Andrews is listed once in the cast credits, playing the parts of both Victor and Victoria, Hoffman is listed twice, both as Michael Dorsey and as Dorothy Michaels, as if they were two separate and distinct people.

When the story opens, Michael, like the Victoria character, cannot find work. The resemblance ends there because the flaw lies not with those who might hire him but in the character himself, an inflexible actor with such dogged dramatic integrity and such a prominent ego that he has become virtually unhirable. He will not, for example, walk to the center stage to die just to allow the audience to see him more clearly, because the dying character realistically could never walk there. On another level, he will not sit down when he plays the role of a tomato on commercial TV because tomatoes cannot sit.

It is extremely important to know what kind of a person Michael is in order to see what kind of a person Dorothy will become. When Michael, as Dorothy, gets a job on a soap opera, he achieves the same artistic ends he has always wanted, but using different (more feminine) means. Michael, as Dorothy, no longer argues with directors; instead, he takes the indirect route: listens, agrees, and *then* does what he wants.

Playing the part of a female (he says it is the hardest role of his life), Michael learns what being a woman is really like: the cost in terms of clothing and cosmetics; the sexual harassment from directors and male actors; the inability to hail a cab successfully; the demeaning attitude toward women as evidenced when the show's director calls all the male actors by name but reduces the females to anonymity with "Sweetheart," "Honey," and, of course, "Tootsie."

The liberated Dorothy rebels, does not permit the soap opera's male star (known as "the tongue") to kiss her, changes lines, and in standing up for her rights on the show becomes a cult heroine with her picture on the covers of *TV Guide*, *Cosmopolitan*, and *People*.

Michael starts as an exploiter of women, standing up his former girlfriend, Sandy (Teri Garr) to be with his soap opera colleague Julie (Jessica Lange). He changes, however, as he learns to listen to the woman within him.

The "real" females in the film are treated equally well. Sandy, insecure as she is, learns to face disappointment when Michael favors another; Julie, exploited by the soap's director is able to break off the affair and go on with her own life. In addition, she is totally accepted as an unwed mother. In an extremely well-acted moment, Julie, unable to accept Dorothy in what she believes would be a lesbian relationship, yet undeniably drawn to her, admits that she really loves her (emotionally) while she cannot love her (physically).

The best line in the film belongs to Michael, when he sums it all up with, "I was a better man as a woman with a woman than I've ever been as a man with a woman." It is because of this realization and the fact that Dorothy and Julie were initially (girl)friends that Michael and Julie can take up a loving heterosexual relationship as the film ends.

While some feminists may cavil because the strongest female portrayal this year is by a male, they are overlooking the fact that the true ability to empathize, to put oneself into another's shoes, may be the only way truly to understand anyone else, especially anyone of the other (called "opposite") sex.

That is not the only way, however. Molly Haskell (1983) cites much of what is missing from contemporary films. She questions the real confusion about how women should be shown: "as victims of a patriarchal and still heavily male-oriented society . . . or as vanquishers of mighty odds?"

She questions the lack of stories about coming of age and rites of passage, the absence of female versions of *Diner* and *Four Friends*, and promises:

They are coming, certainly the women who live not just through and for men but for themselves; women who insist on seeing as well as being seen. Until these women have come to write, direct, and act in the stories that will illuminate our interior landscape, chart our "passages," and make us accept the unacceptable, change will come in isolated segments. For the bottom line is that most adults have given up on movies altogether, and those who haven't see only four or five movies a year. To talk of sexism in such a context is almost meaningless. (27)

Is television any better?

Television

If you can write a nation's stories, you needn't worry about who makes its laws. Today television tells most of the stories to most of the people most of the time.
George Gerbner
(quoted by Harry Waters in *Newsweek*)

Three 1982 television movies are telling new stories to audiences and in so doing are transcending the stereotypical depiction of women that has been prominent in so much prime time until now: *Games Mother Never Taught You* (CBS), with Loretta Swit, *Having it All* (NBC), starring Dyan Cannon, and *I Was a Mail Order Bride* (CBS), with Valerie Bertinelli.

Games is the fascinating adaptation of a nonfiction handbook by Betty Lehan Harragan, which instructs women in the strategies used by men to play (and win) power struggles in the business world. For example, understanding both the rules and terminology of team sports allows men to practice and apply the same rules and language metaphors in the organizational network.

Thus when a secretary is catapulted into a seat on the board of directors, she has to learn fast: what to wear, what to say (and how to say it), and whom to befriend—or else. Plagued by troubles at home and more troubles at work, she learns the rules and, more important, wins.

Credit for this skillful presentation and for the production of *Having it All* goes to a former college professor turned independent TV producer, Tristine Rainer, according to Patricia Bosworth (1982). Rainer, who spent several years from her first reading of *Games* to its successful on-the-air production, had far less trouble breaking into the big-boy TV network with *Having it All*, which, Rainer claims, was originally inspired by a friend who actually had two husbands—one on the west coast and one on the east. As Rainer notes, "It seemed like the ultimate fantasy. What woman hasn't dreamt of having two sexy men in love with her?" (214).

Of course, women must have sufficient money and sufficient (plausible) freedom in order to be successful bigamists, and Thera, the 40-year-old, wealthy fashion designer heroine has both. More important for television plotting, she is a resourceful victim rather than the villain in her bigamy. She has not committed bigamy deliberately (that would allow a woman too much motivation); rather, when she believed that her philandering New York husband was getting a quickie divorce, she responded by wedding a younger, free-spirited California cutie. Once the knots are tied, however, she does enjoy both men thoroughly, with only a modicum of guilt, stating, "It's unrealistic to think any one man can satisfy all your needs."

Suspense builds as close call follows close call, à la restoration comedy, until the two men ultimately meet and all is discovered. Both promptly divorce Thera who must then face life alone. How will she survive when she can no longer be fulfilled by men? Slowly and gradually she learns, listening to advice from her widowed mother, taking time to be good to herself—as in preparing a meal just to please her own palate.

The film could, and should, have ended here, with Thera standing tall and proud. In typical fashion, however, Thera gets back together with her original (philandering) husband while the west coast sweetie finds someone closer to his own age.

Kate Tosconi is better able to handle the autonomous life in a film with a most deceptive title, *I Was a Mail Order Bride*. Kate, a reporter for *Contemporary Woman's Magazine*, takes on the assignment of advertising for a husband in order to get a good feature story. Not only does she get a handsome lawyer to respond to the ad, she becomes involved in a convoluted plot that pits her as sexual aggressor against a reluctant male. He is reluctant because, unbeknown to her, he has bet his law partner he can remain celibate throughout the courtship.

Undomestic Kate (both sewing and cooking are handled admirably by her father and her boyfriends) is cheerfully willing to aggress, but she is furious when she discovers that the man's reticence is based on a bet rather than on memories of his painful, recent divorce. She feels used, and writes the story. He feels used and sues for libel. Their verbal sparring comes to resemble the comic clashes of Hepburn and Tracy; of course, all ends well.

At least three TV heroines have had it all: work, love, autonomy. A fourth goes too far for even feminist belief: *Rodeo Girl* (CBS), starring Katherine Ross.

Sammy and Will Garrett are both rodeo performers. Will rides the broncos while wife Sammy ropes calves and rides in the barrel races. When she wants to try doing more in an all-girl rodeo, she asks Will's permission. From that first step, she gains strength, taking on bigger professional obstacles until she, too, can ride the broncos. The only flaw in the story, as in her life, is that she becomes pregnant. Does that stop her? No. Sammy wants the baby and she wants to bust broncos. So she does both. In the land of happy endings, Sammy wins professional trophies and has a baby girl; and Will, who left when he couldn't bear to watch his pregnant wife bucking and heaving, returns to the happy household.

All of these films have positive assertions: women get and enjoy it all (albeit unrealistically); struggles are relatively easy to resolve; rewards are assured. In the framework of comedy, not meant to be taken seriously, this works well.

More sober films can dissolve into unrelieved tragedy, as in *My Body, My Child* (ABC), starring Vanessa Redgrave, which considers the plight of a middle-aged, pregnant woman who is misadvised by her gynecologist into taking fetus-threatening drugs. The film seriously examines such crucial theses as women in the hands of unsympathetic, judgmental male doctors, and their ignorance of their own bodily functions. It does not tell the audience what the heroine's decision will be on the question of whether or not she should have her pregnancy aborted.

Children's Programming   Films intended for younger audiences also often grapple with more genuine problems than are seen during prime time. The 1982 ABC After-School Specials, shown bi-monthly in the late afternoons, examine VD, pregnancy, and difficult relationships. A typical example is *Between Two Loves*, in which two teenagers find their love threatened by a violin competition they both enter. He loses; she wins and states, "I'm sorry you lost, but I'm not sorry I won. I had every right to compete."

Teenage relationships are also the focus of at least three new situation comedies: *Square Pegs, Facts of Life*, and *Family Ties*.

In a recent interview for the *School Press Review*, the author of *Pegs*, Anne Beatts, is quoted as saying that she thinks the show differs from other television teen-coms because the viewer is asked to identify with girls rather than with boys. The two heroines, one gawky with glasses and the other too plump, are scholastically a cut above their Weemawee High School peers, but desperate to be popular with their more vacant classmates. The show is not so much about the goals of being popular as it is about the pains of trying to fit in—at any stage in life. As Beatts attests, "All life is high school" Lisabeth 1982, (7). She is fighting the adage that high school is the best years of our lives in a show that deliberately tries not to be slick. The moral, Beatts says, is that "it is ok to be lame."

Another teen-centered show, *Facts of Life*, is set in the closed environment of a boarding house for high-school girls. In this matriarchal world headed by a wise dorm mother played by Charlotte Rae, plots attack hypocrisy, the sexual double standard, and many of the affectations of social class. The characters range from an underprivileged tom-girl on scholarship to the school to the wealthy, egotistical daughter of an industrialist, with all kinds of conflicts between the two.

Family Ties focuses both on teenagers and on value judgments in a generational conflict where conservative youngsters set up their standards against the more liberal life views of their parents.

Prime Time Series   Programs centering on adults are more stereotypical. While Gloria no longer lives with Daddy, Archie Bunker, or with her "meathead" husband, for that matter, she still lives in a paternal world working for a rather dippy veterinarian in *Gloria* (CBS).

Knots Landing, *Dynasty*, and *Falcon Crest*, cloned from *Dallas*, all have the same breathtakingly beautiful and wealthy women acting out every role from Cinderella to the Wicked Witch of the West as they worry about who will marry or be impregnated next.

Laura Holt (Stephanie Zimbalist), who is as gorgeous as anyone on TV, looked as though she would break the stereotype, on *Remington Steele*, but she only caused a hair-line fracture. When Holt opens a detective agency, she discovers that clients have no confidence in a female private eye, so she invents a boss: R. Steele. Clients then flock to the door. When a real mystery man appears and takes over Steele's identity, Holt fades into the background and the male takes over. Unable to stick with a tough, competent female private eye, the script writers have made Remington steal the show. This was not the original intention, however; something changed between the pilot and the premiere. According to Tom Shales (1982), a pilot episode screened for the press "featured an intelligent, competent woman continually coming to the aid of a handsome but incompetent man in the detective agency she ran." By the time the premiere was aired, the woman had become weaker, a type-cast female who fled screaming from a corpse in a closet while the tough man provided her with shelter in his arms. The lesson, according to Shales, is that "networks believe viewers will tolerate only limited upsetting of the sexual stereotype applecart."

Laura is now reduced to a sex object, and the relationship between her and Steele brims with sexual promise, unfulfilled lest it complicate their "professional" relationship. As she makes fewer and fewer of the agency's decisions, Holt finds herself with only one decision left: whether or not to succumb to Remington's charms. So far, not.

A ten-year study of the portrayal of working women has faulted television as only rarely reflecting reality (NCWW studies . . . 1982). Among the conclusions reached were that while 60 percent of TV working women are professionals, only 20 percent of women in real life are. While 73 percent of TV women are under age 40, in real life only 56 percent are. The study found that the portrayal of the wealthy woman has risen from less than 1 percent in the early 1970s to 23 percent in the 1980s; and that television misleads young girls with stories of instant success regardless of the market.

In addition, the medium is faulted for not showing two-income couples sharing their work; for portraying the husband's work as more important than the wife's; and for not considering working women's issues: stretching the pay check, going to work when the children are sick, trying to get promoted to a better job.

Of all the programs of 1982, the strongest answer to these complaints can be found in *Cagney and Lacey*, which is being watched very closely by the critics. As Barney Rosenzweig, executive producer of the show, said to Marilynn Preston (1982): "It's so hard to get the networks to accept two women leads. . . . If *Cagney and Lacey* doesn't make it, it'll be too bad for women on TV for a long time."

Here are two on-the-beat female detectives struggling in a grimy city against whatever crime and corruption comes their way during a particular episode. Running throughout each story is a sense of personal worth and dignity, reminiscent of the characterizations on *Lou Grant*.

Both women are dedicated to their work; in fact, Cagney regularly gloats that this is the job she has always wanted and has worked hard to get. The women are nice looking but Lacey, for one, is not gorgeous. Interestingly, according to Preston, the original actress who played Cagney in the pilot was replaced because the producers feared she projected a lesbian image. They, however, do not admit this, stating that they paired Sharon Gless and Tyne Daly to create more contrast between the two women who originally had been depicted as both being blue-collar and street-smart. Chris Cagney is from upstate New York, sophisticated and single, while Mary Beth Lacey is blue-collar and married. As Preston notes, "When Cagney goes home to make thinner thighs, Lacey goes home to make meat loaf."

Relationships are portrayed realistically. Lacey's husband is supportive, not only in doing dishes and helping with the kids, but in showing care, interest, and attention to his wife when she needs his emotional backing after a hard day on the job.

Cagney can be mean and petty as she lets her ambitions rule her judgment; Lacey can show fear, as when she has to catch a criminal by working her way across a construction beam high above the street. These are no Charlie's Angels, but flesh and blood people with jealousies, personality conflicts, and lives that do not flow smoothly.

Daytime Television   Life is also pretty rocky for the much-harried characters of daytime TV, watched by over 55 million viewers. This year, *All my Children* topped *General Hospital* to become number one in the soap opera ratings. Credit for this turn-about has been given to one character and her development. Opal (Dorothy Lyman), is an abrasive, gum-chewing, hard-boiled hillbilly with a frizzy hairdo, tight golden Spandex pants; a single-dimensional fool who initially appeared last summer as racist, sexist, ignorant, and lazy, has changed from caricature to character. Patricia Bosworth (1983) has praised Lyman's skill in depicting Opal's metamorphosis from an idle, indolent woman (who sends her kid out to work rather than get a job herself) to reluctant salesclerk, then housemaid, and now the owner of her own hard-won business, The Glamorama, a unisex beauty spa.

Opal is impatient with phonies or pretense. Angry and frustrated about her daughter's life as well as her own, she is a victim, suffering the aftermath of a disastrous marriage to an unrehabilitated criminal and the loss of a run-a-way son.

Opal is also gutsy, determined to survive. So are all the other women on the program—all twenty-eight of them (counting major and minor figures) who seem to cover the entire job market from nurses to models to reporters, waitresses, secretaries, cooks, restaurant owners, boutique owners, business executives, and so on ad infinitum.

The problems of all these women, however, are only peripherally related to their occupations. That is, jobs are only important if they interfere with the love relationships (at least eight triangles and uncountable pairings at last look). Also the goals still revolve around marriage, even for Opal who would happily give up her Glamorama for a rich husband.

Cinderella is older, but she certainly isn't any wiser.

Fiction

The Cinderella traipsing across the written page is not wiser, either. More often than not, she is going to the Ball for the second time, seeing no other options open to her.

Critic Kathryn Weibel (1977) studying images of women in popular culture noted that popular fiction aimed at male readers (crime novels or Horatio Alger success stories) only rarely centers on male-female relationships (secondary to overcoming great dangers, competing victoriously over other men, and winning great fortunes). Women's literature, on the other hand, has continued "to portray marriage as the good woman's Great Reward and courtship as her Great Adventure" (9). It was not until the "raised conscious-ness" of the 1970s that popular culture really began to focus on the theme of the disillusioned wife and mother, in such books as Sue Kaufman's *Diary of a Mad Housewife*, Eleanor Bergstein's *Advancing Paul Newman*, Anne Roiphe's *Up the Sandbox*, and Alison Lurie's *War Between the Tates*.

Romantic Novels   In 1982 another theme came to the fore: carrying on after loss. The protagonist no longer examines her marriage per se—how she got there or how she survived the experience once she achieved her goal—but figures out what to do when it is all over.

In the most limited works, the romances, loss has spurred a whole new publishing phenomenon: Second Chance at Love (Berkley/Jove). In all of the six novels that are issued every month, the departure of husband number one (shortly before the story opens and through absolutely no fault of the heroine) sets the stage for the sexually titillating search for husband number two—a return to courtship with the archetypal hero modeled on Jane Eyre's Rochester.

The second Mr. Right arrives as close to page one, chapter one as possible. Between these two points, the heroine dallies. She does have some differences from her predecessors: she need no longer be a virgin, but cannot sleep around—Mr. Right must be the only one to enjoy her favors. She may have a career. In Katherine Granger's *Man's Persuasion*, heroine Casey Adams has "worked her way up from chambermaid to become Boston's most fashionable caterer," while in Anne Reed's *The Starlit Seduction*, "Fragile-as-a-flower" Jennifer Denning is "determined to resume the teaching career her ex-husband had ridiculed."

Recent research by Harlequin (which accounts for at least 50 percent of the romance market) has shown that 15 percent of romance readership is women in management-level jobs. This is the reason that fictional governesses, nurses, and secretaries in love with their bosses have given way to career women. But the plots are still sheer stock: boy meets girl, and misunderstandings and jealousies interfere with the path of true love, but, as the cover of every Second Chance at Love book attests: "The heart doesn't count the years—or the tears. And if romance is grand the first time, there is nothing more precious than your Second Chance at Love."

More Serious Fiction   While the solution to loss is simple in formula fiction—just replace the missing person with another, better and brighter than before—there are no such glib answers in the more serious novels of 1982. The heroines are usually older and more willing than either their romantic counterparts or their historical predecessors to take on the self-examination that springs from life's traumatic moments. Often they are mothers who must concern themselves with something other than their own gratification. They have learned something of life from their "first chance at love."

Three works that examine the alternatives of such women are Maureen Howard's *Grace Abounding*, Gail Godwin's *A Mother and Two Daughters*, and Anne Tyler's *Dinner at the Homesick Restaurant*.

Grace Abounding is the weakest of the three because the author tells rather than shows her characters' development. In section one, Maud Dowd, a 43-year-old widow, lives in a large house in Connecticut with her 13-year-old daughter Elizabeth. Maud spends her days visiting her old, sick mother, indulging in quite graphic sexual fantasies about the married shopkeeper down the road, and spying on two eccentric old-maid sisters who live next door.

Section two opens ten years later. Maud has remarried (but not the shopkeeper), lives in New York, has received a PhD from Columbia, and is now a successful children's therapist. Elizabeth, grown, married, and pregnant, has inexplicably given up a promising career as a singer.

It is too fast. The reader feels cheated in not having experienced the intervening years with the characters, and has difficulty believing that the women in section one have actually turned into the women in section two merely on the author's say-so.

More fragmentation occurs as additional characters are introduced and abruptly dropped, many of them quite interesting women: Maud's mother and the mother's companion, and the eccentric sisters next door, for example.

A far more successful depiction of women struggling with mother-daughter relationships and personal growth may be found in Gail Godwin's *A Mother and Two Daughters*, which charts the progress of three women following the sudden, untimely death of their husband-father.

Cate, the older daughter, is the most militantly feminist of the three. Ever the family rebel, twice divorced, moving from one academic job to another, she turns down what appears to be an ideal Prince Charming in order to avoid escaping her own history, as she tells her suitor:

"I mean my future history . . . the whole pattern of my life as it defines me. What I am, what I mean to be. The thing is, I know it would be good with you, but. . . ." How could she convey to this man how much his offer had touched her, tempted her, honored her, yet also make him see why, outside of a storybook, it would be doomed to failure. "I would feel as if I had retired from the struggle without having finished facing it." (260)

Cate does not seek easy answers to life's difficult questions as she continually assesses and reassesses her relationships. About marriage, she says, "Nobody who is first and foremost a family member has a hope in hell of becoming a whole person" (466). About having a child, she concludes, "A flesh-and-blood baby means you have to go back into the failed world and take what you can get till that baby grows up. The baby keeps you hostage in the world" (477).

At a climactic moment, Cate denigrates her sister's accomplishments, accusing Lydia of never having left the dollhouse. Cate judges and judges, and finds almost everybody else wanting. But Cate suffers for each of the conclusions she reaches, having chosen a most difficult road. Lydia and their mother, Nell, accomplish less and suffer less. Lydia is more conservative than Cate. Although she leaves her husband, Lydia soon takes up a lover who bodes well to be husband number two. Her rebellion takes the form of returning to school, and her success can be measured in spoonfuls as she dispenses recipes on national television.

All three women show their independence throughout the book as they struggle both against the outside world and with each other, carrying over the relationships of childhood into the exchanges of their adult lives.

While the characters also mature in *Dinner at the Homesick Restaurant*, these are never truly free from the fetters of their childhood. Tyler tells of two brothers and a sister, deserted by their father and raised by their angry mother. The story is both remembered by the 85-year-old mother from her deathbed and presented by the omniscient narrator.

The mother sees herself as a passive person, an old maid, the unwitting victim of a most charming traveling salesman who one day inexplicably abandoned her. Her passivity appears in her initial acceptance of his proposal, her willingness to leave her family and settle where he would, and in her inability to question, let alone stop, his desertion. She never attempts to find him once he leaves, and never answers the letters he irregularly sends over the years.

The children recall a violent, furious mother who had a strong hand in shaping them. They cannot understand her years of silence, concealing the fact that the father had left for good, never discussing the reasons for his departure.

While the mother's death provides a framework for the story, the father's desertion is the fulcrum for the action. When he finally does return for the mother's funeral, the reader is shocked, never having expected to meet him.

Why did he leave in the first place? Simply because his wife had seen through him. When he discovered that he could no longer charm the old maid to whom he had brought so much happiness during courtship and the early years of marriage, he left, unable to face seeing romance killed by reality. Significantly, the moment he decided to go was triggered by an accident during a family outing. He had bought a bow and arrows to entertain the children, but this romantic pastime was shattered by reality when the mother was inadvertently shot. He decided to go; she, wounded stayed, surviving this literal wound as she did all the other, more serious wounds in her life.

In Alice Walker's *The Color Purple*, Celie (who has no last name) is another survivor. She lives through the death of her mother, copes with being raped by her stepfather, has both of her babies taken from her (and possibly killed), and is forced into a bitter marriage with an abusive husband. The continual and brutal indignities to which he subjects her form the spectrum of the novel. What saves Celie and sets her apart from most fictional heroines is a female support system.

The novel opens in a world invisible to much of white America, that of rural black women. Here the miserable Celie has only one outlet: writing and reading letters. In fact, letters make up the entire novel—first from Celie to God, then from her long-lost sister Nettie to Celie, and finally from Celie back to Nettie after Celie discovers that her sister's correspondence from Africa has been hidden from her for years by her evil husband.

The men in the story are a breed apart, cruel and incomprehensible. They are the enemy; it is the women who are the salvation. Celie's husband's mistress saves Celie, offering her love (physical as well as emotional) and the opportunity to leave him and start her own business. Women help women to help themselves survive.

One of the most blatantly successful women in a popular novel of 1982 was Ann Marie O'Brien, a widow who became mayor of a great metropolitan city and the heroine of Eugene Kennedy's *Queen Bee*. Ann Marie learns the political ropes as she moves from being an apolitical parent to a city hall worker following in the footsteps of her mentor, Mayor Thomas H. Cullen (à la Chicago's Richard J. Daley), until she reaches the ultimate and becomes mayor herself. The name of the game is power, of course, but perhaps because Ann Marie, alone of all the characters discussed here, is the creation of a male author, her power is too often considered and concentrated only in terms of her sexuality. Men leer at her breasts when she speaks at city council meetings; others plan to blackmail her by uncovering her affair with a television commentator and notorious womanizer. Kennedy also attributes more of her rise to luck and coincidence than to innate skill, possibly a commentary on the book's role model, Jane Byrne of Chicago.

Kennedy maintains, however, that his work is pure fiction, not fictionalized biography. If so, *Queen Bee*, like so many other novels of 1982, gives rise to some important questions. Why are so many contemporary novels about successful widows and divorcees? Do the authors find it impossible to envision a wife and/or mother who is also successful outside the home?

Even when a woman has never married, as is the case with 41-year-old Rosie Deane in Sonia Gernes's *The Way to St. Ives*, she is freed from a restrictive male when her brother dies. In addition, she is freed from some of the more stringent rules of the Catholic church as she learns to fend for herself in the modern world.

Women who may not have lost their husbands yet, but are in the process of doing so are examined in Barbara Shoup's *Nightwatch*, in which two women from quite opposite backgrounds furnish emotional support for each other during the endless days they spend waiting in the hospital for news about their cancer-ridden husbands and learning to cope with that news once it arrives.

In one of the few novels written from the point of view of a young unmarried woman, the theme of loss still prevails. This time it is loss of a mother in *A Novel Called Heritage*, by Margaret Mitchell Dukore, winner of the 1982 Maxwell Perkins Award. The book is structured on letters to a book editor, which interrupt the chapters of a quasi-autobiographical novel by an extremely precocious 18-year-old. The unusual narrative method allows the reader to enjoy two distinct but interlocking stories at the same time.

Narrator Anne Sarah Foster blurs fact and fiction as she relates a bizarre tale of her mother's suicide. Anne was only ten years old at the time, but the novel explores her mother's history up to the time of her death and the odd household that followed it: Anne, her younger sister, her father, the father's first wife, his mistress, and the mistress' mother.

It is never really clear why Anne's mother married the man she did, giving up a highly promising acting career to seduce an already married, 51-year-old pudgy small-town drama professor. It is also never quite clear why she committed suicide, but she leaves an indelible memory to Anne and two important lessons: don't live your life by another's words (as actresses do); write your own script, and no matter what happens in your life, USE IT!

Thus Anne, following her mother's advice, "uses" the suicide, uses her father's eventual breakdown and institutionalization, even uses the editor to whom she is trying to sell her story—all within the construct of the novel. Anne will never, like her mother, be defeated by life. She will "use it."

The women in Ntozake Shange's first novel, *Sassafrass, Cypress, and Indigo*, are also able to "use it"—to use their struggles to gain strength. Three black sisters who grow up under the aegis of an ambitious but understanding mother leave home to carve out niches for themselves in the larger world. Mother has always been self-sufficient, a weaver, and her daughters master this skill as well as their own individual arts: writing, dancing, and playing the violin.

Again, the situation is a fatherless home, the father having died long before the story opens (and, as a seafaring man, having spent little time at home to begin with). This work is a celebration of being female, with all kinds of female concerns woven into the tale, including poetry and even recipes. The most celebratory moment occurs on the day that the youngest daughter,

Indigo, a rather mystical child who conducts long, imaginary conversations with fifteen dolls she has crafted herself, reaches her first menstruation. The language is triumphant as the older woman advises Indigo:

There in the garden, among God's other beauties, you should spend these first few hours. Eve's curse threw us out of the garden. But like I told you, women tend to beauty and children. Now you can do both. Take your blessing and let your blood flow among the roses. Squat like you will when you give birth. Smile like you will when God chooses to give you a woman's pleasure. Go now, like I say. Be not afraid of your nakedness. (17–18)

Indigo carries the celebration to those she feels closest to, her dolls, and creates a party for them that Shange details as "MARVELOUS MENSTRUATING MOMENTS (As Told by Indigo to Her Dolls as She Made Each and Every One of Them a Personal Menstruation Pad of Velvet)." This work is both more personal and more political than most mainstream fiction.

Lesbian Novels   As a genre, lesbian literature is also more personally and politically oriented.

To the Cleveland Station, by Carol Anne Douglas, presents a heroine so caught up in her feminism that she regards marriage as a betrayal of feminist principles, and sees men, even the most understanding and gentle of them, as almost another (incompatible) species. Thus Brenda Anne Daugherty (BAD) leaves her husband when she becomes an intellectual lover of women, long before she has an actual physical experience with them. The novel focuses on the doomed love affair between Brenda and Andy, a black lesbian from Cleveland who has suffered both the horrors of being raped and the nightmares of electric shock treatments by a physician who wanted to "cure" her sexual choices.

Sheila Ortiz Taylor's *Fault-line* is a lesbian novel with a lighter tone, outrageously zesty, and a cast of characters including a white lesbian mother of six children, a six-foot tall black drag queen, and 300 rabbits. The novel as a whole is not nearly as memorable as some of its eminently quotable parts:

Once you agree to make yourself responsible for a man's laundry you sensitize yourself to his defects. You begin to notice his tendency to pee on the toilet seat. You begin to wish he preferred Kleenex to handkerchiefs. And finally you fail to understand why he interprets your growing inability to compose poetry as a sign of your freedom.

I am raising my children to do their own laundry. Otherwise friendship is not possible. (105)

The focus of many of 1982's crop of lesbian novels does not revolve around sex, as those unfamiliar with feminist lesbian fiction might assume. Rather, the stress serves to explain (not justify) why the authors (through their characters) made the choice they did, examining themselves as women, questioning their own roles and their interactions with others. Narrators may have started out believing the middle-American party line, willing to be Cinderellas, but eventually and inevitably they changed. The 1982 lesbian literature explores, not exploits, these changes.

The exploitation of lesbian sexuality may be found in soft-core pornography, where it is depicted amid heterosexual couplings and team orgies (excluding male homosexuality). These books are primarily aimed at men, although many women read them and a whole new crop is springing up: the Jennifer books from Pinnacle, the Nicole series from Jove, and proposals for similar books are in the works from Bantam, NAL/Signet, and Playboy.

All follow very explicit rules: the covers show near naked women and fully clothed men; the women all have glamorous professions (models, stars of X-rated films, photographers); all are fabulously rich (no fear of economic dependency); all enjoy each and every sex act and are never troubled by impotent partners, pregnancy, or herpes. Strong, independent (sexy) women are looking for even stronger (sexier) men. No slave motifs allowed.

Nicole and her pals fit the bill. As the world's "most wanton—and wanted—women," they aggressively go from sex act to sex act, over and over, and under and under, again and again. The language is explicit; for example, in the very first paragraph of Morgan St. Michel's *Nicole in Captivity*, the heroine and her best friend (also gorgeous, rich, etc.) sit in a restaurant and discuss "the care and feeding of the hungry, furry little beasts hidden between [their] thighs."

The sexual exploitation, which is the hallmark of this genre, becomes even more glaring when the women try to entice two sailors at the next table by their shockingly direct language and behavior: revealing intimate glimpses of their anatomy, eating food lasciviously, and masturbating to orgasm on the restaurant chairs. The growth of the pornography industry and its widespread availability remain continuing issues for those who resent the denigration of women within popular culture.

Science Fiction

Science fiction has, of course, always been the antithesis of sexually provocative literature. While the pulp magazines may have featured scantily clad females escaping the evil intentions of bug-eyed monsters, the stories inside the magazines were far more concerned with adventure than with sex, and never, for example, considered what the monsters would actually have done with the women once caught. (What could King Kong really have done, sexually, with Fay Wray?) Originally and chastely marketed as a literature for adolescent males, SF offered ideas in lieu of orgasms.

Three approaches to these ideas, according to Isaac Asimov, have categorized the genre: gadget, adventure, and social SF. The women's movement has made a difference in all three.

In typical gadget fiction, women have been literally portrayed as machinery. One example is Ira Levin's *Stepford Wives* (1972) where androids became perfect helpmates, content to shop, care for children, wash the floors, clean the house, and enjoy their husband's beds. The real wives had been murdered and replaced with these paragons.

Anne McCaffrey was ahead of most of her contemporaries when she used gadgetry to create a cyborg in *The Ship Who Sang* (1961), uniting a deformed female child and a space ship. The heroine became something far more than human, with senses able to experience the wonders of the galaxy as she traveled from planet to planet.

In 1982 Tanith Lee answered Ira Levin's substitution of a machine for a human woman by positing a perfect, handsome, and sensitive android male in *The Silver Metal Lover.* In addition, Lee's work explores not only the feelings and motivations of the teenage heroine who falls in love with him, but the realistic mother-daughter conflict as the youngster cuts the umbilical cord to form her first romantic attachment.

No motivations were ever examined in early works of adventure science fiction, where women became the object of the adventure, to be saved when they were too stupid or too inept to save themselves. Today this has changed, and women have their adventures fighting barbarians, piloting spaceships, and conquering new worlds. In 1982 Jessica Amanda Salmonson edited a second anthology, *Amazons II*, devoted entirely to stories of female prowess, daring, and swordplay. Jo Clayton's *Moongather* begins the first volume of a trilogy dealing with a strong-willed, adventurous young heroine who topples guards, traitors, and menacing creatures, and vanquishes all the various bad guys. The biggest SF adventure blockbuster this year with a female heroine is Robert Heinlein's *Friday*, one of three works by top SF authors consistently to reach the best-seller lists. (The other two, Asimov's *Foundations Edge* and Arthur C. Clarke's *2010: Odyssey Two* have nothing of note to say to the women's movement in the portrayal of female characters.)

The ultimate "girl Friday," Heinlein's heroine is described as being as "thoroughly resourceful as she is strikingly beautiful . . . one of the best interplanetary agents in the business . . . and . . . an Artificial Person . . . the ultimate glory of genetic engineering."

Is this Wonder Woman the answer to a feminist's or a chauvinist's dream? Early in the book, Friday, acting as a secret courier, is captured by the enemy, gang-raped, and mutilated (one nipple is cut off). Heinlein, however, refuses to give any credence to possible pain and horror. As in television violence, all ends well: the nipple can be regenerated. The author even tries to absolve the males from guilt and responsibility by (unbelievably) making Friday muse that she might not have minded one of the rapists, under different circumstances, and by later depicting this rapist as a "regular guy" who would have been killed if he hadn't "gone along" with it all. Only a male (and an insensitive one at that) could seriously write these rationalizations.

Heinlein has been faulted in the past for giving with one hand what he takes away with another. In *Podkayne of Mars* (1963) he created the very first adolescent heroine in SF, and then had her spouting such lines as, "It's a mistake for a girl to beat a male at any test of physical strength" (56) and "We were designed for having babies. A baby is lots more fun than differential equations" (127). It is more interesting to note that while Heinlein has dedicated *Friday* to thirty-one women, all thirty-one are listed only by first name. Some are obvious: Ursula must be LeGuin; Vonda is McIntyre; but what about the identities of Ann, Anne, Barbie, Betsy, Bubbles . . . ?

Many of these no-last-name women are the ones writing the most important kind of SF for women: social SF, which extrapolates from the present world to envision alternative or future possibilities. Social SF asks, "What if?"

What if there were a world populated only by women? How would it function? How could the inhabitants procreate? These and more questions were answered in Philip Wylie's *The Disappearance* (1951), John Wyndham's novella *Consider Her Ways* (1956), Joanna Russ's short story "When it Changed" (1972) (which later evolved into her angry novel *The Female Man*), and Suzy McKee Charnas's *Walk to the End of the World* (1974) and *Motherlines* (1978).

What if time travel were possible and contemporary women could visit the past? This has been answered in *Shadow of Earth* (1979), by Phyllis Eisenstein, where a contemporary heroine must survive in a medieval culture; in *The Mirror* (1979), by Marlys Millhiser, where a modern girl changes places with her own grandmother; and in Octavia Butler's *Kindred* (1979) in which a modern black woman must survive and function on a Southern slave plantation.

What if there were an androgynous world, composed of creatures that were both male and female? Theodore Sturgeon answered this in *Venus Plus X* (1960) and Ursula K. LeGuin went even further in *The Left Hand of Darkness* (1969) creating a world where, through monthly sex determination, a person may be mother to some children and father to others.

In 1982 the theme most often repeated is the role of the exceptional woman in a male-dominated society, which has been examined by both Marion Zimmer Bradley and Anne McCaffrey.

In Bradley's book, *Hawkmistress!*, teenage tom-girl Romilly has telepathic rapport with birds and animals but finds herself caged in by parental and societal restrictions that prohibit her from working with hawks and lock her into a loveless engagement. She rebels, runs away, dons boys' clothing, and in a book filled with romantic adventure and narrow escapes, reinforces the themes of parent-child conflict as well as adolescent growth toward freedom, power, and responsibility.

In a similar vein, Anne McCaffrey's Killashandra in *Crystal Singer* is also kept from her goal; she will never realize the career as a skilled soloist for which she has trained so long. Leaving the music center, she undergoes a series of adventures as she works her way toward the mysterious and dangerous job of cutting bare crystal from mountainsides through sheer vocal power.

A neat combination of some of the best features of gadget, adventure and social SF (most works have elements of all three in varying degrees of balance) is C. J. Cherryh's *Port Eternity*. This tells an adventure story of a space flight on a ship owned by the opulent Lady Dela Kirn, and crewed, to suit her whimsy, by cloned servants designed to be persona from Arthurian myth: Lancelot, Elaine, Percivale, Gawain, Modred, Lynette, and Vivien. The tale focuses on Elaine as she discovers the truth about her programming and helps the others to break conditioning when their space ship "Maid of Astolat" is threatened.

Freda Bright's *Options* was not marketed as SF, but it is based on an extrapolation. "What if" the same woman could go through her life twice, taking two distinct, mutually exclusive roads: marriage and a career? Interestingly, Bright does not opt for either choice, portraying both as flawed. As the novel ends, married Kit is seeking a divorce; career woman Kate is about to get married.

The biggest "What if" in all science fiction is what if we (men or women) are not really alone? On the simplest level, this has evolved into stories about talking animals. Thus humans go outside of themselves to communicate with others: dolphins, pets, any creatures that may provide a different world perception.

On a more sophisticated level are the tales of telepathy, ranging from communication with infants (in utero or newborn, and often considered aliens to the adult world in either case), through mind-to-mind reading (as women are linked in Sally Miller Gearhart's *The Wanderground*, 1979). Ultimately, the authors examine the linking of many minds to form a new entity that is more than the sum of its parts (Theodore Sturgeon's *More than Human*, 1953), and is possibly united with a higher consciousness or God (Arthur C. Clarke's *Childhood's End*, 1953).

Of course there are the many tales of communication with creatures from other planets and life forms from other galaxies, E. T. cetera.

Communications with aliens leads to the possibility of studying them, learning from their lifestyles much that can be set up as a mirror against one's own. Jacqueline Lichtenberg, who had been examining sex roles in the relations of two human mutations, the Simes and the Gens, in her Zeor series has turned to look at a relationship closer than friendship but different from sexual love in *Molt Brother*. Here a reptilian female (a Kren named Arshel) swears "bhirhir" with a human male, binding the two for life in a brother-sisterhood that would be life threatening if severed. The work adds a new dimension to the possibilities of emotional rather than physical coupling as the two work and play together and help each other to mate, each with its own species.

All of this is an attempt to understand that which is different from oneself: the other. As Ursula LeGuin (1975) described the phenomenon in a critical article in *Science Fiction Studies*:

The question involved here is the question of the Other—the being which is different from yourself. This being can be different from you in its sex, or in its annual income; or in its way of speaking and dressing and doing things; or in the color of its skin, or the number of its legs and heads. In other words, there is the sexual Alien, and the social Alien, and the cultural Alien, and finally the racial Alien. . . .

If you deny any affinity with another person or kind of person, if you declare it to be wholly different from yourself—as men have done to women, and class has done to class, and nation has done to nation—you may hate it, or defy it; but in either case you have denied its spiritual equality, and its human reality. You have made it into a thing, to which the only possible relationship is a power relationship. And thus you have fatally impoverished your own reality. You have, in fact, alienated yourself. (3)

In SF it is not only possible to communicate with the other; it is possible to become the other. "What if" you could be a person of the opposite sex? Bron, the central character of Samuel R. Delany's *Triton* (1976), a blatant male supremist with an identity crisis, does just this in his search to overcome his sexist male ideology (the same thing could have happened to Michael Dorsey if *Tootsie* had been science fiction).

In the real world, such empathy is limited. When Steven Doloff (1983), a New York literature professor, asked his classes to respond to the film *Tootsie* by writing a paper on how each would spend a day as a member of the opposite sex, he was in for a surprise. The results, originally printed in the *Washington Post*, showed a great disparity of choice. Women tried everything they thought men were doing and enjoying: going places *alone*, staying out *all night*, throwing clothing on the floor, leaving dishes in the sink. They engaged in sports, cruised for dates, and deliberately accosted women. At least two women fantasized sex with imaginary girlfriends, wives, or strangers to examine what sex is like for a man.

Males did the opposite. Not one allowed himself to be touched sexually. Few even saw themselves dating. Rather, they led mundane lives as either housewives or workers who did their job, ate dinner, watched TV, and went directly to bed every night. The male students "seemed envious of very little that was female and curious about nothing." Doloff notes that one student crumpled up the paper after ten minutes, complaining, "You can't make me write about this." Others spent their day as a woman frantically seeking a sex-change operation to turn them back into males. Doloff concluded that sexist self-images and stereotypes are not nearly as vestigial as we would like to believe. Rather, we still carry their burden.

Mainstream works—movies, television, and fiction—are tied to reality, tied to reflecting what is while wishing for what might be. Thus men's roles, reflective of men's lives, are seen as positive and desirable. Women's roles (also reflective of reality) are negative, to be escaped at all costs. That has always been the message, and it remains so in the depiction of women in popular culture, circa 1982. Only SF offers alternatives: unconventional living arrangements, group marriages, matriarchal societies, even the construction of new languages.

In the novel *1984* (especially significant with the year so nearly upon us), author George Orwell posited the language Newspeak, which, by eliminating certain words and grammatical forms, could limit thinking. Currently, linguist and author Suzette Hayden Elgin is constructing a women's language to be set within the framework of a patriarchal novel to provide a subversive force by enabling women to say (and think) ideas impossible to formulate or express in the male-constructed tongue.

Science fiction is continually asking questions: about our language, about our roles, about what we will become. Will we, for example, become more like men, and take on all their faults as well as their virtues? Will we avoid becoming like men and instead bring new values to society and in this process also cause men to change? Science fiction asks the right questions and proposes many answers.

Doloff's students were asked the right question, but—embedded in reality—saw and responded to what is; SF sees and responds to what might be, and thus provides the most positive depiction of women in popular culture, not only for 1982, but for at least the twenty years preceding.

References

BOSWORTH, PATRICIA. 1982. Two S*M*A*S*H*I*N*G TV movies. *Working Woman*, November, pp. 212–14.

BOSWORTH, PATRICIA. 1983. The many faces of Dorothy Lyman. *Working Woman*, January, pp. 111–13.

DOLOFF, STEVEN. 1983. Students swap sex roles for imaginary day. *Chicago Sun Times*, February 1. Reprinted from the *Washington Post*.

HASKELL, MOLLY. 1983. Women in the movies grow up. *Psychology Today*, January, pp. 18–27.

How to tell a real woman. 1983. *People*, January, pp. 120–26.

KAEL, PAULINE. 1982a. The current cinema. *New Yorker*, February 22.

KAEL, PAULINE. 1982b. The current cinema. *New Yorker*, May 3.

LEGUIN, URSULA K. 1975. American SF and the other. *Science Fiction Studies*, November, pp. 208–9.

LISABETH, LAURA KING. 1982. BEATTS, a former square peg finds her niche. *School Press Review* 58, no. 1 (Fall):4–7.

NCWW studies 10 years of TV portrayal of working women: Rarely reflects reality. 1982. *Media Report to Women*, January-February, pp. 16–18.

PRESTON, MARILYNN. 1982. "Cagney and Lacy" deserves a closer look. *Chicago Tribune*, November 15.

SHALES, TOM. 1982. "Remington Steele": Originality loses its spark. *Chicago Sun Times*, October 23.

SEITZ, MICHAEL. 1982. Scheming flyboys and honest outlaws. *Progressive*, October, pp. 54–55.

SISKEL, GENE. 1983. Better films, more theaters: A winning year? *Chicago Tribune Arts and Books*, January 2, pp. 3–4.

WEIBEL, KATHRYN. 1977. *Mirror, mirror. Images of women reflected in popular culture*. New York: Anchor.

Bibliography

Behar, Phyllis. "Are Soaps Good for Your Health? The Experts Say Yes!" *Soap Opera Digest*, December 21, 1982, pp. 32–36.

Blooston, George. "Soft Porn in Soft Covers." *Publishers Weekly*, September 10, 1982, pp. 60–63.

Bumiller, Elisabeth. "America's Working Woman. Television Looks a Little Different Now." *TV Guide*, August 21, 1982, pp. 5–6.

Constantine, Peggy. "Soft-core Porn Hot in Soft Covers." *Chicago Sun Times*, February 1, 1983.

Friend, Beverly. "Virgin Territory: The Bonds and Boundaries of Women in Science Fiction." In *Many Futures, Many Worlds*, edited by Thomas Clareson. Kent, Oh.: Kent State University Press, 1977.

———. "Women's Role in Science Fiction: A Course Proposal." *Media Report to Women*, March 1, 1982.

Greenfield, Jeff. "Looking for a Happy Marriage on TV? Forget It!" *TV Guide*, April 17, 1982.

Nelson, Martha. "The Sex Life of the Romance Novel." *Ms*, February 1983, pp. 97–103.

Nightingale, Rosemary. "True Romances." *Miami Herald*, January 5, 1983.

Storch, Charles. "Female Execs Finding Room for Romances, Publisher Finds." *Chicago Tribune*, January 30, 1983.

Waters, Harry. "Life According to TV." *Newsweek*, December 6, 1982.

Resources

Movies

Best Friends. Written by Valerie Curtin and Barry Levinson, directed by Norman Jewison. With Burt Reynolds and Goldie Hawn.

Officer and a Gentleman, An. Written by Douglas Day Stewart, directed by Taylor Hackford. With Richard Gere and Debra Winger.

Personal Best. Written and directed by Robert Towne. With Patrice Donnelly and Mariel Hemingway.

Tootsie. Written by Larry Gelbart and Murray Schisgal from a story by Don McGuire and Larry Gelbart, directed by Sidney Pollack. With Dustin Hoffman, Jessica Lange, and Teri Garr.

Victor/Victoria. Written and directed by Blake Edwards. With Julie Andrews and James Garner.

Additional Movies

Dialogue with a Woman Departed. Written and directed by Leo Hurwitz. A three-hour, forty-five-minute film attempting to capture the spirit of Hurwitz's dead wife and co-worker Peggy Lawson.

Fast Times at Ridgemont High. Written by Cameron Crowe, directed by Amy Heckerling. With Jennifer Jason Leigh, Phoebe Cates, and Robert Romanus. Adaptation from Crowe's book about the year he spent undercover as a California high school student follows the course of teen lives with emphasis on their growing sexual awareness and its attendant problems.

Heartaches. Written by Terrance Hefferman, directed by Donald Shebib. With Margot Kidder and Annie Potts. Canadian film about two women hitting the road in search of meaning and self-discovery.

I'm Dancing as Fast as I Can. Written by David Rabe, directed by Jack Hofsiss. With Jill Clayburgh. A television producer who has experienced a psychotic withdrawal rises from her madness to cut a documentary about an inspirational woman poet.

Not a Love Story. Directed by Bonnie Sherr Klein with the participation of Linda Lee Tracey. Canadian documentary about pornography.

Six Weeks. Screenplay by David Seltzer based on the novel by Fred Mustard Stewart, directed by Tony Bill. With Dudley Moore and Mary Tyler Moore. Precocious little girl whose days are numbered finds perfect husband for mommy. But he's already married.

Television Series

All My Children (ABC). Written by Agnes Nixen, produced by Jacqueline Babbin.

Cagney and Lacey (CBS). With Sharon Gless and Tyne Daly.

Facts of Life (NBC). With Charlotte Rae.

Family Ties (NBC). With Meredith Baxter Birney and Michael Gross.

Gloria (CBS). With Sally Struthers and Burgess Meredith.

Remington Steele (NBC). With Stephanie Zimbalist and Pierce Brosnan.

Square Pegs (CBS). With Amy Linker and Sarah Jessica Parker.

Additional Television Series

Cheers (NBC). With Ted Danson, Nick Colasanto, and Shelley Long. Wisecracking waitress out-talks the jocks in the neighborhood pub.

It Takes Two (ABC). With Patty Duke Astin and Richard Crenna. Marital trials and tribulations among a lawyer-wife, doctor-husband, and two teenage children.

Joanie Loves Chachi (ABC). With Erin Moran and Scott Baio. *Happy Days* spin-off follows the love and singing careers of a young couple.

Mama's Family (NBC). With Carol Burnett and Vicki Lawrence. Sketches of family life spun off from the *Carol Burnett Show.*

St. Elsewhere (NBC). With Ed Flanders, David Birney, David Morse, and Cynthia Sikes. *Hill Street Blues* in a hospital.

Television Specials

Games Mother Never Taught You (CBS). With Loretta Swit.

Having it All (ABC). With Dyan Cannon.

I Was a Mail Order Bride (CBS). With Valeria Bertinelli.

My Body, My Child (ABC). With Vanessa Redgrave and Joseph Campanella.

Rodeo Girl (CBS). With Katherine Ross and Bo Hopkins.

Additional Television Specials

Born Beautiful (NBC). With Erin Gray and Lori Singer. Two models battle to succeed in their field.

First Time (ABC). With Susan Anspach, Jennifer Jason Leigh, and Harriet Nelson. Three women come of age at different stages in their lives.

Memories Never Die (CBS). With Lindsay Wagner. A woman tries to pick up the pieces of her life with her family after being institutionalized.

Sister, Sister (NBC). With Diahann Caroll, Irene Cara, and Rosalind Cash. Three black sisters contend with their problems while dominated by the memory of their late tyrannical father.

The Royal Romance of Charles and Diana (CBS). With Catherine Oxenberg and Christopher Baines. The CBS version of the royal couple.

ABC After-School Specials

January to June 1982:
My Mother Was Never a Kid
A Matter of Time
The Unforgiveable Secret
Daddy, I'm a Momma Now
Schoolboy Father
The Gymnast

July to December 1982:
Sometimes I Don't Love my Mother
Between Two Loves
VD Loves Everybody
The Unforgiveable Secret

Fiction

Douglas, Carol Anne. *To the Cleveland Station*. Tallahassee: Naiad Press, 1982.

Dukore, Margaret Mitchell. *A Novel Called Heritage*. New York: Scribners, 1982.

Gernes, Sonia. *The Way to St. Ives*. New York: Scribners, 1982.

Godwin, Gail. *A Mother and Two Daughters*. New York: Avon, 1982.

Granger, Katherine. *A Man's Persuasion*. New York: Berkley Second Chance at Love, 1982.

Howard, Maureen. *Grace Abounding*. Boston: Little, Brown, 1982.

Kennedy, Eugene. *Queen Bee*. New York: Doubleday, 1982.

Reed, Ann. *Starlit Seduction*. New York: Berkley Second Chance at Love, 1982.

Shange, Ntozake. *Sassafrass, Cypress, and Indigo*. New York: St. Martins, 1982.

Shoup, Barbara. *Nightwatch*. New York: Harper & Row, 1982.

St. Michel, Morgen. *Nicole in Captivity*. New York: Jove, 1982.

Taylor, Sheila Ortiz. *Faultline*. Tallahassee: Naiad, 1982.

Tyler, Anne. *Dinner at the Homesick Restaurant*. New York: Alfred A. Knopf, 1982.

Walker, Alice. *The Color Purple*. New York: Harcourt, Brace, Jovanovich, 1982.

Additional Fiction

Atwood, Margaret. *Bodily Harm.* New York: Simon & Schuster, 1982. After her life in Toronto is shattered by illness and the defection of her lover, a journalist flees to a Caribbean island and finds herself involved in a revolution.

Balantyne, Sheila. *Imaginary Crimes.* New York: Viking, 1982. Sonya Weiller is raised by a series of sadistic housekeepers after the death of her mother and withdraws into a fantasy life in the face of continued misery and loss.

Betts, Doris. *Heading West.* New York: Alfred A. Knopf, 1982. Psychological thriller about a bright, unmarried librarian who is kidnapped and carried-off by a haunted, taciturn, violent man.

Brown, Rita Mae. *Southern Discomfort.* New York: Harper & Row, 1982. A blonde, 27-year-old Montgomery aristocrat falls in love with a 15-year-old black aspiring boxer in 1918.

Buissard, Janine. *A New Woman.* Boston: Little, Brown, 1982. During the six-month period between her husband's departure and their divorce, a woman experiences emotional death and rebirth.

Cameron, Anne. *The Journey.* New York: Avon, 1982. Two strong, determined heroines set off on a Western adventure to find a better life.

Conran, Shirley, *Lace.* New York: Simon & Schuster, 1982. Four elegant jet-setters meet in New York to answer the plea of a world-famous movie actress: "Which one of you bitches is my mother?"

Douglas, Ellen. *A Lifetime Burning.* New York: Random House, 1982. A 62-year-old woman keeps a journal in an attempt to understand why her husband of thirty-two years has stopped sleeping with her.

Gowar, Antonia. *Cashing In.* Boston: Houghton Mifflin, 1982. New woman MBAs manipulate the world of high finance just as skillfully as male MBAs do.

Greenberg, Dan. *What Do Women Want?* New York: Wyndham Books, 1982. He doesn't know.

Hailey, Elizabeth Forsythe. *Life Sentences.* New York: Delacorte, 1982. Heroine with a paralyzed husband is made pregnant by a knife-wielding rapist.

Kidwell, Catherine. *Dear Stranger.* New York: Warner, 1982. Military bride who has ended a long-distance marriage after two years sets up meeting with her first husband after a thirty-year time lapse.

Levin, Jenifer. *Water Dancer.* New York: Poseidon Press, 1982. A long-distance swimmer learns to know herself through the arduous process of training.

McDermott, Alice. *A Bigamist's Daughter.* New York: Random House, 1982. Woman editor of a vanity press becomes involved with a male author writing a book defending bigamy.

[Michael, Judith] (Judith Barnard and Michael Fain). *Deceptions.* New York: Poseidon Press, 1982. Gorgeous identical twins (one the jet-set owner of an antique shop in London, the other a quiet housewife in Evanston) switch roles and husbands to take-on each other's lives.

Piercy, Marge. *Braided Lives.* New York: Summit, 1982. Jill Stuart, growing up in 1950s Detroit, longs to escape her working-class roots and sordid family life.

Rosen, Norma. *At the Center.* Boston: Houghton Mifflin, 1982. Brave confrontation of hard questions about abortion.

Sarton, May. *Anger.* New York: W. W. Norton, 1982. Stormy marriage of an emotionless banker and his half-Italian, half-Swedish opera-singer wife.

Smith, Robert Kimmel. *Jane's House.* New York: William Morrow, 1982. Jane dies and husband Paul brings home a new wife to live in her house and nurture her two children.

Steele, Danielle. *Once in a Lifetime.* New York: Dell, 1982. Romantic flashbacks on life and marriages of a famous novelist as she lies in a hospital following an auto accident.

Swados, Elizabeth. *Leah and Lazar.* New York: Summit, 1982. An artistic young woman sets out to discover herself in New York after she has freed herself from the influence of her older brother.

Woodiwiss, Kathleen. *A Rose in Winter.* New York: Avon, 1982. Typical romance about a young girl who is auctioned off to a mysterious high-bidder against her will.

Science Fiction

Bradley, Marion Zimmer. *Hawkmistress!* New York: DAW, 1982.

Bright, Freda. *Options.* New York, Pocket Books, 1982.

Cherryh, C. J. *Port Eternity.* New York: DAW, 1982.

Clayton, Jo. *Moongather.* New York: DAW, 1982.

Heinlein, Robert A. *Friday.* New York: Holt, Rinehart & Winston, 1982.

————. *Podkayne of Mars.* New York: Avon, 1963.

Lee, Tanith. *The Silver Metal Lover.* New York: DAW, 1982.

Lichtenberg, Jacqueline. *Molt Brother.* New York: Playboy, 1982.

McCaffrey, Anne. *Crystal Singer.* New York: Ballentine, 1982.

Salmonson, Jessica Amanda, ed. *Amazons II.* New York: DAW, 1982.

Additional Science Fiction

Auel, Jean M. *The Valley of the Horses.* New York: Crown, 1982. The series that opened with *Clan of the Cave Bear* continues the story of Ayla who, because of her early years in a patriarchal society that devalues women, is disconcerted to meet a man raised in a matriarchal society which grants equality to both sexes.

Dibell, Ansen. *Summerfair.* New York: DAW, 1982. Volume three in a five-volume series continues the conflicts among the strong male and female characters as Duke Pedross tries to protect the empire he is building.

Herbert, Frank. *The White Plague.* New York: Putnam, 1982. Vengeful molecular biologist who has lost his wife and children in an IRA bomb attack creates a selective virus that attacks only women.

Goldstein, Lisa. *The Red Magician.* New York: Timescape, 1982. A young Jewish girl comes of age during the Holocaust in a town in eastern Europe where the rabbi has genuine magical powers.

Kingsbury, Donald. *Courtship Rite.* New York: Timescape, 1982. Three brother-husbands and their two wives search for the third wife to complete the marriage group, but are thwarted by political powers.

McKillip, Patricia A. *Stepping from the Shadows*. (New York: Atheneum, 1982. The story of the emergence into womanhood of a painfully shy girl is structured through the revelation and integration of her three separate personalities.

Nelson, Ray Faraday. *The Prometheus Man*. Virginia Beach, Va.: Starblaze/Donning, 1982. In a world where merit is supreme, Holly McClintok obtains a job and divorces her loser husband after she passes and he fails their final exams.

Piserchia, Doris. *The Dimensioneers*. New York: DAW, 1982. Cornelia, reluctant inmate of an orphanage, survives her imprisonment by making frequent trips to other planets through a time-space tunnel.

Schwartz, Susan M., ed. *Hecate's Cauldron*. New York: DAW, 1982. Collection of original stories about witches and witchcraft.

Psychology: A Feminist Perspective on Family Therapy

Rachel T. Hare-Mustin

Nowhere do the inequities in society affect more women in their daily lives than in the family. Yet women in families—mothers, daughters, sisters, wives—are often overlooked by those who see the need for changes in approaches to therapy for women. Family therapists who focus on the interests of the entire family over those of the individual and who seek to restore family functioning by reinforcing traditional models may be perpetuating unhappiness and conflict. In fact, family therapists have the opportunity to intervene in many ways to change the oppressive consequences of stereotyped sex roles.

The Emergence of Family Therapy

From its early beginnings in the 1950s, the field of family therapy has grown to a significant and separate mental health specialty dealing with a range of problems including temper tantrums, school phobias, child and marital abuse, delinquency, alcoholism, sexual relations, marital conflict, and divorce, as well as associated problems of depression, anxiety, and psychotic disorders. Interest in family and marital therapy is reflected in the number of books and articles that have appeared in the past decade, in the establishment of family therapy training institutes, and in the increased membership in professional associations of those who identify themselves as family and marital therapists (Olson, Russell, and Sprenkle 1980). There has also been proliferation of programs and workshops on family therapy and a significant increase in the amount of family therapy training required in general psychiatry residency programs (Sugarman 1981).

    In family therapy, the entire family rather than the individual is regarded as the unit of treatment. Typically, the members are seen together in the

Appreciation is expressed to Sharon Lamb for her many thoughtful comments and keen observations associated with the preparation of this chapter.

treatment session, but even when not all are present, the therapist thinks in terms of family interactions and relationships. The hallmark of the field has been relationship-oriented treatment, and the theoretical approach that has made this possible is family systems theory. The family is regarded as a system that affects individuals who in turn affect the system. This differs from traditional approaches to behavior that use the view of science involving linear-reductionistic thinking. In linear causality, event A affects event B, such as childhood affecting adulthood, but B does not affect A. In circular causality, B also affects A. To illustrate, one can look at nagging behavior from these contrasting perspectives. Using the individual-centered focus of linear causality, A, the nagger, is said to be doing something to B, the nagged one. But in the transactional approach represented by circular causality, what B, the nagged one, is doing to A, to influence or cause A's nagging behavior is equally considered. The ideas of circular causality and feedback borrowed from cybernetics have led to family therapy representing a wholly new paradigm for conceptualizing human behavior rather than being merely the application of a new technique to an individual-oriented treatment model (Weiner 1948).

Family therapists avoid diagnosis that uses pejorative labels such as passive aggressive and implies that the problem lies within the individual. Instead they use schemas for understanding families' ways of relating, such as a circumpolar schema that includes three dimensions: family cohesion, family adaptability, and communication (Olson, Russell, and Sprenkle 1980); or the dichotomized schema of enmeshed and disengaged families (Minuchin 1974). In addition, family therapists often take a preventive orientation, recognizing that changes in the membership of a family by birth, death, separation, or different activity cause a realignment of relationships and responsibilities. As the stress research of Holmes and Rahe (1967) indicates, ten out of the top fourteen stressors for individuals have to do with gaining or losing a family member. These often predictable events in the family life cycle allow therapists to predict crises and engage in prevention of family stress around their occurrence.

The pioneers in family therapy could be described as untrained in this field. Most of them were males who came from a psychoanalytic background and were engaged in research on the problems of schizophrenics or delinquents and their families in the late 1940s and early 1950s. On the West Coast, Jackson, Bateson, Haley, and Weakland were working on problems of family communication at the Mental Research Institute, while in the East, several researchers were observing families independently, among them Wynne, Lidz, Ackerman, Bowen, and Minuchin. Research as well as therapy initially centered on the mother-child interaction, with the child-centered, child guidance approach holding the mother to blame for the child's problems (Hare-Mustin 1978). Kagan (1979) has observed that the idealization of the mother-infant bond, a view that children are highly vulnerable and early influences are immutable, is a result of Freudian theory and is peculiarly American. In fact, children have been found to be remarkably robust, and later influences can override early experiences.

The early family reseachers were innovators and mavericks. They were struck by the resistance of families to change, a kind of homeostasis where the disturbed member was almost necessary for the family system to keep functioning (Haley 1980; Hoffman 1981). As family systems theory developed, and with it a deemphasis on women as the cause of pathology and a shift from preeminence conceded to the masculine sex by Freudian theory, more women professionals emerged as active in the field, following Satir's early participation; these include Carter, Coleman, Hare-Mustin, Hoffman, Madanes, LaPierre, McGoldrick, Palazzoli, Papp, Penn, Silverstein, and Walters.

The origins of family therapy are quite different from those of feminist therapy. Feminist therapy grew out of the theory and philosophy of consciousness raising. It emphasizes equality in the relationship between therapist and client with therapists examining their own values concerning women and seeking to validate the female experience. Feminist therapy goes beyond nonsexist therapy in its analysis of the forms of social, economic, and political oppression that affect women (Gilbert 1980; Donovan and Littenberg 1982). Women are encouraged not only to become aware of the oppressiveness of traditional roles, but to gain experiences that enhance self-esteem as they try new behaviors (Hare-Mustin 1978).

The new emphasis on the relational context in family therapy would seem compatible with feminism, which has rejected intrapsychic explanations of pathology and focused on the social and political influences on individual behavior. Still, however, much of family therapy remains limited by a traditional perspective. Five years ago, in my analysis of a feminist approach to family therapy, I pointed out that "although family therapy recognizes the importance of the social context as a determiner of behavior, family therapists have not examined the consequences of traditional socialization practices that primarily disadvantage women" (Hare-Mustin 1978, p. 181). Since that time, there have been some changes in the practice of family therapy but only a handful of articles that have examined the field from a feminist perspective (Caust, Libow, and Raskin 1981; Gurman and Klein 1980; Hare-Mustin 1979a, b, 1980; Libow, Raskin, and Caust 1982).

This chapter examines ideas about the American family that influence therapists and reviews three major approaches to family therapy. It then considers couple therapy, therapy with nontraditional families, and finally, analyzes family therapy from a feminist perspective.

The American Family

The two basic functions of the family have been described as socialization of children and stabilization of adult personalities (Parsons and Bales 1955). Emphasis on distinct sex roles, identified by Parsons as the instrumental role for men and the expressive role for women, has led to these being used as criteria for differentiating normal and pathogenic families (Peal 1975). Although most Americans have applauded the apparent decline in the power of class, genealogy, and tradition to determine social position, they have apparently clung to sexual classification as the last remaining insurance against social disorder (Rosenberg 1982). The traditional family is one in which the husband is the good provider and head of household, the wife is housekeeper and mother, and the children are subject to parental control (Bernard 1981). Bane (1976) notes that the family does not provide equality—individual rights lose in the service of the family—but she extolls the idea of the family as a private refuge. This view is not unlike that held in the early nineteenth century when the family evolved from a domestic economic unit to a retreat from the community, presided over by the mother (Weitz 1977). Women have been expected to pay the price of the family's survival, often subject to isolation and emotional overload or contradictory demands between family roles and occupational requirements. Typically, the fact that housework, with its low status and diminished visibility, supports the wage labor force goes unacknowledged.

Family life in the 1950s, when family therapy began, was far different from any other decade. The later ages at which young people marry today are more similar to the ages at which they married during most of this century. Today's one- and two-child families are more consistent with the long-term trend of the declining birth rate in the United States (Cherlin 1979). The stereotypical image from the 1950s of employed husband, full-time housewife, and two school-age children applies to less than 10 percent of American families today (Wattenberg and Reinhardt 1981), when the most prevalent type of family has two wage earners and two parents. Abortion is not a recent phenomenon, as it was widespread in the nineteenth century, terminating an estimated 20 percent or more of all pregnancies in the United States, compared with 30 percent today; the great majority were sought by married women (Degler 1980). The fact that one-fifth of all children live with a single parent, 90 percent with the mother, may be due to increased divorce and early sexuality, as one-third of all girls and one-half of boys of all races are sexually active by their sixteenth birthday (Gerstel 1982; Haskins 1982).

The high birth rate between the mid-1940s and early 1960s means that on reaching adulthood, people born during that time face greater competition and fewer opportunities than their predecessors or successors (Norton and Glick 1979). Women in this group are in a marriage squeeze, so postponement of marriage may be contributing to their role expansion.

Family therapists are likely to acknowledge the variations in family relationships and structures ranging from single-parent to commune families, reconstituted families from previous marriages, and gay and cohabiting couples, but the majority of services are still offered to individuals in a marriage and family relationship (Olson, Russell, and Sprenkle 1980). Marriage remains the preferred state in America as 96 out of every 100 adults marry, but the emphasis on self-fulfillment has meant a lower tolerance for unhappy marriages. Of the 38 percent who divorce, 83 percent of the men and 75 percent of the women remarry within three years (Goldenberg and

Goldenberg 1980). Only 15 percent of women whose marriages terminate after age forty remarry (Norton and Glick 1979).

Women's Employment Outside the Home   The most dramatic change in work and family patterns in this century has been the entry of women into the world of paid work. Now over half the married women are employed outside the home and the average married woman is employed for twenty-five years (Packwood 1982; Scanzoni 1979). Sex differences defined by domestic activities have been carried into the occupational world to isolate women in certain kinds of jobs, typically, those with low pay. Women are restricted because the family cycle has depended on their remaining at home for some periods or engaging in part-time work connected with bearing and caring for children. Incomes have reflected differentials in status with society's ranking system depending on the husband's income. Married women working outside the home are still defined by their role in the family (Weitz 1977).

Women are the absorption point for stress produced by the intersection of work and family systems although few therapists address this problem (Pleck 1977). Household tasks segregated by sex have been maintained with only slight adjustments to women's work outside the home. Although there has been more discussion of sex-role preferences in the family, evidence of actual changes in behavior is lacking (Scanzoni and Fox 1980). Acceptance of asymmetrical permeable boundaries between work and family roles is so widespread as to be unquestioned by family members and therapists. Men's individual achievements are seen as benefitting the family, women's as interfering with the family. For women, intrusion of the family role into the work role leads to negative stereotypes about women workers and is a source of stress on the job. For husbands, there is permeability in the other direction, as they can take work home or use family time to recuperate from occupational stresses. When both partners follow the male work model, especially in what are called "greedy occupations" in which professional and managerial employees are expected to be totally committed to the organization and strive to advance, extraordinary strain is generated (Handy 1978). In general, employment outside the home is associated with improved mental health for married women despite role overload (Perlin 1975). Although there is a strong correlation for men between earnings and mental health, the mental health of women is unrelated to their earnings (Kessler and McRae 1982). Women with higher earnings do not have less anxiety or depression than women with lower earnings but men with higher earnings do. However, employed mothers show greater satisfaction and self-acceptance, and fewer physical symptoms than those at home (Hoffman 1976). The impact of maternal employment on young children has shown that girls gain in achievement, social adjustment, self-esteem, and their valuation of women. It may cause father-son strains, however, with sons showing less admiration for their fathers (Hoffman 1979). Pleck (1977) has noted that although maternal employment has long and incorrectly been thought to harm children psychologically, it was rarely asked whether paternal employment might do so as well.

Female-Headed Families   Since one of every seven families is headed by a woman, the female-headed family cannot be regarded as a rare situation (Wattenberg and Reinhardt 1981). The impoverished condition of one-half of such households has led to concerns about the feminization of poverty (Cashion 1982). This is true particularly in light of the fact that the plight of the single mother worsens at the same time the father enjoys a higher standard of living (Wattenberg and Reinhardt 1981). Only 14 percent of divorced women are granted alimony, and fewer than half are actually paid it regularly because of husbands' refusal to abide by the agreement. Alimony and child support are the primary source of income for only 7 percent of female-headed families. Children in female-headed families have as good adjustment and self-esteem as those with two parents, except when the former are stigmatized because of poverty and negative attitudes of adults (Cashion 1982).

Feminist View of the Family   As Thorne (1982) has pointed out, "Critical analyses of the family, and efforts to change traditional family arrangements, *have* been central to the women's movement. . . . Of all the issues raised by feminists, those that bear on family—among them, demands for abortion rights and for legitimating an array of household and sexual arrangements, and challenges of men's authority and women's economic dependence and exclusive responsibility for nurturing—have been the most controversial" (p. 1, emphasis in original). Women's lives change radically when they have children, and mothers of young children are often overburdened and report little satisfaction from their role (Hare-Mustin 1983). The child's view of the mother is solely of someone who does or does not live up to the child's expectations, so it is not surprising that therapists themselves find it hard to deal with mothers. The mythic nature of motherhood includes both idealization and deprecation, the mother being identified as the cause of almost every serious psychological disorder (Hare-Mustin and Broderick 1979; Hare-Mustin, Bennett, and Broderick 1983). Recent analysis of feminist writings shows a convergence of ideas of the all-powerful mother with those of conservative writers, the former extolling perfectability, the latter, destruction (Chodorow and Contratto 1982).

As feminists have broken through the assumptions of female pettiness, frivolousness, and pointlessness of purpose, they have also recognized the gratifying and humane elements of women's traditional work, with the family serving as a source of resistance to other social institutions as well as an agent of socialization (Elshtain 1982; Flax 1982). The problem is that as modern families have tended to insulate themselves, this has created the illusion that the family is independent of the economy, the state, and the mental health system. In fact, the family has become the battleground for inequity sanctioned in the larger society. Defenders of the idealized family as a haven demand that the family and women make up for the indifference and hostility of the outer world. Rather than the family today being a refuge from activities that occur in common work and crowded urban areas, the anonymity and freedom of urban life may be a refuge from the intimacy, intensity, and responsibility of the private world of the family. One can occupy urban space without having demands made upon one.

The functionalist views of Parsons (1955) pervade interpretations of the family with the implication that a particular sexual division of labor is inevitable and mutually exclusive. Feminists have pointed out that the language of roles conveys that the roles are both fixed and dichotomous and separate but equal (Thorne 1982). Uncritical use of terms like "sex roles" obscures differences of power between men and women, as well as the presence of conflict, and exaggerates other differences between them. Thus the sexual division of labor makes men and women dependent on one another. The fact that women now spend a smaller proportion of their lives in mothering activities raises questions about sex role differences, which in the past derived from women's being often and unpredictably pregnant (Hoffman 1977). Although these differences may be biologically based, they are not unchangeable. Functionalism cannot explain why some institutions exist rather than others, such as why women rather than men care for children beyond the suckling period.

Adults teach children traits that they believe will be helpful to the children when they have grown up. Despite the advent of the women's movement, the general pattern of sex typing of playthings and of childrens' chores has continued, as has stereotyping in childrens' literature and television. Fathers seek more gross motor behavior from sons than daughters, and play more roughly with sons (Hoffman 1977). It has been found that fathers more than mothers treat sons and daughters differently (Lamb and Lamb 1976), a fact of which therapists and others who encourage fathers to shift to more involvement in parenting seem unaware. The formulation of dominant mother/ineffectual father is typically made without regard for the underlying inequality that leads to such a situation. Failure to question assigned sex roles of all family members is one of the most pervasive shortcomings of family therapy, as becomes evident in the following examination of the major therapeutic approaches.

Schools of Family Therapy

A recent study of the theoretical framework of family therapists found three dominant orientations: communications/Satir; structural/strategic; and psychoanalytic/historical (Green and Kolevzon 1982). They have in common the practice of clarifying roles and relationships, endorsing appropriate self-disclosure, and favoring involvement of all family members in the therapeutic process. An additional orientation, the behavioral approach, has been widely used in marital therapy. It should be remembered in analyzing these four perspectives that they intersect in various ways, and many family therapists are influenced by more than one.

Communication Approach   The communication approach focuses on the ways family members send and receive messages. Family communications theorists have sometimes been divided into three groups (Foley 1974): (1) communication and cognition, associated with Jackson and Watzlawick (Watzlawick, Weakland, and Fisch 1974); (2) communication and power, associated with Haley (1976, 1980); and (3) communication and feeling, emphasized by Satir (1967). These theorists all conceptualize personality in terms of interaction, which thus places them within the family systems approach.

Satir's communications theory is most distinct from the others. Her emphasis on the expression of feelings and the importance of therapists' own growth and development provides a bridge between psychoanalytic and communication approaches. As in psychodynamic systems, she emphasizes that therapists' effectiveness is dependent on their understanding of their position in the family in which they grew up (family of origin). The communications and the psychoanalytic schools advocate the use of cotherapists to relate in different ways to the family, the sharing of therapists' perceptions, and preference for growth rather than resolution of specific family problems. They also advocate taking a family history and believe change can be facilitated by helping family members talk about and show their feeling about themselves and each other.

Communications approaches fail to challenge critically sex role inequities or the impact of the larger society on women and the family. On the face of it, encouragement of the expression of feelings would seem to reinforce women for the way they have been socialized. In fact, this therapeutic maneuver is based on Freudian notions of the negative effect of repression, with the consequent assumption that the free and open expression of feelings will solve problems and make people feel better. The encounter-group movement provides evidence for the ineffectiveness and often harmful results of such a position (Lieberman, Yalom, and Miles 1973).

Psychoanalytic/Historical Approaches   Feminists have produced a number of critiques of psychoanalysis and how it has disadvantaged women, which do not need to be repeated here (Albee 1981; Brodsky 1980; Hare-Mustin 1983). Nevertheless, it is sobering that in a recent survey, 300 family therapists ranked Freud second of the ten most influential theorists on family therapy (Sprenkle, Keeney, and Sutton 1982). Bowen, one of the pioneers in the field, sees the essence of family therapy as having the parents come to terms with their relationships with their own parents and extended families and being able to function autonomously from the "undifferentiated family ego mass," the emotional connectedness and influence among family members (1978). Bowen's emphasis on rational independence as opposed to emotionality fails to acknowledge that women are socialized to be more emotional and intuitive than men. His definition of "differentiation" as "growing away" further disregards the considerable research that shows that women do not "grow away," but use family members as important resources.

The Differentiation of Self Scale of Bowen, which measures the degree to which people are able to distinguish between feelings and thoughts and apply intellectual processes to study their own emotional functioning, is little more than a masculinity-femininity scale with females at the devalued end (Hare-Mustin 1978). The separation of intellect from emotions appears a typically male idea. Bowen's technique is to work with the most rational person to maintain the person in the face of emotional pressure. Frequently he sees only this person and assumes this person will in turn change the family by taking a firm stance. He assumes that problems such as juvenile delinquency arise because families rely on emotional processes in decision making.

The extent to which Bowen's theory supports the traditional approach to the family is seen in a recent edited volume by his followers (Carter and McGoldrick 1980). As in Bowen's own work, most of the examples of therapy are individual-oriented, the key to successful family therapy being how, according to Bowen, "individuals differentiate from their families of origin." Although dealing with the life cycle, these therapists do not seem familiar with developmental theory literature, including the more recent work focusing on women's development (Rossi 1980). The emphasis on firm boundaries around the newly married couple to separate from their families of origin reflects the male-culture's perspective that values independence and separation. On the positive side, there is consideration of women who have careers or choose not to have children.

In acknowledging that it is difficult for contemporary parents to make space for children, with women shifting more toward the nondomestic sphere but men not shifting toward the domestic sphere, Bradt (1980) takes a feminist perspective. This makes less comprehensible his position that the decision not to have children is a selfish one, given the overload for women that he has identified.

From a feminist perspective, the typical limitations of Bowen's theory are seen in Braverman's (1981) discussion of the ego loss for parents when a child "differentiates," that is, becomes separate and seeks distance from the parents. From this individual-oriented psychoanalytic framework, the therapist points in a stereotyped way to the overly involved parent as the mother and the distant one as the father. Although attending well to transactional aspects, the author disregards the social context of and environmental demands on family members in terms of sex role norms and expected behaviors.

A related historical/psychodynamic approach (Boszormenyi-Nagy and Spark 1973) has been called ethical because it extolls obligations to others. It does not offer the kind of feminist analysis that might question the equity of such obligations, obligations Nagy sees as bonds of loyalty transcending generations. The unquestioned determinism of biological-emotional gender roles he uses, noted earlier (Hare-Mustin 1978), continues with his examples of debt and entitlements:

These may vary greatly even between two siblings; e.g., it may be imperative for one to become a success, the other to become a failure. According to the legacy of this family, the son may be entitled to approval, the daughter only to shame. Thus the legacy may fall with gross unfairness on the two. But whatever the specific terms, they derive their weight from the fact that the children were born of their parents. The children are ethically bound to accommodate their lives somehow to their legacies. (Boszormenyi-Nagy and Ulrich 1981, p. 163)

Nagy holds that liberation from the cycle of destructive action can occur only through finding evidence of trustworthiness in and exonerating previous generations. Otherwise the adult offspring are locked into traditional roles.

Nagy's therapy rejects the use of relabeling, believing it is not the therapist's task to put things in a better light or to decide the ultimate justice of an issue, a position at variance with a feminist orientation. One of his goals for therapy of the "constructive complementarity of male-female roles" fails to question the traditional role system.

From time to time therapists have attempted to integrate family systems theory and psychoanalysis such as Pearce and Friedman's (1980) proposal that individual psychodynamics be considered as a subsystem of the family. Such integration may not be helpful to women to the extent that it seeks causes of unhappiness in early life and emphasizes individual pathology.

Psychoanalytic therapists in family work tend to emphasize the therapeutic relationship itself. The unrequited love that women have often felt for their therapists has been criticized by feminists who believe that encouragement of such dependency and longings does not foster good mental health in the patient and often leads to her sexual abuse by the therapist (Hare-Mustin 1983). Feminist therapists think the "transfer" of such feelings is not likely to solve women's problems, favoring instead the encouragement of independence and competence.

While expressing allegiance to family systems therapy, some therapists hold views that are basically psychoanalytic in nature and denigrating of women. An article entitled "The Paranoid Wife Syndrome" defines this as "wives presenting a paranoid delusional system of thought as expiation for their feelings of failure as women and intensive aversive reactions to their husband's character traits" (Williams, Trick, and Troum 1981, p. 75). The therapists go on to state that such women reveal a pattern of failure regarding developmental tasks essential to female maturity, such as caring for their husbands and seeking fulfillment in traditional female roles. Pains are taken to point out that these wives had mothers who were lacking in empathy. The goals for treatment are markedly sexist, being to increase the wife's sense of femininity and defuse her predilection to anger, while helping the husband meet his own needs by being supported by the therapist.

Another such article is one on the incest taboo, which focuses on sexual abuse within the home and loosening of sexual boundaries in remarried families (Perlmutter, Engel, and Sager 1982). The abuser's behavior is explained as stemming from his perception of his own maternal deprivation and suppressed anger toward the mother. The authors seem oblivious of the larger societal issue that has to do with male dominance and treatment of women. The article is also illustrative of the kind of male-oriented language used by some therapists, such as "mother of shapely 15-year-old" (p. 84); "Juanita was aware that she was voluptuous despite her silent prayers not to grow up" (p. 85); "fears were diffused and Juanita's attractiveness was acknowledged" (p. 86).

Brief family interventions can be used despite a psychoanalytic orientation. A good example of relabeling is a case where a little girl was fearful before going to school each morning. Although the therapist saw the fears in oedipal terms as rivalry for the father, he did not interpret this but taught her parents how to set limits to help her experience herself as angry rather than a fragile little thing who needed coddling (Weltner 1982b). On the whole, however, by focusing on historical and unconscious origins of family and marital conflict, the psychoanalytic family approach tends to view human experience in pathological terms.

Systems Approaches   Although virtually all family therapists claim they are dealing with the entire family system, the new paradigm for viewing the family in terms of relationships is most evident in structural and strategic approaches to family systems. Communication approaches other than those emphasizing feelings are also in this category.

Systems therapists do not believe that awareness of one's place in one's family of origin makes for a skilled therapist, as there are other ways to learn about family systems. Nor are expressions of feelings, associated with women's socialization, considered useful therapy. Haley (1976, 1980) believes that the free expression of feelings may be appropriate at religious revival meetings, but in therapy it is incoherent, disorganized, abrasive, and interminable, and most important, does not produce change.

By emphasizing the effects of behavior and communication of members on each other, systems therapy rejects the view that problems reside within the individual and the medical model as an explanation of the individual's problems. Diagnostic labels are viewed as an inaccurate representation of the interactional system and therefore not useful. Symptoms in family members are seen as a result of difficulties in the family system, rather than an individual's "fault." As in feminist therapy, family therapists relabel or reframe difficulties to shift members' perception of the problems.

This approach is best developed in the communications work of the Mental Research Institute (Watzlawick, Weakland, and Fisch 1974), the structural family therapy of Minuchin (Minuchin 1974; Minuchin and Fishman 1981), and in the strategic approach of Haley (1976, 1980), Madanes (1981), and the Milan group (Palazzoli et al. 1978). Although the theory behind these approaches is not inherently sexist, they all tend to be oriented toward control and power, and a tit-for-tat approach that fails to consider the inequity between members of the family system. However, a family systems typology such as Beavers's (1981), which characterizes "optimal families" as having parents sharing power flexibly shows awareness of sex role stereotypes. His typology identifies sex role stereotyping as more apparent in "adequate families," "males being powerful and unemotive, counterpoised by less powerful, more emotive (sometimes depressed) females" (p. 302).

More than any other, Minuchin's (1974, 1981) structural approach emphasizes clear generational boundaries and redesigning the family to approximate the traditional family with its authority differences of parents and children and age-related expectations. Minuchin sees his role as a conductor directing change, in contrast to the reactor-type therapist who is more passive and aims merely to free families to realize their potential (Barker 1981). Minuchin's tendency to ally with the father to strengthen his position in the family has been modified over the years, and his recent work emphasizes the importance of the therapist not rendering the parents, especially the mother, incompetent. He believes that as an expert, the therapist needs a mixture of wisdom, technology, humor, and ignorance, because in systems terms, too much helpfulness defines the clients as helpless.

Minuchin has emphasized that the family context affects the individual's inner processes and that changes in the family change the individual. A central belief of the structural approach is that pathology is a function of faulty family organization, and the family organization should be confronted, largely to strengthen boundaries between the generations of parents, children, and grandparents. Change is promoted by direct experience rather than intellectualization, such as by the therapist forming alliances to support one or more family members who then can do or say something that would not ordinarily be possible.

While the structural approach emphasizes family structure, the strategic school is more paradoxical, putting emphasis on the "symptom" or presenting problem and the repeated communication patterns that must be interrupted if the system is to reorganize itself. Some therapists combine the two approaches, initially dealing with the family in a structural way, then switching to a strategic approach when resistance mounts or a strong tendency against changing is noted (Fraser 1982). Haley (1976, 1980), the best known theorist of the strategic school, sees the therapist as having responsibility for planning a strategy for solving the client's problem. Haley has been an iconoclast, challenging the mental health establishment and theories of the organic causes of mental illness, as well as psychodynamic theories that hold the individual has something wrong independent of the social situation. He rejects the negative Freudian view of human nature that explains problems as due to repression of hostility, anxiety, hatred, and incestuous passion. He has also criticized therapists' blaming parents for their children's problems, although one could argue that the family systems approach merely shifts to blaming "the family." Haley believes that disturbed behavior is basically protective of the family organization. He observes the family status hierarchy, and defines success for a young person as finding work and intimate relationships outside the family. He never raises questions about family boundaries for women, however. Feminist therapists may respect the client's ideas about how therapy is conducted, but systems therapists believe the client should not decide how therapy is to be conducted.

The strategic approach of Madanes (1981) redefines emotional problems into relational or mechanical problems and uses suggestion as well as pretend suggestion. In acknowledging that family participants are not equal, Madanes is aware of status differences based on age, control of resources, and community-vested authority and responsibility, noting that many therapists make the mistake of treating the family as a group of members of equal status. Madanes falls into a similar pattern, however, saying there are typically two comparable family hierarchies and no victims, each of the marital pair being one-up in some regard, even if it is one-up in helplessness. This seems a sophistic approach: a hierarchy based on control of money and one based on knowledge of relatives are not inherently equal. Systems theory holds helplessness is interactional as a symptomatic behavior that protects the other spouse by defining him or her as the competent one. By redefining helpless behavior as being helpful or protective, one denies that there are genuine injustices or victims as in child or spouse abuse, whatever the victim's part in maintaining the interaction. On the other hand, the view that problems can result from an excess of helpfulness does draw attention to the fact that symptoms or weaknesses are also ways of getting power.

Milton Erickson (Haley 1973), from whom the strategic approach evolved, was skillful at designing task interventions to take into consideration a client's social situation, but his use of the community is not apparent in most strategic work.

Stereotyped case examples that are sexist as well as boring tend to appear in much of family therapists' writing. Typical is Hoffman's (1980) case of a nagging domineering mother and a passive father trying to change their son. Sexism is apparent in assuming mother and daughter are in natural competition for the father, or in pointing to the problem of father controlling son's access to money when mother works and has money of her own (Haley 1980). A task Madanes (1981) assigns is for a mother to pretend incompetence in handling the children so an uninvolved father can step in. This of course reinforces the stereotyped traditional view of the father as only a disciplinarian and the mother as one who cannot handle disruptive children.

By reinforcing existing conditions, some paradoxical tasks are intended to use resistance to produce change, but since success is not inevitable, they can encourage family patterns that feminists believe should be changed. A particularly unfortunate example is one of the husband who is excused from chores being given the task of directing how things should be done at home, which he is doing anyway (Fisher, Anderson, and Jones 1981). Therapists believe they are helping the wife by taking responsibility off her shoulders, but they are merely making the man's control more overt. Their hope is that the husband will back down from the responsibility, but it is not clear that this is accomplished, or that the task challenges stereotyped behaviors.

Behavioral Couple Therapy   The ideal marriage provides companionship and love, yet marital conflict ranks as a major problem for which people seek mental health services. Recent surveys report that between 42 and 75 percent of married people seek help for marital problems (Gurman and Klein 1980). In their analysis of marital and family conflicts from a feminist perspective, these authors draw attention to the cultural, political, and social variables that relate to women's relative lower status and the limited satisfactions inherent in the wife role. As they note, the currently popular life span-developmental perspectives such as Levinson's are career-oriented, based on research on men; they focus on the first job, job change, the job mentor, increasing job responsibility, and turning away from the job in later years. When women are included, as in Erikson's work, female development is defined as centered on relationships with males. The assumption that women benefit more from marriage than men is not supported by findings that married women are more than twice as likely to be depressed as married men or single women, or that health statistics favor married men in terms of longevity and health (Brodsky and Hare-Mustin 1980; Sobel and Russo 1980; Weissman 1980).

Behavioral approaches stress the power of rational processes and new skills in therapeutic change. Assertiveness training has helped women, but deficits in communication skills are seen by behavioral therapists as the primary cause of marital conflict. The solutions have been described as glib, perfunctory, and reduced to contingency contracting which is often sexist (Liberman et al. 1980). Behaviorists disavow expressing feelings, including anger, (Jacobsen 1981). Feminists, in contrast, feel that women need to understand and acknowledge their legitimate anger against society and the institutions that oppress them, including appropriate anger at one's therapist (Hare-Mustin et al. 1979). The emphasis on reciprocity in a couple's developing a new contract would seem on the face of it egalitarian, but it ignores the differences in status and resources available to men and women (Sager 1976). The goal of increasing collaboration of the couple can lead to women making the primary accommodations, as they have been socialized to do. What Jacobsen (1981) holds out as a typical example of behavior exchange procedures is so dramatically inequitable as almost to need no comment. With the therapist's encouragement, the wife asks that the husband cook once a week, assume full responsibility for the children on Sundays, and vacuum all the carpeting once a week. The husband asks that the wife help him choose clothes whenever he goes shopping for them, give him back rubs at night if he asks for them, and initiate sexual activity when she wants it. What is exchanged is family work done by the wife for the personal pleasure of the husband, thus underscoring and reinforcing sex-stereotyped roles and privileges.

In a case of a depressed husband, the therapist assigned a task for the woman to initiate sex three times a week, and to be responsible for the man achieving a climax (Madanes 1981). The goal was not mutual pleasure, it was to make the man feel desirable to his wife, as he was depressed because she had become successful in her career and was not home much. The wife was told she was being neglectful, despite the fact that for twenty-five years of their marriage she had sat every day and listened to his problems at work. What is communicated is the wife can have success in her career but she must also always be "there" for her husband, clearly maintaining an inequitable situation. Therapists working with couple therapy seem unable to free themselves from seeking solutions through reinforcing traditional sex role behaviors.

They offer virtually no examination of the inequities in the family and the larger society. Research that reports on couples who are satisfied with their marriages overlooks the fact that without consciousness raising, women may be accepting their traditional lot and blaming themselves rather than outside sources such as the marriage for their unhappiness (Frank, Anderson, and Rubinstein 1980). In couple therapy, discussion of role behaviors that does not challenge the separation of assigned roles has questionable usefulness.

Some therapists attempt to be even-handed in marriage and divorce counseling (Elbaum 1981; Lazarus 1981; Luther and Loev 1981), but this is not enough. By failing to examine the inequities in marriage, they neglect the special needs and vulnerabilities of women. Although they are becoming increasingly aware of the stresses of dual-career marriages in showing that both men and women are stressed, they often disregard research that shows the stress is far greater for the woman (Hare-Mustin 1982). They also tend to give too much consideration to the husband who may have to support his wife's ambitions by helping out doing what they call "women's work," a term that perpetuates domestic stereotypes (Price-Bonham and Murphy 1981).

Marriage enrichment programs, although not actually therapy, reach large numbers of couples with their message of loving and negotiating. By emphasizing individual responsibility and understanding, such well-meaning programs never address the inequities of relationships or the lack of support for certain choices on the part of the larger society.

As a branch of behavior marital therapy, treatment of sexual dysfunction accepts the traditional structure and values of sexual encounters. In a feminist analysis, Seidler-Feller (1982) points out that sex therapists perpetuate a patriarchal bias that negates their avowed egalitarianism by assuming usual sex roles as the basis for sound functioning. The power aspects of the male's position are ignored, but there is concern about women's growing power to weaken male sexual desire and functioning. Too often, treatment programs for the wife are designed from male assumptions about sexual stimulation and fantasy. She observes, "In a culture which tolerates male sexual aggression (and condones sexuality with aggression) and where sex therapy ignores (and thereby sanctions) it, a woman's best (and perhaps only) defense against a sexual ritual of subordination may be sexual dysfunction" (p. 10). It has been pointed out that therapeutic film products often used in treatment to enhance sexual functioning such as "Fuck-O-Rama" are crassly sexist (Szasz 1981).

Nontraditional Families   Remarried and single-parent families are frequently seen in family therapy. Postdivorce therapy often focuses on the obstacles fathers face in maintaining or beginning good relationships with their children (Moreland et al. 1982). This has the merit of shifting some of the burden from the one-parent (mother) families, although it also reflects the preeminence of fathers' needs. Criticism of the woman for fighting an exspouse (Whiteside 1982) is typically made without awareness that her economic plight worsens after divorce at the same time the father enjoys a higher standard of living. Studies of child support and alimony show that women do not receive adequate economic support for child rearing, and court judgments bear little relationship to the father's ability to pay (Wattenberg and Reinhardt 1981).

In another case that emphasizes the mother's attempts to pull her husband back, the therapist focuses on increasing the mother's competence and encouraging her assertiveness (Isaacs 1982). Some therapists stress the need of the single parent to be involved with the larger community. In describing the number of problems such a mother faces, Weltner (1982a) recognizes that one is the lack of validation that is generally available from another adult in the household, however traditional, especially when children attack the mother. His analysis is unfortunately marred by his use of labels that encourage stereotyped thinking.

Some family therapists feel that ethnic and class characteristics should be noted but not challenged, in contrast to feminist therapists who are likely directly to confront sexist behavior as well as the influence of class and race (Donovan and Littenberg 1982). The work of Minuchin, Montalvo, and their co-workers grew out of programs for youths who were delinquent or in need of supervision and their families described in *Families of the Slums* (1967), and reinforced traditional patterns of authority. In discussing the life cycle of the multiproblem poor family, Colon (1980) emphasizes that mother-headed families have great external resources. Apparently he is unaware of research like Belle's (1982), which shows that the ties of an extended family are often more draining than supportive for low-income mothers. There is also a clear implication in much of the therapeutic work with single-mother families that not having a man present is harmful to children, despite lack of research evidence for this.

Often authors will go to pains to emphasize that women in other ethnic groups are not oppressed, such as in the Mexican-American family (Falicov and Karrer 1980), or they present a nationally idealized view, such as the jig is an Irish metaphor for sexual experiences and the Irish woman is independent and dominant like the Virgin Mary (McGoldrick and Pearce 1981). It is suggested that Irish males may at times find a female therapist intimidating because Irish men fear women and hate their blasted martyrdom.

Black middle-class families may be different from black lower-class families as Bagarozzi (1980) argues, but it is difficult to accept his unsupported assertions that most black families have egalitarian structures, and that there are fewer sex-linked roles and tasks in black families than in whites.

In sum, family therapists have tended to accept and support ethnic and class differences rather than challenge their sex role stereotypes, in part due to romantic notions of egalitarianism and the idea that all value orientations are equally valid (Libow, Raskin, and Caust 1982; McGoldrick and Pearce 1981; McGoldrick, Pearce, and Giordano 1982). The prevailing tenet is that therapeutic intervention must be culturally consonant to be effective. This provides further evidence of many family therapists' apparent lack of awareness of the disadvantages of widespread sex-stereotyped behavior in their own or other cultures and the unwillingness to confront such behavior.

A Critique of Family Therapy

A comparison of family and feminist therapies reveals that feminist therapy is more like psychodynamic family therapy in many regards than like family systems therapy (Libow, Raskin, and Caust 1982). The techniques used by feminist therapists grew out of the same psychoanalytic tradition that influenced the pioneers in family therapy, although the philosophy of the former emphasizes the sharing of power, confirming and modeling women's experience, and the social context rather than the medical model. Feminist therapy uses linear causality and is likely to explore historic reasons for behavior, as Bowen theory and other psychoanalytic approaches do. From a feminist perspective, the negative aspect of family systems therapy's view of the family in terms of self-reinforcing and homeostatic interaction is that it treats participants as equals, ignoring distinctions between the oppressor and the oppressed.

In terms of what produces change, many feminist therapists, like Freudians, believe insight produces change, and they direct energy toward understanding and demystification. The systems family therapist does not believe insight necessarily produces change, accepting that it is just as likely that insight will follow change as precede it. Haley (1976) has emphasized the destructive futility of "pointing out" to clients what the therapist observes. Similarly, the idea that expressing feelings will produce change is based on the psychoanalytic theory of repression. Instead, systems family therapy is more like behavioral assertive training, which allows the female therapist to break out of the nurturant-reactive feminine stereotype (Caust, Libow, and Raskin 1981). Strategic family therapists regard all therapy as an influence process; thus they consider open disclosure by a therapist as much a technique to further therapy as is lack of disclosure. Therapists who impose paradoxical injunctions and task assignments from a directing stance are more likely to be called manipulative than those who work indirectly or in an insight-oriented stance (Libow, Raskin, and Caust 1982). Yet therapists such as Whitaker, who use mystification and playfulness, may evade the usual standards of judgment by a "gentle" sexism that masks an authoritarian approach, which is more insidious and difficult to identify than that of more straightforward therapists (Keith and Whitaker 1981). Family therapy is regarded as a collaborative effort typically based on an explicit or implicit contract established between therapist and family. Similarly, many feminist therapists advocate the use of a contract to make explicit the goals and shared nature of therapy (Hare-Mustin et al. 1979).

Feminists view symptoms as the consequence of oppression in a sexist society; family systems therapists view symptoms as a result of difficulties in relationships in the family unit, often also considering the social context but failing to recognize its sexism. Both avoid the medical model and blaming the victim. Both reframe and relabel behavior in order to shift its meaning and promote change. Positive relabeling is emphasized by family therapists who believe most problems in families are caused not by fear, hostility, and incestuous feelings, but by excessive concern for one another (Haley 1980; Palazzoli et al. 1978). Concrete change in behavior is of interest to feminists as it is to family therapists. Although feminist therapists may feel that the woman can be changed as an individual, family therapists would say that that is impossible unless the system in which she is functioning is also changed.

Community Influences   Those concerned with the prevention of mental illness question whether therapy merely postpones or aborts long-term broader and more extensive solutions and radical societal change (Albee 1981). Zwerling (1981) has criticized family therapies that focus on adaption and reduction of conflict, as well as those that are based on techniques for changing the family symptom without reference to the relationship of the family to the community.

The family has been regarded by some not so much an institution as a mechanism through which society exerts control, in part through the responsibilities it assigns to the women for the health and education of children under traditional patriarchy (Donzelot 1980). Feminists have observed that families and schools are implicated in the reproduction of unequal social relations (Elshtain 1982).

The simplistic idea that urban residential neighborhoods are natural communities is more often flawed than not, and "the romanticization of 'community' must be tempered with the realization that one of the most pernicious ideological bases for the perpetuation of racism in the United States has been the appeal for 'the preservation of the community'" (Zwerling 1981, p. 337). The sexist community has not supported changes in the family when such changes have become apparent in schools, neighborhoods, and the paid workplace. Although family network therapy seeks improved family functioning through involving a broader network (Speck and Attneave 1973; Rueveni 1975), such networks may also hinder change and impose additional burdens on the family (Belle 1982). The development of women's self-help groups encouraged by feminists has been independent of the family therapy movement (Brodsky and Hare-Mustin 1980; Hare-Mustin et al. 1979).

Therapists' Attitudes and the Traditional Family   Research has shown that men continue to be more traditional than women, which has consequences for family therapy since most therapists are male and are themselves in traditional marriages (Hare-Mustin, Bennett, and Broderick 1983; Hare-Mustin and Broderick 1979; Rice and Rice 1977; Scanzoni and Fox 1980). There is further evidence that many therapists, particularly males, engage in sex role stereotyping (Brodsky and Hare-Mustin 1980; Broverman et al. 1970; Sherman 1980; Sobel and Russo 1981). Gender bias can be evident not only in what the therapist does, but in what the therapist fails to do, such as not responding to issues of bias or being unaware of inequality (Sheridan 1982). In a study of therapists' practices and knowledge about women clients, male therapists were found to be more biased than female. In addition, a significant correlation was found between sex bias and lack of information or misinformation about women (Sherman, Koufacos, and Kenworthy 1978).

Family therapy may well attract professionals whose values are those of supporting the traditional family. In a study of seventy therapists who worked with delinquent youth, the author found that those who said family therapy was their preferred mode of treatment were significantly more conservative in their attitudes toward women than those preferring other methods such as individual or group therapy. Another study of over 300 family therapists found that the highest-ranked goals for family therapy were differentiation and negotiation (Sprenkle and Fisher 1980). These are unquestionably male values, stressing individuality and that decisions be fair and equal. The lowest-ranked goal was physical care-taking, typically the mother's major responsibility, with loyalty also near the bottom of the list. Case examples show that blaming the mother for family problems persists, as in one therapist's description, "Her inability to control their child and her passivity in general has 'driven' her husband from the home to the bar or bowling alley" (Stollak 1981, p. 308).

The father is perceived as least enthusiastic about therapy and family therapists view him as the most responsible for cancelling appointments (LeFave 1980). As a consequence, therapists tend to schedule sessions for the father's convenience and often initially focus on him; to the extent that he is paying for the sessions, he controls them. In such subtle ways, aspects of the family system that the therapist may wish to change are in fact strengthened.

Family therapists often show more interest in adults than children, and typically pay little attention to sibling relationships. Kahn and Bank (1981) are an exception to this. They point out how adult sisters can be a resource for each other, which is in direct contrast to traditional views that emphasize sibling competition, jealousy, and anger. Their case example shows how a lesbian daughter finally achieves acceptance from her father.

Cotherapist teams of husbands and wives often base their treatment on idealization of their own marriage. A team where the wife is more senior in experience, training, and credentials is rare, thus reinforcing sex role stereotypes of the man being more qualified. Low and Low (1975) presented an unintended disquisition of how husband-wife cotherapy may be detrimental to women as cotherapists as well as clients. More recently, Hoffman and Hoffman (1981) described working together, noting that their effectiveness reached an all-time high when the wife finished her doctoral degree. They believed they had a flexibility and reciprocity in expected roles, but then the wife became aware that clients attributed her most successful interventions to her husband.

The overt use of sexist language has largely disappeared from family therapy writing in the last few years. Some authors still think it is sufficient to acknowledge the inequity of using the generic masculine pronoun and continue its use for "convenience" (Haley 1980, p. 9). A remarkably effective device Minuchin and Fishman (1981) use is to alternate by chapters the use of "he" and "she" for the therapist. Specific gender assumptions are often masked by nonspecific language (in terms of gender) as in pejorative expressions such as "the domineering partner." One has yet to see "domineering" explicitly applied to the man, testimony of the continued influence of psychodynamic theory that sees most problems as a result of a domineering mother (Thorne, 1982). Similarly the use of labels such as frigid for a woman, rather than inquiring about how much and what kind of sexual stimulation she receives is an indication of sex bias, as is the use of first names and diminutives with women but not with men (Hare-Mustin 1979b).

The use of nonsexist language may be negated by stereotyped illustrations that typically make the woman look more foolish than the man, as in, "One may resent the choice of his wife not to join him in a particular activity. Or she may be irritated by her husband's wearing an old pair of pants that should have been thrown away" (Nelson and Friest 1980, p. 401).

Training Issues   Training women as well as men to be nonsexist requires the development of new thinking and new modes of behaving. Certainly it needs to include addressing sex role issues early in professional development (Caust, Libow, and Raskin 1981). Principles for therapy with women have been developed by the American Psychological Association, which recognize that therapists and counselors who work with women need special skills and knowledge with regard to biological, psychological, and social issues that impact on women in general and on particular groups of women (*Counseling Psychologist* 1979; Hare-Mustin 1983).

Family systems therapy has emphasized the importance of learning by doing and the use of videotaping and live supervision of family sessions, rather than supervision involving subsequent selective and incomplete recall of the session by the therapist.

Among the many training conferences offered around the country for practitioners in family therapy, mention should be made of one called *The Women's Project in Family Therapy* (1982) presented since 1980 by four women family therapists. They have included topics such as "The Dilemma of Women in Families," "Mothers and Daughters," and "Women and Success." Carter represents the Bowen approach, which urges the woman to work on her family of origin and differentiate herself, the relationship with the mother being regarded as the prototype for all subsequent relationships. Silverstein focuses on the problems of fusion and unrelatedness, acknowledging that motherhood is not an identity for all time. In exhorting women to strive for expanded roles and opportunities, Papp emphasizes the need for courage but not the solutions for women.

Walters's approach is closest to a feminist position, as she observes that family therapists tend to perpetuate stereotypes by asking the mother for *change* and the father for *involvement*, thus by implication ascribing the problem to her failure and his lack of participation. As Walters notes, despite the innovative methods of family systems therapists, their notions of family structure are wedded to traditional role models. Through their conferences, this group seeks to encourage women family therapists and increase therapists' awareness of conflicts faced by women and their families.

Evaluation of Family Therapy Outcome   Studies of the effectiveness of
marital and family therapies show that they are at least as effective as and
probably more so than other therapies such as individual therapy for marital
and family problems, and often even for problems presented as individual or
intrapsychic (Gurman and Kniskern 1978, 1981). How to assess accurately the
outcome of successful therapy is a problem for all approaches, since the values
of therapists and family members influence these ratings. Certainly, marital
and family stability can no longer be used as a measure of successful marriage
or family functioning. New criteria are needed, including those that define
healthy functioning for women such as mastery, competence, independence,
and coping skills as well as measures to assess such functioning (Brodsky and
Hare-Mustin 1980). Gurman and Klein (1980) address some of the problems
associated with assessing change in therapy. Since males have been found to
hold more sexist attitudes, they point out that the male therapist cannot be the
sole evaluator of therapy outcome nor can the husband be. Assessments based
on spouse agreement, which perpetuate the assumption that conformity between spouses is a sign of a happy marriage, are questionable, as is the use of
normative behaviors that perpetuate the expectation that the woman should
adjust to the situation. Families that appear functional by conventional assessment may be restricting the introduction of new behaviors that are in the
long-range interests of women. Family systems approaches that emphasize the
good of the whole family overlook the fact that some members, such as women,
may be disadvantaged by the outcome of family therapy (Hare-Mustin 1980).

Conclusion

Feminists have been concerned about the family because it is the primary
beneficiary and focus of women's labor as well as the source of women's most
fundamental identity, that of mother. Family therapy, increasingly the treatment of choice for many problems in living, focuses on relationships among
people and provides opportunities for social change unavailable in other
therapeutic approaches. By recognizing the predictable crises in the family life
cycle, family therapists can also take a preventative orientation, frequently
intervening to reduce stress in the family.

The two main orientations to family therapy, psychodynamic and systems theory, both focus on family relationships; however, they are so different
conceptually and operationally that they remain mutually independent (Sluzki
1981). Interest in the *genesis* of the symptom is the focus of the psychodynamic
therapist, while the systems therapist is more interested in how patterns of
symptoms are *maintained*. The latter view holds that, regardless of their origin,
symptoms or conflicts can only persist if maintained by ongoing interactional
patterns, and in fact these patterns have become in Gordon Allport's (1937)
sense, functionally autonomous. The patterns can be disrupted by reframing,
positive connotation, symptom prescription (such as requiring a person who
has headaches to have headaches), and paradoxical interventions such as

encouraging a child who has tantrums to continue a tantrum. Advances in family systems theory now view the goal of treatment as not just to restore previous functioning but to move the system to a new level of family functioning. The systems approach to family therapy is congruent with feminist approaches that emphasize the social and economic determinants of behavior and focus on concrete behavior changes.

Although there is increasing sensitivity to sex role issues and women's position in the family, many therapists still are unaware of and insensitive to the inequity in the traditional family and the extent to which women are historically and currently asked to subordinate their individual interests to the good of the family. There is still a tendency to equate women with the family, while men are allowed an individualized and separate status. As has been shown, the unquestioned reinforcement of stereotyped sex roles takes place in much of family therapy.

In part this results from the prevalence of the relativity view of families, that is, that all values are equally valid, and also from the fact that therapists are themselves part of the same traditional sexist culture. The change in the traditional family to the two wage earner family should require therapists to examine their traditional assumptions. They need to question the glorification and deprecation of motherhood, the home as a domestic haven, the prevalence of marital conflict and depression in married women, and the inequitable distribution of power and work in the family. The feminist perspective is increasingly being expressed and receiving attention among family systems theorists and leaders in the field who are pointing out that models of family functioning must examine the differentials in status and resources available to family members, and the measures of successful family therapy outcome need to include new criteria for women.

References

ALBEE, G. W. 1981. The prevention of sexism. *Professional Psychology* 12:20–28.

ALLPORT, G. W. 1937. *Personality: A psychological interpretation.* New York: Holt.

BAGAROZZI, D. A. 1980. Family therapy and the black middle class: A neglected area of study. *Journal of Marital and Family Therapy* 6:159–66.

BANE, M. J. 1976. *Here to stay: American families in the twentieth century.* New York: Basic Books.

BARKER, P. 1981. *Basic family therapy.* Baltimore: University Park Press.

BEAVERS, W. R. 1981. A systems model of family for family therapists. *Journal of Marital and Family Therapy* 7:299–307.

BELLE, D. 1982. Social ties and social support. In *Lives in stress: Women and depression,* edited by D. Belle. Beverly Hills: Sage.

BERNARD, J. 1981. The good provider role. *American Psychologist* 36:1–12.

BOSZORMENYI-NAGY, I., and SPARK, G. M. 1973. *Invisible loyalties: Reciprocity in intergenerational family therapy.* New York: Harper & Row.

BOSZORMENYI-NAGY, I., and ULRICH, D. N. 1981. Contextual family therapy. In *Handbook of family therapy*, edited by A. S. Gurman and D. P. Kniskern. New York: Brunner/Mazel.

BOWEN, M. 1978. *Family therapy in clinical practice.* New York: Jason Aronson.

BRADT, J. O. 1980. The family with young children. In *The family life cycle: A framework for family therapy*, edited by E. A. Carter and M. McGoldrick. New York: Gardner Press.

BRAVERMAN, S. 1981. Family of origin: The view from the parents' side. *Family Process* 20:431–37.

BRODSKY, A. M. 1980. A decade of feminist influence on psychotherapy. *Psychology of Women Quarterly* 4:331–44.

BRODSKY, A. M., and HARE-MUSTIN, R. T. 1980. Psychotherapy and women: Priorities for research. In *Women and psychotherapy: An assessment of research and practice*, edited by A. M. Brodsky and R. T. Hare-Mustin. New York: Guilford.

BROVERMAN, I. K.; BROVERMAN, D. M.; CLARKSON, F. E.; et al. 1970. Sex role stereotypes and clinical judgments of mental health. *Journal of Consulting and Clinical Psychology* 34:1–7.

CARTER, E. A., and MCGOLDRICK, M. 1980. *The family life cycle: A framework for family therapy.* New York: Gardner Press.

CASHION, B. G. 1982. Female-headed families: Effects on children and clinical implications. *Journal of Marital and Family Therapy* 8:77–85.

CAUST, B. L.; LIBOW, J. A.; and RASKIN, P. A. 1981. Challenges and promises of training women as family systems therapists. *Family Process* 20:439–47.

CHERLIN, L. 1979. Work life and marital dissolution. In *Divorce and separation: Context, causes and consequences*, edited by G. Levinger and O. C. Moles. New York: Basic Books.

CHODOROW, N., and CONTRATTO, S. 1982. The fantasy of the perfect mother. In *Rethinking the family: Some feminist questions*, edited by B. Thorne and M. Yalom. New York: Longman.

COLON, F. 1980. The family life cycle of the multiproblem poor family. In *The family life cycle: A framework for family therapy*, edited by E. A. Carter and M. McGoldrick. New York: Gardner Press.

Counseling Psychologist. 1979. 8, no. 1.

DEGLER, C. 1980. *At odds: Women and the family in America from the revolution to the present.* New York: Oxford University Press.

DONOVAN, V. K., and LITTENBERG, R. 1982. Psychology of women: Feminist therapy. In *The women's annual: 1981—The year in review*, edited by B. Haber. Boston: G. K. Hall.

DONZELOT, J. 1980. *The policing of families.* London: Hutchinson.

ELBAUM, P. L. 1981. The dynamics, implications and treatment of extramarital sexual relationships for the family therapist. *Journal of Marital and Family Therapy* 7:489–95.

ELSHTAIN, J. B. 1982. "Thank heaven for little girls": The dialectics of development. In *The family in political thought*, edited by J. B. Elshtain. Amherst: University of Massachusetts Press.

FALICOV, C. J., and KARRER, B. M. 1980. Cultural variations in the family life cycle: The Mexican-American family. In *The family life cycle: A framework for family therapy*, edited by E. A. Carter and M. McGoldrick. New York: Gardner Press.

FISHER, L.; ANDERSON, A.; and JONES, J. E. 1981. Types of paradoxical intervention and indications/contraindications for use in clinical practice. *Family Process* 20:25–35.

FLAX, J. 1982. The family in contemporary feminist thought: A critical review. In *The family in political thought*, edited by J. B. Elshtain. Amherst: University of Massachusetts Press.

FOLEY, V. 1974. *An introduction to family therapy*. New York: Grune & Stratton.

FRANK, E.; ANDERSON, C.; and RUBINSTEIN, D. 1980. Marital role ideals and perception of marital role behavior in distressed and nondistressed couples. *Journal of Marital and Family Therapy* 6:55–63.

FRASER, J. S. 1982. Structural and strategic family therapy: A basis for marriage or grounds for divorce? *Journal of Marital and Family Therapy* 8:13–22.

GERSTEL, N. 1982. Domestic life: The new right and the family. In *The women's annual: 1981—The year in review*, edited by B. Haber. Boston: G. K. Hall.

GILBERT, L. A. 1980. Feminist therapy. In *Women and psychotherapy: An assessment of research and practice*, edited by A. M. Brodsky and R. T. Hare-Mustin. New York: Guilford.

GOLDENBERG, I., and GOLDENBERG, H. 1980. *Family therapy*. Monterey, Calif.: Brooks/Cole.

GREEN, R. G., and KOLEVZON, M. S. 1982. Three approaches to family therapy: A study of convergence and divergence. *Journal of Marital and Family Therapy* 8:39–50.

GURMAN, A. S., and KLEIN, M. H. 1980. Marital and family conflicts. In *Women and psychotherapy: An assessment of research and practice*, edited by A. M. Brodsky and R. T. Hare-Mustin. New York: Guilford.

GURMAN, A. S., and KNISKERN, D. P. 1978. Research on marital and family therapy: Progress, perspective, and prospect. In *Handbook of psychotherapy and behavior change*, edited by S. L. Garfield and A. E. Bergin. New York: John Wiley & Sons.

GURMAN, A. S., and KNISKERN, D. P., eds. 1981. *Handbook of family therapy*. New York: Brunner/Mazel.

HALEY, J. 1973. *Uncommon therapy: The psychiatric techniques of Milton H. Erickson*. New York: W. W. Norton.

HALEY, J. 1976. *Problem-solving therapy*. San Francisco: Jossey-Bass.

HALEY, J. 1980. *Leaving home: The therapy of disturbed young people*. New York: McGraw-Hill.

HANDY, C. 1978. Going against the grain: Working couples and greedy occupations. In *Working couples*, edited by R. Rapoport and R. Rapoport. New York: Harper & Row.

HARE-MUSTIN, R. T. 1978. A feminist approach to family therapy. *Family Process* 17:181–94.

HARE-MUSTIN, R. T. 1979a. Family therapy and sex role stereotypes. *The Counseling Psychologist* 8, no. 1:31–32.

HARE-MUSTIN, R. T. 1979b. Sexism in family therapy. *American Journal of Family Therapy* 7, no. 4:81–83.

HARE-MUSTIN, R. T. 1980. Family therapy may be dangerous for your health. *Professional Psychology* 11:935–38.

HARE-MUSTIN, R. T. 1982. *Stress and its impact on women in their dual roles: Professional and family.* Unpublished manuscript.

HARE-MUSTIN, R. T. 1983. An appraisal of the relationship between women and psychotherapy: 80 years after the case of Dora. *American Psychologist* 38:593–601.

HARE-MUSTIN, R. T.; BENNETT, S. K.; and BRODERICK, P. C. 1983. Attitude toward motherhood: Gender, generational and religious comparisons. *Sex Roles.* 9:643–61.

HARE-MUSTIN, R. T., and BRODERICK, P. 1979. The myth of motherhood: A study of attitudes toward motherhood. *Psychology of Women Quarterly* 4:114–28.

HARE-MUSTIN, R. T.; MARECEK, J.; KAPLAN, A. G. et al. 1979. Rights of clients, responsibilities of therapists. *American Psychologist* 34:3–16.

HASKINS, W. J. 1982. A black responsibility. *New York Times*, October 4.

HOFFMAN, L. 1980. The family life cycle and discontinuous change. In *The family life cycle: A framework for family therapy*, edited by E. A. Carter and M. McGoldrick. New York: Gardner Press.

HOFFMAN, L. 1981. *Foundations of family therapy: A conceptual framework for systems change.* New York: Basic Books.

HOFFMAN, L. W. 1976. The decision to become a working wife. In *Family roles and interaction*, 2d ed., edited by J. Heiss. Chicago: Rand McNally.

HOFFMAN, L. W. 1977. Changes in family roles, socialization, and sex differences. *American Psychologist* 32:644–57.

HOFFMAN, L. W. 1979. Maternal employment: 1979. *American Psychologist* 34:859–65.

HOFFMAN, L. W., and HOFFMAN, H. J. 1981. Husband-wife co-therapy team: Exploration of its development. *Psychotherapy: Theory, Research and Practice* 18:217–24.

HOLMES, T. H., and RAHE, R. H. 1967. The social readjustment rating scales. *Journal of Psychosomatic Research* 11:213–18.

ISAACS, M. G. 1982. Helping mom fail: A case of stalemated divorcing process. *Family Process* 21:225–34.

JACOBSEN, N. S. 1981. Behavioral marital therapy. In *Handbook of family therapy*, edited by A. S. Gurman and D. P. Kniskern. New York: Brunner/Mazel.

KAGAN, J. 1979. Family experience and the child's development. *American Psychologist* 34:886–91.

KAHN, M. D., and BANK, S. 1981. In pursuit of sisterhood: Adult siblings as a resource for combined individual and family therapy. *Family Process* 20:85–95.

KEITH, D. V., and WHITAKER, C. A. 1981. Play therapy: A paradigm for work with families. *Journal of Marital and Family Therapy* 7:243–54.

KESSLER, R. C., and MCRAE, J. A., JR. 1982. The effect of wives' employment on the mental health of married men and women. *American Sociological Review* 47:216–27.

LAMB, M. E., and LAMB, J. E. 1976. The nature and importance of the father-infant relationship. *Family Coordinator* 25:379–85.

LAZARUS, A. A. 1981. Divorce counseling or marriage therapy? A therapeutic option. *Journal of Marital and Family Therapy* 7:15–22.

LEFAVE, M. K. 1980. Correlates of engagement in family therapy. *Journal of Marital and Family Therapy* 6:75–81.

LIBERMAN, R. P.; WHEELER, E. G.; and DEVISSER, L. A. J. M. et al. 1980. *Handbook of marital therapy: A positive approach to helping troubled relationships.* New York: Plenum Press.

LIBOW, J. A.; RASKIN, P. A.; and CAUST, B. L. 1982. Feminist and family systems therapy: Are they irreconcilable? *American Journal of Family Therapy* 10, no. 3:3–12.

LIEBERMAN, M. A.; YALOM, I. D.; and MILES, M. B. 1973. *Encounter groups: First facts.* New York: Basic Books.

LOW, P., and LOW, M. 1975. Treatment of married couples in a group run by a husband and wife. *International Journal of Group Psychotherapy* 25:54–66.

LUTHER, G., and LOEV, G. 1981. Resistance in marital therapy. *Journal of Marital and Family Therapy* 7:475–80.

MADANES, C. 1981. *Strategic family therapy.* San Francisco: Jossey-Bass.

MCGOLDRICK, M., and PEARCE, J. K. 1981. Family therapy with Irish-Americans. *Family Process* 20:223–41.

MCGOLDRICK, M.; PEARCE, J. K.; and GIORDANO, J., eds. 1982. *Ethnicity and family therapy.* New York: Guilford.

MINUCHIN, S. 1974. *Families and family therapy.* Cambridge: Harvard University Press.

MINUCHIN, S., and FISHMAN, C. 1981. *Family therapy techniques.* Cambridge: Harvard University Press.

MINUCHIN, S.; MONTALVO, B.; GUERNEY, B. G., JR. et al. 1967. *Families of the slums.* New York: Basic Books.

MORELAND, J.; SCHWEBEL, A. I.; FINE, M. A. et al. 1982. Postdivorce family therapy: Suggestions for professionals. *Professional Psychology* 13:639–46.

NELSON, R. C., and FRIEST, W. P. 1980. Marriage enrichment through choice awareness. *Journal of Marital and Family Therapy* 6:399–407.

NORTON, A. J., and GLICK, P. C. 1979. Marital instability in America: Past, present, and future. In *Divorce and separation: Context, causes and consequences*, edited by G. Levinger and O. C. Moles. New York: Basic Books.

OLSON, D. H.; RUSSELL, C. S.; and SPRENKLE, D. H. 1980. Marital and family therapy: A decade review. *Journal of Marriage and the Family* 42:239–59.

PACKWOOD, R. 1982. The equal rights amendment. *Congressional Record* July 1.

PALAZZOLI, M. S.; CECCHIN, G.; PRATA, G. et al. 1978. *Paradox and counter-paradox.* New York: Jason Aronson.

PARSONS, T., and BALES, R. F. 1955. *Family, socialization, and interaction process.* Glencoe, IL.: Free Press.

PEAL, E. 1975. "Normal" sex roles: An historical analysis. *Family Process* 14:389–409.

PEARCE, J. K., and FRIEDMAN, L. J., eds. 1980. *Family therapy: Combining psychodynamic and family systems approaches.* New York: Grune & Stratton.

PERLIN, L. I. 1975. Sex roles and depression. In *Life-span developmental psychology: Normative life crises,* edited by N. Datan and L. H. Ginsberg. New York: Academic Press.

PERLMUTTER, L. H.; ENGEL, T.; and SAGER, C. J. 1982. The incest taboo: Loosened sexual boundaries in remarried families. *Journal of Sex and Marital Therapy* 8:83–96.

PLECK, J. H. 1977. The work-family role system. *Social Problems* 24:417–44.

PRICE-BONHAM, S., and MURPHY, D. C. 1981. Dual-career marriages: Implications for the clinician. *Journal of Marital and Family Therapy* 7:181–88.

RICE, D. G., and RICE, J. K. 1977. Non-sexist "marital" therapy. *Journal of Marriage and Family Counseling* 3:3–10.

ROSENBERG, R. 1982. *Beyond separate spheres: Intellectual roots of modern feminism.* New Haven: Yale University Press.

ROSSI, A. S. 1980. Life-span theories and women's lives. *Signs: Journal of Women, Culture, and Society* 6:4–32.

RUEVENI, U. 1975. Network intervention with a family in crisis. *Family Process* 14:193–203.

SAGER, C. 1976. *Marriage contracts and couple therapy.* New York: Brunner/Mazel.

SATIR, V. 1967. *Conjoint family therapy.* Palo Alto: Science and Behavior Books.

SCANZONI, J. 1979. A historical perspective on husband-wife bargaining power and marital dissolution. In *Divorce and separation: Context, causes and consequences,* edited by G. Levinger, and O. C. Moles. New York: Basic Books.

SCANZONI, J., and FOX, G. L. 1980. Sex roles, family and society: The seventies and beyond. *Journal of Marriage and the Family* 42:20–33.

SEIDLER-FELLER, D. 1982. A feminist critique of sex therapy. Unpublished manuscript.

SHERIDAN, K. 1982. Sex bias in therapy: Are counselors immune? *Personnel and Guidance Journal* 61, no. 2:81–82.

SHERMAN, J. A. 1980. Therapist attitudes and sex-role stereotyping. In *Women and psychotherapy: An assessment of research and practice,* edited by A. M. Brodsky and R. T. Hare-Mustin. New York: Guilford.

SHERMAN, J.; KOUFACOS, C.; and KENWORTHY, J. A. 1978. Therapists: Their attitudes and information about women. *Psychology of Women Quarterly* 2:299–313.

SLUZKI, C. E. 1981. Process of symptom production and patterns of symptom maintenance. *Journal of Marital and Family Therapy* 7:273–80.

SOBEL, S. B., and RUSSO, N. F. 1981. Sex roles, equality, and mental health. *Professional Psychology* 12:1–5.

SPECK, R. V., and ATTNEAVE, C. 1973. *Family networks.* New York: Vintage Books.

SPRENKLE, D. H., and FISHER, B. L. 1980. An empirical assessment of the goals of family therapy. *Journal of Marital and Family Therapy* 6:131–39.

SPRENKLE, D. H.; KEENEY, B. P.; and SUTTON, P. M. 1982. Theorists who influence clinical members of AAMFT: A research note. *Journal of Marital and Family Therapy* 8:367–69.

STOLLAK, G. E. 1981. Variations and extensions of filial therapy. *Family Process* 20:305–09.

SUGARMAN, S. 1981. Family therapy training in selected general psychiatry residency programs. *Family Process* 20:147–54.

SZASZ, T. 1981. *Sex by prescription.* New York: Penguin Books.

THORNE, B. 1982. Feminist rethinking of the family: An overview. In *Rethinking of the family: Some feminist questions,* edited by B. Thorne and M. Yalom. New York: Longman.

WATTENBERG, E., and REINHARDT, H. 1981. Female-headed families: Trends and implications. In *Women and mental health,* edited by E. Howell and M. Bayes. New York: Basic Books.

WATZLAWICK, P.; WEAKLAND, J.; and FISCH, R. 1974. *Change: Principles of problem formulation and problem resolution.* New York: W. W. Norton.

WEINER, N. 1948. *Cybernetics.* New York: John Wiley & Sons.

WEISSMAN, M. W. 1980. Depression. In *Women and psychotherapy: An assessment of research and practice,* edited by A. M. Brodsky and R. T. Hare-Mustin. New York: Guilford.

WEITZ, S. 1977. *Sex roles: Biological, psychological, and social foundations.* New York: Oxford University Press.

WELTNER, J. S. 1982a. A structural approach to the single-parent family. *Family Process* 21:203–10.

WELTNER, J. S. 1982b. One- to three-session therapy with children and families. *Family Process* 21:281–89.

WHITESIDE, M. F. 1982. Remarriage: A family developmental process. *Journal of Marital and Family Therapy* 8:59–68.

WILLIAMS, A. R.; TRICK, O. L.; and TROUM, R. A. 1981. The paranoid wife syndrome: Diagnosis and treatment. *Journal of Marital and Family Therapy* 7:75–79.

The women's project in family therapy. 1982. Washington, D.C.

ZWERLING, I. 1981. Family therapy and the alienation syndrome. *Journal of Marital and Family Therapy* 7:331–38.

Scholarship and the Humanities

Heather McClave

> *Being so caught up,*
> *So mastered by the brute blood of the air,*
> *Did she put on his knowledge with his power*
> *Before the indifferent beak could let her drop?*
> > W. B. Yeats, "*Leda and the Swan*"

> *I have to learn alone*
> *to turn my body without force*
> *in the deep element.*
> > Adrienne Rich, "*Diving into the Wreck*"

The courage to explore what has never been defined is bringing the study of women decisively into its own. Where previous work in the field often depended on a male point of view, treating women in dialectical terms as Other, current writing is immersed more fully in the actual experience of women, which it seeks to describe in unitary terms from within.

The feminist critique of what we have inherited continues, as it must, in order to redress the skewed perspective that highlights men in heroic relief against a dull, indistinguishable blur of women. This effort is essential, not merely because academic disciplines are still presumptuously narrow and demeaning, but because the self-alienating attitudes they enforce still dominate our lives and dreams. Yet at the same time, the struggle to reform this system fixes the vigilant critic in place: as Elaine Showalter (1981) insists in her comprehensive review, "the feminist obsession with correcting, modifying, supplementing, revising, humanizing, or even attacking male critical theory keeps us dependent upon it and retards our progress in solving our own theoretical problems." Vanguard developments, she suggests, such as the formulation of women-centered criticism or "gynocritics," may emerge at least in part from a proposed "wild zone" where women are uniquely themselves, distinct from men (183–85, 200–1).[1] We have yet to learn, of course, whether any difference of this kind constitutes a special female essence.

What is authentic for women? This remains the most pressing question in the field, and it prompts us to account for our subjects and ourselves in strikingly personal terms that draw on our common experience. There could hardly be a greater contrast in approach and intent than the one we now find between feminist work on women—so conscious of individual traces surfacing out of buried generations—and fashionable academic theories that try to objectify human perceptions into autonomous texts and processes. At this stage, it seems crucial to have women avow the substance of their lives, less to provide varied role models, I think, than to certify that a history exists.

Three obvious trends in women's studies dramatize the importance of literal evidence as the base of believable truth. Most prominently, we see the ongoing gathering of data that shares and celebrates women's experiences in biographies, essays, journals, diaries, and letters. In a related development over the past several years, certain scholars such as Carolyn Heilbrun (*Reinventing Womanhood*), Carol Gilligan (*In a Different Voice*), and Rachel Brownstein (*Becoming a Heroine*) have made the author an active presence in the text, confiding rather than confessional, very much in control. The effect of this disclosure, startling to those who take Olympian detachment for granted, is not only to fuse the private life openly with the public work, but also, more radically, to make that life the base and measure of learning. Finally, on a broader scale, literary critics and historians are beginning to concentrate on subjects closer to home, including popular culture and the twentieth century.

All these trends show a sense of being deeply involved with the world, a condition that some writers, such as Starhawk (1982a), describe in spiritual terms as "immanence—the awareness of the world and everything in it as alive, dynamic, interdependent, and interacting" (177). It is here in the real, among densely combining elements, that the modern quester searches for her self, diving into a contained world of water and wreck, as Adrienne Rich does, instead of yearning for illusive free flight in the open air as Keats's nightingale or Shelley's skylark.

What women seek in these depths is authenticity, a core of being that gives meaning and motivation to the self and gives shape to the actual person underlying all her attributed images. Among the books available for review this year, two contrasting schools of thought address this concern directly. The first, more popular school, represented by writers such as Nina Auerbach, Annis Pratt, Simon Shepherd, and Starhawk, extends essential identity into general forms of myth and archetype. For Auerbach, an eloquent advocate, "Women's freedom is no longer simple initiation into historical integrity, but the rebirth of mythic potential" (1982, 12).

The second school sees mythmaking as dangerously regressive. Watchful of nostalgias for lost Edens, or lost mothers, Barbara Rigney says women "must go beyond mythology itself in order to find the self" (1982, 35), while Sally McNall (1981) bemoans the waste of women's inner forces when they are projected onto spurious icons, counseling, "If we learn to outgrow the power of the maternal archetype to fill us with terror or impossible longing, then perhaps we may learn to understand that power as our own strength" (125).[2]

In her excellent study of heroines in English novels, Rachel Brownstein (1982) also cautions her readers against self-perfecting "fictions of the feminine," which isolate the self in the futile discipline of trying to become an unattainable ideal. Alternatively, she proposes a more realistic and rewarding investment in "self-awareness" (295), pointing out, "It is not megalomaniacal to want to be significant; it is only human. And to suspect that one can be significant only in the fantasy of fiction, to look for significance in a concentrated essence of character, in an image of oneself, rather than in action or achievement, is, historically, only feminine. Or mostly" (xv). Brownstein speaks knowingly to the compulsive "good girl" in so many women who fail to cope with life because they want to make everything "just right," who hate themselves and the rest of the world because nothing measures up to their adamant expectations. As Sylvia Plath notes with poignant desperation in the journals released last year (McCullough 1982), "I have this demon who wants me to run away screaming if I am going to be flawed, fallible. It wants me to think I'm so good I must be perfect. Or nothing" (176).

Plath's tacit sense of the absolute as all against the void of nothing confirms an important link between false and true versions of authenticity. In wishing for impregnable perfection, an ideal that reflects society's demands on women even as it defends fiercely against them, she is expressing at the same time an urgent desire for wholeness, for literal self-fulfillment.

The two approaches I have been considering come together on this point. By means of communal myth or individual mind, both schools are trying to locate some field and force which can unify the self into a conscious whole.

This effort takes on even larger implications when we realize that much of what scholars are saying and doing in women's studies involves a general vision and process of synthesis. Thematically, holistic thinking has become a premise as well as a goal, as the following statements by several authors will illustrate:

[S]uppose that women are, in fact, complete human beings. Then it seems logical to ask whether those virtues promulgated by a masculine theological perspective are not in themselves questionable (Rabuzzi 1982, 49).

The appeal of popular women's fiction lies largely in the unparalleled opportunity it presents not only for a release of the usually repressed, but for a temporary healing of the splits in personality, a provisional integration of parts (McNall 1981, 9).

A feminist semiotics of American women's poetry must consider not only the way an individual piece refuses assimilation in the puzzle but also the way it demands such assimilation (Walker 1982, xii).

Recently, analyses of sexual difference have stressed interrelationship as well as opposition, difference *between* as well as difference *from*. Feminist critical attention has shifted from recovering a lost tradition to discovering the terms of confrontation with the dominant tradition (Abel 1981, 174).

Alert to other alliances, Nina Auerbach examines Victorian myths of women, which, like archetypes, heroines, and historical role models, are composite forms, syntheses of different aspects. She brilliantly fuses the two faces of angel and demon, showing that their superficial "polarity reveal[s] a fundamental identity" (1982, 4).[3] Going even further to integrate seeming disparities, Linda Bamber (1982) gives a splendid analysis of "shaping connections" between men and women in Shakespeare, in which women—while inevitably "Other" for men—become revealing and indispensable complements (5, 11).

Over time, the methodology of women's studies has made synthesis the norm, both by combining separate disciplines such as literature, history, and psychoanalysis, and by applying familiar approaches to new subjects such as frontier diaries, lesbian writing, Goddess worship, and housework. In this spirit, Audre Lorde (1982) coins the term, "biomythography," for her memoir, *Zami*, while Laurel Thatcher Ulrich (1982) argues for a historical outlook that focuses on patterns of continuity instead of on disruptive turning points. Present debates on "mainstreaming" signal yet another phase of this evolving synthesis, as scholars begin to assess women in the contexts of ethnicity, race, gender, class, and sexual orientation.

Closely allied to the search for authenticity is the assumption that the integral self is enormously powerful. The current emphasis on recovering the inherent power of women, or discerning how it was there all along, explicitly revises earlier unilateral views on victimization. Here are some representative statements:

> For women, the symbol of the Goddess is profoundly liberating, restoring a sense of authority and power to the female body and all the life processes—birth, growth, love-making, aging, and death (Starhawk 1982a, 179).

> To insist upon women's power in the past, and in the present, is to challenge the most dominant and most entrenched of social relations (Newton 1981, xix).

> Women emerge in these analyses no longer as the passive victims of male authorial desire but rather as powerful figures that elicit texts crafted to appropriate or mute their difference.
> . . . Female characters and female authors alike emerge as ingenious strategists who succeed in devising some mode of assertion (Abel 1981, 174, 178).

> . . . it seems more plausible to read the novel [*Dracula*] as a fin-de-siècle myth of newly empowered womanhood, whose two heroines are violently transformed from victims to instigators of their story (Auerbach 1982, 24).

So much has been accomplished during this first stage of women's studies—compiling information, adapting and developing approaches to the material, changing attitudes toward traditional concepts and values—that we can now begin to measure certain pressing limitations along with the general progress of the field. As a discipline, women's studies can be rather insular and self-referential at times, too dependent on a few recent voices for sanction.[4] This seems a predictable and temporary problem, given the novelty of the field, the reductive discourse in current academia, and the tremendous challenge scholars face of reformulating the terms of human experience.

Women's studies has already changed our ways of perceiving the world, of reading and writing texts, of sharing our knowledge among colleagues and students, and of dealing with our lives. Even so, these are still the early intimations of our journey as we dive, of necessity, into the wreck, and learn to consolidate new wholes.

Literature

The books under review for this year continue to reflect the connection women have traditionally made between work and life. In all areas of the humanities, scholars are using biographical materials to account for the personal motives of their subjects and the consequent lines of force in their work. Biography in various forms—diaries, journals, letters, and narratives—remains a major concern in itself.

For the most part, literary criticism in women's studies is organized by standard categories of author, period, genre, or theme. Women novelists get the greatest attention, which is logical, even fair; but it leaves a disturbing gap where wide-ranging explorations of women poets and short story writers should be.

Four of the best books about literature deal with issues of women's power. Nina Auerbach's superb exposition (1982) probes the Victorian cultural imagination to redeem the dark underside of the Angel of the House, where she finds "an explosively mobile, magic woman, who breaks the boundaries of family within which her society restricts her" (1). Her analysis links demonic mermaids, spinsters, and fallen women as disruptive figures with heroic capabilities of self-regeneration. In *Thomas Hardy and Women*, Penny Boumelha (1982) notes a related duality in Hardy's portrayal of women as both victims and sexual destroyers, and shows how he came to question biologically determined sex roles and the double standard. Musing on whether current scholars are so ambivalent about women's power that they prefer to study it at a safe remove in the past, Judith Lowder Newton (1981) takes a backward look, cogently tracing a line of resistance in women novelists from Fanny Burney through George Eliot as they substituted female ability—marked by the competent autonomy of the heroine—for conventional feminine influence (xviii, 10). Combining thoughtful readings of English novels with lively personal commentary, Rachel Brownstein (1982) warns against a deceptive ideal of power: the self-actualizing immanence of the fictive heroine, who "perfects herself into art, out of life" (xxii).

Annis Pratt (1981), in her interesting but scattered treatment of *Archetypal Patterns in Women's Fiction*, reveals how some heroines-in-training drag or divert their feet when "growing up" means taking on social roles that infantilize and alienate them. Yet looking at classical literature in *Heroines and Hysterics*, Mary Lefkowitz (1981) suggests that in certain situations, helpless women gain critical independence, whereby "as outsiders, they can comment as observers on what is happening around them" (3). In contrast to Pratt, Lefkowitz maintains that normative mythic "patterns also persist in literature composed by women" (45).

Three studies focus on women in sixteenth- and seventeenth-century English drama with varying success. Simon Shepherd (1981) provides a useful overview of warrior women in early English literature with the conclusion that such images may indicate a resistance within some Puritan sects to patriarchy and antifeminism. Irene Dash (1981) considers *Wooing, Wedding and Power: Women in Shakespeare's Plays* with worthwhile attention to how characters have been changed in performance, but the book is marred by repetition and by undue reliance on Simone de Beauvoir and Virginia Woolf as unquestioned authorities on aspects of women that are still controversial. Arguing that Shakespeare, as a man, could only see women as Other, Linda Bamber (1982) makes an elegant and persuasive case that "in every genre except history he associates the feminine with whatever it is outside himself he takes most seriously" (6).

Psychology, canonical and revised, is by now an established influence in literary criticism. To ongoing debates about the place of women in Freud's theories, Judith Van Herik (1982) contributes an intriguing assessment in which she demonstrates how Freud linked femininity with Christian "illusion," and masculinity with both the Jewish renunciation of wish and the postreligious scientific attitude (2, 55). Dianne Sadoff (1982) draws on Freud's concepts of "primal fantasies" to isolate informing metaphors of the primal scene in Dickens, of seduction in George Eliot, and of castration in Charlotte Brontë (2). Although the book makes many telling points, especially on Dickens, the premise is dubious (how closely can we afford to read fiction as psychobiography?) and the outcome is increasingly banal. If we say, as Sadoff does, that "'seduction,' like 'incest,' can signify activities ranging from caring and nurturing that gratify infant needs to overt child abuse" (67), how useful is our term? If we think, in reading *The Mill on the Floss*, that "Maggie's father . . . soothes her with the language of love which signifies desire" (70) do we understand more or less? An impressive pioneering study of popular American fiction by women uses psychological insights to better advantage, as Sally McNall (1981) distills a central theme for two centuries of literature: "the young woman's ambivalence about growing up to be a woman," which entails the strategic evasion of mothers and motherhood (3, 9, 71, 81, 86).

While enlarging the field of known writing by women, scholarship in American literature continues to reevaluate the canon in feminist terms. In a broad, thoughtful survey (Fleishman 1982), various critics examine such issues as heroines in Cooper, Hawthorne's feminism, the evolution of Stowe's social ideals, androgyny in Hemingway, and women in Richard Wright. Carol Wershoven (1982) begins with a promising subject, *The Female Intruder in the Novels of Edith Wharton*, but says little that is new and fails to question Wharton's marked dichotomy between childish women and powerful men.

Elizabeth Hampsten (1982) offers an informative though erratic inspection of the private writings of midwestern women in which she casts doubt on the concept of regionalism as it is applied to documents that reflect little sense of specific place: "Women describe where they are in relation to other people more than according to a spot on the map and its attendant history and economics" (29–30, 40). Yet another book, *Teaching Women's Literature from a Regional Perspective* (Hoffman and Rosenfelt 1982), shows the exciting potential of rooting academic classes in a regional approach, where students do historical research firsthand and learn to relate their findings to their own lives.

In general, the few critical books available on American women's poetry serve to reinforce feminist and mainstream maxims while attempting to establish new norms. They accomplish a good deal in specific readings of verses, but their ambitions cast shadows which raise false hopes. Cheryl Walker (1982) seeks to identify common preoccupations among American women poets before the twentieth century. Her method is instructive, treating representative works by different poets in terms of a particular theme, then concentrating in some breadth on a given poet. Yet the "tradition" she posits is rather vague and negative, full of predictable features such as ambivalence toward power and repressed passions—and not clearly distinct from what one encounters in writing by men during the same period. Joanne Diehl (1981) proposes to regard Dickinson both as a latter-day Romantic and as a woman, but ultimately explores her subversive relation to English Romanticism with little regard for gender after a fine opening section on the woman poet and her muse. Barbara Mossberg (1982) does another turn on the agonistic pivot to show identity conflicts closer to home, explaining in persuasive terms that while Dickinson's "identity as a daughter may be impelled by psychological needs, . . . her identity as a daughter is also conceived by her as a strategy to further her poetic career" (86).

In recent years, psychology has taught us an enormous amount about literary texts we thought we knew. Yet this muscular school of thought, which views poetry dynamically as an oedipal struggle for selfhood, seems now as constricting as the quietist school of the past, which viewed the same poetry contemplatively as an achieved statement of being. Women, who presumably have a different orientation toward relationships and the world—or at least a different experience of them—must bring their own examples to bear on the self-revealing task of literary criticism.

Two other books concerning American women's poetry are of particular note. The first, *May Sarton: Woman and Poet* (Hunting 1982), provides an absorbing collection of essays and interviews that addresses the range of Sarton's achievement as a novelist, poet, autobiographer, and person. For the most part, these are introductory pieces that offer directions for subsequent scholarship, already long overdue. Sarton's own voice, conveyed largely through the interviews, has impressive authority whether she reflects on her own writing or on current trends, as in the following excerpt:

In much of feminist poetry today there is not enough self-criticism—I feel. People are much too pleased with what I would call half finished work—full of talent, full of energy and everything else, but somehow it has stopped too soon. These poets think that the poem is finished when from my point of view it's only just begun. When you get down that strong feeling, that's just the beginning. (243)

The second book, a long essay, really, Jan Clausen's *A Movement of Poets* 1982, includes a similar opinion within a much broader context, working to improve feminist poetry and its associations with mainstream culture from within. This probing and incisive critique suggests a significant coming of age in women's writing in which feminist poets can examine their premises without fearing to break rank with their political cause. With unflinching candor, Clausen challenges familiar feminist assumptions: that individuals can speak accurately for the mass as "we"; that poetry should be "useful" in the service of political ends; that poetry should be "accessible," often enough a synonym for easy reading; that feminist writing is sufficient unto itself; and that criticism of it "is politically suspect—or irrelevant" (7, 21, 23, 28, 33, 35). Citing forceful statements by some current poets, Clausen admonishes us to avoid the wishful lure of rhetoric, and looks for sustaining poetry to be drawn out of a depth of experience and a complexity of vision (26). She calls on us to expect more from our writers while freeing them from dogmatic constraints, and points toward the emerging voices of women of color as the most notable development of this period in the field.

The autobiographical materials that appeared this year converge strongly on the twentieth century, with a time frame running effectively from the late nineteenth century to a minute ago. The first volume of *The Diary of Beatrice Webb*, scrupulously edited by Norman and Jeanne MacKenzie (1982), is a fascinating portrait of a Victorian life in action—a woman examining herself and the world with the curious detachment of a naturalist, fully aware of the competing pulls of progressive zeal and regressive need:

> But at times a working life is a weary work for a woman. The brain is worn and the heart unsatisfied, and in those intervals of exhaustion the old craving for love and devotion, given and taken, returns and an idealized life of love and sympathy passes before one's eyes. (177)

By contrast, one waits in vain for thoughtful observations in Charlotte Wolff's coyly unself-conscious autobiography, *Hindsight* (1980). Where one craves revealing details on Wolff's personal development as a lesbian, on her professional work as a therapist, and on her social encounters with such people as Virginia Woolf, one only hears a gruff Anaïs Nin recording how various parts of her looked in the mirror.

Despite massive cuts and Ted Hughes's irresponsible loss and ill-judged destruction of the late notebooks, *The Journals of Sylvia Plath* (McCullough 1982) bring a refreshingly robust voice into the open. For readers acquainted only with the sharp distillations of Plath's poetry, this rich, often ebullient prose will fill in the larger person—and her tremendous potential—behind the flat popular image. Anne Truitt's *Daybook* 1982 is a beautiful journal by a woman rare as much for her maturity as for her sensibility. A sculptor and painter, she started writing the journal in an effort to deal with visceral feelings she was stealthily displacing into her art: ". . . the more visible my work became, the less visible I grew to myself. In a deeply unsettling realization, I began to see that I had used the process of art not only to contain my intensities but also to exorcize those beyond my endurance" (42). In the course of her experiment, Truitt manages to integrate diverse aspects of her inner life while continuing to appreciate the outer world with equal interest and compassion. Less analytically inclined, Audre Lorde (1982) evokes her past with unusual power, chronicling her experiences as a child and young adult with all her senses. Her approach is most compelling in the first half of her story, where she can revel in self-awareness without seeming distractingly self-centered.

Robin Morgan (1982) ponders a number of general concerns such as aging, abuse, agoraphobia, and the applications of learning to life. There is a personal, meditative tone to these pieces, yet they seem like collegian essays, self-consciously intelligent, well stoked with literary allusions. I found myself wanting her real voice to break through. In *Ariadne's Thread*, Lyn Lifshin (1982) presents a spotty pastiche of excerpts from journals by contemporary women, organized according to topics such as work, self, family, love, and friendship. The title, apparently adopted from one of the entries, is unfortunate for a book with feminist import, when we remember that Ariadne gave the thread to Theseus so that he could find his way out of the Labyrinth—after which he married, and later abandoned her. Individual journals have more and less appeal, but as a group they articulate an impressive range of women's attitudes and experiences.

Biography must be one of the most demanding genres, requiring detached objectivity and passionate identification at the same time. Most of the works read this year convey essential information about women of substance and style; but few try to draw out inferences about the effects of being female, or to assert a distinctly feminist perspective on their materials; and almost none achieve the incalculably difficult ideal of bringing their subjects to life.

Three books on major writers cover an indicative range of accomplishment. The best of these, Judith Thurman's *Isak Dinesen* (1982), gives a vividly detailed account that allows Dinesen's life and work to evolve, shaped comprehensively by inner revelations from diaries and letters, by recollections of family, friends, and acquaintances, and by discreet authorial conclusions. By contrast, Stephen Trombley is intrusively self-serving in *All That Summer She Was Mad* (1982), where he argues, against the accepted view, that "the Virginia Woolf of *Three Guineas* was perfectly sane" (2). Trombley's method is exasperating, as he questions the validity of lay judgments determined by Leonard Woolf and others, and then proceeds to pronounce his own. Overall, this treatise merely capitalizes on feminist concerns, relying on dubious interpretations and pompous assurances to simulate a scholarly approach. In *Katherine Anne Porter*, Joan Givner (1982) renders a great service to those who have sifted through conflicting versions of the Porter myth and wondered what the truth really was. She solves numerous nagging puzzles, and feelingly sketches in the somber background of a much glorified public image. Still, the book lacks a direct focus, so that it seems at the mercy of its material. Worse, Givner sometimes makes superficial associations that undercut her own reliability: "Once Gay [Porter's sister] was accused of stealing a ring. Perhaps this accounts for Porter's use of the theft of a precious object as a recurring motif in her fiction" (56).

Several other biographies serve either to introduce us to new women or to deepen our sense of those we already know. Nancy Boyd's *Three Victorian Women Who Changed Their World: Josephine Butler, Octavia Hill, Florence Nightingale* 1982), treats these doughty pioneers of English social reform in terms of their achievements and of their motivating Christian ideals. Unfortunately, Boyd accepts such faith at face value, and does not speculate on how a religious mantle can be used to transform virtuously repressed women into vigorous public activists. F. B. Smith (1982) writes a fuller and more critical appraisal of the "Lady with the Lamp" in *Florence Nightingale*, but emerges more with an assortment of data than with a defined portrayal of character. J. C. Furnas (1982) speaks like an avid member of the family in his doting, leisurely study of the Anglo-American actress, *Fanny Kemble;* he is particularly evocative when describing plantation life in the American South.

No one reading Henry Adams's famous memoir could possibly gauge the identity of his wife, whom he flatly ignored as he traced successive sites where his hopes were blasted. In *The Education of Mrs. Henry Adams*, Eugenia Kaledin (1981) combines facts with intuition in describing the sad life of "Clover" Hooper Adams. While Kaledin draws us effectively into a complex and wrenching family drama, she relies too heavily on inference and generalization when she cannot substantiate historical fact; and she does not, to my mind, distinguish clearly enough between adverse cultural influences and family pathology in determining the causes of Clover Adams's behavior.

Some biographies depend on a close understanding of a person's work to illuminate the life in sufficient depth. Celia Bertin's *Marie Bonaparte* (1982) fails on this count, and diverts readers with trivial, if often engaging details: "Mimau and Nelly dressed her in a white silk dress with a blue sash, the Greek colors. Her hat was also blue and white. The outfit did not suit her, but she didn't mind" (92). One wonders wistfully about the content of Bonaparte's thought about her analysis with Freud and her subsequent career as a psychoanalyst. The inner life eludes Léonie Rosenstiel, too, as she contemplates the great musician and teacher, *Nadia Boulanger* (1982), but she writes an arresting narrative full of pertinent information. Happily, there remains a stunning example of suiting method to subject to Elisabeth Young-Bruehl's extraordinary *Hannah Arendt* (1982), which organizes the philosopher's life in terms of her work, thought, and relationships.

Two books concern American radicals involved with the Socialist weekly, the *Masses*, published between 1911–1917. Leslie Fishbein's *Rebels in Bohemia* (1982) gives an enlightening survey of Greenwich Village activists, depicting their central personalities, high ideals, and habits, along with certain glaring lapses: "They claimed to be feminists yet often failed to comprehend that liberated women might not view birth control and free-love arrangements merely as a means of freeing male rebels from the constraints of the bourgeois family" (5). In *"Friend and Lover,"* Virginia Gardner (1982) concentrates on one of the best-known rebels, Louise Bryant, graphically projecting the shape but not the center of the person Bryant's lover, John Reed, characterized as "wild and brave and straight" (13).

Finally, there are two impressive books on American women of style. Jane Smith (1982) brings back to light a formidably ambitious woman in *Elsie de Wolfe*, the story of a modestly talented actress who became the first and fabulously successful interior decorator, a lesbian who lived with a socially prominent theatrical agent for over thirty-five years and then married an English lord at the age of sixty. Knowledgeable descriptions of elegant trappings make as real as possible a woman more invested in things than people. Where Elsie de Wolfe seems heroic in her drive, skill, and egotistical magnetism, Edie Sedgwick, the subject of Jean Stein and George Plimpton's *Edie* (1982) seems merely pitiful and decadent. The narrative method is original and absorbing, building on excerpted statements by friends, relatives, teachers, and Edie herself. The effect is like watching a snuff film in slow motion, frame by frame, as an entranced audience chants its adulation of a woman who made a spectacle of herself, hoping desperately to see in the mirrors of other people's eyes that she was real. No one seems to have cared much about what went on inside.

History

As a group, historians are still contributing the most to women's studies, constantly assimilating new data and reshaping our sense of the past. Two noticeable trends in this field will make women's history increasingly accessible to us, as scholars draw closer parallels between past and present, and come to regard the twentieth century in light of what they are learning about its antecedents.

Fine examples of historical recovery and reconstruction continue to appear, substantiating in fact the long procession of women's lives that we could previously only imagine. In *Good Wives* (1982), Laurel Thatcher Ulrich investigates the daily reality beneath the pervasive ideal of the "good wife," limiting her study to women in northern New England from 1650–1750. The position of wife, she finds, "was complementary and at the same time secondary to that of her husband," so that while the Colonial wife had less status than her husband, she could perform a wider range of tasks and assume a greater measure of authority than her nineteenth-century successor, who was relegated to a more exclusive sphere of "women's work" (5, 8). Despite marked differences, the Colonial period exhibits surprising parallels to the nineteenth century in terms of "the magnification of motherhood, the idealization of conjugal love, and the elevation of female religiosity" (240).

Mary Ryan (1981) instructively combines social and women's history to focus on the family in Oneida County, New York, from 1790–1865. Her main concern is the way in which family structures and values changed as the culture moved from an agrarian to an industrial economy. This transition is dramatically evident in the local operations of The Female Moral Reform Society: "Although female moral reform seemed to hark back to an older household order . . . , it also gave birth to some inventive social and familial forms. Most important, these associated women enhanced the power of their sex and devised novel methods of sexual control, to be lodged not in legal and religious institutions but in the mandate of public opinion and the character of individuals" (127).

In *Out to Work*, a major study made possible by recent research, Alice Kessler-Harris (1982) explicates the conversion of women's work into wage labor from Colonial America to the present. Two themes figure prominently in the book, as Kessler-Harris probes how women's "wage work simultaneously sustained the patriarchal family and set in motion the tensions that seem now to be breaking it down" (ix): first, the perpetuation of the myth that women's wage work was temporary, a way of preparing for a future at home; second, the persistent segmentation of the work force into sex-stereotyped jobs. "As it turned out," the author patiently concludes,

moving toward, even achieving, equality at work proved to be the beginning, not the end, of the battle. Each step on the road to equality—equal pay, an end to discrimination in hiring and training, access to promotion—exposed a deeply rooted set of social attitudes that tried to preserve women's attachment to the home and hindered a commitment to the job world. (315)

Surveying without illusions the place prepared for American women, Susan Strasser (1982) enumerates the strenuous chores of housework over the past century in her aptly named *Never Done*. Graphically documenting these facts of life while demonstrating their implications, Strasser reviews such matters as household tasks and equipment, the effects of industrial development, the gradual shift from economic self-sufficiency to dependency as the home production of goods waned into mere consumption, and theories of household efficiency and child rearing. She is especially attentive to the ways in which housework has been simultaneously glorified and dismissed in our culture, ensnaring women in successive double binds. Women who have worked at home, for instance, have not generally been thought to be "working" at all (4). Furthermore, once the "separate spheres" ideology hardened into dogma in the nineteenth century,

The qualities that defined the ideal wife—dependence, gentleness, emotionality—destroyed the ideal mother, who performed heavy housework duties and prepared children for the demands of the outside world. (183)

For some, home was a southern plantation. Catherine Clinton (1982), in *The Plantation Mistress*, counterbalances the northern bias of women's studies with compelling descriptions of plantation routines, family customs, social isolation, sexual double standards, health problems, and life with and among slaves. Like Mary Chesnut in *A Diary from Dixie*, Clinton draws implicit parallels between plantation mistresses, other free women, and slaves, emphasizing that "These women were merely prisoners in disguise. However

comfortable their surroundings, however elaborate the rhetoric that celebrated them, however sheltered they were from the market economy and class
oppression, plantation mistresses spent much of their lives under constraint
and in isolation: fettered nonetheless" (109).

Estelle Freedman (1981) looks at the acknowledged penal system in
America to see why separate women's prisons originated in the nineteenth
century. She notes how prisons, which were once used simply to detain
people, became places of reform; and how double standards in the classification of crime made the female criminal a "fallen woman," hence a hopeless
case: "Because she had denied her own pure nature, the female criminal was
more depraved than her male counterpart" (8–10, 17). The change Freedman
describes in social attitudes toward female offenders is remarkable, as the
nineteenth-century reformers first tried to "uplift" fallen women and condition them (in the improbable setting of a cell) to homely values; while the
Progressives extended social services in an attempt to control the environmental causes of crime. Ruth Rosen (1982) presents a related study on prostitution
during the Progressive Era where she considers the profession in terms of both
class and gender. Dexterously combining the overview of a social historian
with inside reports from the women themselves, she treats prostitution as a
revealing index of women's experiences, which "tends to *mirror changes in the
family, women's lives, and sex roles*" (173).

Like Freedman and Rosen, Rosalind Rosenberg (1982) examines some of
the critical consequences of the shift in perception that took place during the
Progressive Era, as people began to question social and biological determinism, and to explain human behavior as the interaction of environmental
influences and individual traits. Rosenberg analyzes the revolutionary work of
women social scientists "who launched the modern study of sex differences,"
(xiii) challenging the entrenched belief that social roles were rooted in biology
(xiv). Helen Thompson, for example, compared men and women matched
according to their backgrounds, and found that while differences between the
sexes persisted, there were no *consistent* differences, and thus no basis either for
distinctive male and female types, or for ordained male and female roles. Susan
Ware (1981), in *Beyond Suffrage*, focuses on another group of extraordinary (and
hitherto neglected) women who held critical positions in the government
during the New Deal. Sketching in personal dynamics along with public
achievements, she delineates the binding affinities of class, education, and
ideology these women shared, which strengthened the empowering network
they formed with Eleanor Roosevelt at its strategic center. They believed "that
women had special roles to play in society," (14) and they served their causes
by "setting an example" (129). Unfortunately, like many women of accomplishment, they isolated themselves from the mass of their sex by assuming
they were exceptions. As a result, they failed to address the systematic
oppression of women or to gather capable recruits to succeed them.

In Her Own Words, edited by Morantz and colleagues (1982) taps oral
history to compare three generations of women in medicine. After an excellent

introduction by Regina Morantz on the history of women healers in America, interviews with three female physicians depict family backgrounds and influences, professional ideals and goals, and various experiences of being a woman in a male-dominated field. The subjects share a common sense of medicine as "giving, caring," which they regard as particularly female (51, 81). While some suggestive generational contrasts emerge between an early pioneer operating within the philosophy of separate-but-equal institutions and her less idealistic successors, the sample here is too small to justify any definite conclusions.

Two smartly designed books inaugurate a promising series on American Women in the Twentieth Century. Organized into decades, *Holding their Own* by Susan Ware (1982) and *The Home Front and Beyond* by Susan Hartmann (1982) cover in trenchant detail the activities and options of American women during the 1930s and 1940s. Both studies survey their periods in terms of work, home, and popular culture, with special emphasis on the prevailing forces of the time—for Ware, the Depression and the interplay of feminism and social reform; for Hartmann, the Second World War. Like Kessler-Harris, Ware and Hartmann point up the incessant pressures on women to maintain gender-divided roles that relegated them primarily to the home just as they were struggling to gain access to protected male professions and wage scales. Hartmann notes, ". . . as women moved into the public sphere, they were reminded that their new positions were temporary, that retaining the traditional feminine characteristics was essential, and that their familial roles continued to take precedence over all others" (23). Hartmann is especially sensitive to differences of class and race which have persistently discriminated against black women. Basically, these books accomplish what they set out to do very well. Still, I would like to have seen sections on marriage, child rearing, sexual attitudes, and the treatment of women in medicine and psychology. Such subjects would add a valuable depth of specific experience to overviews weighted in favor of public and statistical expressions of women's lives.

Two commendable books appeared this year on the socialization of women in Victorian England and some of its results. Carol Dyhouse (1981) documents the ways in which girls were brought up by families and schools to conform to cultural definitions of femininity. We see some tragic consequences in the lives of women teachers who chose to remain single in order to keep their jobs: "It was inordinately difficult for women to separate their sexuality from what they had learned about 'femininity'—from associations of fragility, passivity and dependence. So they frequently denied both at the same time" (72). Janet Murray (1982) presents a marvelous anthology of "lost voices from nineteenth-century England" that addresses central Victorian concerns such as women's nature and mission, household duties, marriage and motherhood, single women, women's education, and work. Complemented by Murray's superb introductions and editorial notes, these excerpts offer vigorous models of achievement that can still teach and direct us today. As Murray exhorts:

We need to recover the history of these women in order to be renewed by an awareness of their vitality, and to replace in our own imaginations the false images of passive victimization with our true heritage of women's struggles and women's strengths. (16)

Religion

Women's studies in religion offsets stringently male frames of reference as it restores and extends potent representations of women's spirituality. In *Jesus as Mother*—the most conventional work of those under review this year—Caroline Walker Bynum (1982) explores the feminization of Christian imagery and rituals during the High Middle Ages. Through careful analyses of religious texts, Bynum shows how a growing interest in female metaphors accompanied a new devotion to Christ's gentle humanity, in contrast to earlier emphases on God's severe judgment. While men used more female imagery in their writing, women mystics concentrated Church rituals in aspects of Christ that made God seem more accessible to believers. In retrospect, however, the Church seems to have co-opted women piecemeal as metaphorical functions—such as childbearing, nursing, surrendering in sex—without improving their inferior status in the world.

Kathryn Allen Rabuzzi (1982) deliberately puns on Eliade's famous meditation on *The Sacred and the Profane* in her book, *The Sacred and the Feminine*, but, typically, makes nothing of it; she simply exploits the title instead of amplifying its meaning. Ostensibly, Rabuzzi sets out to illuminate "the Land of Happily Ever After," which women are encouraged to expect without having any real sense of what it is (5). She eclectically scans literature, history, and casual anecdotes for references to an argument that never develops beyond familiar truisms about how women are misperceived and mistreated. What she posits, finally, is a "theology of housework," which sounds to a skeptical reader disturbingly like an academic rendition of *The Total Woman:*

Whereas, on the surface, a woman picking up last night's paper, several dirty coffee cups . . . may simply appear to be straightening her living room, she may actually be enacting her own psychic environment. (100–2)

Ritualized housework not only sets a housewife in the context of female ancestors, placing her in the larger family of women, it also determines her place in the largest context of all: the world. The process by which such placement occurs is cosmization, the creation of world out of chaos. (105)

There are, of course, many respected traditions that teach us to see everything as holy, but I cannot begin to associate Rabuzzi's breezy, jargon-ridden pep talk with a dignified, sacramental attitude toward life. A much better book, though again rather spotty in its argument, *Lilith's Daughters* by Barbara Hill Rigney (1982) surveys contemporary writers such as Sally Miller Gearhart, Annie Dillard, and Margaret Atwood, and proposes an adaptive model strikingly different from Rabuzzi's: "Women writers have perhaps never before been so free to challenge the sacred, to revise and reinterpret the traditional, or to exercise the mythopoetic function in creating new symbols for spiritual transcendence" (3).

The three remaining books treat pagan aspects of women-centered religion, and assure us that women are looking behind Christianity as well as within it for spiritual fulfillment. In this area, as in the aspects of black studies and lesbian studies presented this year, standard scholarship is supplemented by works that cannot be called scholarship in any formal sense, but that contribute to the kinetic energy and scope of the field. Such writing has an essential place in the discourse of women's studies, because it draws in further dimensions of women's lives phrased as personal narratives, speculations, or statements of rhetoric and faith. Against the generic objectivity that most scholarship assumes, these voices assert specific points of view and question the premises of any humanistic discipline that would exclude them. At best, they inform and correct the field; at worst, they fail to communicate on a reasonable level, or they keep themselves contemptuously aloof while demanding privileged status from those they disdain. Internal criticism is inevitable and often enriching in any healthy discipline, but it should have a constructive purpose; gratuitous remarks either fall away with no effect or sap the general strength.

In *The Female Experience and the Nature of the Divine*, Judith Ochshorn (1981) argues that the male prerogatives that seem a given in our culture actually came late to Western civilization and coincide with the emergence of monotheism (14). She then goes on to describe the androgynous vision in polytheistic religions of the ancient Near East where images of women were attributed comparable power to those of men. In the course of presenting interesting research, she expands our mythological repertory so that we can imagine women more vividly as dynamic forces.[5] Charlene Spretnak has edited a large collection of essays, many of which had been published between 1975–1981. Like Ochshorn, Spretnak sees patriarchal religion as a comparatively recent development, dating from 4500 B.C., in contrast to evidence of goddess worship dating from 25,000 B.C. (xi–xii). Overall, the book is concerned with women's power, usually as expressed through an identification with the Goddess incarnate in this world. As Starhawk (also known as Miriam Simos) insists in "Witchcraft as Goddess Religion":

> The importance of the Goddess symbol for women cannot be overstressed. The image of the Goddess inspires women to see ourselves as divine, our bodies as sacred, the changing phases of our lives as holy, our aggression as healthy, our anger as purifying, and our power to nurture and create, but also to limit and destroy when necessary, as the very force that sustains all life. (51)

Taken as a group, the essays are stimulating, though overly redundant. Starhawk's own book, *Dreaming the Dark: Magic, Sex and Politics* (1982b), continues in the same mode, proclaiming the fundamental unity of the world in the face of our superficial estrangement, and trying to show us how to "find the dark within and transform it, own it as our own power" (xiv).

Black Studies

June Jordan (1981), in her eloquent set of essays from 1964 to 1980, gives us a prophetic clue to the tone and content of the few books available in black studies this year. Where she once passionately refused to become absorbed in the destructive hatred of self and others (xi), and defined black feminism in terms of "positive self-love" that allows "a steady-state deep caring and respect for every other human being" (144), she now concludes that "The expression of hatred for your enemies is sometimes the only way to end self-hatred" (184). Similarly, where she once celebrated her shared identity with a larger group, she now recognizes the need for each person to find and act on a private truth of feeling, "without apology" (187). Other writers begin where Jordan leaves off, wanting to settle issues of accountability, wanting to purge themselves of unwarranted pain.

Current discussions on racism in conferences on women's studies confirm what we can readily see in the writings that surface in black studies: the need for more common ground between black and white women. In the books considered here, black women express their grief and outrage at feeling ignored by white women in the field. Indeed, from what I have read, white women say remarkably little about missing black people or wishing to understand them and their points of view.

There is significant work to be done in every area of women's studies that will not only take women of all colors into serious account, but will also develop some synthesis of how their lives and achievements relate to each other. In terms of black studies, this means that much more scholarship must come out on particulars of the black experience in America, and further efforts must be made to fuse all the parts we know into some representative whole.

All scholars can contribute to this enterprise by disregarding false barriers between fields and by educating themselves more thoroughly. Someone well versed in literature, for example, should notice the intriguing affinities between Virginia Woolf and Zora Neale Hurston. At this stage, perhaps for want of a viable dialogue with whites, some black scholars are spending too much time imagining what whites think about blacks instead of dealing directly with their own impressions. Would it not be more worthwhile for blacks to share their reactions to whites instead? Or to discuss the stereotypes they see being imposed on blacks and assumed by them? Or to explain how blacks within the community perceive differences among themselves, and thus break down the monolithic association by color? Or to convey how they feel about other people of color, such as Native Americans, Chinese Americans, and Chicanas? Research in this area could use much more breadth and resiliance.

Ain't I a Woman (1981), by Bell Hooks (also known as Gloria Watkins), is a case in point. Hooks provides an informative survey of black women's attitudes toward feminism from the 1950s on, emphasizing the terrible frustrations of feeling invisible within two worlds:

> No other group in America has so had their identity socialized out of existence as have black women. We are rarely recognized as a group separate and distinct from black men, or as a present part of the larger group "women" in this culture. (7)

However forceful, the book is too polemical, generally indicting black men as sexist and white women as racist, and disparaging the efforts of writers such as

Adrienne Rich and Catharine Stimpson to address racial issues in depth. This stance reduces the impact of the book, since it serves primarily to defend the speaker instead of revealing her positions more fully (102, 123–35, 139, 143–5). Hooks also ignores the dynamic role of lesbian feminism in her description of the women's movement, which seems a major oversight in a historical study.

Trudier Harris (1982) traces the evolution of domestics in black American literature, interspersing plot summaries of relevant texts with references to folklore, history, psychology, and sociology. In examining the changing postures of black domestics toward their white employers on a scale that runs from white-identified "mammyism" to black-identified militance, Harris seems to assume that blacks and whites are fundamentally incompatible. From this vantage, no alliance is possible: a "mammy" seriously involved with whites is a lost black, rather than someone bridging two worlds; while a militant who kills whites is a self-fulfilling heroine, rather than a criminal who increases racial friction. As Harris tells us, without clearly distinguishing between her own opinion and that of the literature she is reviewing:

> Direct confrontation, overt physical violence, and ultimate denial of the power of the white world to control Blacks are the traits of the final stage in the progression of domestics from mammies to militants. Maids in this category . . . are without mercy and without guilt. . . . [Characters who kill] are militants who use their revolutionary activity to benefit all black people. (34)

I am troubled by the tacit endorsement of random violence as a form of social progress said to "benefit all black people." Does it really? Is it commendable or socially productive to be "without mercy and without guilt?" To me, these are dangerous and regressive features that imply a psychological stunting of growth, because the militant fixes on the most hated aspects of the oppressor and imitates them, instead of turning away and asserting positive independence. I would like to have seen Harris deal with these issues more concretely, since they go well beyond the context of "trickster psychology" in which she casts them.

Finally, an indispensable addition to this field, *But Some of Us Are Brave*, edited by Hull and colleagues (1982), presents a definitive set of essays on such subjects as black feminism, confronting racism, black women and the social sciences, creative survival, and black women's literature. Through such a book, and through the concerted efforts of teaching and writing that it reflects, the concept of a black feminist analysis becomes an exciting reality. Following the essays, which themselves give detailed citations for further research, the book includes nearly two hundred pages of essential bibliographic materials.

Lesbian Studies

Two books on lesbian studies complement each other in a basic way.[6] The first, *Nice Jewish Girls*, edited by Evelyn Torton Beck (1982), focuses on the particular difficulties of Jewish lesbians. Being omitted from Jewish law, a

Jewish lesbian feels uncreated, an alien blank in the ritualistic lives of Jews. Noting examples of anti-Semitism in lesbian literature, a Jewish lesbian feels adversely recognized—and still excluded—by lesbians. While the writers of these essays and narratives struggle to incorporate elements of their Jewish heritage, the lack of a comparable lesbian heritage becomes acutely evident. As Savina Teubal comments wistfully in "A Coat of Many Colors":

> Belonging is a form of identification. One may identify as a lesbian, but lesbianism has little reclaimed history and no traditions. There are no celebrations to mark the stages in the life of a lesbian, her initiation or her union with another, no coming-of-age rituals, weddings, or lesbian gatherings at the birth of a child. Even at her death, a lesbian's life-long commitment to another woman may be contested or made invisible by omission. (87)

The second anthology, Margaret Cruikshank's *Lesbian Studies* (1982), shows by example how scholars can begin to search for women's hidden lesbian history. If we consider *But Some of Us Are Brave, Nice Jewish Girls*, and *Lesbian Studies* as a group, we must confront the hard truth that lesbian studies is still a frightening subject in this culture and only a tentative field in academia. It is here that teachers describe the incalculable anxiety of "coming out" to their students and colleagues; of guiding students through honest and fair discussions of the literature; of coping with the volatile feelings that erupt in class. Reading these accounts of lives that are so vulnerable, whether closeted or open, we know the courage and the cost of being in the vanguard of civil rights.

Music History and Art History

Three landmark books on women musicians and artists reveal a fine heritage from our foremothers. Sally Placksin (1982) compiles a richly informed, anecdotal history of noted performers from 1900 to the present. Giving us incisive glimpses of both individuals and ensembles, she presciently closes with a selected discography so that readers will be able to gratify their inevitable enthusiasm for this music with living sounds. Charlotte Streifer Rubenstein (1982) completes an even broader survey in *American Women Artists: From Early Indian Times to the Present*, which again—and here in splendid color—cultivates our awareness of what women have achieved. Offering a cameo succession of lives in brief, Rubenstein brings us strongly into our own time, but does not probe the continuities between past and present, which would promote a more coherent sense of tradition. *Feminism and Art History* (1982), edited by Norma Broude and Mary Garrard, addresses persuasively such diverse topics as goddess imagery in ancient Egypt, Artemisia Gentileschi's rendering of *Susanna and the Elders*, and themes of virility and domination in early twentieth-century painting. These essays are superb demonstrations of how a feminist point of view can make even the most familiar objects seem vitally expressive.

Conclusion

Women's studies has emerged as a field of undeniable consequence. Already, significant work has met and inspired crucial questions, and affected the lives of several generations. What we must do now is consolidate these gains in substantive school curricula, and extend our learning into communities that will implement it through binding social action.

Notes

[1] This excellent volume of *Critical inquiry*, devoted to the subject of writing and sexual difference, should be read in its entirety.

[2] Emerson makes a related point at the end of his essay, "Nature."

[3] See also Alice Ostriker, "The thieves of language: Women poets and revisionist mythmaking," *Signs* 8 (Autumn 1982):68–90; and Cynthia A. Davis, "Self, society, and myth in Toni Morrison's fiction," *Contemporary Literature* 23 (Summer 1982):323–42, for interesting ideas on women's uses of myth.

[4] Most commonly those of Chodorow, Dinnerstein, Smith-Rosenberg, Faderman, and Gilbert and Gubar.

[5] See also Catherine Keller, "Of swallowed, walled, and wordless women," *Soundings* 3 (Fall 1982):328–39, for a pertinent discussion of women giving birth to themselves through words; and Sharon W. Tiffany, "The power of matriarchal ideas," *International Journal of Women's Studies* 5 (March-April 1982):138–47, for a brief review of these issues from an anthropological perspective.

[6] See also Catharine R. Stimpson, "Zero degree deviancy: The lesbian novel in English," *Critical Inquiry* 8 (Winter 1981):363–79, for perceptive comments on the better-known lesbian novels.

References

ABEL, ELIZABETH. 1981. "Editor's introduction," *Critical Inquiry* 8 (Winter):173–78).

AUERBACH, NINA. 1982. *Woman and the demon: The life of a victorian myth*. Cambridge: Harvard University Press.

BAMBER, LINDA. 1982. *Comic women, tragic men: A study of gender and genre in Shakespeare*. Stanford: Stanford University Press.

BECK, EVELYN TORTON, ed. 1982. *Nice Jewish girls: A lesbian anthology*. Watertown, Mass.: Persephone Press.

BERTIN, CELIA. 1982. *Marie Bonaparte: A life*. New York: Harcourt, Brace Jovanovich.

BOUMELHA, PENNY. 1982. *Thomas Hardy and women: Sexual ideology and narrative form*. Sussex: Harvester Press.

BOYD, NANCY. 1982. *Three victorian women who changed their world: Josephine Butler, Octavia Hill, Florence Nightingale.* New York, Oxford: Oxford University Press.

BROUDE, NORMA, and GARRARD, MARY D., eds. 1982. *Feminism and art history.* New York: Harper & Row.

BROWNSTEIN, RACHEL M. 1982. *Becoming a heroine.* New York: Viking.

BYNUM, CAROLINE WALKER. 1982. *Jesus as mother: Studies in the spirituality of the high middle ages.* Berkeley: University of California Press.

CLAUSEN, JAN. 1982. *A movement of poets: Thoughts on poetry and feminism.* Brooklyn: Long Haul Press.

CLINTON, CATHERINE. 1982. *The plantation mistress: Woman's world in the old south.* New York: Pantheon.

CRUIKSHANK, MARGARET. 1982. *Lesbian studies: Present and future.* Old Westbury, N.Y.: Feminist Press.

DASH, IRENE G. 1981. *Wooing, wedding, and power: Women in Shakespeare's plays.* New York: Columbia University Press.

DIEHL, JOANNE FEIT. 1981. *Dickinson and the romantic imagination.* Princeton: Princeton University Press.

DYHOUSE, CAROL. 1981. *Girls growing up in late victorian and Edwardian England.* London: Routledge & Kegan Paul.

FISHBEIN, LESLIE. 1982. *Rebels in bohemia: The radicals of the Masses, 1911–1917.* Chapel Hill: University of North Carolina Press.

FLEISHMANN, FRITZ, ed. 1982. *American novelists revisited: Essays in feminist criticism.* Boston: G. K. Hall.

FREEDMAN, ESTELLE B. 1981. *Their sisters' keepers: Women's prison reform in America, 1830–1930.* Ann Arbor: University of Michigan Press.

FURNAS, J. C. 1982. *Fanny Kemble: Leading lady of the nineteenth-century stage.* New York: Dial Press.

GARDNER, VIRGINIA. 1982. *"Friend and lover": The life of Louise Bryant.* New York: Horizon Press.

GILLIGAN, CAROL. *In a different voice.* Cambridge: Harvard University Press.

GIVNER, JOAN. 1982. *Katherine Anne Porter: A life.* New York: Simon & Schuster.

HAMPSTEN, ELIZABETH. 1982. *Read this only to yourself: The private writings of midwestern women, 1880–1910.* Bloomington: Indiana University Press.

HARRIS, TRUDIER. 1982. *From mammies to militants: Domestics in black American literature.* Philadelphia: Temple University Press.

HARTMANN, SUSAN. 1982. *The home front and beyond: American women in the 1940s.* Boston: Twayne.

HEILBRUN, CAROLYN. 1979. *Reinventing womenhood.* New York: W. W. Norton & Co.

HOFFMANN, LEONORE, and ROSENFELT, DEBORAH, eds. 1982. *Teaching women's literature from a regional perspective.* New York: Modern Language Association.

HOOKS, BELL. 1981. *Ain't I a woman: Black women and feminism.* Boston: South End Press.

HULL, GLORIA T., SCOTT, PATRICIA BELL, and SMITH, BARBARA, eds. 1982. *But some of us are brave*. Old Westbury, N.Y.: Feminist Press.

HUNTING, CONSTANCE, ed. 1982. *May Sarton: Woman and poet*. Orono, Me.: National Poetry Foundation, University of Maine at Orono.

JORDAN, JUNE. 1981. *Civil wars*. Boston: Beacon Press.

KALEDIN, EUGENIA. 1981. *The education of Mrs. Henry Adams*. Philadelphia: Temple University Press.

KESSLER-HARRIS, ALICE. 1982. *Out to work: A history of wage-earning women in the United States*. New York: Oxford University Press.

LEFKOWITZ, MARY R. 1981. *Heroines and hysterics*. New York: St. Martin's Press.

LIFSHIN, LYN, ed. 1982. *Ariadne's thread: A collection of contemporary women's journals*. New York: Harper & Row.

LORDE, AUDRE. 1982. *Zami: A new spelling of my name*. Watertown, Mass.: Persephone Press.

MACKENZIE, NORMAN, and MACKENZIE, JEANNE, eds. 1982. *The diary of Beatrice Webb*. Vol. I, 1873–1892. Cambridge: Belknap Press of Harvard University Press.

MCCULLOUGH, FRANCES, ed. 1982. *The journals of Sylvia Plath*. New York: Dial Press.

MCNALL, SALLY ALLEN. 1981. *Who is in the house? A psychological study of two centuries of women's fiction in America, 1795 to the present*. New York: Elsevier North-Holland.

MORANTZ, REGINA; POMERLEAU, MARKELL; STODOLA, CYNTHIA; and FENICHEL, CAROL HANSEN, eds. 1982. *In her own words: Oral histories of women physicians*. Westport, Conn.: Greenwood Press.

MORGAN, ROBIN. 1982. *Depth perception*. Garden City, N.Y.: Anchor/Doubleday.

MOSSBERG, BARBARA ANTONINA CLARKE. 1982. *Emily Dickinson: When a writer is a daughter*. Bloomington: Indiana University Press.

MURRAY, JANET HOROWITZ. 1982. *Strong-minded women: And other lost voices from nineteenth-century England*. New York: Pantheon.

NEWTON, JUDITH LOWDER. 1981. *Women, power, and subversion: Social strategies in British fiction, 1778–1860*. Athens, Ga.: University of Georgia Press.

OCHSHORN, JUDITH. 1981. *The female experience and the nature of the divine*. Bloomington: Indiana University Press.

PLACKSIN, SALLY. 1982. *American women in jazz*. New York: Seaview Books.

PRATT, ANNIS. 1981. *Archetypal patterns in women's fiction*. Bloomington: Indiana University Press.

RABUZZI, KATHRYN ALLEN. 1982. *The sacred and the feminine: Toward a theology of housework*. New York: Seabury Press.

RIGNEY, BARBARA HILL. 1982. *Lilith's daughters: Women and religion in contemporary fiction*. Madison: University of Wisconsin Press.

ROSEN, RUTH. 1982. *The lost sisterhood: Prostitution in America, 1900–1918*. Baltimore: Johns Hopkins University Press.

ROSENBERG, ROSALIND. 1982. *Beyond separate spheres: Intellectual roots of modern feminism*. New Haven: Yale University Press.

ROSENTIEL, LÉONE. 1982. *Nadia Boulanger: A life in music*. New York: W. W. Norton.

RUBENSTEIN, CHARLOTTE STREIFER. 1982. *American women artists: From early Indian times to the present*. Boston: G. K. Hall.

RYAN, MARY P. 1981. *Cradle of the middle class: The family in Oneida County, New York, 1790–1865*. Cambridge: Cambridge University Press.

SADOFF, DIANNE F. 1982. *Monsters of affection: Dickens, Eliot, and Bronte on Fatherhood*. Baltimore: Johns Hopkins University Press.

SHEPHERD, SIMON. 1981. *Amazons and warrior women: Varieties of feminism in seventeenth-century drama*. New York: St. Martin's Press.

SHOWALTER, ELAINE. 1981. Feminist criticism in the wilderness. *Critical Inquiry* 8 (Winter):179–205.

SMITH, F. B. 1982. *Florence Nightingale: Reputation and power*. New York: St. Martin's Press.

SMITH, JANE S. 1982. *Elsie de Wolfe: A life in the high style*. New York: Atheneum.

SPRETNAK, CHARLENE, ed. 1982. *The politics of women's spirituality*. Garden City, N.Y.: Anchor/Doubleday.

STARHAWK, 1982a. "Consciousness, politics, and magic." In *The politics of women's spirituality*, edited by Charlene Spretnak. Garden City, N.Y.: Anchor/Doubleday.

STARHAWK, 1982b. *Dreaming the dark: Magic, sex and politics*. Boston: Beacon Press.

STEIN, JEAN, and PLIMPTON, GEORGE, eds. 1982. *Edie: an American biography*. New York: Alfred A. Knopf.

STRASSER, SUSAN. 1982. *Never done: A history of American housework*. New York: Pantheon.

THURMAN, JUDITH. 1982. *Isak Dinesen: The life of a storyteller*. New York: St. Martin's Press.

TROMBLEY, STEPHEN. 1982. *All that Summer she was mad*. New York: Continuum.

TRUITT, ANNE. 1982. *Daybook: The journal of an artist*. New York: Pantheon.

ULRICH, LAUREL THATCHER. 1982. *Good wives: Image and reality in the lives of women in northern New England 1650–1750*. New York: Alfred A. Knopf.

VAN HERIK, JUDITH. 1982. *Freud on femininity and faith*. Berkeley: University of California Press.

WALKER, CHERYL. 1982. *The nightingale's burden: Women poets and American culture before 1900*. Bloomington: Indiana University Press.

WARE, SUSAN. 1981. *Beyond suffrage: Women in the new deal*. Cambridge: Harvard University Press.

WARE, SUSAN. 1982. *Holding their own: American women in the 1930s*. Boston: Twayne.

WERSHOVEN, CAROL. 1982. *The female intruder in the novels of Edith Wharton*. East Brunswick, N.J.: Associated University Presses.

WOLFF, CHARLOTTE. 1980. *Hindsight: An autobiography.* London: Quartet.

YOUNG-BRUEHL, ELISABETH. 1982. *Hannah Arendt: For love of the world.* New Haven: Yale University Press.

Bibliography

Asbell, Bernard, ed. *Mother and daughter: The letters of Eleanor and Anna Roosevelt.* New York: Coward, McCann & Geoghegan, 1982. Well edited and evocative, though meagerly illustrated.

Dallman, Elaine, ed. *Woman poet.* Vol. 1, *The west.* Reno: Women-in-Literature, 1980. The first of a new series of regional anthologies, including poetry, short essays, and interviews; suggestive, but rather shallow.

Dallman, Elaine, ed. *Woman poet.* Vol. 2, *The east.* Reno: Women-in-Literature, 1981. Poets include Audre Lorde, Robin Morgan, Marie Ponsot, Joan Larkin, June Jordan, and Sara Miles.

Foley, Helene P., ed. *Reflections of women in antiquity.* New York: Gordon & Breach, 1981. Fine essays on such topics as the socioeconomic roles of women in Mycenaean Greece, Sappho's poetry, women in Athenian drama, women in Theocritus.

Kerber, Linda K., and Mathews, Jane Dehart, eds. *Women's America: Refocusing the past.* New York: Oxford University Press, 1982. Classic essays by scholars such as Julia Cherry Spruill, Lyle Koehler, Anne Firor Scott, Kathryn Kish Sklar, and Blanche Wiesen Cook; useful as a textbook, but it needs more of an overview than it offers.

Kuhn, Annette. *Women's pictures: Feminism and cinema.* London: Routledge & Kegan Paul, 1982. Lively, but difficult study examines films as texts or constructs.

Maxwell, Margaret F. *A passion for freedom: The life of Sharlot Hall.* Tucson: University of Arizona Press, 1982. Graphic descriptions of growing up in the early West; otherwise, more an occasional piece.

May, Keith M. *Characters of women in narrative literature.* New York: St. Martin's Press, 1981. A frustrating book: full of thoughtful opinions, but so broad a survey as to render them superficial.

Miller, William D. *Dorothy Day: A biography.* New York: Harper & Row, 1982. Unsatisfyingly chatty and indiscriminate: the person of Dorothy Day eludes this book.

Schoen, Carol B. *Anzia Yezierska.* Boston: Twayne, 1982. A useful survey of Yezierska's career with critical synopses of her work.

Shorter, Edward. *A history of women's bodies.* New York: Basic Books, 1982. A provocative, eerily voyeuristic book full of unsubstantiated opinions.

Simon, Kate. *Bronx primitive: Portraits in a childhood.* New York: Viking, 1982. An evocative memoir of growing up as a Jewish immigrant in New York.

Skelton, Geoffrey. *Richard and Cosima Wagner: Biography of a marriage.* Boston: Houghton Mifflin, 1982. Informative; but Cosima Wagner remains a shadowy figure in her husband's drama.

Smith, Stevie. *Me again*. New York: Farrar, Straus & Giroux, 1981. Canny and conversational materials. One sees a winning mind, especially in the essays and letters.

Staircar, Tom, ed. *The feminine eye: Science fiction and the women who write it*. New York: Frederick Ungar, 1982. Definitely an acquired taste: to my mind, these essays were amazing in how much they missed.

Stauffer, Helen Winter, and Rosowski, Susan J., eds. *Women and western American literature*. Troy, N.Y.: Whitston, 1982. Useful set of short, introductory essays on women's experiences in the West.

Todd, Janet, ed. *Women and literature*. Vol. 2, *Men by women*. New York: Holmes & Meier, 1981. Lively and informative essays, largely on novels by English women.

Vallier, Jane E. *Poet on demand: The life, letters and works of Celia Thaxter*. Camden, Me.: Down East Books, 1982. Restores a figure of historical interest, but makes rather commercial use of Emily Dickinson without comparing them adequately.

Washington, Ida H. *Dorothy Canfield Fisher: A biography*. Shelburne, Vt.: New England Press, 1982. Rather flat and sketchy.

Westbrook, Arlen G. R., and Westbrook, Perry D., eds. *The writing women of New England, 1630–1900: An anthology*. Metuchen, N.J.: Scarecrow Press, 1982. A sampler of brief excerpts from nineteen American women writers. This would have been more appropriate fifty years ago, when less was known, and available.

Wijesinha, Rajiva. *The androgynous Trollope: Attitudes toward women amongst early victorian novelists*. Washington, D.C.: University Press of America, 1982. Studious readings, more a thesis than a book.

Violence Against Women

Freada Klein

The discrepancy between knowledge about the forms of violence against women and the resources devoted to coping with them reveal much about our nation's policy-making process. Specifically, the following patterns come to light: the fragmentation of research from services, the abandonment of problems shortly after their identification, the relative unimportance to policy makers of social problems that affect women, and the conflict of values that leads to allowing sexual violence to go unchecked.

Reading the literature of 1982 on violence against women reveals two highly distinct, almost mutually exclusive domains (e.g., Newsbriefs . . . 1982; Schechter, 1982). Feminist literature resounds with the difficulties of mere survival. Most important are the external constraints—funding losses, challenges to legal advancements, and the erosion of a political climate conducive to broad social change—that are reflected in internal debates centering on how to respond. Programs face pressures to become more "acceptable": to replace the focus on women with a focus on the family and/or the perpetrators of the violence; to replace collectives with hierarchies; to replace experienced activists with inexperienced professionals; and to replace women of color, lesbians, and former clients with representatives of business and government on their staffs and boards.

Scholarly journals (e.g., Cate et al. 1982; Schumm et al. 1982), in contrast, continue to publish results of basic research, validation studies, causal models, and case studies with virtually no acknowledgement of two critical events. First, their publications and, in many cases, whole careers would not have been possible without the existence of a dedicated feminist movement that raised the issues they study. Second, research results are seldom made accessible to service providers. Activists are rarely allowed, let alone invited, to help determine what needs to be studied, how it should be studied, and by whom. The source of the problem, though, does not lie with researchers. The

230

policy-making process ensures the division of research from services by equating expertise with professional credentials, by valuing research more highly than provision of service, and by funding the efforts separately.

Social scientists have documented the evolution of social poblems to the national agenda and their subsequent withering from attention. One author describes a five-stage process (Downs 1973). It ends not with elimination of the problem, but rather with boredom from media oversaturation and the concomitant realization that eradication would require a powerful group in society relinquishing some of its privilege. This model fits sexual violence all too well.

Currently, sufficient evidence exists that rape, battering, sexual harassment, and sexual abuse of female children is rampant, and is a product of social forces as well as of individual responses to cultural conditions. The next step constitutes a quantum leap: are we willing, as a society, systematically to change these conditions known to produce violence against women? Every direct-service provider faces this dilemma. Victims and perpetrators alike are patched up through shelter or counseling or reeducation and sent right back into the milieu that created them.

There is profound refusal on the part of our society to adopt broad policy initiatives based on what we know. Although the National Institutes of Mental Health (NIMH) have found an important cause-and-effect relationship between television violence and real life aggression, television violence is at an all-time high; within the last few years, it has increased 25 percent (*Response* . . . 1982).

Similarly, we know that sexual abuse of women in prisons is coming to light as a common occurrence. Yet coed prisons are currently being advocated as a way to reduce the discipline problems created by overcrowding and homosexuality among inmates. The sexual abuse of women is more tolerable than homosexuality.

Stress resulting from unemployment and financial difficulties has been identified as a major correlate of family violence. Services are being cut just as these economic conditions worsen. The subject of stress prompts more questions. Recent evidence suggests that women suffer more financial troubles than men—greater unemployment, loss of recent gains made through affirmative action programs, and reduction in training programs and educational aid that allowed women access to higher-paying nontraditional positions. In addition, the single greatest occupation for women, clerical work, has been documented as engendering extremely high stress. Among 130 professions, clerical workers have the second highest stress rate, according to a study by the National Institute of Occupational Safety and Health (Nine-to-Five, personal communication). Lack of respect for the occupation, the strain of balancing work and family obligations (the greater the number of children, the greater the rate of coronary heart disease), and the uncomfortable design of video display terminals were all considered contributing factors. Faced with this evidence—the growing poverty of women and the stressful nature of "women's work"—why aren't women committing violence in record numbers?

Other contradictions of our culture reveal themselves in the experiences of individuals. Michael Morgenstern, author of *How to Make Love to a Woman*, stood trial for allegedly punching his girlfriend. A California state senator, known for his vehement opposition to abortion and his "pro-family" views, was recently charged with child abuse. In Illinois, a former nun who refused an abortion after she became pregnant as the result of a rape was fired from the school where she worked because she was an unwed mother.

These daily life experiences reveal the same messages as are implicit within national policy: individualism and maintenance of male prerogatives take priority over epidemic rates of violence against women.

Sexual violence is socially determined and can therefore be eliminated. A recent interdisciplinary review of the literature (Stark-Adamec and Adamec 1982) on male aggression toward women noted:

. . . there has to be a climate in which aggression is both condoned and reinforced, a climate in which asymmetrical sex roles are adopted and the female devalued, for men to choose aggression as a response to stress and to choose a woman as the target of the aggression.

Every act of sexual violence is a choice—on the part of an individual to commit it, and on the part of society to allow it to continue. The literature and activist efforts of 1982 indicate growing recognition of this element of choice and vastly uneven responses.

Rape

Research on rape seems to be dwindling. The lag time involved between funding, conducting studies, and publishing findings means the scarcity of literature in 1982 is probably not solely attributable to decreases in research funds available in that year. Replacing the scores of reports on incidence, victim or offender characteristics, and counseling techniques that were prevalent from the mid-1970s through 1981 is a new emphasis on rape in relation to embedded societal conditions. Men's attitudes, rape and racism, date rape, and rape in institutions became current focal points of study.

Three publications appearing in 1982 focused on men as rapists (Why don't all men rape? 1982), as significant others to rape victims (Rodkin et al. 1982), and their attitudes toward rape in general (Beneke 1982). Pauline Bart cited an important new study by a male UCLA graduate student (Why don't all men rape? 1982). Men were interviewed who responded to an ad in the *Los Angeles Free Press* asking those to call who had committed rape, but not been caught. Although the study prompts questions regarding methodology, important information was gained. In sum, the rapists were primarily white and middle class; and they felt that raping had few negative effects in their lives and many positive ones.

A recent report dealt with the importance of a support group for the male significant others of women who had experienced rape (Rodkin et al. 1982).

Sufficient experience now exists to formulate a series of developmental phases through which these men pass. Specific attention is given to the impact of their response on the relationship. Setting out "to explore and map a significant portion of the territory that constitutes men's consciousness of rape, and to think hard about the assumptions that supported the consciousness I found" (xiii), Timothy Beneke (1982) interviewed a range of men. Included are men representing different walks of life, men who admit to having committed rape; husbands, lovers, and friends of women who have been raped; and professionals who work with the victims such as lawyers, doctors, and policemen.

Beneke explores "rape signs" ("A rape sign is a way of expressing ideas and feelings about rape without acknowledging them to ourselves" [7]); "rape language" ("the way men talk about sex and women" [11]); and "pornographizing" ("the process by which men relate to women, images of women, the visual presence of women, stories about women, women in any way as PORNEA, which is Greek for 'low whore'" [24]). He shares the feminist analysis of rape that it is "a *man's problem* and one that results directly from the way men regard women in American culture" (169) (original emphasis).

A particularly interesting feature of the book is an interview with Andrea Rechtin, a sexual assault counselor and advocate for a program in Oakland, California. After reading the interviews presented in the book, she summarizes succinctly, "[t]he underlying assumption in these interviews is that if somehow *women* would change their behavior, men might stop raping" (157) (original emphasis). She points out that while many of the interviewees have become sensitized to rape as a problem and may be able to recite the realities rather than the myths, their core belief in women's responsibility for the assault has remained unaltered.

Beneke concludes by suggesting several changes that are prerequisites to confronting rape. His recommendations appeal to global values. "For men who care about women or (finally) themselves, violence against women benefits no one. It mystifies and poisons relations between men and women and vitiates the potential for trust, love, and surrender" (171). Yet his hopes are diametrically opposed to the content of his interviews: men benefit from rape and have no immediate reason to change.

The links between rape and racism are finally being treated with reasoned inquiry instead of simplistic generalizations. Deriving from experience with Third World victims at the Washington, D.C., Rape Crisis Center, one author (Ross 1982) suggests that myths specifically pertaining to women of color compound those that normally surround sexual assault. These myths include:

1. Third World women are more sexually active; or the reverse, more sexually submissive.
2. Rape only exists in the ghetto.
3. Third World women are exceptionally strong under stress and not affected by the rape.
4. Third World people are more accustomed to violence in their daily lives—therefore rape is not a serious offense for Third World women.

5. All Third World women are immoral and deserving of violence.
6. Intraracial crime is irrelevant or not important.
7. Sexual assault is mostly interracial; we don't do it to ourselves. (47)

Using data from 443 cases, one researcher tested two popular sociological explanations of interracial (black offender/white victim) rape (LaFree 1982). The two models were the normative model and conflict theory. The former assumes "legitimate interracial contact" and "attitudinal and behavioral changes in white women as well as black men. . . . In contrast, the conflict model assumes no prior interaction between victims and offenders" (316). "Conflict theorists . . . argue that sexual access, like other scare resources, is determined in large part by power relationships between societal subgroups" (315).

In comparing interracial and intraracial rape from National Crime Panel data, no differences were found between racial groups "with regard to physical injury, medical attention, or victim resistance" (323). These findings led the author to reject both explanatory models. Instead he speculated that interracial rape cases with black offender and white victim are attributable to "a white-dominated sexual stratification system [that] has enshrined the white female as a symbol of sexual attractiveness, freedom, and power" (325).

Date rape, particularly on college campuses, has begun to receive some attention. A survey of 447 female undergraduates over a five-year period found that 65 had been raped and 82 had reported attempted rapes. Just over half of the rape victims experienced more than one attempt. Apparently, a significant number of young women have come to believe that this is a normal part of dating, as many of these self-reported victims continued to date their assailant (Wilson and Durrenberger 1982).

A review article reported another recent survey (Barrett 1982). Dr. Mary Koss interviewed 1,846 male and 2,016 female college students. Over one-half of the women surveyed reported experiencing some form of sexual aggression at some time in their lives; one out of eight had already been raped. Of the men surveyed, 4.3 percent admitted to some use of violence to obtain sex, while an additional 27 percent used lesser degrees of physical and emotional force when women refused sex with them. Koss believes date rapists in her study had "oversubscribed" to male roles (130).

The acceptance of rape as part of daily life was reflected in two additional studies. In comparing samples of women who were raped "only once" versus those sexually assaulted on more than one occasion, "multiple incident subjects" were found to be poorer and more transient than women reporting one incident (Ellis, Atkeson, and Calhoun 1982, 221). A dissertation (Stoks 1982) explored how physical design characteristics affect rape in urban settings. A linear equation was designed to predict precisely where rapes are likely to occur in urban public places; the model was applied five times and predicted four actual sites accurately. If this information is used to aid in the planning and design of cities, it is an important step; however, it seems that the topic itself suggests that rape is inevitable and is perpetrated only by strangers in public places.

Stories of sexual abuse by those in positions of authority and power outside of workplaces came to light recently. Carol Ann Wilds, an inmate in an Indiana prison, is serving time for killing her husband who forced her into prostitution and beat her up in her sixth month of pregnancy, threatening to kill the baby. In 1981 Wilds filed suit against the Indiana Department of Corrections for negligence in allowing women inmates to be sexually coerced by guards, supervisors, and staff. (A similar suit was previously successful against the Wisconsin penal system.) The filing of the suit prompted investigation by a local journalist. Of the twenty-four inmates interviewed, all had witnessed or were aware of cases of sexual abuse; one-third reported experiencing harassment or coercion themselves. Another reporter uncovered several additional cases, including several pregnancies being attributed to prison employees (Jones 1982).

Two final studies round out our knowledge of rape and its consequences. Recidivism rates (measurement of return to criminal activity after serving a prison term) are traditionally used to evaluate rehabilitation efforts; however, clinical study of convicted rapists and child molesters indicates that these may not be dependable (Groth, Longo, and McFadin 1982). The number of "undetected sexual assaults," that is, admitted to by respondents for which they were not apprehended, ranged from 0 to 250.

It would appear from this study that sexual offenders avoid detection approximately twice as often as they are apprehended for their crimes. The rapists, who had an average of three rape convictions on record, and the child molesters, who averaged two convictions on record, admitted to an average of five similar offenses for which they were never apprehended. (456)

These findings are sobering reminders that official statistics bear little resemblance to the actual number of rapes taking place, and that effective rehabilitation remains an unrealized goal.

With so many women being raped, the question of long-term effects on their lives becomes increasingly important. A follow-up study was conducted on women who had sought treatment in a hospital emergency room after being raped (Nadelson et al. 1982). One to two and a half years later, the women, ranging in age from 18 to 60 years, were still facing consequences: 50 percent reported they were fearful of being alone, 75 percent reported still being suspicious of others, and many reported feeling restricted in their daily lives, episodes of depression, and sexual problems. All of these attitudes were attributed by the respondents to the experience of rape.

Marital Rape

For the first time, marital rape in and of itself has been the subject of scholarly attention. Marital rape refers to a husband's use of force or the threat of force to obtain sexual intercourse. As with other forms of sexual violence, research first attempts to document its prevalence.

Although marital rape seems to occur in marriages across demographic and socioeconomic lines, it seems more prevalent in relationships charac-terized by other forms of violence as well. Studies from battered women in shelters have revealed that anywhere from 36 to 59 percent have been raped by battering husbands (Finkelhor and Yllo 1982; Lystad 1982). Some researchers are advocating the adoption of the term forced sex instead of marital rape, partly because women themselves tend to avoid describing their experiences as rape, even when .the behavior fits the legal definition (Finkelhor and Yllo 1982).

A random sample study conducted in Boston found 10 percent of the women who had been married or living as a couple reported experiencing "physical force or threat to try to have sex" (Finkelhor and Yllo 1982, 461). In this study, three major concerns mitigated women's attempts to resist sexual abuse from their partners.

First, many of the women felt that they could not prevent their partner's aggression, no matter how hard they tried. . . . Second, many of the women feared that if they resisted they would be hurt even worse. . . . Third, many of the women believed they were themselves in the wrong. . . . Many saw sex as an obligation. (475)

Diana Russell's *Rape in Marriage* (1982) is a major contribution to the emerging field. Her study is based on a random sample of 930 women residents of San Francisco who were interviewed about all experiences of sexual vio-lence. The volume focuses on a subset of the study:

Eighty-seven women in our sample of 930 women 18 years and older were the victims of at least one completed or attempted rape by their husbands or ex-husbands. This constitutes 14 percent of the 644 women who had ever been married (286 of the 930 women had never been married). This means that *approximately one in every seven women who has ever been married in our San Francisco sample was willing to disclose an experience of sexual assault by their husbands that met our quite conservative definition of rape.* (57) (Original emphasis)

Russell also examines the overlap between wife rape and wife beating. Of the 644 women who had ever been married, 10 percent experienced both forms of violence; 4 percent experienced rape only, and 12 percent experienced beating only (89). By looking at the 175 marriages in which rape and/or battering occurred, she found that 37 percent involved both, 14 percent involved rape only, and 49 percent involved battering (90).

Russell concurs with other feminists who study and work against sexual violence that wife rape "is one of the consequences of the unequal power relationship between husband and wife . . ." (355). Violence and predatory sexuality, two "male problems," are also cited as origins of wife rape (357). By positing a continuum of abuse, she points out the variety of forces that contribute to a "considerable amount of marital sex . . . . [being] closer to the rape end of the continuum" (356):

Many men believe their wives do not have the right to refuse their sexual advances and though many of these men may be unwilling to rape their wives, they are nevertheless willing to have intercourse with them even when they know it is totally unwanted. And we have seen that many women feel obliged to accommodate their husband's sexual wishes no matter how repelled they are by them. (356)

Although she suggests only one solution—making marital rape illegal—Russell recognizes that this would entail important changes on many levels and in many areas of consciousness.

Battering

Research on battering has also progressed from incidence studies and psychological descriptions to attempts to synthesize the literature and apply it in practical settings. Recent publications indicate that the problem is in the public eye; the result is that victims are seeking services and that human service and criminal justice system personnel are replacing their mythology with more realistic appraisals. Stress, financial and unemployment problems, and violence and abuse are the three major problems families face, according to the biannual survey of the Family Service Association. The survey is based on problems brought by 62,610 families to responding agencies between autumn 1979 and summer 1981 (*Response* 1982).

A review of the literature on the predictors of family violence cited over the past ten years was published recently (Schumm et al. 1982). Four factors were identified that relate to the incidence of family violence, including battering and child abuse: "the appearance of a *cycle* of violence"; "the notion that family violence is more common in low socioeconomic status homes"; "family stress accompanying . . . unemployment or part-time employment among men and the resultant financial difficulties"; and "social isolation" (319–20). These four factors were then tested on a nonclinical sample comprised of 181 adolescent family members from intact midwestern rural and urban families. These predictor variables were unable consistently to account for differences among violent, verbally violent, and both verbally and physically violent families. The authors discuss the implications of these findings:

. . . repeated citation of relatively poor initial research in a new area of inquiry leads us to emphasize and overvalue variables that may not explain much about the dependent variable considered. . . . [T]he present research indicates that these broad social indicators have minimal predictive value in distinguishing violent from nonviolent families. For the policymaker, it could mean having to design programs that cover the entire population instead of just a small portion of the people. (334–35)

Another literature review indicates that causal studies of family violence cumulatively point to a combination of factors as responsible for the problem (Lystad 1982). These can be generally grouped under headings relating to an individual's functioning within the social group and within cultural norms.

The question of why women stay in abusive relationships is still the subject of inquiry (Kalmuss and Straus 1982). Based on a sample of 2,143 adult men and women, the authors conclude that economic rather than psychological dependence traps women in violent marriages.

In-depth interviews with adult women who grew up witnessing their mothers being battered formed the basis for a dissertation (Lombardi 1982). Four groups of hypotheses emerged from the data: (1) children are involved in the conjugal conflict in a protective role or otherwise feel placed in the middle; (2) with normal intrafamily support being absent, social supports are too limited and/or unresponsive to the needs of children in violent homes; (3) when the mother is a victim of battering, children are emotionally neglected and at risk themselves of physical and sexual abuse; and (4) children who witness battering suffer low self-esteem, have poor parent-child relationships, and are ill prepared for the establishment of positive adult relationships.

Violence in the intimate relationships of college students was found to be of substantial existence (Cate et al. 1982). Nearly one fourth of the 355 students surveyed reported involvement in violent relationships. Abuse was usually present after the establishment of some degree of commitment, and was felt to be provoked by anger. Quite alarming was the finding that the violence was not always seen by participants as detrimental to the relationship.

Casework formed the basis for distinguishing between an episode of violence and the chronic battering syndrome (Bern 1982). As a batterer progresses from an incident to chronic abuse, the behavior becomes part of his self-definition, supported by "societal norms, sexism, and societal reactions to deviants" (45). Effective intervention becomes increasingly difficult.

Maria Roy has edited a book called *The Abusive Partner* (1982). Sections cover contributing factors to abuse (alcohol and drugs; environmental and nutritional factors; pornography) and several treatment approaches (the collective model, conjoint therapy, and police crisis intervention). A section of particular interest focuses on a trend analysis of 4,000 cases of batterers from New York City and its suburbs. Roy's findings include: most battering husbands are between twenty-six to thirty-five years of age with a substantial number falling between thirty-six and fifty years; most marriages are supported by two incomes; violence occurred immediately or soon after the relationship began in over 70 percent of cases; most abuse is physical, without weapons, but resulting in an array of injuries; over 80 percent of the batterers witnessed or experienced violence in their families of origin while only 33 percent of the battered women reported similar histories; and the three most prominent catalysts for episodes of violence were arguments over money, jealousy and sexual problems (31, 34, 35).

The problems encountered when attempting to apply research results to clinical practice were explored in a recent article (Gelles 1982). Six limitations were discussed:

(1) Most studies are based on caught cases . . . (2) lack of comparison groups . . . (3) lack of generalizability . . . (4) simplistic theoretical models (single variable) . . . (5) the woozle effect (simple empirical results or statements repeated until they are accepted as law without verification) . . . and (6) the perpetuation of myths (into clinical practice) (12–13)

Far too little attention is paid in the academic literature to the specific needs of racial and ethnic minorities. One important exception discusses effective clinical strategies that are respectful of the needs of American Indian families (Red Horse 1982). The Indian Child Welfare Act of 1978 mandates human service professionals to protect Indian children from two risks: personal safety and cultural genocide. The former refers to children from families where alcohol, drugs, and/or violence is present. These conditions lead to Indian children being removed from their kinship systems and relocated in foster homes, which accounts for the second risk. A cultural network model of family therapy is proposed that relies on age-integration. A "developmental day care service" is described that would meet the social and emotional needs of all ages; it would also preserve the "vital features of cultural and structural integration of Indian extended kinship systems" (17). The model avoids the inadequate outreach and follow-up that characterize traditional child welfare programs. In addition, "four principles of clinical service that represent a foundation for successful therapy with Indian families" are identified: developing spiritual leadership; becoming immersed with the family and community as a whole; the examination and articulation of family behaviors usually taken for granted; and reconstituting the extended family system (18–19).

Two publications by the U.S. Commission on Civil Rights explored various aspects of domestic violence. One reviews statutes and the response of various actors in the criminal justice system to cases of battering (Gerebenics 1982). Not surprisingly, much of the report documents failures—of police to enforce new laws, of prosecutors to regard intrafamily violence with the same seriousness as they regard stranger violence, and of judges to consider women's safety to be as important as preserving marriage, when making sentencing recommendations. Specific findings and recommendations include the inappropriateness of pretrial diversion programs and mediation-arbitration techniques for resolving cases of battering. Both are felt to convey to abusers and victims alike the message that the criminal justice system does not consider family violence to be serious. On the contrary, shelters are seen as providing "vital and essential support services for battered women" (96). As discussed in this chapter's introduction, these findings are being disregarded by both policymakers and funders.

Federal initiatives are examined in the Commission's second report (*Federal Response* 1982). Unfortunately, this report was largely obsolete by the time of its publication. Specifically reviewed are programs funded by the Law Enforcement Assistance Administration (LEAA), Comprehensive Employment and Training Act (CETA), and the Community Services Administration (CSA), all of which are now defunct. The Federal Office of Domestic Violence is also closed. Two funding avenues also described, Housing and Urban Development (HUD) and Title XX, have been the targets of significant budget cuts (U.S. Commission on Civil Rights, 1982).

Research on premenstrual syndrome (PMS) will have an impact on the handling of battering cases in which women fight back. The evolving theory is that women can be driven to violence through hormonal changes (Brozan

1982). Feminists will undoubtedly express much concern over the reemergence of biological determinism in any form. If PMS is used as a defense for battered women who kill their batterers, it will change the act from one of rational self-defense to one of irrationality.

Lystad's review of the literature cited above also includes a lengthy section on prevention of family violence based on a system of psychological, social, and cultural supports. Her recommendations are presented in some detail as they indicate both the state of our current knowledge about contributors to battering and child abuse, and the magnitude of change required to eradicate the problems.

Special help to families with mentally ill and substance-abusing members; educational programs for teenagers and young adults, dealing with family functioning and child care; interpersonal networks for nuclear families; parent education in the use of nonviolent techniques for raising children and especially in the positive reinforcement of the child's strengths and capabilities; education of educators in the rights and responsibilities of children in social and physical interactions in the classroom and the playground; liberation of women and men to perform and enjoy family tasks as they choose; increased opportunities for men and for those women who want to work; sensitization of parents (mothers, fathers, step-parents) to the need of female as well as male children for positive self-images of themselves, including respect for the personal space of others and the ability to say *no* to intrusions; and reduction in the frequency and intensity of violence displayed in the mass media. (24)

Child Sexual Assault and Incest

Researchers and clinicians have long studied child sexual assault and incest. Recent literature reflects growing recognition of feminist insights; specifically, the academic community now considers variables of power and sex roles in their commentaries.

Links were explored between experiences of sexual abuse as children and adult life situations. Whereas 20 percent of the population of convicted drug offenders at one institution reported sexual abuse as children, 57 percent of a population of convicted sex offenders reported experiencing sexual assault (Lystad 1982). Forensic Mental Health Associates in Washington, D.C. revealed that 70 percent of children who run away, 75 percent of prostitutes, and 55 percent of all juvenile offenders have been sexually assaulted as children (*Response* 1982). Multipersonality disorders (MPD) have been linked to childhood sexual abuse as well; the degrees of dissociation range from daydreaming to flipping back and forth among a number of personalities. A review of 100 years of the literature on MPD indicated that 60 percent of its sufferers were identified as sexually abused children (*Response* . . . 1982).

Voices in the Night (McNarron and Morgan 1982) is an eloquent if painful collection of women's writings on their experiences of incest. The editors, both incest survivors, point out that a collection that breaks the silence surrounding incest is a profound step; many victims were met with "eyes averted, voices unheard" as they attempted to end their isolation (11). Various forms are used to communicate the memories and impact of those memories on survivors' lives—journal entries, poetry, short stories, and letters. More than forty entries weave a portrait of the range of incest perpetrators, age at onset, family size, and environment. *Voices in the Night* represents the best form of consciousness raising; there is bound to be a piece in the book that connects to one's own past. Above all it reminds us what statistics merely mask: incest is not just a social problem, it is the lives of real women and girls that are marked by fear, pain, and scars.

The majority of new material on incest and child sexual assault presents counseling approaches. Group therapy techniques with sexually abused adolescents are reviewed, with emphasis on eliciting the themes of violation, loss, anger, and hope for the future (Lubell and Soong 1982). Group art therapy and expected stages of growth for young incest victims is also explored (Carozza and Heirsteiner 1982).

Work with adult women who were victims of childhood or adolescent incest reveals significant information on both the experience and its consequences. Long-term effects fall into eight categories: social, psychological, physical, sexual, family relations, self-esteem, relations with men, and relations with women (Courtois and Watts 1982, 277). The presenting problem bringing a woman into therapy may correspond to any of these. Counselors' attitudes and assumptions are critical to gaining trust: "[m]any clients are caught in significant conflict and trust no one because no one was trustworthy in their families" (277). The authors go on to recommend several useful techniques: writing letters to family members, structured interviews, guided imagery, and group therapy (using psychodrama, self-help, or structured around open-ended statements).

The *Handbook of Clinical Intervention in Child Sexual Abuse* (Sgroi 1982) compiles information on patterns, investigating cases, treatment modalities, perpetrators, the role of law enforcement, and implementing intervention programs. Aimed at professionals who encounter child sexual abuse, it is based on methods and cases of the Connecticut Sexual Trauma Treatment Program between 1977 and 1979.

Sgroi's position is that aiding victims is only accomplished through involving the entire family in treatment. While this may be shared as an eventual goal, its feasibility is questionable. A five-phase pattern in child sexual abuse is identified: engagement, sexual interaction, secrecy, disclosure, and suppression.

The authors mention that child sexual assault is motivated by the adult's need to feel powerful or in control, abuse is planned, and the adult's age, authority, and power allow him to coerce the child into sexual compliance.

Despite growing documentation of the exploitative character of child sexual assault, a "pro-incest lobby" still exists. Their three major assertions are: (1) incest is so prevalent that a taboo is meaningless; (2) guilt and social intervention do more harm than the act; and (3) the act is less destructive than seductive behavior by parents. Nicholas Groth has offered an effective counter to those who defend the "right" of children to have sex with adults: "No child is damaged by being denied the privilege of sex with an adult" (Dunwoody 1982, 13).

The leader of a therapy group for incest perpetrators has written with insight an article focusing on normal male characteristics that produce and excuse incest (Snowdon 1982). His initial shock at the "ordinary men" in his group led to taking a critical look at male socialization. Yet this ordinariness was transformed by offenders into an excuse for their behavior. Denial and turning themselves into victims of "a provocative child or a bad mother" are common tactics:

. . . Through the stories they tell, they construct their fearful version of family—*Lolita*, *The Wicked Witch*, and *Santa Claus*. . . . *Lolita* is the first of their three deceptions. . . . Not only do they cast girls as sex objects, but also as aggressors, as "demon nymphettes." . . . The second deception offenders use is *The Wicked Witch*. . . . "My wife made me do it, it was her fault" is the spoken or unspoken message. . . . The third deception offenders use is *Santa Claus*, whom each of them pretends to be, the man who is known for giving children presents, for giving them "what they like and what they ask for." (58, 60, 61, 62)

Snowdon believes that it is men who are responsible and should be held responsible for incest. He concludes, "[w]e have the power to stop being "ordinary guys" and become something much better—men with whom children and women can be safe" (63).

Prevention as currently applied to child abuse and neglect in general derives from the classic public health model. This model's limitations were discussed in a recent article (Giovanni 1982). Prevention in the public health conception includes the identification of stages (i.e., primary, secondary, and tertiary), clarity about the condition itself, and the search for a single cause. The author points out the poor fit of these criteria to the dynamic and complex phenomenon of child abuse. Intriguing ethical questions are posed concerning what should be the goals and therefore the criteria for evaluation of service and prevention programs. For example, "Should the success of a program to prevent child abuse be measured only by a reduction in abuse—not in other social ills that may affect families?" (30). Such questions challenge researchers and policy makers to scrutinize their assumptions and to ask themselves, "Am I inadvertently advocating that certain levels of child sexual assault are acceptable?" If the data cited in this section are accurate, child sexual assault and incest are linked not only to other social ills, but to the structure of the family and the exercise of power within it.

Sexual Harassment

A wealth of new material on sexual harassment found its way into the professional literature in 1982. The general focus was recognizing the existence of sexual harassment in both educational institutions and a variety of work settings. In addition, the responsibility of management to clean up the problem and guides for intervention were discussed.

Sexual harassment was documented among many groups: nurses (Duldt 1982), autoworkers (Gruber and Bjorn 1982), construction workers (Housing . . . 1982), and patients victimized by doctors (Carlova 1982).

Two small surveys of workplaces were also reported. Of 439 college alumnae (graduating between 1945 and 1980) polled, the authors report that "less than 40 percent" had experienced sexual harassment (Hopkins and Johnson 1982). If sexual harassment affected men, it is doubtful that the finding would be similarly trivialized; for example, unemployment figures are not reported as "only 12 percent of the labor force is out of work." A survey of women autoworkers concluded what feminists have speculated since the mid-1970s: black women and those with low job status are disproportionately the targets of coercion (Gruber and Bjorn 1982).

Confusion over what actually constitutes sexual harassment and the place of sexuality in the work environment still abounds. A recent book, *Sex in the Office*, subtitled "Power and Passion in the Workplace" (Horn and Horn 1982), is one illustration. The authors point out that the increased numbers of women in the labor force and the growing importance of work in many individuals' personal lives have resulted in work environments becoming the sites for meeting mates. Their recommendation is that management intervene only in cases of sexual harassment, yet they gloss over the consequences of mutual relationships that do not continue. Office romances, they feel, contribute energy and excitement that are potentially good for the couple, their co-workers, and the company. Such optimism ignores the complexity of sexual harassment and the reality that women usually suffer deteriorating working conditions, transfers, and even firings when workplace affairs terminate. Effects on co-workers are also inaccurately portrayed. Although ambiguous in terms of legal standing, it is known that participants in sexual relations at work may receive benefits that should have been given to nonparticipants (Baxter 1982). For example, women in voluntary or coercive sexual relationships with their supervisors may be promoted over better qualified candidates, or may be allowed business travel when their coworkers are not.

A *Wall Street Journal* poll attempted to grapple with the continuum of sexual relations at work (Feinberg and Levenstein 1982). On the basis of 112 respondents, four categories emerged: sexual harassment, legitimate courtship, sexual relations between two unmarried people, and illicit affairs. The majority of respondents (fifty-seven) said yes when asked, "Do you believe in a policy of absolute hands-off in cases of simple romance?" As the third and fourth categories were inquired about, the majority shifted to advocating management intervention. Favoritism, "scandal mongering," and lowered morale of other employees were cited as some of the adverse effects of seemingly mutual sexual liaisons.

Male and female perspectives on sexual harassment continue to be divergent. A random sample of 172 members of the Administrative Management Society indicated that while only 9 percent of the men knew of sexual harassment incidents within their organizations, 39 percent of the women knew of cases (McKendrick 1982).

Most recent literature concerned itself with the steps management should take to minimize its liability in cases of sexual harassment. Articles recommended one or more of the following: adoption of policies prohibiting sexual harassment; development of grievance procedures and investigative mechanisms; clear sanctions imposed on offenders; training programs for employees, managers, and complaint handlers; the development of good two-way communication channels; and in-house counseling for sexual harassment victims (Kirkpatrick and Nason 1982; Faley 1982; Petersen and Massengill 1982; Stevens 1982a; Sexual harassment . . . 1982; Dreyfack 1982; Waks and Starr 1982a).

Some authors (Waks and Starr 1982b) are quite clear that the problem with sexual harassment is monetary cost rather than the abuse and discrimination itself:

Employers would be wise to take action regarding this very widespread problem, to avoid such direct costs as paying: (1) back wages and attorney fees in the event of losing a suit, and (2) large verdicts in the event a state court tort action is available to the victim. There are also indirect costs, such as lowered morale and increased absenteeism. (357)

For all those managers worried only about their profits, new assistance has arrived. Sexual harassment defense insurance plans, underwritten by Lloyd's of London, are available to United States businesses and universities. Coverage is for 90 percent of legal defense costs up to $100,000 per claim or $300,000 per year. Damages, however, are not covered (Insurance pays . . . 1982; Gilpin 1982).

Two articles took up the subject of slander, libel, and defamation of character in sexual harassment cases. While one focused only on avenues of complaint for the accused (Stevens 1982b), the other raised the possibility of legal grounds for the victim (Kandel 1982). Kandel went on to point out, "The internal communications necessary to investigate the incident may contain the roots of claims for libel or slander" (309).

Speculation about future trends in sexual harassment litigation revealed two directions: increasing complaints based on the work environment being hostile, intimidating, and/or discriminatory (Faley 1982) and the use of arbitration (Wolkinson and Liberson 1982).

Despite this flood of concern about management liability, a survey of corporate Equal Employment Opportunity and Affirmative Action officers revealed that sexual harassment has low priority. Rather, their concerns are primarily with the impact of Reagan administration policies (Macleod 1982).

Only one piece explored the effects on the lives of the women experiencing sexual harassment (Crull 1982). Based on case analysis of 262 women who sought assistance from the Working Women's Institute in New York, the article reveals the enormous impact of harassment. Ranging in age from sixteen to sixty-five years, these women were subjected to verbal and physical force. One-third quit their jobs, and of those who resisted advances, over two-thirds suffered retaliation. Lowered self-confidence and productivity, and an array of physical and emotional symptoms of stress were reported by the women.

Sexual harassment on campuses received specific attention during 1982, with surveys conducted at a number of institutions. More than 40 percent of the 467 women surveyed at the University of Washington suffered sexual harassment from male students and professors; 5 percent were subjected to rape or attempted rape (*hersay* 1982). The newsletter of the Project on the Status and Education of Women reports that there has been an increase in rape and sexual violence on United States campuses (*On Campus with Women* 1982).

In Phyllis Crocker's (1982) introduction to her excellent "Annotated bibliography on sexual harassment in education," she reminds us why the issue is important:

. . . [f]or a woman, the injury of sexual harassment occurs when she is confronted by an educator whose concern is not with her intellectual growth but with the satisfaction of his own sexual needs and desire for power. . . . It affects all women who must try to study and grow in institutions of higher education that fail to provide women with an environment in which academic progress is based on intellectual achievement and not on gender. (91)

Her collection includes books, pamphlets, articles, reports, and cases from writers with diverse perspectives. This well organized bibliography will aid women to understand their rights and to network with others who have taken steps to change their campus climate.

Campus administrators, like workplace managers, began to generate a list of steps institutions can take to minimize liability and/or prevent sexual harassment. The particular difficulties of locating and stopping the offense in higher education were discussed; included are issues of academic freedom and the sensitivity of the student-mentor relationship (Betts and Newman 1982). Implementing policies, procedures, sanctions, and training in the school setting were addressed by some authors (Deane and Tillar 1982; Joyce 1982). One article went beyond the basics and recommended the establishment of an office with a professional staff member "to monitor and investigate all grievances"; employing a counselor for victim assistance; and "[o]ffer workshops for campus personnel, including students and the community, to create an atmosphere of consciousness about sexual harassment" (Betts and Newman 1982, 51).

"The politics of sexual harassment," written by women involved in the sexual harassment case at Clark University, points out that low awareness compounds the problem (Fairness Committee 1982). The uneasiness of women with the case reflects the depth of all women's internalization of social and sexual stereotypes. Due to the harasser's long standing as an activist on progressive issues, the implicit hierarchy of the issue's importance came to the fore—is sexual harassment as politically reprehensible as nuclear proliferation? His maleness meant even feminists could ask him directly if he was guilty; his "no" seemed sufficient, and the women bringing the charges were not spoken with.

Pornography and Violence Against Women in the Media

Despite the studies published in 1980 and 1981 that "consistently found that exposure to sexually violent media increases men's aggression and hostility to women, and increases their acceptance of violence against women" (Klein 1982, 283), no new research results appeared. Instead, general commentaries on violence in the media (Experts warn . . . 1982; Fifteen-year study . . . 1982), the growth of pornography (Beale 1982), and debate over whether censorship or boycott is an appropriate strategy to cope with pornography (Meehan 1982) were the subjects of articles.

One recent analysis of existing research deserves note, however. After reviewing data collected since 1970 on the relationship between pornography and men's attitudes and behaviors toward women, Susan Gray (1982) concludes that "anger is a greater social problem than pornography, particularly in men who are unable to resolve that anger and to distinguish it from sexual arousal and control over women" (387). What she never squarely faces, though, is that anger toward women is endemic in our culture. Although Gray recognizes that pornography can and does evoke the male anger underlying violence against women, her position is that the anger is not eradicable. Instead, she suggests that pornography is allowed to remain unchallenged and that we develop "cultural mechanisms to encourage socially acceptable forms of resolving this anger or directing it more appropriately . . ." (395). A very basic point is missing: until the recent wave of feminism exposed, analyzed, and critiqued violence against women in its myriad forms, including pornography, it *was* socially acceptable. Feminism's challenge remains transforming the prevailing view of violence against women from inevitable to eradicable.

Activism

The feminist antiviolence movement itself was the focus of several important pieces of work in 1982. Although all of the authors were concerned with the battered women's movement, their impressions are generalizable to other efforts.

By applying theories on the evolution of social movements to the recent groundswell of attention to the problem of battered women, an interesting article predicts what is already taking place (Tierney 1982). Namely, the general abatement of interest in the issue and the changing nature of the movement itself. Specifically foreseen are two developments:

(1) The trend toward conventional, social service-oriented programs that is already evident will continue, and the emphasis on feminist concerns will decline. . . . (2) Outside support should change the character of the battered women's movement itself. . . . Conventional, social service-oriented organizations staffed by professionals, with relatively limited goals, will ultimately come to speak for the movement. (216)

A major accomplishment is the publication of *Women and Male Violence* (1982). Susan Schechter has painstakingly documented the emergence and evolution of the battered women's movement in the United States. For all of those who believed the incidence of battering suddenly increased or professionals discovered the problem, the record is set straight. Extensive interviews with activists and excerpts from the literature, correspondence, and files of early shelters provide the basis for her portrait. In the first half of the volume the movement's roots, early projects, and coalitions are described. Its uneasy relationship with the criminal justice system and government funding are also discussed. Featured in the second half are an analysis of violence against women, the dual focus of services and politics, and suggestions for an organizing agenda for the coming years.

Schechter is particularly adept at portraying the complexity, richness, and on-going contradictions of launching a feminist movement aimed at eliminating violence against women in a society whose fabric promotes that violence. The current debate over services versus politics was a dilemma from day one. In the words of an activist involved with Women's Advocates, one of the first of this country's shelters:

We were driven away from the main issue, which is: How are we going to stop violence against women? . . . Are we going to change the situation? Or are we just going to build a social service to meet the needs of abused women only to a point. (111)

The success of the battered women's movement in bringing the problem to public attention contained the elements of its co-optation: funding became available, but only with strings that curtailed the definition and therefore possible solutions to battering.

So, while services allowed feminists to mobilize for themselves and other battered women, they also made activists juggle increasingly complicated and sometimes contradictory demands and constituencies. (243)

Organizing in the 1980s, according to Schechter, will require clarity about external constraints and building internal movement strength. She foresees organizing to protect services, forming progressive alliances, and encouraging a resurgence of community outreach and education as the major tasks. In the face of external pressures and internal divisions, *Women and Male Violence* also reminds us of the movement's incredible accomplishments: "The battered women's movement has given women back their lives and dignity" (311). "Most significantly, the battered women's movement has created a vision of a better life for women and an alternative to enduring degrading brutality" (320).

The theme of analyzing problems from inside and outside the movement was echoed in a piece by Gail Sullivan (1982). Outside problems include the criminal justice system; funding agencies; social service agencies; the influence of the above agencies on organizational structure and development; homophobia; and the Right Wing. Internal problems cited are lack of clear political direction; more and more services; services rather than empowerment; services instead of organizing; pursuit of careers through the movement; and the conservative influence of fundraising (Sullivan 1982).

An interview with Mary Morrison, executive director of the National Coalition Against Domestic Violence, offered specific illustrations of these pressures (Lootens 1982). Morrison's cataloguing of problems included shelters facing pressures to become more like social service agencies; the dilemma of serving more women and children or offering more comprehensive services; traditional agencies not being held accountable for their negligence in handling cases; lesbian-baiting of shelters; and confidentiality of records and casework only covering professionals. Positive responses to changing conditions were also chronicled. For example, thanks to funding cutbacks, safe-home networks are being replaced by shelters rather than being totally dissolved; independent economic bases are being developed to support shelters (e.g., the Ford Foundation grant supporting five demonstration programs especially for rural women and women of color); and coalition work has grown at an encouraging rate.

The conference of the National Coalition Against Domestic Violence held in Milwaukee last August included discussion papers on several important topics. Intended to promote dialogue, they were: Obstacles to Unity, Shelters for Empowerment, An Examination of The Role of the Battered Woman in the Movement, Rural Women: Defining Our Own Standard, three perspectives on class issues, Women Of Color in the Battered Women's Movement: Organizing for Power, Issues Relating to American Indian Women, Breaking the Racism Cycle, Lesbians in the Battered Women's Movement, Violence in Lesbian Relationships, Working with Men Who Batter, Programming for Children, and The Co-optive and Repressive State Versus the Battered Women's Movement.

Taken together, these papers reflect two aspects of the movement. First, they are topics that evoke the most controversy within shelters and the movement as a whole. Second, they represent the attempt of shelter activists to define their own long-term political goals while working amid the daily crises that comprise their service work and those crises that stem from a shortage of resources to perform their tasks. It is precisely this context—the tension between survival and short-term victories on the one hand versus self-definition and long-term social change goals on the other—that is critical to an understanding of the advances and setbacks of activism on all forms of violence against women.

Legal Arena

Activists' efforts in the legal arena continue to be marked by creativity and persistence. A review of legal periodicals indicates that movement-inspired reforms have evoked a flood of debate. Specific cases are reported, as are general themes: self-defense criteria in rape cases (Kates and Engberg 1982), comparing Canadian and United States rape laws (Backhouse and Schoenroth

1982), the battered wife syndrome as expert testimony (Thar 1982), and liability for teacher-student sexual harassment (Winks 1982).

Unevenness at best, however, is the most accurate descriptor for the criminal justice system's handling of cases of violence against women in 1982. In Florida, a twenty-four-year-old man convicted of raping and beating a twenty-one-year-old woman spent 120 days in jail; the judge feared that he would "stand the chance of violent sexual abuse" if sent to prison (News from all over 1982b). A former college professor who bludgeoned his wife to death has been sentenced to tutor prisoners in *psychology* for twenty-two months instead of serving prison time (*New Directions for Women* 1982). Wisconsin Judge William Reinecke felt a five-year-old sexual assault victim was "the aggressor in this incident" (of sexual assault by her mother's boyfriend, whom the judge described as one who "didn't know enough to refuse"). He went on to blame the victim and excuse the perpetrator by identifying her as "an unusually sexually promiscuous young lady" (News from all over 1982a).

With regard to rape law, Pennsylvania became the first state to enact legislation protecting the confidentiality of the counselor-victim relationship. Senate bill 532 makes it "illegal for a rape crisis counselor to release information or to be subpoenaed to testify to anything that has been said in a counseling session" (Russ 1982, 8). The new law stems from a case in 1980 when Pittsburgh Action Against Rape's director, Anne Pride, refused to release a client's file to a judge; she was found to be in contempt of court. Pennsylvania's supreme court agreed to review the matter shortly before Pride was to report to jail. Although the incident ends favorably with the new legislation, the two years of struggle took its toll:

The number of anonymous phone calls to PAAR's hotline shot up sharply, from 32 percent in August '79 to 61 percent after the confidentiality issue became known. Some women discontinued badly needed counseling for fear their records would not be kept private. (8)

Two setbacks in rape rulings are noteworthy. A Washington state appeals court ruled that a woman was not really raped when she submitted to sex with a man who she thought was carrying a pistol because the object turned out to be a toy (*hersay* 1982). In Massachusetts, one of three doctors convicted in 1981 of raping a nurse was released after serving six months, exactly half the time it took for the case to come to trial.

Specific incidents of campus rapes appeared frequently in the popular literature in 1982. For example, a group rape resulted in a fraternity being shut down at Duke University. The fraternity's response was to sue the University for $320,000 in damages. A fraternity at Columbia University did not need to sue. They only received a public warning after an investigation of an incident in which a first-year Barnard student was subjected to verbal and sexual abuse while trapped in a closet for more than two hours.

Marital rape law changes both by statute and by court rulings. In 1982 Wisconsin became the eleventh state that considers rape by a husband or cohabitor illegal (National Center 1982a). In the District of Columbia a statute against sexual assault, including marital rape, passed unanimously. Disapproval of the Moral Majority and some members of Congress led to the law's overturn by Congress, however. Senator Denton of Alabama commented about the marital rape provision of the new federal criminal code, "Damn it, when you get married you kind of expect you're going to get a little sex" (News from all over 1982b).

Legal activity on the issue of battering fell into three categories: funding through legislation, other new legislation or litigation, and challenges to existing legal practices.

To date, at least seventeen states have some form of legislation imposing a tax on marriage licenses, divorce proceedings, or both. In 1982, Kentucky, Mississippi, and Oregon passed their laws, and California increased its fee (National Coalition 1982). The challenge to the fee brought in 1981 by a wedding chapel in Nevada (on grounds that it would hurt their business) was dismissed in 1982 for lack of standing (National Center 1982b). A challenge to the tax in Illinois, however, was supported. The Cook County circuit court judge ruled that the method of collecting the funds is illegal (Taylor 1982). A bill in Colorado to fund domestic violence programs through a check-off on tax returns, although defeated, represents a new direction for program funding. A five-year-old struggle to fund such programs and rape crisis centers was successful in June in Pennsylvania. Approximately $1.5 million will be available in fiscal year 1982–1983 from an additional ten dollars imposed by the court on all convictions and pleas of guilty or nolo contendere; the fee applies to all crimes with the exception of motor vehicle violations (National Coalition 1982).

New legislation and litigation continue to proliferate. Connecticut took steps to remove the family exclusion clause that currently prevents battered women from receiving compensation through the Victim Compensation Board; women who are not cohabiting by mutual consent now qualify for reimbursements. Although activists deem it a farce in practice, Connecticut police and hospital emergency rooms are now mandated to report suspected cases of battering to the Department of Human Resources. Iowa's unmarried women are now covered by the same protective orders and injunctions available to married women in cases of battering (National Coalition 1982). The Missouri state supreme court handed down a strong decision upholding protection of battered women. Judges are now required to enforce the domestic violence law that permits ordering an abuser to leave home and allows for the arrest of violators (National Center 1982b). A superior court judge in California ruled that battered women may bring a class action against the Los Angeles police for frequent refusals to arrest battering husbands. The complaint requests a police training program and shelters (*off our backs* 1982).

Challenges to battered women's legislation or trial practices, although largely unsuccessful, continue to be filed. Two conflicting decisions on the subject of the admissibility of expert testimony on the battered woman syndrome in self-defense murder cases were handed down in 1982. The Ohio supreme court in *State* v. *Thomas* restricted the admissibility of such testimony on the grounds that it is prejudicial and not currently accepted as scientific knowledge. In *Hawthorne* v. *State*, the first district court of appeals in Florida felt quite differently. The court held that the testimony on the psychological ramifications of domestic violence might aid a jury in evaluating a specific case. Information on why a woman might remain in an abusive relationship could help the jury, according to the decision, distinguish murder from self-defense (National Center 1982b).

Sexual harassment related legal events reflected the same growing recognition of the problem found in the management literature. The case at Clark University involving women faculty, staff and students' complaints against the male chair of the sociology department, settled out of court for $95,000. It is interesting to note that the University's press release neglects to mention the settlement, merely stating that an agreement had been reached between Professors Bunster, Stanko, and Peck. Peck's statement, not quite an admission of guilt, does, however, acknowledge that conduct in which he engaged "was perceived and/or experienced by Ximena Bunster and Elizabeth Stanko as sexually harassing or retaliatory behavior" (*Equal Times* 1982, 7). Peck returned to Clark in September as a professor, but no longer as the sociology department's chair. Bunster was forced to look elsewhere for work and Stanko is on sabbatical. The settlement also included the establishment of a full-time post for a grievance counselor, despite the University's claim that its existing procedure was adequate.

Two United States Supreme Court Title IX decisions (the federal law prohibiting discrimination of any form in federally funded educational institutions) will affect the outcome of future campus sexual harassment charges. While employees were held to be covered by Title IX in one decision (Riprap 1982), a later decision limits the power of the Department of Education to act only when a discriminatory program is supported directly by federal funds (*hersay* 1982). Previously, the agency had the discretion to withhold all federal funds from an institution found to engage in discriminatory practices.

The California supreme court ruled that a victim of job discrimination has the right to sue for punitive and compensatory damages (*hersay* 1982). In all other states without a similar provision, and under federal employment discrimination law (Title VII), punitive damages are not recoverable.

A recent New Hampshire supreme court decision (*Monge* v. *Beebe Rubber Co.*) indicated a conflict between the power of an employer to terminate employees "at will" and the Equal Employment Opportunity Commission guidelines on sexual harassment. The court ruled that firing a woman for failure to submit to a foreman's sexual advances mitigated the employer's power, and constituted a breach of the implicit employment contract (Kandel 1982).

Defamation suits filed by charged harassers against complainants have prevented some women from taking legal action; however, a recent suit (*Barnes* v. *Oody*) by two men failed. Two women had claimed sexual harassment; their employer (the federal government) had investigated and suspended the two men for thirty days; because the procedure was deemed fair, it was decided that defamation had not occurred (*Aegis* 1982).

Several cases of sexual harassment came to light last year. Eight women miners are suing the Consolidation Coal Company in federal court for $5.5 million in damages resulting from invasion of privacy. A peephole in their bathhouse was apparently used for spying by men in the office. It is alleged that the company knew about the practice for years but took no action (*New Directions for Women* 1982). A United States Manpower Development specialist pleaded guilty to threatening to cut off CETA funds from the Fond Du Lac Indian Reservation unless its female director slept with him. The case was resolved with a $500 fine (*hersay* 1982). "Unorthodox recruitment techniques" were the charges leveled against an inspector general of the Agriculture Department; he apparently exchanged information about job openings for sexual favors (*hersay* 1983). A military court exonerated a woman sailor who was absent without leave after she was threatened with an initiation rite that involved the injection of grease, oil, and coffee grounds into intimate body areas (*hersay* 1982). Finally, $250,000 in legal settlement was awarded two New York women who were forced to have sex with their licensed PhD psychologists (*New Directions for Women* 1982).

An emerging issue in child sexual assault cases is the development of trial techniques that recognize the intimidation and questions concerning the credibility of child witnesses. A landmark law that allows for the admission of hearsay in some cases was passed in the state of Washington. Specifically, statements made by the child victim to another person are admissible. The law also extends the statute of limitations from three to five years (*Aegis* 1982). Videotaped testimony is now admissible in Wisconsin's civil courts, provided all parties agree (Sexual abuse . . . 1982). The United States Supreme Court ruled unconstitutional the Massachusetts statute requiring judges to exclude the general public from courtrooms during testimony of minors in sexual assault cases (*Aegis* 1982). Brought by the press as a First Amendment issue, the decision is a setback for those interested in creating conditions that encourage the prosecution of child sexual assault.

In another decision affecting children, the United States Supreme Court upheld a New York criminal statute that prohibits the production or distribution of pictures showing children under age sixteen engaging in sex or lewd conduct (*Aegis* 1982). Although the decision may help reduce the amount of "kiddie porn" on the market, its ambiguity could lead to restriction of valuable sex education materials.

Services

The dismantling of all human services was a popular theme of feminist and mainstream media. Direct services to victims were cut in many locations, as were services that provide training and employment opportunities for women that might enable them to leave violent relationships (National Coalition 1982;

Churchman 1982). The *New York Times* reported that one-quarter of the nation's rape crisis centers have closed under Reagan.

Violence-against-women services are attempting a variety of mechanisms to stay afloat. In addition to funding through legislation described above, several other creative approaches are noteworthy. The high costs of maintaining shelters have given way to safe-home networks in many communities; battered women and their children are housed for a shorter time in private residences. Some programs have launched businesses to support their work. The Women of Color Task Force of the National Coalition Against Domestic Violence initiated a self-sufficiency employment training and small business project to assist battered women and shelters. Five programs from four states were selected as demonstration models, to be funded for two years by the Ford Foundation. The small businesses are a wholesale nursery specializing in houseplants (Hilo, Hawaii); a computer service (Bemidji, Minnesota); and a second-hand store (Ansonia, Connecticut). The employment programs are apprenticeship provision (Marshall, Minnesota) and job readiness skills (Louisville, Kentucky) (National Coalition 1982). Women from shelters in Boston formed the Greater Boston Housing Task Force for Women in Crisis; their goal is to form a corporation for housing and economic development.

Efforts to be multiracial in staff composition and client population continue to be a critical part of services. Committees for women of color are found within many state and regional coalitions. Recognizing and changing subtle and blatant racism on the part of white members has finally emerged as a frequent subject at conferences and in the literature of the violence-against-women movement (Landerman and McAtee 1982).

Conferences are a vehicle for services to exchange fundraising ideas, service delivery approaches, and strategize about continuing to raise consciousness on the incidence and dynamics of sexual violence. Literally hundreds of workshops and conferences were held in 1982. The National Coalition Against Sexual Assault and the National Coalition Against Domestic Violence each held summer conferences running several days. State coalitions of rape crisis centers and/or battered women's shelters continued to be formed. Montana held a conference on incest, bringing together human service and criminal justice personnel with feminists from around the state. Materials produced for the conference and emerging from it formed the basis of the Montana Incest Prevention Coalition.

Services seem to have expanded in 1982 in three areas: (1) programs for men who batter; (2) family violence programs on military bases; and (3) support groups for incest survivors. In addition, the Employee Assistance Program of the Association for Flight Attendants now offers services for battered women. Ninety percent of the Association's 23,000 members are women. The program is being funded as a three year demonstration project by the National Institute of Alcohol Abuse and Alcoholism (*Response* 1982).

One service, Santa Cruz Women Against Rape, lost all of its funding ($19,400) from the California Office of Criminal Justice Planning. Women

Against Rape's original grant proposal had included a statement that they would participate in data collection if it did not interfere with their contracts with clients. Evaluation forms arrived only after funding had been granted, and included requirements to categorize callers by race, age, type of crime, and number of incidents. After two consecutive months of reporting all of their crimes as rape (instead of differentiating among statutory rape, attempted rape, etc.) and all ages and races as unknown, their funding was removed (*Aegis* 1982).

Resistance

Resistance to violence against women takes many forms. Individuals learn and practice self-defense. Support is mobilized for women who kill or confront their assailants and then themselves confront criminal charges. Group activities continue to focus on two goals: increasing awareness of the forms of violence against women and ending practices that promote sexual violence.

A Tacoma, Washington woman was initially charged with first-degree manslaughter after she allegedly shot and killed the man she says previously raped her and who was returning to attack her again. Public outcry resulted in charges being dropped (*hersay* 1982; Self-defense . . . 1982). The Chicago Take Back the Night group began picketing Chicago Bulls' games after a basketball player pleaded guilty to aggravated assault against a nursing student. Original charges had included rape, attempted rape, and false imprisonment (Assailant . . . 1982).

New technology has brought new sexual violence. Several pornographic video games are now on the market. One that has gained some attention is "Custer's Revenge," which features General Custer raping a Native American woman. The sexist and racist nature of the game has prompted concerted protest. Although the manufacturer of the game, American Multiple Industries, claims it is really not rape, Atari has filed suit to stop its distribution and sale (*hersay* 1982). A Seattle video game store canceled an order totaling several thousand dollars after local protests (*hersay* 1982). Another video game has also prompted outrage: "Beat 'Em and Eat 'Em" involves a prostitute on a street corner and a masturbator on a rooftop above her (News 1982b). Pornography shops around the country have been targets of picketing, tours, and civil disobedience. In Washington, D.C. the Anti-Swine Brigade padlocked shut one shop for a few hours; New Mexico women spraypainted "Porno Stinks" on porn shop walls and nearby streets, using a paint with a skunk-like odor (News 1982b). Women Against Pornography in New York demonstrated at "Sexpo '82," the first northeast trade show for pornography.

Two campaigns by San Francisco's Women Against Violence in Pornography and the Media resulted in successful settlements with major manufacturers. Famolare was targeted for an ad that featured a woman stumbling in high heels as a man shot a gun near her. Not only did they agree to cease the ad's use, but Famolare fired the advertiser and replaced him with a woman committed to responsible advertising. Women Against Pornography in New York honored Famolare after the company signed a statement opposing violence in advertising. Demonstrations against Esprit de Corps, a San Francisco clothing manufacturer, were organized because of an ad depicting a woman lying on her back on an ironing board, smiling, while a man pressed an iron to her crotch. The campaign resulted in a written apology and a verbal agreement to refrain from violence against women in future advertising (News 1982a; *Aegis* 1982). Even in Nicaragua there is a decree outlawing sexism in advertising.

Conclusion

Revealing and confronting the myriad forms of male violence perpetrated against women continue to characterize the literature and activities of 1982. Despite worsening economic conditions and a conservative national mood, important advances were made. Three trends deserve note. First, the gap between research findings and feminist analysis is narrowing. For the first time, the link between the relative power and privileges of men in this society with acts of violence were at least noted in the majority of scholarly literature on all forms of sexual violence. Second, the boundaries between types of violence have become more fluid. For example, battering and incest are being looked at under the rubric of family violence; marital rape fuses the once distinct problems of rape and wife abuse; and sexual abuse in institutions or perpetrated by professionals against clients or patients is merging the issues of sexual harassment and rape. Finally, the movement exhibits growing sophistication in its legislative and educative strategies, and in its quest to resolve internal dilemmas.

All of these trends are evident in daily events. The term "violence against women," once known only to activists, is emerging into regular use in the mass media. Its use signifies growing awareness that one incident or depiction of sexual violence is not isolated; it blurs the boundaries and sees the whole; and it begs the question, "why has sexual violence been rampant, hidden, and tolerated?"

References

Assailant is shooting baskets for bulls. 1982. *Off Our Backs*. December, p. 10.

BACKHOUSE, C., and SCHOENROTH, L. 1983. A comparative survey of Canadian and American rape law. *Canada—U.S. Law Journal* 6:48–88.

BARRETT, K. 1982. Date rape: A campus epidemic? *Ms.*, September, 48.

BAXTER, R. 1982. Judicial and administrative protections against sexual harassment in the work place. *Employee Relations Law Journal* 7:587–83.

BEALE, L. 1982. Survey on "sleaze" genre of films. *Los Angeles Times*, March 7.

BENEKE, T. 1982. *Men on rape*. New York: St. Martin's Press.

BERN, E. 1982. From violent outbreak to the spouse abuse syndrome. *Social Casework* 63:41–45.

BETTS, N., and NEWMAN, G. 1982. Defining the issue: Sexual harassment in college and university life. *Contemporary Education* 54:48–52.

BROZAN, N. 1982. Premenstrual syndrome is at issue in three recent court trials involving violent acts by women. *New York Times*, July 12.

CARLOVA, J. 1982. The impairment doctors won't talk about. *Medical Economics* 59:92–100.

CAROZZA, B., and HEIRSTEINER, S. 1982. Young female incest victims in treatment. *Clinical Social Work Journal* 10:165–75.

CATE, R.; HENTON, J.; KOVAL, J., et al. 1982. Premarital abuse: A social psychological perspective. *Journal of Family Issues* 3:79–90.

CHURCHMAN, D. 1982. Women's service centers are cutting back or closing across US because of Federal funding cuts. *Christian Science Monitor*, March 3.

COURTOIS, C., and WATTS, D. 1982. Counseling adult women who experienced incest in childhood or adolescence. *Personnel and Guidance Journal* 60:275–79.

CROCKER, P. 1982. Annotated bibliography on sexual harassment in education. *Women's Rights Law Reporter* 7:91–106.

CRULL, P. 1982. Stress effects of sexual harassment on the job: Implications for counseling. *American Journal of Orthopsychiatry* 52:539–44.

DEANE, N., and TILLAR, D. 1982. Dealing with sexual harassment. *AGB Reports* 24:43–48.

DOWNS, A. 1973. Up and down with ecology: The 'issue-attention cycle.' *The Public Interest*.

DREYFACK, M. 1982. Sexual harassment: Can you afford not to clamp down. *Supervision* 44:8–10.

DULDT, B. 1982. Sexual harassment in nursing. *Nursing Outlook* 30:336–43.

DUNWOODY, E. 1982. Sexual abuse of children: A serious, widespread problem. *Response* 5:14.

ELLIS, E.; ATKESON, B.; and CALHOUN, K. 1982. An examination of differences between multiple- and single-incident victims of sexual assault. *Journal of Abnormal Psychology* 91:221–24.

Experts warn girls may be limiting their career potentials by failing to spend as much time with computers as boys. 1982. *Business Week*, June 21, p. 102.

Fairness Committee. 1982. The politics of sexual harassment. *Aegis: Magazine on Ending Violence Against Women*, Summer, pp. 5–15.

FALEY, R. 1982. Sexual harassment: Critical review of legal cases with general principles and preventive measures. *Personnel Psychology* 35:583–600.

FEINBERG, M., and LEVENSTEIN, A. 1982. Sex and romance in the office and plant. *Wall Street Journal*, November 29.

Fifteen-year study of U.S. prime-time television audiences. 1982. *Newsweek*, December 6, p. 136.

FINKELHOR, D., and YLLO, K. 1982. Forced sex in marriage: A preliminary research report. *Crime and Delinquency*, July, pp. 459–78.

GELLES, R. Applying research on family violence to clinical practice. *Journal of Marriage and the Family* 44:9–20.

GEREBENICS, G. 1982. *Under the rule of thumb: Battered women and the administration of justice.* Washington, D.C.: U.S. Commission on Civil Rights.

GILPIN, C. 1982. Sexual harassment defense coverage protects employers against suits. *Rough Notes* 125:18, 38.

GIOVANNI, J. 1982. Prevention of child abuse and neglect: Research and policy issues. *Social Work Research and Abstracts* 18:23–31.

GRAY, S. 1982. Exposure to pornography and aggression toward women: The case of the angry male. *Social Problems* 29:387–98.

GROTH, N.; LONGO, R.; and MCFADIN, J. 1982. Undetected recidivism among rapists and child molesters. *Crime and Delinquency*, July, pp. 450–58.

GRUBER, J., and BJORN, L. 1982. Blue-collar blues: The sexual harassment of women autoworkers. *Work and Occupations: An International Sociological Journal* 9:271–98.

hersay. 1982. Women's News Institute, San Francisco, September 7, 13, 20; October 11, 25; December 13, 27.

hersay. 1983. Women's News Institute, San Francisco, January 3.

HOPKINS, C., and JOHNSON, D. 1982. Sexual harassment in the work place. *Journal of College Placement* 42:30–35.

HORN, P., and HORN, J. 1982. *Sex in the office.* Reading, Mass.: Addison-Wesley.

Housing breakthrough? Sex bias called "pervasive." 1982. *Engineering News*, February 25, pp. 67–68.

Insurance pays legal costs in sexual harassment cases. 1982. *Chronicle of Higher Education*, September 8, p. 7.

JONES, A. 1982. One woman who chose to say no. *Nation*, April 17, pp. 456–59.

JOYCE, R. 1982. Defusing sexual harassment in the work place. *School Law Bulletin* 13:1, 13–15.

KALMUSS, D., and STRAUS, M. 1982. Wife's marital dependency and wife abuse. *Journal of Marriage and the Family* 44:277–86.

KANDEL, W. 1982. Sexual harassment law: Beyond Title VII. *Employee Relations Law Journal* 8:309–14.

KATES, D., and ENGBERG, N. 1982. Deadly force self-defense against rape. *University of California at Davis Law Journal* 15:873–906.

KIRKPATRICK, R., and NASON, J. 1982. Employment law litigation and the changing limitations on personnel management: Three illustrations. *Journal of Retail Banking* 4:62–71.

KLEIN, F. 1982. Violence against women. In *The women's annual: 1981 The year in review*, edited by B. Haber. Boston: G. K. Hall.

LAFREE, G. 1982. Male power and female victimization: Towards a theory of interracial rape. *American Journal of Sociology* 88:311–28.

LANDERMAN, D., and MCATEE, M. 1982. Breaking the racism barrier: White antiracist work. *Aegis: Magazine on Ending Violence Against Women*, Winter, pp. 16–25.

LOMBARDI, J. 1982. Growing up with violence: An analysis of retrospective accounts of female offspring. PhD dissertation, University of Maryland, College Park.

LOOTENS, T. 1982. Interview with Mary Morrison. *Off Our Backs*, November, p. 17.

LUBELL, D., and SOONG, W. 1982. Group therapy with sexually abused adolescents. *Canadian Journal of Psychiatry* 27:311–15.

LYSTAD, M. 1982. Violence in the home: A major public problem. *Urban and Social Change Review* 15:21–25.

MACLEOD, J. 1982. Current EEO concerns of personnel people. *EEO Today* 9: 155–60.

MCKENDRICK, J. 1982. Viewpoint: Men versus women. *Management World* 11: 11–13.

MCNARON, T., and MORGAN, Y. 1982. *Voices in the night—Women speaking about incest*. Minneapolis: Cleis Press.

MEEHAN, M. 1982. Coalition for better television's boycott of RCA and NBC has potential appeal. *Los Angeles Times*, March 18.

NADELSON, C.; NOTMAN, M.; ZACKSON, H. et al. A follow-up study of rape victims. *American Journal of Psychiatry* 139:1266–70.

National Coalition Against Domestic Violence. 1982. *End violence in the lives of women*. Milwaukee: Coalition Resource Office.

National Center on Women and Family Law. 1982a. Marital rape packet. New York: The Center.

National Center on Women and Family Law. 1982b. Challenges to battered women's legislation. New York: The Center.

News. 1982a. *Off Our Backs*, March, p. 18.

News. 1982b. *Off Our Backs*, November, p. 12.

Newsbriefs and announcements. 1982. *Aegis: Magazine on Ending Violence Against Women*, Summer, pp. 49–55.

News from all over. 1982a. *Ms.*, April, p. 18.

News from all over. 1982b. *Ms.*, October, pp. 23–24.

New Directions for Women. 1982. September-October, p. 3.

On Campus with Women 34, no. 1, Association of American Colleges, Washington, D.C.

PETERSEN, D., and MASSENGILL, D. 1982. Sexual harassment—a growing problem in the workplace. *Personnel Administrator* 27:79–89.

RED HORSE, J. 1982. Clinical strategies for American Indian families. *Urban and Social Change Review* 15:17–19.

Response to family violence. 1982. Washington, D.C.: Center for Women Policy Studies.

RIPRAP. 1982. *Equal Times*, June 13, p. 4.

RODKIN, L.; HUNT, E.; and COWAN, S. 1982. A men's support group for significant others of rape victims. *Journal of Marital and Family Therapy* 8:91–97.

ROSS, L. 1982. Rape and Third World women. *Aegis: Magazine on Ending Violence Against Women*, Summer, pp. 39–48.

ROY, M., ed. 1982. *The abusive partner—An analysis of domestic battering.* New York: Van Nostrand Reinhold.

RUSS, M. 1982. Pennsylvania rape victims win victory in courts. *New Directions for Women*, September-October, p. 8.

RUSSELL, D. 1982. *Rape in marriage.* New York: Macmillan.

SCHECTER, S. 1982. *Women and male violence.* Boston: South End Press.

SCHUMM, W.; MARTIN, M.; BOLLMAN, S.; and JURICH, A. 1982. Classifying family violence. *Journal of Family Issues* 3:319–40.

Self-defense case dismissed. 1982. *Off Our Backs*, December, p. 10.

Sexual abuse: Prosecution and prevention. 1982. *Off Our Backs*, December, p. 10.

Sexual harassment: Guarding against legal problems. 1982. *Effective Manager* 5:4–5.

SGROI, S., ed. 1982. *Handbook of clinical intervention in child sexual abuse.* Lexington, Mass.: D. C. Heath.

SNOWDON, R. 1982. Working with incest offenders: Excuses, excuses, excuses. *Aegis: Magazine on Ending Violence Against Women*, Summer, pp. 56–63.

STARK-ADAMEC, C., and ADAMEC, R. 1982. Aggression by men against women. *International Journal of Women's Studies* 5:1–21

STEVENS, G. 1982a. The "cruel trilemma": Sexual harassment under Title VII and the tangible job benefit. *American Business Law Journal* 20:109–17.

STEVENS, G. 1982b. Sexual harassment of female employees and the law of slander. *EEO Today* 9:163–71.

STOKS, F. 1982. Assessing urban public space environments for danger of violent crime—especially rape. PhD dissertation, University of Washington.

SULLIVAN, G. 1982. Funny things happen on our way to revolution. *Aegis: Magazine on Ending Violence Against Women*, Spring, pp. 12–21.

TAYLOR, M. 1982. Cook County Circuit Court Judge Joseph M. Wosik rules county's method of collecting funds for new state program that funds shelters for victims of domestic violence is illegal. *Chicago Tribune*, August 19, Section 2, p. 3.

THAR, A. 1982. The admissibility of expert testimony on battered wife syndrome: Evidentiary analysis. *Northwestern University Law Review* 77:348–73.

TIERNEY, K. 1982. The battered women movement and the creation of the wife beating problem. *Social Problems* 29:207–19.

U.S. Commission on Civil Rights. 1982. *The federal response to domestic violence.* Washington, D.C.: The Commission.

WAKS, J., and STARR, M. 1982a. Sexual harassment in the work place: The scope of employer liability. *Employee Relations Law Journal* 7:369–88.

WAKS, J., and STARR, M. 1982b. The "sexual shakedown" in perspective: Sexual harassment in its social and legal contexts. *Employee Relations Law Journal* 7: 567–86.

Why don't all men rape? *Off Our Backs*, October, p. 4.

WILSON, W., AND DURRENBERGER, R. 1982. Comparison of rape and attempted rape victims. *Psychological Reports* 50:198.

WINKS, P. 1982. Legal implications of sexual contact between teacher and student. *Journal of Law and Education* 11:437–77.

WOLKINSON, B., and LIBERSON, D. 1982. The arbitration of sex discrimination grievances. *Arbitration Journal* 37:35–44.

Resources

Below are listed organizations and print and nonprint materials that pertain to each form of violence against women. The emphasis is on practical materials, identified by those working in each field.

ODN Productions, Inc., 74 Varick Street, Room 304, New York, NY 10013. ODN has produced several excellent film series; each consists of several short films designed to elicit discussion and materials to assist facilitators. *The Acquaintance Rape* prevention series is aimed at high school and college audiences, and focuses on rape between people who know each other. *Time Out* is a series for working with men who batter. *In Need of Special Attention*, a 17-minute film, assists hospital emergency room staff in establishing protocol for battered women. *No More Secrets*, a 13-minute film, features children 9 and 10 years of age, and focuses on talking openly about sexual abuse and prevention techniques.

Rape

Modern Talking Picture Services, 5000 Park Street North, St. Petersburg, FL 60062. Three films can be obtained on a five-day, free-loan basis: *Rape: Caring for the Adult Female Victim* for medical personnel, the *Acquaintance Rape* series described above, and *Rape: Victim or Victor.*

Molmen, Marcia. *Avoiding Rape without Putting Yourself in Protective Custody.* Grand Forks, N. Dak.: Athena Press, 1982. After a brief introduction to the myths and realities of rape, this book contains extensive discussion and photographs of self-defense techniques and strategies.

Sexual Assault Crisis Service (SACS), 135 Broad Street, Hartford, CT 06106. The "outreach project report," an in-depth description of the process of developing this rape crisis center into a multiracial, multicultural project, is now available.

Washington, D.C. Rape Crisis Center, P.O. Box 21005, Washington, DC 20009. As one of the first rape crisis centers in the United States, this center played an important role in fostering communications between early projects. In addition to publishing *How to Start a Rape Crisis Center*, a valuable resource for new programs, they are currently involved in developing services and community education programs tailored to the needs of women of color.

Battering

Casa Myrna Vasquez, 342 Shawmut Avenue, Boston, MA 02118. *The Gathering— Newsletter for Women of Color Working on the Issue of Domestic Violence* is published three to four times per year. This shelter program has also produced other publications, including *Outreach Strategies to Third World Women.* Write for more information.

Center for Women Policy Studies, 2000 P Street NW, Washington, DC 20036. *Response to Violence in the Family* is published six times per year.

National Center on Women and Family Law, 799 Broadway, Room 402, New York, NY 10003. The center provides technical assistance on legal issues affecting battered women; they also work on marital rape and child custody legislation and litigation. A variety of publications is available, including resource packets on battering, marital rape, and child custody; the *Women's Advocate* (newsletter); and *Legal Advocacy for Battered Women*. Write for order forms and for Service Request Policy if seeking legal assistance.

National Coalition Against Domestic Violence (NCADV), 1728 N Street NW, Washington, DC 20036. The NCADV has provided a powerful voice in the development of the battered women's shelter movement through its production of technical assistance materials and its sponsorship of conferences. Regional caucuses and the issues committees promote information sharing. A number of publications, including the quarterly *NCADV Voice* are available. Many materials are available from the Resource Development Office, 1228 W. Mitchell Street, Milwaukee, WI 53204; of special note is the *Domestic Violence Manual*. ($19.50)

Park Slope Safe Homes Project, P.O. Box 429, Van Brunt Station, Brooklyn, NY 11215. *Developing Community Based Services for Battered Women and their Families* is a 150-page manual describing the implementation of a safe-home network. Topics covered include organizing and training volunteers, establishing a hotline, program philosophy, and community education. ($5.00)

Pennsylvania Coalition Against Domestic Violence (PCADV), 2405 N. Front Street, Harrisburg, PA 17110. One of the oldest and most active state coalitions, PCADV has produced many materials on subjects including counseling, advocacy, program development and management, and police training. Write for publications list.

Southern California Coalition on Battered Women, P.O. Box 5036, Santa Monica, CA 90405. A bibliography, statistics, legal information, and a training notebook have been produced by this organization. In addition, materials from the now-defunct National Clearinghouse on Domestic Violence are obtainable through the Southern California Coalition.

Marital Rape

National Clearinghouse on Maritial Rape (NCOMR), Women's History Research Center, 2325 Oak Street, Berkeley, CA 94708. The clearinghouse has published a pamphlet on the Greta Rideout case in Oregon ($1.00), a brochure on marital rape, and a discussion of the impact of California's marital rape law ($5.00). Send a self-addressed, stamped envelope for materials and for information about membership in the clearinghouse.
(See National Center on Women and Family Law, in Battering section above, for their materials on marital rape.)

Child Sexual Assault

Montana Incest Prevention Coalition, 24 South Fourth East, Missoula, MT 59801. A variety of print and nonprint materials was produced from an innovative statewide conference that brought together feminists, human service workers, criminal justice personnel, health care providers, and educators. Of particular note is a videotape of a panel of incest survivors discussing the impact of their experiences and the benefits of a self-help support group model. Write for more information.

National Center on Child Abuse and Neglect, U.S. Department of Health and Human Services, Washington, DC 20013. The Center has funded research and has volumes of reports and literature available. A 13-minute film, *No More Secrets* demonstrates ways children can say no to adults' unwanted touches.

National Legal Resource Center for Child Advocacy and Protection, 1800 M Street, Washington, DC 20036. Guidelines for using the judicial system in child sexual assault cases, written for attorneys, are contained in *Child Sexual Abuse: Legal Issues and Approaches*. ($3.00)

Sexual Harassment

Massachusetts Department of Education, Division of Curriculum and Instruction, Chapter 622 Project, 1385 Hancock Street, Quincy, MA 02169. The Department has produced two materials on sexual harassment aimed at high school students: *It's no Laughing Matter*, a 25-minute color slide/tape exploring sexual harassment in a vocational high school, a comprehensive high school, and an after school job; and *Who's Hurt and Who's Liable*, a curriculum and guide for school personnel.

National Organization for Women, Legal Defense and Education Fund, 132 W. 43rd Street, New York, NY 10036. A number of reports, legal briefs, and articles are available on selected topics, including sexual harassment. Write for publications list.

Pornography and Sexual Violence in the Media

Earthworks, 431 W. Rustic Road, Santa Monica, CA 90402. A 29-minute video, *Taking Back the Night: Feminist Perspectives on Pornography*, documents the conference held by Women Against Violence in Pornography and Media. Rental fee is $25; purchase price is $150.

Women Against Pornography (WAP), 358 W. 47th Street, New York, NY 10036. WAP initiated touring pornography shops to encourage women to understand the messages conveyed by books, films, and peep-shows. A bimonthly newsletter, *Newsreport* is available. *Sex Roles for Sale: Sex Stereotyping in the Media* is a new slide show for teenagers. It contains 44 slides, cassette, lesson plan, and bibliography; both violent and positive sex role imagery are depicted. Write for membership, newsletter, and slide show information.

Women Against Violence Against Women (WAVAW), 543 N. Fairfax Avenue, Los Angeles, CA 90036. In 1975 WAVAW began to protest the sexual violence in record album advertising. Their boycott of record companies has in some instances brought about changes in company policy. They are a national membership with chapters across the country. Over the years WAVAW's slide show has been updated and broadened to cover other forms of media violence. Write for the address of a local chapter and information on their newsletter, slide show, and other materials.

Work

Karen Sacks

In 1982 the political Right won its battle to defeat the ERA but lost the war to implement its social program to remove women from the workforce and restore a nuclear family under the control of a male breadwinner. Instead of looking backward, women are facing their very difficult economic realities and pursuing strategies to gain living wages, ameliorate the double day, and end discrimination in public programs and policies.

Both in the United States and overseas, the conservative and patriarchal image of women as full-time homemakers supported by a male wage-earner is increasingly out of step with the double work days of paid and unpaid work that most women experience. It is also out of step with the single parenthood and single old age that growing numbers of middle-class as well as working-class women have to face (Ehrenreich and Stallard 1982; Sacks and Rubin 1982; Task Force on Economic Issues 1982; Welch 1982). Poverty is a woman's issue (Pearce and McAdoo 1981). Female-headed families are half of all families below the poverty level, and over half of all women who head families with preschool children are in the labor force. A major cause of women's poverty is the low wages earned by the large majority of working women, combined with their increased responsibilities as single parents. Female-headed families are growing at ten times the rate of male-headed families (Chapman 1982; Children's Defense Fund 1982b; National Commission on Working Women 1983; Rubin 1982).

Feminization of the Working Class

Karen Nussbaum, Executive Director of Nine to Five/National Association of Working Women, recently pointed out, "The typical American worker is no longer a man in a hard hat. She is a woman at the typewriter—or, rather, at a keyboard" (Yencket 1982). A recent sociologic study of the American class structure found that women make up more than half of those in working-class jobs. Together with minority men, they make up a "sizeable majority" of this class, which in turn is a majority of the labor force (Wright et al. 1982). The National Commission of Working Women refers to women in these clerical, service, and manufacturing jobs as "the 80 percent" to underline the high proportion of women in such work.

Table 1.
Occupations of Employed Women by Race, December 1982
(16 years of age and over)

Major Occupation Group	All Women	Black and Other	Black
Number (in thousands)	43,570	5,724	4,615
Percent	100.0	100.0	100.0
Professional and technical workers	18.4	15.7	14.6
Managers and administrators (except farm)	7.5	4.2	3.6
Sales workers	7.4	3.7	3.2
Clerical workers	34.2	29.9	30.4
Craft and kindred workers	2.0	1.5	1.3
Operatives, (except transport)	8.3	12.6	11.8
Transport equipment operatives	0.7	0.7	0.8
Nonfarm laborers	1.2	1.3	1.3
Private household workers	2.4	5.4	6.4
Service workers (except private household)	16.9	24.4	26.0
Farmers and farm managers	0.4	0.1	[1]
Farm laborers supervisors	0.5	0.6	0.7

[1] Less than 0.05 percent.

Source: U.S. Department of Labor, Bureau of Labor Statistics. Unpublished data. Prepared by the Women's Bureau, Division of Statistical and Economic Analysis, December 1982.

As of December 1982, women made up 43.4 percent of the labor force; and 53 percent of all women were in the labor force (Table 1). Over the year the labor force (which includes the officially unemployed as well as employed persons) grew by almost two million, of which 68 percent were women. Women's overall unemployment rate was 10.3 percent, while that of black women was 18.6 percent and Hispanic women 15.1 percent. For the first time in over thirty years, men's unemployment rate outstripped women's, reflecting the severity of the recession in heavy industrial sectors (U.S. Department of Labor 1982).

The work lives of these women have begun to receive proportional scholarly attention. Wertz (1982) found a dramatic return in social science research to concern with the lives of working-class women. They had been eclipsed by some thirty years of almost exclusive focus on professional and managerial women. Kahn-Hut, Daniels, and Colvard's *Women and Work* (1982) is an excellent and unified collection of this new sociologic research. *Out to Work* (1982) by Alice Kessler-Harris synthesizes recent historical research on working-class women to show the radical transformations wrought by two centuries of gradual change. Susan Strasser's *Never Done* (1982) treats the changing technology and labor of unwaged domestic work since colonial times, and their impact on work and family social relations.

Working-class women are also becoming visible in studies of women in international development and women and migration. Beneria and Sen (1982) show that economic exploitation is a class as well as a gender issue for Third World women. More than half of the "new immigrants" are women who come to the United States in search of work to sustain their families (Mortimer and Bryce-Laporte 1981).

Feminism and Economics

What are women's perceptions of their situations? Is feminism on the rise, or are women turning away from it? Do women see themselves as oppressed workers? Would they rather be traditional homemakers? Are there class differences among women regarding feminism? Despite Right Wing rhetoric, the issue is no longer *whether* women (or mothers) should work. Today's women seem to find it normal and expected to combine wage work and motherhood (Frankel, Monogue, and Paludi 1982). How do women respond to these heavy social expectations?

Some writers, focusing on more affluent, younger, and white women, present a disconcerting picture, indicating that women are more satisfied with their circumstances in the workplace, do not feel discrimination, or are reluctant to rock the boat (Bolotin 1982; Crosby 1982). The same cannot be said, however, for working-class women in the labor force. Although still in a fledgling stage, organized women clerical and service workers have become increasingly outspoken in pursuit of pay equity, occupational mobility, health, and safety (Sexton 1982). Such a class contrast is incomplete, however, for there is a great deal of activity and a new militance among women professionals. Gender and working-class interests have been joined on economic issues by the organized women's movement (Coalition of Labor Union Women 1982; Eisenstein 1982). A very broad coalition of such groups published an analysis of the negative economic impact of the Reagan budget on women, joining others opposing policies of taking from women, children, minorities, and workers, and giving to the rich (Children's Defense Fund 1982a; Coalition on Women and the Budget 1982).

Summary and Overview of Issues

While the issues of equal pay, access, and promotion are shared by all working women, there are some important distinctions in the ways they affect women in different occupations. The majority are in occupations that are predominantly female, namely clerical, service, and specific manufacturing industries. Here, the major issues are those raised by runaway shops (and offices, to a lesser extent), automation, and work reorganization. In offices this most frequently translates into problems around deskilling of clerical work, its lack of mobility, assembly-line organization and pacing, low pay, and increased racial segregation within an already female workforce (Murphree 1982; Nine to Five 1982; Nussbaum 1982). In microelectronics, apparel, and textile manufacturing, areas where women make up the bulk of the production workforce, job flight and job loss loom very large for both American and Third World women workers. Automation, combined with extraordinary mobility by multinational corporations in these industries has forced women workers to become increasingly mobile, emigrating internationally as well as regionally within their home countries. Women manufacturing workers now face similar problems, solutions of which require overcoming racial and ethnic divisions across national and linguistic boundaries.

For the most part, women in the professions and in management (with notable exceptions in nursing and librarianship) are in occupations that are predominantly male. Here, women have made significant gains; however, these have not been followed by equality in promotion, prestige, or pay. This has led to a situation that could be described as the emergence of a two-track system within many professions, with white men continuing to predominate on a "fast track" and women on a second-class track, with much less mobility, pay, and control over their work.

Despite these differences, both groups of working women are acting with vigor to improve their economic situations. Tactics and strategies differ with the circumstances. Where women are a minority in an occupation, affirmative action suits predominate, especially class action suits and demands for equal pay and promotion through union or professional association channels. The most active constituency at present seems to be college faculty. Among clerical and health care workers, who are almost all women, and among public sector employees where women predominate and where they are in the forefront of activity, collective bargaining combined with union-sponsored litigation for equal pay for work of comparable value have emerged as the major strategies for economic equity. Unions have been weak or absent in many of the occupations and industries where women are concentrated. Spurred perhaps by declining memberships due to massive unemployment in heavy industry, perhaps by the changing character of the workforce, or perhaps by the self-generated militance of women workers, many unions are giving more serious attention to organizing among clerical, health care, and public sector workers. In addition, some professionals, most notably nurses and librarians, are pursuing unionization and litigation for a combination of sex equity and wage and professional needs.

Automation and Runaway Shops

Advocates of automation argue that the new technology will eliminate boring and repetitive work, while unions and clerical workers' organizations argue that it is leading to deteriorating working conditions and job losses for women workers, as management uses it to speed up the work and to supervise workers more closely. Office technology has occupied the center of the debate about the microelectronics revolution's impact on women, in part because clerical workers are organizing and becoming increasingly effective on their own behalf (Gregory 1982). Yet women also hold almost one-third of all manufacturing jobs (Eckart 1982) and are the majority of production workers in electronics, textiles, and apparel. Here, the new wave of automation has joined the older problem of runaway shops—flight of factories from higher- to lower-waged regions—while in clerical work, automation is just now beginning to generate a new problem in the runaway office.

Office Automation and Deskilling   Two contrasting views of automation appeared in a special issue of *Scientific American* on the mechanization of work. In a historical overview, Joan Wallach Scott (1982) shows how the mechanization of factory work as well as that of telephone operators and clerical workers led to its transformation from men's to women's work, with a corresponding decrease in pay, status, and mobility. Scott argues that women's economic gains are due to their own efforts, and that technology's role has been in creating the conditions that enabled women to act collectively.

Vincent Giuliano (1982) takes a positive view of office automation— although he does not even mention women as workers. He sees three stages to the evolution of office work. First, preindustrial stage has little division of labor and an emphasis on smooth interpersonal relations. Second, the industrial office has finely divided labor, assembly-line organization, routine jobs, and a push for ever greater productivity in information processing. The third stage, or information-age office, would use the latest computer technology to reintegrate labor, substitute work stations for the assembly line, facilitate people working at home, and allow restoration of the work satisfaction and interpersonal values of the preindustrial office.

An International Conference of Office Work and the New Technology, organized by the Working Women's Educational Fund (1983), brought together European and American management, clerical workers, unionists, and researchers. Keynote speaker Harley Shaiken from Massachusetts Institute of Technology pointed out that the real question automation posed was a human one: progress for whom and for what goals? He noted a conflict between management goals of greater productivity, supervision, and control over workers, and workers' goals of improved bodily, mental, and economic health.

Several corporate speakers agreed that business had tended to apply an industrial model and that this had eliminated and deskilled many clerical jobs. Some felt that more progressive companies were now using the new technology to increase the scope of workers' abilities (Yencket 1982).

This view was contested by sociologist Roslyn Feldberg's research in two large information-processing companies. With her co-worker Evelyn Glenn, she found assembly-line work common, with data-entry workers required to enter information exactly as written even when they recognized errors. She added a strong caution about the work station as well. Citing a situation in which such an approach had reintegrated the job of customer representative, Feldberg showed that the computer was then used to apply assembly-line criteria and monitor workers' productivity. As a result, assisting a customer on a complicated and time-consuming matter was detrimental to the daily "production" quota on which the worker's performance was evaluated.

European unionists joined clerical workers in stressing the importance of worker involvement in design and introduction of computers as a way of eliminating some of their health hazards, enhancing the work, and reintegrating subdivided jobs. Olov Ostberg, a Swedish representative, noted, "In the final analysis it's the worker-management interaction that is most important" (Moberg 1982).

Runaway Shops and an International Women's Workforce   The contemporary world of women's waged work is international, multiracial, and multiethnic by design (Safa and Leacock 1981). Helen Safa traces three stages in the development of the workforce in the apparel industry to indicate that the movements of capital and workers in this industry link women around the world. In the first stage companies relied on a native-born, largely rural population; this was followed by a second stage of family labor by an immigrant labor force; and finally, a third, contemporary stage of runaway shops (Safa 1981).

Some of the most mobile industries internationally employ a largely female production workforce. These are still labor-intensive industries whose profits depend heavily on finding new sources of ever more poorly paid women workers throughout the world, and hiring minority and immigrant women at substandard wages in American-based production work (Duggan and Rocamora 1981; Guma 1982; Asia— 1982).

Increasing numbers of Asian, Caribbean, and Latin American women have been forced to emigrate in search of work. Many of the plants that sprang up in their nations were birds of passage that moved on to new sources of labor when government tax incentives ended or when they found cheaper labor and better incentives elsewhere. Indeed, immigration has been linked to such plant movement. Since employment opportunities are few and wages are low in many Third World countries, large numbers of women migrate both within their own countries and internationally in the hopes of finding decent employment (Sassen-Koob 1981; Bolles 1981).

While most of the international job flight to date has taken place in manufacturing, information-processing jobs may soon follow suit. Thanks to satellite telecommunications, work can now be processed in distant—and low-waged—areas and relayed to central offices on other continents. Several banks have already made plans to move to low-waged states, and other companies that have performed information processing overseas for some time are contemplating expanding their operations (Gregory 1982).

Job Loss and Automation   Automation is threatening women's jobs in the growing clerical sector as well as in the declining manufacturing sector, and in the Third World as well as in the United States. Several recent reports point to a decline in microelectronics and garment-manufacturing jobs internationally as well as domestically. Rising wages in Korea, Taiwan, Hong Kong, and Singapore combined with new forms of automation have decreased the long-range importance of low wages as a competitive advantage in microelectronics manufacturing. Some companies are now moving to still lower-waged nations such as Thailand, the Philippines, and even China, while others are bringing more of their production back home, but with automated systems rather than human labor (Asia— 1982).

Between 1969 and 1978, eight international microelectronics firms cut back their production work forces by some 20 percent; Japanese television manufacturers have decreased theirs by 50 percent. In the United States, Western Electric, AT&T's manufacturing division, eliminated 24,000 jobs when they changed to solid-state switching gear. In textiles, computer systems are being used in pattern layout in combination with electronically controlled laser cutting. This has resulted in a loss of skilled, mainly men's jobs. The introduction of microprocessor controlled sewing machines on a large scale could have disastrous consequences for sewing work, which is virtually all done by women (Eckart 1982).

The situation in the clerical and information-processing industries is also alarming. In France, one study suggests that a 30 percent decline in the number of banking and insurance jobs is likely by 1990. The British Association of Science, Technology and Managerial Staffs estimate that there has already been a decrease in banking and insurance jobs from 1.1 million to some 600,000 in that country. In the United States, between 1973 and 1979 AT&T cut back on the number of telephone operators by 40 percent, a loss of 40,000 jobs, mainly for women (Eckart 1982). One sour note in Giuliano's (1982) case for a work-station approach to office work is that it eliminates a large number of jobs. He cites as commonplace, "staff reductions of as much as 50 percent," and notes as well that automation in the preceding decade has already eliminated many keypunch, stenography, and typing jobs.

Part-Time Work, Underemployment, and Homework   Employers frequently treat the growing phenomenon of job-sharing (where two part-timers share one full-time job) as part-time work. Such workers seldom receive the fringe benefits, like insurance and paid vacations, that make up a significant proportion of full-time workers' total compensation. Between 1972 and 1982 the number of part-time workers increased 50 percent nationally, according to one report, such that one in five job-holders are now part-timers (Diggs 1982). Unfortunately, it is not known how much of this represents the underemployment of those who seek full-time work, and how much is due to voluntary part-time on the part of teenagers or full-time workers who are moonlighting. One Long Island data-processing firm has an all-woman work force of whom 85 percent are part-timers who work their own hours and are paid on piecework rates. Most are married women who find flex-time a great advantage in managing their two jobs; however, they lose benefits like paid vacations (Trimble 1982). Flex-time and part-time work can help women cope with their double day, provided they receive prorated benefits. Without them, such work is doubly oppressive: the domestic and the waged exploitation reinforce each other.

Like flex-time and job-sharing, homework is also potentially attractive to women who need to earn an income while taking responsibility for caring for small children. Many older forms of homework, particularly sewing and home manufacture, were outlawed long ago because they were so exploitative. Most computer home work is now legal, and it is growing. Several major banks and insurance companies are expanding pilot projects that involve workers doing "information-manipulation" jobs with home-based terminals (If home is . . . 1982). One analyst estimates that as many as fifteen million such jobs could presently be done at home; another estimates that there will be five million home-based terminal workers in ten years (If home is . . . 1982).

Companies see supervision as a major problem in this work, although the computers themselves can be used to monitor output and error. Unions are opposed to such monitoring and even more opposed to piece rates for this work because of the ways in which they have been used to drive down the levels of wages. Despite such objections, one large insurance company (Aetna) is going ahead with plans to pay piece rates to home computer workers, to deny them benefits—worth between $2000 and $3000 per year—available to full-time workers, and to charge them $2400 for terminal rental. Aetna argues that such workers could earn "up to" $3000 more than regular salaried workers (If home is . . . 1982).

Proponents of homework argue that it allows mothers to combine wage work and child care in their own homes (Giuliano 1982). Opponents argue that competition among women, who are already crowded into a sex-segregated labor market, would reduce wages, and that the substitution of piece rates (made easy to calculate by the computers themselves) for hourly rates would further decrease them while intensifying the work. Earlier in the century, portable sewing machines encouraged manufacturers to farm out sewing at piece rates to married women in great need of money. Most of these women worked long hours for low wages because they had no choice. While sewing by machine was indeed faster and easier than manual sewing, employers used this against women in setting the rates. Scott (1982) notes, "The sewing machine transformed such households into miniature sweatshops," and data terminal homework could have similar consequences.

Health and Safety in the Office   The image of office work as clean and safe is coming under scrutiny as office workers begin to speak up. They are finding that work at video data terminals (VDT) for long periods of time is responsible for increased back and eye problems. There is also mounting concern about irradiation and incidents of pregnancy problems and miscarriages among VDT operators (Moberg 1982). Most attention has focused on stress, however, which is beginning to be recognized as an occupational hazard of office work. A long-term medical study found that the rates of heart disease among women clerical workers was almost twice that of other women workers (Gregory 1982). A National Institute of Occupational Safety and Health (NIOSH) study found higher stress levels aong women VDT operators at Blue Cross than among other occupational groups, including air traffic controllers. In a San Francisco study comparing stress levels among traditional clerical workers, VDT operators, and reporters and editors who used VDTs for an equivalent amount of time, the clerical workers who used VDTs scored highest and the professionals lowest on all scales, suggesting that stress stems from an interaction between VDTs and work organization (Moberg 1982). Terminal operators also have high rates of eye strain, migraines, muscle pain, anxiety, and depression (Gregory 1982).

Women in the Professions and Management

The news is somewhat mixed for women in these occupations. While there is great variety in the jobs included under this heading, most require some form of formal postsecondary education and certification. Thus the nature of an educational program and institution plays a large role in determining employment opportunities in salaried careers. The good news is that women now make up slightly more than half of all students enrolled in higher education (Astin and Snyder 1982). The bad news, as Randour, Strassburg, and Lipman-Blumen (1982) found, is that a much less favorable picture emerges when educational statistics are broken down. As one moves from two- to four-year schools, and from undergraduate to graduate and professional training, the proportion of women declines. Likewise, there are relatively more part-time than full-time women students. At all levels, most women are still concentrated in lower-paid and traditionally female fields, with over half of all women MAs and over one-third of all women PhDs being in education. There has, however, been a substantial movement of women into traditionally male areas of business and engineering, law, and medicine (where over a quarter of all recent entrants are women). While a wage gap still exists between men's and women's salaries in these well-paid fields, it tends to be smaller than average.

Management   Ann Harlan and Carol Weiss (1982) studied the changes in management careers for women now that entry-level barriers have been significantly dented. While women have increased their total percentage to 25 percent of all management positions (17 percent in the private sector), they are still concentrated in the lower levels and earn only 55 percent of what their male counterparts do.

Their three-year study had several surprising findings. They discovered that the problems and psychological profiles of male and female managers in similar positions were basically the same. Both were high achievers with good self-esteem. This countered notions that women's psychology had something to do with their lack of success; and it was revealed that men could also have psychological weaknesses. Both sexes also faced career barriers in lack of access to mentors and to blocked career mobility. A second set of findings countered the myth that a "critical mass" of women in management would by itself decrease bias against women. Indeed, they found that jobs with large numbers of women tended to become thought of as "women's jobs" and to lose male recruits, power and prestige. In addition, women continue to face subtle biases in evaluation and promotion. Where a man may be evaluated as assertive and rewarded by his supervisor, the same behavior in a woman may be negatively evaluated, for example, as aggressive. In general, Harlan and Weiss found that women received less feedback than men on their work. Most interesting was their report that middle-level management tended positively to evaluate and promote nonthreatening women who lacked the skills and characteristics that top management sought for the upper levels—a *Catch-22* for women caught facing timid immediate supervisors who serve as gatekeepers for the upper levels.

Professions   In a provocative article subtitled, "Women get a ticket to ride after the gravy train has left the station," Carter and Carter (1981) examined a variety of professional and technical fields in which women have begun to be a significant numerical presence. They asked about what made it possible to breach the barriers, and what is happening to the occupations now that women are in them. Their examinations of the histories of law, medicine, college teaching, computer programming, allied health, and middle management suggested that women have been able to enter these fields in real numbers because their own efforts have coincided with a shift in control over occupational recruitment and performance from the professionals themselves to those who employ them, be they top corporate executives, boards of directors, or hospital or university administrators. Employers are contesting professional control over work organization, job definition, and division of labor into several specialized sub-jobs in an effort to cut costs and to increase productivity. The consequence of these moves, the Carters showed, is growth of a two-track professional structure, with the men retaining their position in the better-paid, more autonomous, and more mobile fast track, and with women entering a developing second-class track with lower pay, less opportunity for advancement, and less control over their work. In short, women are entering professional careers that are in the process of becoming deprofessionalized, and less attractive to new male entrants. The two-track system then, is an unstable halfway house.

Race and Gender

While much attention has been given to occupational segregation by sex, unfortunately all too little has been written about racial segregation within the female occupational ghetto. Historians have discussed the earlier exclusion of black women from most manufacturing, sales, and clerical work (Kessler-Harris 1982). Karen Anderson (1981), in her study of women in World War II, has shown just how resistant the large automobile and aircraft companies were to hiring black women. Forced by labor shortages and by the government to hire white women, they often refused to employ black women even when they could find no one else. Anderson found that black women were consistently steered by employment offices into domestic work despite wartime shortages in heavy industry. She indicates that the breakthroughs they did make during the war came from a combination of individual tenacity and organized struggles waged by themselves and by civil rights groups.

In recent years, black women have gained increased access to clerical occupations, some improvement in access to professional, technical, and managerial positions, and have been able to move out of private household work on a significant scale. In clerical work, where their greatest gains took place numerically, their earnings fell relative to those of white women over the last decade. The ratio of black to white earnings in professional and technical occupations held constant over the decade (Westcott 1982). While statistical data on newer, automated data-processing occupations do not yet exist, there is widespread suspicion that corporations are tracking minority women into these new high-pressure, low-paid, and dead-end clerical occupations (Gregory 1982).

Black women's triple battle—to preserve a degree of community independence from exploitative and racist power holders, to maintain their autonomy in relationships with black men, and to gain decent and equitable waged work—is the theme of three in-depth studies by historians and anthropologists. What happened to free black women in post-Revolutionary War Petersburg, Virginia is the subject of Suzanne Lebsock's study (1982). She shows a community in which over half of all free black households were headed by women who owned property, worked, and exerted a fair amount of autonomy in their relationships with men of the community. This autonomy could not carry across the color line, however, in a society based on the oppression of black people. Nevertheless, Lebsock argues, the inequalities between free black men and women were considerably less than those between their white counterparts. One of the many tragedies of racism, she concludes, is that white society could not benefit from their example.

Jacqueline Jones (1982) deals with black women's work as slaves and in the immediate post-Civil War period. She describes the tension of attempting to maintain African patterns of labor division under a system that forced black women as well as men to work long hours at heavy agricultural labor. Even the few who were domestic servants were often expected to work the fields when needed. Black women's withdrawal from plantation work after the war made clear how much the Southern agrarian economy depended on their labor. For this period, Jones analyzes the complex ways that the need to defend against the dangers of racist attack led to costs as well as to strengths in the organization of men's and women's family and community roles.

Kay Day (1982) provides a contemporary analysis of these triple tensions in South Carolina's Sea Island black communities. She shows that women have a heritage of economic independence and autonomy within their families and communities maintained through their marketing and basket-making activities. The development of urban commerce and the destruction of their produce and fish markets by the city of Charleston forced women into wage work to maintain their autonomy vis-a-vis men, and the autonomy of their communities against the larger white society. Employer patterns of sex and race discrimination channeled them into the most menial and poorly paid domestic and cleaning jobs. Women from these communities captured national attention when they sustained a massive strike against the Medical College of Charleston to change their rock-bottom position in the wage economy (Hoffius 1980).

Organizing for Change

Despite formidable barriers, there have been continuing efforts to turn the situation around. These have been most visible in occupations and industries where women are concentrated, among clerical workers, nurses, and health care workers. Women on college and university faculties have also been active, although they are a minority of such teachers. In response to heightened activity for affirmative action in a variety of occupational sectors, lawyers William Pepper and Florynce Kennedy (1982) have written a guide to be used by nonlawyers in seeking legal remedies to race and sex discrimination.

For the most part, clerical and health workers have pursued pay equity and improvements through union forms, collective bargaining, and union-sponsored litigation, while professional women have used individual and class action suits. Nurses have become increasingly militant, moving toward unionization, strikes, and lawsuits simultaneously.

Women have given increasing attention to recognizing, publicizing, and combatting sexual harassment in the workplace, with a variety of publications addressing the issue (Sexual harassment 1981; Pennsylvania Commission for Women 1981; Arditti et al. 1982). Unlike pay discrimination, there are still few legal recourses in cases of sexual harassment, and the victims, often correctly, fear stigma and further punishment for speaking out. Efforts are underway to make sexual harassment illegal. The State of Michigan has incorporated such provisions into its civil rights law (Harel and Cottledge 1982).

Universities   The Women's Equity Action League (WEAL) has records of 217 administrative complaints and lawsuits against academic institutions in almost every state (Downey and Endy 1981). The literature on discrimination against women in academe has grown large enough to generate at least one annotated bibliography (Farley 1982).

In their survey of the progress made by a decade of affirmative action efforts, Astin and Snyder (1982) found that more women have been hired and that the salary gap has decreased, but that women are still promoted and tenured less frequently than men. In an analysis of sex discrimination lawsuits, Abel (1981) found that most women faculty who went to court did so in a political effort to change discriminatory patterns and procedures. University channels, however, forced them to focus on individual merit and procedure. Governmental agencies also tended to focus only at the individual level. Neither wanted to handle systematic patterns of race or sex discrimination. Current Labor Department proposals would prevent class action suits in the future nationally, and would limit back pay awards to two years (Fields 1982). Despite these barriers, Abel found that political mobilization of both students and faculty often led to improvement for women on campuses. She links continuing success to wider alliances with campus clerical, faculty, and service worker unions, and with women's and ethnic studies programs. A report on what is perhaps the largest pending class action suit—against Cornell University by five ex-faculty women on behalf of two hundred women at Cornell— seems to agree. Although the suit is not settled, results to date include an increased number of newly tenured faculty and a better atmosphere for women on campus (Downey and Endy 1982).

Two case studies analyze a complementary set of strategies to campus-based activity. Sanjek (1982) and Quinn and Smith (1982) discussed the battle that ensued in the American Anthropological Association to implement their long-standing resolution to censure departments that were found to have taken inadequate steps to remedy discriminatory patterns of hiring and promotion.

Comparable Worth   Called the "issue of the 80s," comparable worth, or the pursuit of equal pay for work of comparable skill, effort, and responsibility, has come to be the major strategy for improving women's position in the face of a workforce that is extremely resistant to desegregation. Last year, in the important case of *Gunther* v. *Washington County*, the Supreme Court ruled in favor of women prison matrons who argued that the State of Oregon violated Title VII of the Civil Rights Act by paying them some 30 percent less than male guards whose work was similar but not identical to theirs. Almost immediately after the Gunther decision, some two thousand San Jose city workers in a local of the American Federation of State, County, and Municipal Employees (AFSCME) waged a successful nine-day strike to gain wage raises and incorporate pay equity raises into their union contract (Mutari et al. 1982; Bunzel 1982; Lublin 1982; Newman 1982). They demanded that the city remedy the wage discrimination uncovered by its own job evaluation study.

This study found that jobs in which women predominated paid some 15 percent less than comparable jobs in which men predominated. In addition to wage raises to all workers, the settlement provided some 780 librarians and clerks an additional increase to remedy pay inequities based on sex.

Litigation and collective bargaining have become complementary strategies for pay equity, with labor unions, particularly those with large constituencies of women workers, taking the initiative on both fronts. In a long-standing case brought to the Supreme Court by the International Union of Electrical Workers (IUE) against Westinghouse, the company was charged with paying women less than men for jobs the company had evaluated as equivalent; thus women assemblers were paid some three or four levels below that of, for example, janitors (Newman 1982).

Gunther and the IUE cases have established two important legal principles helpful to future pay equity efforts. Several of the IUE cases have established that litigation is part of the collective-bargaining process, and therefore employers must supply unions with information on sex and race, even when that information is to be used in suits against the employer (Newman 1982). The *Gunther* decision established that wage discrimination based on sex violates Title VII of the Civil Rights Act, even where the jobs are not identical. That decision did not make clear what kinds of evidence would be needed to demonstrate that wage differentials were illegal, and what kinds of defense employers could use to argue that their wage differentials were not discriminatory.

Since then, public employees have been very active in comparable-worth efforts. The state of Minnesota has made law of its commitment (Comparable worth . . . 1982). About twelve states and two cities have done job evaluation studies of their civil service jobs. At least four states and one city are facing sex discrimination charges (Lublin 1982; Dunlop 1982). With some 400,000 women members, AFSCME filed charges against the state of Washington—a pioneer in comparable-worth job studies—to demand implementation. In Connecticut, the state health workers' union bargained for a $1.07 million "pay equity" fund for its workers. The California State Employees Association won the promise of a comparable-worth plan from state officials. The Service Employees International Union (SEIU) has made this a major issue in organizing school and university clerical workers (Dunlop 1982).

A recent federal court decision against Madison, Wisconsin public health nurses represents a setback for comparable worth. Nurses there argued that their jobs were comparable to those of mainly male sanitarians or public health inspectors, but that they were paid less because they were female. The judge accepted their argument for comparability, but ruled against them because they did not persuade her that the city was intentionally discriminatory. The city argued that the market wage for sanitarians was higher and therefore a higher wage was needed to fill vacancies. The requirement to demonstrate intent combined with acceptance of a marketplace argument as a nondiscriminatory reason for pay inequity will make it very difficult to litigate for comparable worth (Comparable worth setback . . . 1982).

The issue is far from being resolved, however. A complaint to the Equal Employment Opportunity Commission (EEOC) by the American Nurses' Association (ANA) on behalf of the University of Pittsburgh School of Nursing faculty in 1977 takes on the marketplace argument from another perspective. This case could potentially upset nationwide university practices of large pay differentials by subject area. The ANA has argued that nursing faculty were paid less than male faculty because they were female. The EEOC demanded salary data for three years from the university, which the university refused to supply. The university has appealed a federal court order for compliance with EEOC's request. That court order argues in favor of cross-school and cross-departmental salary comparisons on the basis that all faculty are primarily teachers and hence do comparable work (Bunzel 1982).

Unionization   While the overall unionization of the labor force has declined, white-collar unionization has grown (Sullivan 1982). Although only 16 percent of working women are members of unions or worker associations, they make up 28 percent of the total membership. Women also account for half the growth of membership in unions since 1960 (Baden and Glassberg 1982). Women and minorities are nevertheless very underrepresented in union leadership positions (Davis 1982). The Coalition of Labor Union Women's (CLUW) Empowerment Project is an attempt to correct this situation by educating and training union women for leadership (Baden and Glassberg 1982).

Hospital workers in general and nurses in particular have used a variety of strategies to improve their low pay and poor working conditions. Patricia Sexton's *The New Nightingales* deals with the ways unionization among hospital workers helps them act on their interests as both workers and women.

Barbara Melosh's *The Physician's Hand* (1982) is a history of nursing that focuses on the conflict between a professional perspective among nursing's leadership and administrators, and a more working-class apprenticeship culture of the rank and file. The rise of the civil rights movement and public employee unions in the 1960s, and health worker unionization and the women's movement in the 1970s have helped nurses begin to resolve their internal conflicts in a militant direction. According to Melosh, nursing leaders' professionalist attitudes contribute to a demand for nurses' right to define the nature of their work and a challenge to traditional deference to doctors. Widespread support for organizing among nurses has pushed the leadership to encourage rank and file efforts to unionize and strike in pursuit of their linked demands for improved patient care, pay equity, and better working conditions.

This year, over 1,200 nurses in San Jose waged a long, although ultimately unsuccessful comparable-worth strike against four hospitals. They demanded pay levels equal to those of mainly male pharmacists (Nurses ask . . . 1982; Cohn 1982).

Hospital workers are increasingly having to deal with professional "union busters" or consulting firms hired by management to defeat unions. A recent federal court ruling overturned an election in which the Federation of Nurses and Health Professionals was narrowly defeated. The judge held St. Francis Hospital in Milwaukee responsible for the campaign of intimidation run by Modern Management (or 2M), one of the country's largest antiunion companies. The hospital was directed to recognize the union immediately because the "long-term coercive effects" of management's tactics made a fair election impossible in the near future (Astin 1982).

In the last few years, clerical workers have organized in growing numbers and visibility. While few are as yet represented by unions, there is a variety of "pre-union" organizations springing up around the country in response to a new mood of militance and working-class feminism. In a case study of one such organization, Roberta Goldberg (1983) found that clerical workers' grievances were widespread and centered around low pay, lack of job mobility, and lack of recognition.

As automation heightens the assembly-line conditions of clerical work, job dissatisfaction can be expected to increase. Clerical workers who had previously relied on education, conciliation, and dialogue with employers may increasingly find themselves turning toward unionization and collective bargaining as necessary steps in improving wages and working conditions. Nine to Five, National Association of Working Women, affiliated with SEIU as District 925 last year. It has organized six hundred workers in six locations thus far, including Equitable Life in Syracuse, where the insurance company employed a major union buster (Moberg 1982; District 925 1982).

Conclusion

It was a year of transition and contradiction. More women were forced to support themselves and their children on their own, and more two-parent households required multiple earners. The New Right urged women to demand a return to a nostalgic ideal of freedom from the double day, but at the price of economic and personal dependence on a wage-earning husband. Working women's organizations and unions encouraged women's independence by organizing to demand the economic wherewithall to provide for themselves and their families. In 1982, the second trend gained force, especially among women, while the New Right social program lost much of its appeal.

The path of economic equity in the workforce contains its own contradictions, however. On the positive side, widespread acceptance of pay equity and active efforts against sexual harassment indicate widespread social acceptance of women's role as workers (While this is progress, there is still a way to go in such acceptance. For example, an important book on union responses to technological change focuses on occupations where women and minorities predominate [Kennedy, Craypo, and Lehman 1982], but the cover design shows a white male arm wrestling with a robot arm.) On the negative side, women's worker role is added to her domestic and child-raising role. Feminists have long pointed out that this gives women two responsibilities to a man's one.

While working women express anger at the unfairness of the burden, they nevertheless attempt to carry it, while pushing for work organizations and family-oriented benefits to ease the burden. It certainly is premature to suggest that working women are using their role as workers radically to transform traditional notions about family and work. Still, there are positive implications about who should share family responsibilities in pursuit of employer-paid health insurance for pregnancy and childbirth, paid parenting leaves, paid sick leave to cover time off to care for dependents, improved family coverage in health insurance, and employer-paid child care. Such steps would force employers to shoulder some of the time and money costs of raising families. They could be first steps in the recognition that raising families is work that is crucial for the whole society and that must be shared.

References

ABEL, E. 1981. Collective protest and the meritocracy: Faculty women and sex discrimination lawsuits. *Feminist Studies* 7:505–38.

ANDERSON, K. 1981. *Wartime women*. Westport, Conn.: Greenwood Press.

ARDITTI, R.; BRUKMAN, G.; DISCH, E. et al. 1982. The politics of sexual harassment. *Off Our Backs* 12, no. 5:9.

Asia— automation is hitting a low-wage bastion. 1982. *Business Week*, March 15.

ASTIN, H. S. 1982. Judge sticks it to union-buster. *In These Times*, February 24– March 9.

ASTIN, H. S., and SNYDER, M. B. 1982. Affirmative action 1972–1982: A decade of response. *Change* 14:26–31.

BADEN, N., and GLASSBERG, E. 1982. *A handbook for empowerment of women*. Washington, D.C.: Coalition of Labor Union Women Center for Education and Research.

BENERIA, L., and SEN, G. 1982. Class and gender inequalities and women's role in economic development. *Feminist Studies* 8, no. 1:157–76.

BOLLES, A. L. 1981. "Goin' abroad": Working class Jamaican women and migration. In *Female immigrants to the United States*, edited by D. M. Mortimer and R. S. Bryce-Laporte. Washington, D.C.: Smithsonian Institute.

BOLOTIN, S. 1982. Voices from the post-feminist generation. *New York Times Magazine*, October 17.

BUNZEL, J. 1982. To each according to her worth? *Public Interest* 67:77–93.

CARTER, M. J., and CARTER, S. B. 1981. Women's recent progress in the professions, or, Women get a ticket to ride after the gravy train has left the station. *Feminist Studies* 7:477–504.

CHAPMAN, J. R. 1982. Poverty viewed as a woman's problem—The U.S. case. In *Women and the world of work*, edited by A. Hoiberg. New York: Plenum.

Children's Defense Fund. 1982a. *A children's defense budget: An analysis of the President's budget and children*. Washington, D.C.: Children's Defense Fund.

————. 1982b. *Employed parents and their children: A databook*. Washington, D.C.: Children's Defense Fund.

Coalition of Labor Union Women. 1982. Women gain in states as "gender gap" grows. *CLUW News* 8:6.

Coalition on Women and the Budget. 1982. *Inequality of sacrifice: The impact of the Reagan budget on women*. Washington, D.C.: National Education Association.

COHN, KAREN. 1982. San Jose nurses stay out. *Union WAGE* 69:1.

Comparable worth, Minnesota enacts law. 1982. *Off Our Backs* 12, no. 6:11.

Comparable worth setback in Madison nurses' suit. *Public Eye* 7, no. 4:1.

CROSBY, F. 1982. *Relative deprivation and working women*. New York: Oxford University Press.

DAVIS, B. 1982. Nonreferral unions and equal employment opportunity. Washington, D.C.: United States Commission on Civil Rights.

DAY, K. 1982. Kinship in a changing economy: A view from the Sea Islands. In *Holding onto the land and the Lord*, edited by C. Stack and R. Hall. Athens: University of Georgia Press.

DIGGS, F. 1982. Job sharing: For many a perfect answer. *U.S. News*, August 23.

District 925. 1982. *Fledgling labor union wins out over huge insurance company, anti-labor consultant*. Washington, D.C.: Service Employees International Union.

DOWNEY, P., and ENDY, D. 1981. A struggle for academic equity. *Graduate Woman* 75:10–15.

DUGGAN, L., and N. ROCAMORA. 1981. Where the runaway shops run to. *Union WAGE* 67:8.

DUNLOP, S. 1982. Bargaining cited as key to achieving pay equity. *AFL-CIO News* 27, no. 38:1.

ECKART, D. R. 1982. Microprocessors, women and future employment opportunities. *International Journal of Women's Studies* 5:47–57.

EHRENREICH, B., and STALLARD, K. 1982. The nouveau poor. *Ms.* 11:217–24.

EISENSTEIN, Z. R. 1982. The sexual politics of the new right: Understanding the "crisis of liberalism" for the 1980s. *Signs* 7, no. 3:567–88.

FARLEY, J. 1982. *Academic women and employment discrimination: A critical annotated bibliography*. New York: Cornell University School of Industrial Relations.

FIELDS, C. 1982. U.S. proposes limits on back pay in bias cases. *Chronicle of Higher Education* 24:11.

FRANKEL, J.; MONOGUE, M. A.; and PALUDI, M. 1982. The employed mother: A new social norm? *International Journal of Women's Studies* 5, no. 3:274–81.

GIULIANO, V. E. 1982. The mechanization of office work. *Scientific American* 247, no. 3:149–65.

GOLDBERG, R. 1983. *Organizing women office workers: Dissatisfaction, consciousness and action*. New York: Praeger.

GREGORY, J. 1982. Technological change in the office workplace and implications for organizing. In *Labor and technology*, edited by D. Kennedy, C. Craypo, and M. Lehman. Pennsylvania State University.

GUMA, K. 1982. Network stalks runaway shops. *Union WAGE* 68:4.

HAREL, G. H., and COTTLEDGE, K. 1982. Combatting sexual harassment: The Michigan experience. *Human Resource Management* 2, no. 1:2–10.

HARLAN, A., and WEISS, C. 1982. *Moving up: Women in managerial careers. Final report*. Working paper no. 86. Wellesley, Mass.: Wellesley College Center for Research on Women.

HOFFIUS, S. 1980. Charleston hospital workers' strike, 1969. In *Working Lives*, edited by M. Miller. New York: Pantheon.

If home is where the worker is. 1982. *Business Week*, May 3.

JONES, J. 1982. My mother was much of a woman: Black women, work, and the family under slavery. *Feminist Studies* 8, no. 2:235–70.

KAHN-HUT, R.; DANIELS, A. K.; and COLVARD, R. 1982. *Women and work: Problems and perspectives*. New York: Oxford University Press.

KENNEDY, D.; CRAYPO, C.; and LEHMAN, M., eds. 1982. *Labor and technology: Union response to changing environments*. Pennsylvania State University.

KESSLER-HARRIS, A. 1982. *Out to work: A history of wage-earning women in the United States*. New York: Oxford University Press.

LEBSOCK, S. 1982. Free black women and the question of matriarchy: Petersburg, Virginia. *Feminist Studies* 8, no. 2:271–92.

LUBLIN, J. S. 1982. Big fight looms over gap in pay for similar "male," "female" jobs. *Wall Street Journal*, September 16.

MELOSH, B. 1982. *The physician's hand*. Philadelphia: Temple University Press.

MOBERG, D. 1982. Terminal boredom and higher stress. *In These Times*, November 10–16.

MORTIMER, D., and LAPORTE, R. S. B., eds. 1981. *Female immigrants to the United States: Caribbean, Latin American and African experiences*. Washington, D.C.: Smithsonian Institute.

MURPHREE, M. 1982. Viewpoint on secretaries. *National Business Woman* 63, no. 6:7–9.

MUTARI, E.; RUBIN, M.; SACKS, K. et al. *Equal pay for work of comparable value*. Chicago: American Library Association.

National Commission on Working Women. 1983. *Women at work: News about the 80%*. Washington, D.C.: National Commission on Working Women Center for Women Policy Studies.

NEWMAN, W. 1982. Pay equity emerges as a top labor issue in the 1980s. *Monthly Labor Review* 105, no. 4:49–51.

Nine to Five, National Association of Working Women. 1982. *Office work in America*. Cleveland: National Association of Working Women.

Nurses ask same pay as men in similar jobs. 1982. *New York Times*, February 14.

NUSSBAUM, K. 1982. The hazards of office automation. *Business and Society Review* 40:45–48.

PEARCE, D., and MCADOO, H. 1981. *Women and children: Alone and in poverty.* Washington, D.C.: National Advisory Council on Economic Opportunity.

Pennsylvania Commission for Women. 1981. *Not for fun, not for profit.* Harrisburg: The Commission.

PEPPER, W., and KENNEDY, F. 1982. *Sex discrimination in employment: An analysis and guide for the practitioner and student.* Charlottesville, Va.: Michie.

QUINN, N., and C. SMITH. 1982. A new resolution on fair employment practices for women anthropologists. *Signs* 7, no. 4:869–77.

RANDOUR, M.; STRASSBURG, L.; and LIPMAN-BLUMEN, J. 1982. Women in higher education: Trends in enrollments and degrees earned. *Harvard Educational Review* 52, no. 2:189–202.

RUBIN, M. 1982. *Women and poverty.* Research summary no. 4. Washington, D.C.: Business and Professional Women's Foundation.

SACKS, K., and RUBIN, M. 1982. Then, now and future woman. *Ms.* 11:130–31.

SAFA, H. 1981. Runaway shops and female employment: The search for cheap labor. *Signs* 7, no. 2:418–33.

SAFA, H., and LEACOCK, E., eds. 1981. Development and the sexual division of labor. *Signs* 7, no. 2 (special issue).

SANJEK, R. 1982. The American anthropological association resolution on the employment of women: Genesis, implementation, disavowal, and resurrection. *Signs* 7, no. 4:845–68.

SASSEN-KOOB, S. 1981. Exporting capital and importing labor: The role of women. In *Female immigrants to the United States*, edited by D. Mortimer and R. Laporte. Washington, D.C.: Smithsonian Institute.

SCOTT, J. W. 1982. The mechanization of women's work. *Scientific American* 247, no. 3:166–85.

SEXTON, P. 1982. *The new Nightingales: Hospital workers, unions, new women's issues.* New York: Enquiry Press.

Sexual harassment. *On Campus with Women* 31:1.

STRASSER, S. 1982. *Never done.* New York: Pantheon.

SULLIVAN, F. L. 1982. Union organizing in the 1980s: The battle cry is "organize!" *Supervisory Management* 27, no. 5:16–21.

Task Force on Women's Economic Issues. 1982. *Expanding the role of women in our own economy.* Washington, D.C.: Report of the House Democratic Caucus Task Force on Women's Economic Issues.

TRIMBLE, J. 1982. Where part-timers are the majority. *U.S. News*, August 23, p. 67.

United States Department of Labor, Bureau of Labor Statistics. 1982. *Employment situation of women, December 1982.* Unpublished data. Prepared by the Women's Bureau, Division of Statistical and Economic Analysis. Washington, D.C.

WELCH, C. E. 1982. Family and the state: An American perspective. *International Journal of Women's Studies* 5:227–35.

WERTZ, D. C. 1982. Social science attitudes toward women workers, 1870–1970. *International Journal of Women's Studies* 5:161–71.

WESTCOTT, D. N. 1982. Blacks in the 1970s: Did they scale the job ladder? *Monthly Labor Review* 105, no. 6:29–38.

Working Women's Educational Fund. 1983. *Highlights of the international conference on office work and the new technology.* Cleveland: Working Women's Educational Fund.

WRIGHT, E. O.; COSTELLO, C.; HACHEN, D. et al. 1982. The American class structure. *American Sociological Review* 47, no. 6:709–26.

YENCKET, J. 1982. Careers: High tech in the office. *Washington Post*, November 10.

Resources

Women Workers

Nine to Five, National Association of Working Women, 1224 Huron Road, Cleveland, OH 44115.

National Commission on Working Women, Center for Women Policy Studies, 2000 P Street N.W., Washington, DC 20036.

Coalition of Labor Union Women, Center for Education and Research, 2000 P Street N.W., Room 615, Washington, DC 20036.

Careers and Jobs for Women

Displaced Homemakers Network, Inc., 1531 Pennsylvania Avenue S.E., Washington, DC 20003.

Wider Opportunities for Women, 1325 G Street NW, Lower Level, Washington, DC 20005.

Women in Management and the Professions

National Association of Women Business Owners, 500 N. Michigan Avenue, Suite 1400, Chicago, IL 60611.

National Federation of Business and Professional Women's Clubs, 2012 Massachusetts Avenue N.W., Washington, DC 20036.

Project on the Status and Education of Women, Association of American Colleges, 1818 R Street N.W., Washington, DC 20009.

Minority Women

National Institute for Women of Color, 1712 N Street N.W., Washington, DC 20036.

Women for Racial and Economic Equality, 130 East 16th Street, New York, NY 10003.

Pay Equity

National Committee on Pay Equity, National Education Association Building, Room 615, 1201 16th Street N.W., Washington, DC 20036.

Comparable Worth Project, 488 41st Street, Room 5, Oakland, CA 94609.

American Library Association, Office of Personnel Resources, 50 East Huron Street, Chicago, IL 60611.

Sexual Harassment

Working Women's Institute, 593 Park Avenue, New York, NY 10021.

Contributors

Barbara Haber, editor for this volume, is curator of printed books at the Arthur and Elizabeth Schlesinger Library on the History of Women in America and a Radcliffe Scholar. Educated at the University of Wisconsin, the University of Chicago, and Simmons College, she is advisory editor for G. K. Hall's Women's Studies publications and author of *Women in America: A Guide to Books, 1963–1975* (G. K. Hall, 1978), which has been updated and issued in paperback by University of Illinois Press (1981). She directed the NEH-funded project "Women in the Community: Where Were They? Where Are They? Where Are They Going?," which has enabled public libraries throughout the country to prepare programs about women for local audiences.

Marjorie Bakken is an associate professor and the undergraduate dean at Wheelock College, Boston, Massachusetts. She worked for several years as a teacher of young children and subsequently taught in and directed a college program for "reentry women" who worked in Head Start and day care centers. She currently teaches courses about adult development and adult learning. Dr. Bakken is vice chair of the Cambridge (Massachusetts) Commission on the Status of Women and is a board member for several day care centers in the Boston area.

Kathleen Barry is a radical feminist and sociologist who teaches feminist theory in the sociology department at Brandeis University. She is the author of *Female Sexual Slavery* (Prentice-Hall; Avon, 1979) and is scheduled to publish a new biography of Susan B. Anthony in 1984. In addition, she is currently involved in organizing the International Feminist Network Against the Traffic in Women.

Joan Bergstrom is professor and chairperson of the Department of Professional Studies in Early Childhood at Wheelock College, Boston, Massachusetts.

284

Over the past twenty years she has been involved in early childhood education and child care. She has a doctoral degree in education from the University of Massachusetts, and in 1980 she received a National Institute of Education Fellowship from Northwestern University. Her extensive professional experience has included responsibilities in a number of teaching, research, and consulting positions. In addition to two audiovisual teaching resources on early education of young children, she has published several books and pamphlets and a number of magazine articles for both professional and parent audiences. Currently, Dr. Bergstrom is involved in writing a guide to children's out-of-school life for families with children six to twelve.

Beverly Oberfeld Friend, Ph.D., associate professor of communications at Oakton Community College, Des Plaines, Ill., teaches science fiction and journalism and advises the student newspaper. A science fiction critic who wrote her doctoral dissertation on *The Science Fiction Fan Cult* (Northwestern University, 1975), Friend has written numerous articles on the treatment of women in SF and has authored a textbook, *SF: The Classroom in Orbit*. In 1982 her syllabus on "Women's Role in SF" won a first place from the Women's Institute for Freedom of the Press.

Rachel T. Hare-Mustin is a noted leader in the fields of family therapy and psychotherapy for women. She has published a leading volume, *Women and Psychotherapy: An Assessment of Research and Practice*, with Annette M. Brodsky. Her articles include "A Feminist Approach to Family Therapy," "Family Therapy May Be Dangerous to Your Health," "An Appraisal of the Relationship between Women and Psychotherapy: 80 Years after the Case of Dora," and research on ethics and attitudes toward motherhood in this country and China. She is director of the counseling and consulting psychology program at Harvard University.

Freada Klein has been working on issues of violence against women for over a decade. Until 1976 she worked locally and nationally with rape crisis centers. At that time, she cofounded the Alliance Against Sexual Coercion, the first organization to provide a comprehensive approach to sexual harassment. Freada currently travels throughout North America conducting trainings on all aspects of violence against women. She is finishing her doctorate in social policy and research at Brandeis University, with a dissertation on the relationship between sexual harassment and work structures.

Heather McClave is a literary scholar and critic. She has taught English and American literature at Harvard University and the Radcliffe Seminars, and has published various studies of American poetry and women's prose.

Susan Reverby is assistant professor of women's studies at Wellesley College. She is an historian of women, medicine, and nursing. She has worked as a health policy analyst and was active in the women's health movement. She is the coeditor of *America's Working Women: A Documentary History* (1976) and

Health Care in America: Essays in Social History (1979) and is the author of a forthcoming book on the history of nursing.

Karen Sacks is research director at the Business and Professional Women's Foundation and a research associate at Duke University, where she studies the workplace and family lives of women workers. She has also taught anthropology and women's studies at the university level for ten years. A long-time feminist activist, her articles have appeared in *Signs, Ms., Monthly Review,* and *American Anthropologist.* She is the author of two books, *Sisters and Wives* and *My Troubles are Going to Have Trouble with Me* (coedited with Dorothy Remy) to be published in 1984.

Peggy Simpson is the economic correspondent for the Hearst Newspapers and Washington political columnist for the *Boston Herald-American.* A Neiman fellow and former president of the Washington Press Club, she is Washington correspondent and contributing editor to *Working Woman* magazine where her column, "Washington," appears monthly.

Jeanne J. Speizer worked as director of the Administrative Skills Program for Women in Higher Education Administration at Higher Education Resource Services (Project HERS), Wellesley College, from 1977 to 1982. She holds a doctorate in education from Boston University and a bachelors degree from the University of California, Berkeley. She recently completed a study of the career paths of approximately 300 women administrators and faculty members in higher education. She is currently a "mature student" at Northeastern University Law School. She plans to combine her knowledge of education with her newly learned legal skills and continue to work as an advocate for the advancement of women.

Index